Lou...

THE...

let you go

CWR, CWR, Waverley Abbey House, Waverley Lane, Farnham, Surrey GU9 8EP

Scripture quotations are taken from:
NIV, New International Version, © 1975, 1978, 1984, by International Bible Society.
NKJ, New King James Version, © 1979, 1980, 1982, Thomas Nelson, Inc., Publishers.
RSV, Revised Standard Version, © 1972, Thomas Nelson, Inc., Publishers.
Amplified, The Amplified Bible, © 1965, Zondervan Publishing House.
TLB, The Living Bible, © 1971, Tyndale House Publishers.
J.B. Phillips, The New Testament in Modern English, revised edition, © 1958, 1960, J.B. Phillips.
KJV, King James Version, © 1984, 1977, Thomas Nelson, Inc.
Moffat, The Bible. A New Translation, © 1950, 1952, 1953, 1954, James A.R. Moffat.
The Message, © 2002, Christian Art Publishers.
Used with permission.

LOVE THAT WILL NOT LET YOU GO
A compilation of excerpts from Every Day with Jesus 1988, 1989, 1990, 1995, 1997 by Selwyn Hughes
compiled by Monica de Vries
© CWR 2003

Concept development, editing, design and production by
Struik Christian Books Ltd
A division of New Holland Publishing (South Africa) (Pty) Ltd
(New Holland Publishing is a member of the Johnnic Publishing Group)
Cornelis Struik House
80 McKenzie Street
Cape Town 8001

Reg. No. 1971/00972/07

DTP by Bridgitte Chemaly
Cover design by Christian Jaggers
Cover photograph by Photo Access
Cover reproduction by Hirt & Carter Cape (Pty) Ltd
Reproduced, printed and bound by CTP Book Printers
PO Box 6060, Parow East 7501

ISBN 1 85345 261 0

SELWYN HUGHES

Love

THAT WILL NOT
let you go

THE GREATEST THING IN THE WORLD

Sometimes, Lord,

in seeming to
give
we are
grasping.
Sometimes
in seeming to
care
we are
clutching.
Open our eyes to
recognise
and our hands to
release
selfish motives.
Then dip these
empty hands
into your Endless Treasure
to give
without gain,
to care
without counting the cost.

SUSAN LENZKES
EDWJ Nov/Dec 1988

January / February
walking the way of love

March / April
God's blueprint for living

May / June
channels of God's love

July / August
balancing the love scales

September / October
overcoming giants

November / December
walking our talking

Love divine

FOR READING AND MEDITATION – 1 CORINTHIANS 13:1–13

'. . . but the greatest of these is love.' (v. 13: NKJ)

All my life I have longed to write on this particular section of Paul's writings, viz. 1 Corinthians 13, but until now I have never felt ready or adequate to do it. From time to time I have commented on various phrases from this sublime passage, but I have never before attempted a full exposition. Just recently, in fact soon after I had passed my sixtieth birthday, the Spirit seemed to nudge me and say as he did to the apostle John in the Revelation: 'Now write what you see . . .' (1:19: RSV).

We begin with the thought that perhaps at no time in history has it been more important to focus our attention on this pregnant passage than now, for unless I am greatly mistaken, today's church, generally speaking, is becoming more preoccupied with power than it is with love. It is eager for miracles and manifestations, often with wrong motives. Not that a longing to see God work in mighty power is wrong; it becomes wrong when the desire for power overtakes the desire for love.

David Wilkerson, author of *The Cross and the Switchblade*, makes this solemn observation, 'I say to you, it is possible to gather Spirit-filled people in one place, praising and lifting up their hands, and still have Christ walking among them as a stranger. We make Christ a stranger when we give the Holy Spirit pre-eminence over him.' Let's make it our prayer on this very first day of our meditations together that the greatest of all our spiritual pursuits will be the pursuit of love.

O God, can it be that our longing for miracles and manifestations of power has become stronger than our longing for love? If it has, then forgive us, we pray. Help us to re-establish our priorities and make love our greatest aim. Amen.

FOR FURTHER STUDY – Psa. 146:1–10; Deut. 7:8; Jer. 31:3
1. What motivates God? / 2. What is the quality of God's love?

The supremacy of love

FOR READING AND MEDITATION – 1 CORINTHIANS 14:1–15

'Eagerly pursue ... this love – make it your aim, your great quest ...' (v. 1: Amplified)

We began yesterday with the thought that some sections of today's Church are in danger of putting power before love. Does this mean we ought to withdraw from seeking after spiritual gifts and concentrate only on love? The answer is 'No'. Some have interpreted 1 Corinthians 13 as Paul's attempt to turn the attention of the Corinthian converts away from the exercise of spiritual gifts, to focus exclusively on love. But Paul is not saying that love should be our exclusive focus; he is saying (so I believe) that love should be our initial focus.

Those who attempt to analyse 1 Corinthians 13 without reference to the preceding chapter fail to understand what Paul is really saying. He is not suggesting that the Corinthian converts should abandon the exercise of spiritual gifts, but rather that they should bring them under control – the control of love. In fact, he ends the twelfth chapter with the words: 'But earnestly desire and zealously cultivate the greatest and best – the higher gifts and the choicest graces. And yet I will show you a still more excellent way – one that is better by far and the highest of them all, love' (12:31: Amplified).

When I encourage you to make love your aim, don't hear me deriding spiritual gifts. I value them and I am glad of them. I am simply seeking to do here, in the midst of a power-conscious church age, what Paul did in the midst of the power-conscious Corinthians – hold aloft the supremacy of love. The real power chapter in 1 Corinthians is not 1 Corinthians 12 or even 1 Corinthians 14 – it is the love chapter in 1 Corinthians 13. For all else fades and fails. Love alone abides and holds the field.

O Father, help me grasp the point that whatever else comes and goes – love remains. Give me this persisting love so that all my values may be held intact – preserved by love. For I live in vain if I do not love. Amen.

FOR FURTHER STUDY – Eph. 3, 4:16; Gal. 5:6

1. What was Paul's desire for the Ephesians? / 2. How is our faith to work?

Love – vital as well as verbal

FOR READING AND MEDITATION – JOHN 15:1–17

'My command is this: Love each other as I have loved you.' (v. 12: NIV)

Before we come to focus on each of the verses that comprise 1 Corinthians 13, we pause on the threshold to consider a few important and related factors. We know from our reading of the New Testament (especially the text before us today) that love was central to the life of our Lord Jesus Christ, and he insisted that love must be central to our own lives also. Was this emphasis lost as the early church developed? Decidedly not. Every one of the New Testament writers lays down this emphasis, particularly the apostles Peter and John. But nowhere is the emphasis on love more clearly seen than in the writings of the great apostle Paul.

Prior to his conversion, however, love was not Paul's strongest point. In his own way he loved God and professed allegiance to him but, at the same time, he was ready to kill those who turned from the Jewish observances to trust instead the atoning sacrifice of Christ. Then came the amazing change. On the Damascus Road he was conquered by the love of Christ – conquered in outlook, in thought, in act, in character. As Henry Drummond points out, 'The observing student of Scripture can detect a beautiful tenderness growing and ripening all through Paul's character as he gets older, but it ought not to be forgotten that the hand that wrote "the greatest of these is love", when we meet it first, was stained with blood.'

Paul was not only converted to love but became one of the greatest exhibitors of it. How could he have written so eloquently of love in 1 Corinthians 13 had it not gripped and mastered his life? Like his Master, he lived by love. And it was not just verbal – it was vital.

O Father, I am so grateful that your Spirit, working through Paul, enabled him to hold aloft the torch of love. Help us, as your church in this 21st century, to make it our highest emphasis also. Amen.

FOR FURTHER STUDY – Acts 9:1–31, 26:1–23; 2 Cor. 5:14
1. How did Paul describe love's motivating power? / 2. Can you echo Paul's testimony?

Depravity in the dictionary

FOR READING AND MEDITATION – 1 JOHN 3:11–24

'This is how we know what love is: Jesus Christ laid down his life for us …' (v. 16: NIV)

We are pausing on the threshold of 1 Corinthians 13 to look at some relevant factors before entering in and examining it verse by verse. Today we look at the word *love*. What particular word is Paul using and what does it mean? No doubt many of you are aware that in the Greek language, there are several words for *love*; unfortunately, in English, we have just one. The English word *love* has a medley of meanings, ranging from the highest to the lowest. A dictionary definition of love runs like this: 'a feeling of deep regard, fondness, devotion or deep affection, usually accompanied by a yearning or desire for a person of the opposite sex'.

This definition reflects very much the ideas of contemporary society and as such, it is sub-Christian. Someone has said, 'If you want to see the depravity of man, look in the dictionary, for words associated with man soon become depraved by that association.' We can see that in the way the word *gay* has been eased out of every-day conversation, for nowadays it is slowly coming to mean just one thing – a homosexual relationship. Freud defined love as sex love, or, to be fair, as almost entirely sex love. Adultery these days is described by some as 'making love'.

How desperately our language needs to be redeemed. We will not be able to understand what Paul is talking about when he uses the word *love*, nor dedicate ourselves to pursuing it, until we know the precise Greek word he is using and the meaning that lies behind that word. For if we go wrong as to the meaning of love, we will go wrong all down the line. Our first step will determine our last.

Father, I see that I cannot look to the world for the real meaning of love, for the world's thinking has been depraved. I would turn from the smog that overhangs our civilisation to breathe the fresh air of the Spirit. Teach me love's true meaning. In Jesus' name. Amen.

FOR FURTHER STUDY – Deut. 10:12–22, 6:5; Psa. 31:23
1. Write out your own definition of Christian love. / 2. What does the Lord require of us?

Agape – the highest form of love

FOR READING AND MEDITATION – ROMANS 5:1–11
'… the love of God has been poured out in our hearts …' (v. 5: NKJ)

We said yesterday that if we are to understand the meaning of the word *love* which is used by Paul in 1 Corinthians 13, then we must look further than a dictionary, for our dictionaries simply reflect the views of earth and not the views of heaven.

Although, in English, we have just the one word *love*, the original language of the New Testament has several words. There is *Eros*, for example – the powerful sexual attraction between people of opposite sexes. Then there is *Philia* – the love that is displayed in the intimate bond that develops between parents and children, brothers and sisters, friends, business partners and so on. The most powerful word for love and the one used consistently by Paul in 1 Corinthians is *Agape*, which has reference to divine love – a love that is unconditional, undeserved and unquenchable.

The Greeks of Paul's day tended to use the word *Eros* to express the idea of love for God and man, but the Christians adopted the word *Agape*. The meaning which the Christians put into the word, however, did not reflect its Greek source. They adopted the word because it was the most suitable one, but they added to it a distinctly Christian emphasis. As Anders Nygren, a Greek scholar, puts it, '*Eros* is a man's way to God; *Agape* is God's way to man. *Eros* seeks to gain its life, a life divine, immortalised; *Agape* lives the life of God, therefore dares to lose it.' Christians put into the word the idea of a love that arises, not on earth but in heaven – a spontaneous love, eager, rushing, overflowing. How beautiful. To be exposed to it is to be transformed by it.

O Father, help me not to come under any dominance other than the dominance of your love. Show me how I can absorb more of your love, so that more of your love absorbs me. Amen.

FOR FURTHER STUDY – Col. 3:1–14, 1:7–8; 1 Tim. 6:11
1. What did Paul exhort the Colossians to do? / 2. What was Paul's word to Timothy?

The difference of two words

FOR READING AND MEDITATION – PHILIPPIANS 1:1–11

'And this I pray, that your love may abound still more and more ...' (v. 9: NKJ)

We continue meditating on the thought that the early Christians put into the word *Agape*, a content that was richer and more beautiful than anything the world could conceive. Nygren said, 'In ancient times two men commented about God: Plato said, God is *Eros*; John the apostle said, God is *Agape*. Just the difference of two words, and yet there was a difference of two worlds.' Two worlds of different meaning went into those two words. And this difference runs straight through all our ethics and all our religions. It divides – and divides them decisively.

All systems range themselves unconsciously on one side or the other, according as they embody *Eros* or *Agape*. *Eros* love is the love that loves for what it can get out of it. It turns everything – even God – into a means to an end. With *Eros* love, we love people for what they give us in return. If there is no return, then love dies. We love others because we see in them something that brings satisfaction to us – their beauty, their physical attractiveness, their sensuality. They meet a need in us, therefore we would like to acquire them. We can love God in this way too – by making him serve our ends. It looks and sounds religious, but it is pure egocentricity.

The cults are rooted in *Eros*. They would not admit to it, of course, but the attitude underlying the cults is this, 'If I serve God, repeat certain slogans and obey certain rules, I will have peace of mind and inner serenity.' Everything they do comes back to them. The centre of their universe is *me*. They do not love God for himself, they love him for what they can get out of him. There is a better way – 'a more excellent way' – *Agape* love.

O God, help me lay hold of this truth before I go deeper and show me how to organise my life, not around myself but around you. Take my Eros love and convert it into your Agape. In Jesus' name I pray. Amen.

FOR FURTHER STUDY – 1 John 4:1–16, 3:16; Eph. 5:1–2
1. How does John define love? / 2. How does he define God?

Is the church sub-Christian?

FOR READING AND MEDITATION – EPHESIANS 3:14–21

'… May you be rooted deep in love and founded securely on love.'
(v. 17: Amplified)

I had thought to move on from what I was saying yesterday, but something compels me to stay with it. You will remember I made the point that *Eros* love is acquisitive – it loves in order to experience pleasurable feelings. With *Eros* love, if there is no return, then love soon dies or fades. How much of the love that we see in our churches, I ask myself, is *Eros* love and how much of it is *Agape*? If we expect to get something out of loving God, then that is *Eros*.

If we go to church, pray, tithe, attend to our Christian duties in order to put God under an obligation to us – to shield us from harm, ward off sickness, provide us with plenty of material goods – then that is *Eros*. In a conference of young people where the speaker gave a talk on the difference between *Eros* and *Agape* love, he asked the audience to raise their hands to indicate which of the two loves controlled and dominated their lives. Two thirds said '*Eros*'. He complimented them on their honesty and then asked them what they intended to do about it. At once several hundred young people dropped to their knees and began to pray. The speaker said, 'I have never known a prayer meeting start so spontaneously and end up so powerfully, for many of those young people came through to a thrilling new understanding of *Agape* love.'

I ask again: how much of our modern-day church life is built around *Eros* rather than *Agape*? Two thirds? Perhaps one of the greatest dangers we face as the people of God is not that we have become anti-Christian but that we will become sub-Christian – disciples who are content to live on a lesser love.

O Father, forgive us that we pervert the Agape *love you pour into us and make it into something else – something in our own image. Again we ask: take our* Eros *love and change it to your* Agape. *In Jesus' name. Amen.*

FOR FURTHER STUDY – John 15:1–13, 13:1; Rev. 1:5–6
1. What was the quality of Christ's love? / 2. How did he demonstrate it?

The judgment of love

FOR READING AND MEDITATION – JOHN 13:31–38

'By this all men will know that you are my disciples, if you love one another.'
(v. 35: NIV)

Now that we have a clear idea of the kind of love Paul is talking about in 1 Corinthians 13 (*Agape* love) we begin our examination of it verse by verse. The chapter divides easily into three parts. In the first part, love is contrasted (vv. 1–3); in the second part, love is analysed (vv. 4–7) and in the third part, love is defended (vv. 8–13).

Paul begins by contrasting love with the things that men and women thought much of in those days – learning, religion and power. These three things were symbolised in the three nations and people that dominated the world at that time – the Greeks, the Hebrews and the Romans. The Greeks were the emphasisers of the power of speech and oratory; the Hebrews were the emphasisers of prophetic wisdom; the Romans the emphasisers of conquest and power. Paul stepped into the midst of them and said: 'If I can speak in the tongues of men and even of angels (the Greeks), but have not love, I am only a noisy gong or a clanging cymbal. And if I have prophetic powers – that is, the gift of interpreting the divine will and purpose (the Hebrews) … and if I have sufficient faith so that I can remove mountains (the Romans), but have not love (God's love in me) I am nothing – a useless nobody' (vv. 1, 2: Amplified).

Can you see what he is saying? He is making the point that though we can speak with eloquence, interpret divine mysteries and wield tremendous power, but have not love, then we say nothing, know nothing and accomplish nothing. In all the annals of history, has ever a more devastating judgment fallen upon the systems of learning, religion and power than this? But it is, I hasten to add, a judgment that love is entitled to make.

Father, make the point even clearer to me as I go about my life day by day – unless I love, I say nothing, know nothing and do nothing. Help me love as you love, dear Lord, for I do not want to live in vain. Amen.

FOR FURTHER STUDY – Rom. 8:28–39; Gal. 2:20; Eph. 5:2
1. What was Paul's persuasion? / 2. What was his conviction?

The arterial highway of life

FOR READING AND MEDITATION – JOHN 17:13–26

'… that the love which you have bestowed upon me may be in them
… and that I myself may be in them.' (v. 26: Amplified)

We ended yesterday with the thought that never before had a more devastating judgment fallen upon the systems of learning, religion and human accomplishment than is to be found in the opening words of 1 Corinthians 13. The world was weighed and found wanting. Paul showed that a more excellent way had arisen, and apart from the way of love, the lesser ways led nowhere. It was not that learning, religion and human accomplishment were unimportant, but unless these areas of life are undergirded by love, they amount to nothing.

It is interesting to note that throughout time, other civilisations have searched for the meaning of life along similar lines to the world of Paul's day. Take India, for example. The late E.S. Jones, a missionary to India, said, 'In her search to realise God, India emphasises three main ways: the way of knowledge (*Gyana Marga*), the way of devotion (*Bhakti Marga*) and the way of works (*Karma Marga*).' It would seem the Hindu's search is along the three ways in which the Mediterranean world searched. Here Paul's judgment of love is just as devastating: 'If I have all knowledge (*Gyana*), all devotion (*Bhakti*), all deeds (*Karma*), but have no love, then I know nothing, am devoted to nothing and accomplish nothing.'

Life founded on half-truths perishes for want of inner sustaining power. I say again, the qualities of knowledge, devotion and action are not to be discounted or ignored. But the point is that unless they are energised by love, they are destined to fail. And why? Because the universe was made for love – and only love abides.

Father, I see that all my ways are ways of futility unless I can go the way of love. Love is the arterial highway of life – help me walk in it this day and every day. In Jesus' name I ask it. Amen.

FOR FURTHER STUDY – John 14:1–23, 15:9, 16:27
1. How do we demonstrate love for Christ? / 2. What was Christ's injunction to his disciples?

walking the way of love

Controlled by love

FOR READING AND MEDITATION – MARK 12:28–34

'And you shall love the Lord your God out of and with your whole heart
and out of and with all your soul … mind … strength …' (v. 30: Amplified)

We saw yesterday that mankind seems to move along three clear paths in the search for meaning and fulfilment – the way of knowledge, the way of devotion and the way of achievement. The judgment of love, however, is that without God's love flowing in to direct and control these areas of life, they amount to nothing.

Let's apply the judgment of love to the modern world of psychology – a world I have explored in some depth over the past few decades. Modern psychology divides man into three areas, intellect, feeling and will. Some teachers lay emphasis upon the intellect and say that thinking is everything. Others lay emphasis upon emotion and say that emotion is everything. Still others lay emphasis upon the will and say that the will is everything. Each has its devotees, but unless the mind, the emotions and the will are controlled by *Agape* love, then the judgment of love says – we are nothing. For if we think everything, feel everything, do everything but have no love, then we think nothing, feel nothing and do nothing.

You see, nothing works out right unless it is controlled by love. Our text for today shows that we are required to love God with our total being. In other words, the mind, feelings and will are to be attached to God, who is love. Then, animated by love, we will feel right feelings, think right thoughts, will take the right actions and become the right kind of person. Love (*Agape* love) is the bond that holds the personality intact. If only the non-Christian psychologists and psychiatrists could see this, I have no doubt that their sincere and well-intentioned efforts would meet with much greater success.

O God my Father, it is clear that the world has missed the way – the way of love. Our confusions and clashes, our personality disorders, all testify to the fact that life is off centre. Bring us back to your centre – the centre of love. For Jesus' sake. Amen.

FOR FURTHER STUDY – 2 Thess. 3:1–5; Jude 21; Matt. 22:37
1. What does the Bible mean by the term *heart*? / 2. What is to be the anchor for the heart?

Pain set to music

FOR READING AND MEDITATION – 1 CORINTHIANS 4:1–17

'… He will bring to light what is hidden in darkness and
will expose the motives of men's hearts …' (v. 5: NIV)

We pause in the midst of looking at Paul's opening words in 1 Corinthians 13 to
remind ourselves that the whole of the letter to the Corinthians was written out of
pain – the pain of a divided church, one group going with Apollos, another with
Cephas and another with Paul. In addition to this, there was the pain of Christians
turning to pagan practices and attitudes, the pain of Christians becoming selfish
and self-centred, and the pain of Christians misunderstanding the spiritual gifts.

Against that background of pain, Paul picks up his pen and writes out of love. You
simply cannot write at such depth unless it is out of a heart of pain – pain which
has been turned to redemption. Someone has described this chapter as 'pain set
to music'. The heartstrings are drawn so tight by pain that they are thus tuned to
the higher notes of love. But before love can sing, it has to cut. This is why, in the first
three verses, Paul cuts away at wrong motives and wrong attitudes, cuts away at
speaking in tongues, miraculous powers, faith that removes mountains, personal
sacrifice or even martyrdom – cuts these all away unless their basis is love.

I don't know about you, but I find these opening words of 1 Corinthians 13 the
most challenging I know. They force me to look at my own motives as I teach, preach
and write. A Christian magazine article here in Britain recently wrote about me
under the title, *Preacher with the world's biggest daily congregation.* I trembled as I
read it, for I realised that unless my ministry was under the control of love, it would
count for nothing.

*O Father, help me as I face the challenge of this day, for I see that you draw a cancelling line through
everything which has no love in it. I stand before you for inspection. Try me and then make me
whole. In Jesus' name I ask it. Amen.*

FOR FURTHER STUDY – James 1:1–12; Psa. 17:3; Zech. 13:9
1. What could the psalmist testify? / 2. Can you echo the psalmist's words?

To whom do we draw attention?

FOR READING AND MEDITATION – JUDE 14–25
'Keep yourselves in the love of God …' (v. 21: NKJ)

We must stay a little longer with the challenge which Paul's opening words in 1 Corinthians 13 brings home to us. What would happen, I wonder, if every Christian community (especially those where the charismatic gifts are in evidence) were to stop and examine how much of their ministry was motivated by love? Assuming that the self-examination was real and honest, I think I know what would happen. Firstly, we would be shocked to discover how much of what we describe as ministry is really manipulation – a veiled attempt to draw attention to ourselves.

In the days when I pastored churches, I can remember many occasions when I would have to sit down with people who had misused a spiritual gift and gently and lovingly correct them. I would say to them, 'Why do you think you allowed yourself to be carried to excess in the way you did?' Time and time again I would hear them say, 'Because it made me feel good to be the centre of attention.' But the basis of ministry in the Christian church is not drawing attention to ourselves but drawing attention to Christ. The church is designed by God to be Christocentric, not egocentric. When we draw attention to ourselves, we are failing to draw attention to him, and, as David Wilkerson said, 'He becomes a stranger in our midst.'

The second thing that would happen if we examined how much of our ministry is motivated by love is that the Spirit would come to our aid in a way that would produce even greater power than we are presently seeing. There is nothing God loves more than openness, honesty and reality. Where truth is, love cannot keep out.

O God, help us not to shrink from the moments of self-examination out of fear that we might find something we do not like. Give us courage to be real and honest and open. Then we know we are on line for real revival. Amen.

FOR FURTHER STUDY – Psa. 139:15–24, 51:6; 1 Cor. 8:3
1. What was the psalmist's prayer? / 2. What does God desire to see in us?

The spectrum of love

FOR READING AND MEDITATION – JOHN 13:1–17

'… having loved his own who were in the world, he loved them to the end.'
(v. 1: NKJ)

After contrasting love with learning, devotion and achievement, Paul then proceeds to tell us what love is all about. Henry Drummond likens this analysis to light passing through a prism. He says, 'As you have seen a man of science take a beam of light and pass it through a prism, as you have seen it come out on the other side of the prism broken up into its component colours – red and blue and yellow, and violet and orange and all the colours of the rainbow – so Paul passes this thing called love through the magnificent prism of his inspired intellect and it comes out on the other side, broken up into its elements. It is what we might call the *spectrum of love*.'

This spectrum of love, like the fruit of the Spirit, has nine ingredients: patience, kindness, generosity, humility, courtesy, unselfishness, good temper, guilelessness, sincerity. Don't look for these exact words in 1 Corinthians 13, for they are not there, but the truth these words represent most certainly is. The first thing that Paul says about love is that it is patient (v. 4: RSV). The dictionary definition of *patience* is this: suffering afflictions, pain, toil, calamity, provocation or other evils with a calm, unruffled temper.

The first emphasis, then, is that love can suffer, can take it. Love is outgoing, and by its very nature involves itself in the pain and suffering of its loved ones. To understand this aspect of love, we have only to look at the cross, where love showed its capacity to take on itself everything that would fall upon the objects of that love. So if love can go to a cross, it can go anywhere. It meets the supreme test and thereby passes all other tests.

Lord Jesus, you who showed your ability to meet the supreme test of the cross, pour into me the same kind of love – the love that is not just tender-hearted but tough-minded, with the capacity to take it and take it cheerfully. Amen.

FOR FURTHER STUDY – Luke 21:10–19; Eccl. 7:8; Heb. 10:36
1. What do we need to have? / 2. What did Jesus say to his disciples?

Trusting, trusting, trusting

FOR READING AND MEDITATION – JAMES 1:1–12

'… count it all joy when you fall into various trials, knowing that
the testing of your faith produces patience.' (vv. 2–3: NKJ)

We continue looking at the first quality of *Agape* love – the power to take things and take them cheerfully. A young girl said to her youth leader, 'It's been a habit of mine to respond negatively to sorrow. For the life of me I can't react to problems with a positive attitude. Why?' The youth leader said, 'You respond negatively to sorrow because the roots of life are in yourself. You are saying, "Though I try I can't." You are trying, trying, trying, instead of trusting, trusting, trusting. You are trying to bring forth fruit without the root.'

Other than *Agape* love, there is no love that is strong enough to enable us to move out of self-centredness and self-concern. If we do not possess *Agape* love (God's love in us), then we have a limited framework of reference in which to operate. We do not have the resources we need to cope with everything that comes.

In a crisis, the three greatest personalities of the New Testament, Jesus, Stephen and Paul, all prayed for their enemies. Jesus said on the cross: 'Father, forgive them; for they know not what they do.' Stephen prayed amid a shower of stones: 'Lord, do not hold this sin against them.' Paul said: 'For I am already on the point of being sacrificed; the time of my departure has come … At my first defence no one took my part; all deserted me. May it not be charged against them!' It was the crowning act in the life of all three.

Why can love be patient? Because it knows that the universe is behind it; that in spite of what the present says, the future belongs to God. Nothing right can come out wrong and nothing wrong can come out right.

My Father, yet again I would ask – fill me so full of Agape love that I will have an infinite capacity to take whatever comes. Help me to see that your word is always the last word and therefore I can wait for it with joy. Amen.

FOR FURTHER STUDY – 2 Tim. 4:6–17; Luke 23:32–34; Acts 7:54–60; Rom. 5:3
1. What did Paul receive during his trial of patience? / 2. What does patience produce?

Another distinctive of love

FOR READING AND MEDITATION – EPHESIANS 4:17–32

'Be kind and compassionate to one another, forgiving each other,
just as in Christ God forgave you.' (v. 32: NIV)

We have seen over the past few days that the first capacity of *Agape* love is patience; the power to take anything that comes. The second capacity of love is that of being kind: 'Love suffers long and is kind', says the inspired apostle (1 Corinthians 13:4: NKJ).

Human love can be patient without being kind. I have met many patient people who did not leave a good impression because their patience was not a gracious, kindly patience. But *Agape* love, that is, the love which flows out of God's heart into ours, will not have this deficiency. It will put up with irritating situations and go on being kind. A Christian who was kept waiting in a department store and became more and more irritated said to the assistant, 'How much longer do I have to wait to be served in this place?' The assistant apologised and explained the reason for the delay, whereupon the man said, 'All right, I will put up with it, but don't expect me to enjoy it.' The Christian was functioning at that moment, not on *Agape* love, but on human love – a love that soon runs out of energy and enthusiasm.

The exciting thing about *Agape* love (God's love in us) is that it has within it the capacity to enable us not only to hang on, but to be kind to those who keep us hanging on. Don't think, however, that this capacity of kindness makes a person a pushover. A young Christian once said to me, 'I am afraid if I am kind, someone will take advantage of me.' The love that is kind will not hesitate to confront any issue that needs confronting, but it will do it in a way that differentiates between the person and the problem. It shows respect for the person while seeking to overcome the problem.

O Father, help me to understand that when I get irritated and frustrated by life, it is a silent witness to the fact I am running on my resources and not yours. Help me to open my being to your invading love – then I can cope with anything that comes. And cope with it kindly. Amen.

FOR FURTHER STUDY – Col. 3:12–17; Rom. 12:10; 1 Pet. 3:8

1. What is to be the pattern for our kindness? / 2. How can we 'put on' kindness?

Love – not sentimentality

FOR READING AND MEDITATION – ROMANS 12:9–21

'Be kindly affectionate to one another … in honour giving preference to one another.'
(v. 10: NKJ)

We spend another day meditating on the thought that *Agape* love is not only patient, but kind. The hard-lipped patience you see in some Christian men and women may enable them to get through the day, but it does not enhance the Christian testimony. These types of people are patient, but not kind in their patience – therefore it is something less than *Agape* love. The kindness that divine love brings with it into our personalities enables us to give back kindness when life is not kind to us. It means we are not just negatively patient but positively kind in the midst of the patience. A well-known hymn puts it this way:

> Able to suffer without complaining
> To be misunderstood without explaining
> Able to give without receiving
> To be ignored without grieving
> Able to ask without commanding
> To love despite misunderstanding
> Able to turn to the Lord for guarding
> Able to wait for his own rewarding.

This kind of love, it must be noted, is not maudlin sentimentality; it is tough as well as tender, strong as well as sensitive. People who do not know better may think of it as a clinging vine, but actually it is a sturdy oak, gnarled but not bowed under the storms of life. I tell you, a love that is patient and kind is the most formidable thing on our planet.

O Father, as the violet leaves its perfume on the heel that crushes it, so let me leave the perfume of divine kindness on all who may hurt me this day. In Jesus' name I ask it. Amen.

FOR FURTHER STUDY – 2 Pet. 1:1–9; 1 Thess. 4:9–10; Jer. 31:3
1. How does God draw us to himself? / 2. What are the steps in the development of our faith?

The purpose of Paul's negatives

FOR READING AND MEDITATION – 1 JOHN 4:1–11

'He who does not love does not know God, for God is love.' (v. 8: NKJ)

We come now to look at four statements that show what love is not. Why does Paul use these four negatives to describe love? Is it just for effect, or is there some other reason behind his choice of expression? I cannot be sure, of course, but I think he is seeking to show that love has to be able to say 'No' as well as 'Yes'. You see, just being positive in life is not enough. You may be positive with the wrong positive and with the wrong spirit behind the positive. You have to be negative to many things in order to be positive to the highest things. A great philosopher once said, 'No one can say "Yes" who hasn't said "No".'

Cast your eye for a moment over some of the characteristics of love which Paul lines up in 1 Corinthians 13: 'Love is patient and kind … Love bears all things, believes all things, hopes all things, endures all things' (vv. 4, 7: RSV). These things could not stand out unless they had a negative backdrop to them: not jealous, not boastful, not arrogant or rude and so on. The very negatives imply a positive. Maturity means that we come to a position in life where we know how to reject as well as accept. To put the statement from the philosopher I referred to above in a different form, 'No man is capable of accepting, who is not capable of rejecting.'

Negativism is bad if it stops at positivism. Behind positivism must be a positive negativism that has said a positive 'No' in order to say a positive 'Yes'. I am not just playing with words. When we are positive in relation to the loving thing, we are negative to the unloving thing.

Gracious and loving Father, make me into a person who knows how to say both 'Yes' and 'No' – 'Yes' to the things that are loving and 'No' to the things that are unloving. In Jesus' name I pray. Amen.

FOR FURTHER STUDY – 2 Cor. 1:13–24; Josh. 24:15; Matt. 5:37
1. What were Joshua's words to the people? / 2. How did Jesus put it?

Living on an even keel

FOR READING AND MEDITATION – ROMANS 12:1–8

'… Do not think of yourself more highly than you ought, but rather think of
yourself with sober judgment …' (v. 3: NIV)

Today we examine the first of the things which Paul says love is not: 'Love is not jealous or boastful' (1 Corinthians 13:4: RSV). Both jealousy and boastfulness show one thing – a deep sense of inferiority and worthlessness. If you are jealous of someone, you most probably (among other things) have feelings of inferiority in relation to that person.

Boastfulness is the obverse side of inferiority and worthlessness – you boast to cover things up. J.S. Bonell says, 'If a man is blatant about his atheism, we may expect to find a desire for a belief in God. If he is constantly protesting his ideas, we may look for an inclination to doubt. If he is suffering from impulses to suicide, we may expect to find deep within him a marked desire to live and accomplish something in which he has been thwarted. If he induces conceit, we may expect to find inferiority. If he is distressed by a feeling of humiliation, we may be sure that pride is present also.'

Agape love (God's love in us) has no inferiority complex – jealousy – nor has it a superiority complex – boastfulness. It is natural and normal and even. An inferiority complex keeps you down in the dumps and a superiority complex brings you into the same condition. A superiority complex is an attempt to lift oneself out of inferiority by a loud assertion of superiority, by boastfulness. But the boastfulness soon gives way and leaves you down in the dumps again. Divine love, or *Agape* love as we are calling it, will not lift you up to false heights nor drop you down into the despairing depths. It is neither up nor down – it is even.

O God, save me from the depths of false inferiority and also from the heights of false superiority. Give me the balanced, even-tempered heart that is so sure, serene and unruffled. Amen.

FOR FURTHER STUDY – Gal. 5:22–26; Prov. 6:34; 1 Cor. 3:3
1. What are the marks of a worldly Christian? / 2. If we live in the Spirit,
what attitudes will we avoid?

Not 'above' or 'below' but 'with'

FOR READING AND MEDITATION – GALATIANS 3:26–4:7

'… you are all one in Christ Jesus.' (v. 28: NIV)

We saw yesterday that *Agape* love saves us from inferiorities and superiorities. Kahlil Gibran puts it this way:

> Only those beneath me can envy or hate me.
> I have never been envied or hated
> I am above no one.
> Only those above me can belittle me.
> I have never been belittled
> I am below no one.

A Christian group I was once with started up a song I had never heard before. They looked around the room at each other, joined hands and sang, 'Not above you, nor below you, but with you.' I could sense that the group meant every word they sang to each other and I tell you, the fellowship and love I experienced among them the one evening I was with them made a deep and lasting impression on me.

Agape love (God's love in us) delivers us from being 'above' or 'below' and enables us to take the position of 'with'. The person who is filled with divine love cannot, by the nature of things, be jealous of another. If there is jealousy, then it is obvious that *Agape* love is not flowing and the heart is under the constraint of a lesser love. For whoever loves his neighbour as himself can neither despise himself nor his neighbour. The dynamic thing about *Agape* love is this – once it invades a heart, it gives a person such a sense of worth that jealousy and boastfulness simply cannot take root.

My Father and my God, I see so clearly that without Agape love, I do not really live – I simply exist. Let this love be illustrated in me this day in all my thoughts and relationships. In Jesus' name I ask it. Amen.

FOR FURTHER STUDY – James 4:10–17; Psa. 10:3; Prov. 25:14, 27:1
1. How does James describe our life? / 2. What is the folly of boasting?

The basis of true humility

FOR READING AND MEDITATION – PSALM 18:16–36

'… Your gentleness has made me great.' (v. 35: NKJ)

We come now to another of Paul's statements in which he points out what love is not: 'Love … is not arrogant or rude' (1 Corinthians 13:5: RSV). The Amplified Bible puts it thus: 'It is not conceited – arrogant and inflated with pride; it is not rude (unmannerly) and does not act unbecomingly.' The word *arrogant* seems at first to be so close to *boastful* that one wonders whether Paul is just being repetitive. Think of it this way – boastfulness is outward and verbal; arrogance is inward and comes across, not so much in our words as in our attitudes.

The rude and arrogant act the way they do because they are unsure of themselves. Only the humble are sure of themselves, and only those who are sure of themselves are humble. One of my favourite passages of Scripture is John 13, and I am pulled back to it time and time again. It says: 'Jesus, knowing that the Father had given all things into his hands, and that he had come from God and was going to God … girded himself with a towel … and began to wash the disciples' feet' (vv. 3–5: RSV).

What was the secret of Christ's humility? In my opinion, it was the consciousness of his greatness. Listen to it again: 'Knowing that the Father had given all things into his hands … that he had come from God and was going to God … girded himself with a towel … and began to wash the disciples' feet.' Only the great are humble; they have to be in order to be great. Believe me, you will never know greatness until you know humility, and you will never know humility until you know greatness – the greatness of who you are in God.

Father, pour your love into me in greater measure than ever before, so that I may know the lowly heart and the kindly attitude. Make me so inwardly great that I can afford to be humble – in speech and in act. In Christ's name I ask it. Amen.

FOR FURTHER STUDY – 1 John 2:1–16; Prov. 11:2; Psa. 138:6
1. What is 'the pride of life'? / 2. What accompanies pride?

The true way to be humble

FOR READING AND MEDITATION – ACTS 20:17–38

'Serving the Lord with all humility, with many tears and trials ...' (v. 19: NKJ)

We spend another day looking at the statement: 'Love is not arrogant or rude.' If we turn this statement from its negative form to a positive one, the thought we come out with is, of course – humility. I have often reflected on the words of Phillip Brooks who, when commenting on humility, said, 'The true way to be humble is not to stoop until you are smaller than yourself, but to stand at your real height against some higher nature that will show you what the real smallness of your greatest greatness is.'

If this is true, then we must stand at our very highest. Look at Christ and then be forever humble. You see, when we lose sight of Christ, then self looms large. A man said to an evangelist, 'I used to believe in God, but now I don't believe in anything except myself. In fact I am coming round to believe that I myself am God.' He gave up believing in the true God and focused his attention on an idol – himself. That is exactly what happens when we lose sight of God – we lose our source of humility.

Agape love (God's love in us) enables us to be truly humble. A lot of what we call humility in the Christian church (as I have said before) is really self-belittlement. True humility flows out of a consciousness of greatness. Those who do not see their greatness in God may act in humble ways, but their humility flows out of wrong motives. They work at being humble in the hope that it will provide them with a sense of greatness. But, as we saw yesterday, the humility of Jesus flowed out of his sense of greatness. All things had been given into his hands, so he chose to use those hands to wash the disciples' feet.

O God, help me never to lose sight of you and my greatness in you, for when I do, I lose the source of true humility. You stooped to serve me – now I shall stoop to serve others. Amen.

FOR FURTHER STUDY – Luke 14:1–11; Prov. 16:19; Rom. 12:3
1. How did Jesus illustrate humility? / 2. How does Paul say we should view ourselves?

Love – the law of our being

FOR READING AND MEDITATION – ROMANS 13:8–14

'Love does no harm to a neighbour; therefore love is the fulfilment of the law.'
(v. 10: NKJ)

We look now at another thing love does not do: 'Love does not insist on its own way'
(1 Corinthians 13:5: RSV). So deeply entrenched in human nature is the desire to
get our own way that only *Agape* love (God's love in us) can give us victory over it.

One writer points out that outside of the help given to us through Jesus Christ,
there are just two ways we can take in order to get the victory over wanting our own
way. One is to retreat into empty silence, where we become a nonentity, everybody's
doormat; the other is to sink into silent, sullen resentment. Many take the first way
– the way of empty silence – and become household drudges; they accept it as a
kind of self-punishment for wanting their own way, a kind of masochism. Those
who take the second way – the way of silent, sullen resentment – are painful to live
with because they are like a time bomb just waiting to explode. Either way is a disaster to the personality and a threat to good relationships.

The best way of not wanting your own way is to allow God's love to invade and
penetrate your heart, for then you are caught up in something beyond yourself – a
higher purpose and a higher plan. You find yourself wanting God's way more than
your own way, for your inner being recognises that his way is always best. You don't
care what happens as far as your way is concerned so long as his way and purposes
are furthered. This saves the self from insistence on its own way and, at the same
time, saves the self from disintegrating. You see, love is the law of our being, and
when divine love flows in and through us, our personalities feel complete. Our inner
being says, 'This is what I was made for.' And how!

*My Father and my God, I see that only your love flowing through me can break the tyranny of self-
preoccupation and give me the outgoing heart that will find itself released, happy and fulfilled.
Flow in, dear Lord – still more. Amen.*

FOR FURTHER STUDY – 1 Cor. 10:1–24; Rom. 14:21; 2 Cor. 10:12; Phil. 2:4
1. What are we not to seek? / 2. What are we to look for?

Giving up our rights

FOR READING AND MEDITATION – PHILIPPIANS 2:1–13

'Each of you should look not only to your own interests,
but also to the interests of others.' (v. 4: NIV)

We continue meditating on the statement: 'Love does not insist on its own way.' The
Amplified Bible puts it like this: 'Love does not insist on its own rights or its own
way, for it is not self-seeking.'

Here in Britain, we teach our children the importance of personal rights. A saying that is often used is, 'An Englishman's home is his castle.' I learned as a boy that
even the King or Queen of England, if they came to the door of my home, would have
to knock and wait to be admitted. Their royal status does not give them the right to
enter into anyone's home uninvited. We British people cling tightly to our rights, but
there comes a time when the law of love compels us to acknowledge a higher right
– the right to give up our rights.

Henry Drummond argues that Paul's statement: 'Love does not insist on its
own rights' means much more than just giving up our rights; it means being willing to recognise that we have no rights at all,' he says, 'it is not hard to give up our
rights. They are often external. The hard thing is to give up ourselves. The more difficult thing still is not to seek things for ourselves at all. After we have sought them,
bought them, won them, deserved them, we have taken the cream off them for ourselves already. Little difficulty, then, to give them up.' If it is more difficult, as Henry
Drummond has said, not to seek something for ourselves than, having sought it, to
give it up, then we are faced with a hard and difficult challenge. Hard and difficult?
Not really, for if we truly understand it, the way of *Agape* love (God's love in us) is
an easier way than any other.

My Father and my God, quietly my ideas and opinions are being overturned – overturned by love.
Help me understand the truth that happiness comes, not through getting, but through giving.
In Christ's name I ask it. Amen.

FOR FURTHER STUDY – Matt. 26:36–39; 1 Cor. 10:31–33; 2 Cor. 8:1–9
1. How did Jesus demonstrate this submission? / 2. What was Paul's motivation?

I don't get ulcers – I give them

FOR READING AND MEDITATION – 1 PETER 1:13–25

'Now that you have purified yourselves … so that you have sincere love
for your brothers, love one another deeply …' (v. 22: NIV)

We come now to another step on the road of love: 'Love … is not irritable or resentful' (1 Corinthians 13:5: RSV). The Amplified Bible puts it like this: 'Love … is not touchy or fretful or resentful.' Time and time again, when talking to people in counselling sessions, they have said to me, 'How can I get rid of touchiness and resentment?' After many years in the Christian ministry, I have come to regard irritation and resentment as two of the biggest evils that can take root in the human heart.

A businessman sat in his office and bellowed at a man on the other end of the line. A friend of the businessman, sitting with him in the office, said, 'If you keep that up, you will get a stomach ulcer.' The businessman said, 'I don't get ulcers, I give them.' He said it with an air of finality – but was it final? Was he only giving ulcers and not getting any? Perhaps his stomach had a tough lining that resisted ulceration, but if I know anything about human functioning, his spirit was certainly becoming ulcerated. And that, to my way of thinking, is a far worse condition than an ulcerated stomach. That which did not show up in the physical would inevitably show up in the spirit. Irritation toward others would produce increased irritation toward himself. Like Haman in the Bible, he would be hanged on the gallows he had prepared for others.

What is the root cause of irritation and resentment? I believe it to be an unsurrendered self. Once the self – the centre of irritation and resentment – is fully surrendered to Christ and *Agape* love is allowed to invade the whole of the personality, then irritability and resentment dissolve as quickly as sugar in hot tea.

O Father, you who are truly Love, invade me this day with Love's strong and mighty power so that my ugly, touchy, resentful self shall be changed and become the beautiful self you purpose for me to be. In Jesus' name I ask it. Amen.

FOR FURTHER STUDY – Heb. 12:1–15; Eph. 4:30–31; Prov. 14:10
1. What results from not drawing on God's grace? / 2. How can we grieve the Holy Spirit?

Fill up and feel the difference!

FOR READING AND MEDITATION – 2 THESSALONIANS 3:1–18

'May the Lord direct your hearts into realising and showing the love of God ...'
(v. 5: Amplified)

We ended yesterday with the thought that the answer to irritation and resentment is a surrendered self. A farmer got up in a testimony meeting and said this, 'If you know how to surrender to God and let the power of his love take hold of you, then you won't short-change yourself.' He meant, of course, that to live any other way than the way of love is to miss getting the best out of life – short-changing yourself. The irritable and resentful are always short-changing themselves, for life was not made to work that way.

The universe was designed by what J.B. Phillips calls 'an Aggressive Lover'. But God is more than just a person who acts lovingly; the Bible puts it in this way: 'God is love' (1 John 4:8). Not just loving, or *has love*, or *does loving things* – he is love. This means that he would violate his own nature if he acted in ways contrary to love. He cannot act against love and still be God; if he did the stars would tumble from the sky and the whole universe disintegrate, for the creation was made for love and can only function effectively when it is sustained by love.

The same applies to you and me; we too were designed to run on love – *Agape* love. If divine love does not permeate and penetrate our beings, we chug along the road of life like a car that is functioning on an inferior grade of petrol. It goes, but it does not go in the way it was designed. Our Creator never intended for us to function on irritation and resentment, so let's allow our Heavenly Mechanic to flush out the inferior grade of love that may be within us and fill us up with *Agape* love. Then – feel the difference!

O God, how foolish I am to splutter and sputter along the road of life, tolerating the intolerable, when I can come to you and fill up with a different grade of love. Help me, dear Lord. Amen.

FOR FURTHER STUDY– 1 John 2:1–11; 2 John 6; Psa. 107:8, 118:1
1. How is God's love made complete in us? / 2. What is his command?

Right – and yet wrong

FOR READING AND MEDITATION – 1 TIMOTHY 6:3–21
'… pursue righteousness, godliness, faith, love …' (v. 11: NKJ)

We come to yet another step in the unfolding of love: 'Love … does not rejoice at wrong, but rejoices in the right' (1 Corinthians 13:6: RSV). It is surprising how easy it is for us to rejoice at wrong. We don't do it consciously, of course, because then we would recognise it and be compelled to do something about it. It goes on unconsciously beneath the surface of our thinking, but it is none the less devastating for all that.

One of the things I am grateful for is that over the years, I have had the privilege of sitting in hundreds of counselling sessions with people and have heard and seen them when they have come to a moment of self-awareness. Time and time again, when people have come to recognise some of the hidden underlying motives that moved them to act and behave the way they did, I have heard them say, 'I could never believe that I was capable of that.' Consciously they would not be capable of it, but unconsciously they were.

I am not giving secrets away when I talk about these things, for whenever I refer to what I have discovered in a private counselling session, I always change a few details so that no one can recognise themselves or say, 'I think I know who he is talking about.' A Christian worker I talked to some years ago was deeply critical of his fellow workers. Consciously he told himself, 'These people are not living the life they should, and ought to be exposed.' He came to recognise, however, that unconsciously he was saying to himself, 'Their wrongness boosts my rightness.' However correct his criticism, he was being driven by another law than the law of love.

O Father, let your love so invade my personality that it will penetrate, not only my consciousness but my unconscious also. I would be inwardly unified and united – united by love. In Jesus' name I ask it. Amen.

FOR FURTHER STUDY – Phil. 1:1–11; Hos. 1:12; Matt. 5:20
1. What are we to break up? / 2. What are we to be filled with?

I wouldn't do that

FOR READING AND MEDITATION – 2 JOHN 1–13

'It has given me great joy to find some of your children walking in the truth …'
(v. 4: NIV)

We continue meditating on the fact that unless our personalities are strengthened and girded by divine love, we can easily fall into the trap of rejoicing at wrong. We do not do it consciously – we do it unconsciously.

I once talked to a young man who had become involved with a group who were concerned about the many obscene and pornographic books and magazines that were appearing on some of the newsagents bookshelves in his town. (The anti-pornography stand, by the way, is something that has my wholehearted support.) However, after a while he began to experience some deep inner conflicts and after many hours of talking and praying together, he came to see that the roots of his problem lay in the fact that he unconsciously delighted in the discovery of pornographic literature, for it satisfied his curiosity concerning sex and at the same time boosted his own estimate of himself, 'I wouldn't do that.' Once he came to recognise this and dealt with it, he was set free from the unconscious conflict and involved himself in a new way with the work he felt called to do.

What is the unconscious motive behind criticism, mote-picking or wanting to expose the wrongs of others? It is this – if I can find wrong in others, it will help to boost my superiority – their wrongness boosts my rightness. And what is the test of whether we are acting by love or by a desire to boost ourselves? It is simple: in pointing out wrong, do I become a more loving person in the process? If so, then love is the basis of my actions. If I become a less loving person, then it suggests I am operating from a motive that is not based on love.

O Father, save me from secretly rejoicing when others show weakness or fall into sin. Help me to rejoice in nothing but good. Then I shall become what I rejoice in. Fill me with love. In Jesus' name. Amen.

FOR FURTHER STUDY – Matt. 7:1–5; Prov. 30:12; Rom. 2:1
1. What human tendency did Jesus point out? / 2. What was his remedy?

Love uses all things

FOR READING AND MEDITATION – LUKE 21:5–19

'... they will lay hands on you and persecute you ... This will result in
your being witnesses to them.' (vv. 12–13: NIV)

Having looked at what love is not, Paul now turns to focus on four aspects of love: 'Love bears all things, believes all things, hopes all things, endures all things' (1 Corinthians 13:7: RSV). The first and the last are similar: 'bears ... endures'. The two central ones are also similar: 'believes ... hopes'. The two at the centre save the first and the last – save them from just bearing and enduring. They therefore become believing and hopeful bearing and believing and hopeful enduring.

It is not a sad, morose, despairing kind of bearing; it is bearing with a smile – the smile of belief and hope. Bearing and enduring have a pulse at their centre, the beats of which are, alternately, belief and hope. This saves bearing and enduring from being stoical and makes them Christian. Stoics are the people who are committed to facing life's problems with the grim determination that nothing will get them down. This attitude produces brittleness in the personality, and you know what happens to things that are brittle – they easily break.

The Christian in whom *Agape* love flows does not break – he bends. When, many years ago, I first came across the verse that is before us today in the Amplified Bible: 'They will lay their hands on you and persecute you ... This will be a time (an opportunity) for you to bear testimony', an entirely new world opened up before me. Before that I had concentrated on trying to analyse problems and explain them, but since then, I have seen that my task is not to explain them, but to use them.

Gracious and loving Heavenly Father, drive this truth so deeply into my spirit this day that it will become one of the turning points of my life and experience. Help me see that your Agape love enables me to bear all things – because I can use all things. Amen.

FOR FURTHER STUDY – Eph. 4:1–8; Col. 3:13
1. What did Paul urge the Ephesians and Colossians to do? / 2. How does it apply to us?

Cosmic optimism

FOR READING AND MEDITATION – ROMANS 8:28–39

'… we know that in all things God works for the good of those who love him …'
(v. 28: NIV)

We continue from where we left off yesterday, with the emphasis that the reason why *Agape* love (God's love in us) bears all things is because it can use all things. Love is so creative that it can wrest from the worst situations something that is positive and good. Evil put Jesus on a cross but Jesus, being love, made that cross redemptive. When God's *Agape* love flows in us and through us, there is nothing, no matter how hurtful or evil it is, that cannot be transformed into good.

Tolstoy, in his book, *My Confessions and My Religion*, says in substance, 'There are those who say: (1) Life is all bad, so get drunk and forget it. (2) Life is bad, but struggle hard against it. (3) Life is bad, so do the logical thing and end it. (4) Life is bad, but live on and accept things as they come.' How sad if that was the full statement on life. The Christian view of life is this: life may at times be hard and difficult, but no matter what comes, we have within us a redemptive energy called love that lifts us above every negative situation and turns every setback into a springboard, every stumbling-block into a stepping stone and every reversal into a leap forward.

There are limitations, of course. Even Jesus recognised that he was thwarted in his own community: 'A prophet is not without honour except in his own country' (Mark 6:4, NKJ). He was thwarted there, but that very limitation became a contribution and spilled over in love, healing and blessing to other parts of Palestine. Christianity has been described as *cosmic optimism*. It is – for love uses everything that comes – good, bad and indifferent.

Lord Jesus Christ, draw closer to me today and let your love flow so deeply into me and through me that together we will turn every bad or evil thing that comes into glorious good. In your dear name I ask it. Amen.

FOR FURTHER STUDY – 2 Cor. 4; Psa. 34:19, 41:3; Isa. 43:2
1. What was Paul's perspective on difficult times? / 2. In which four ways did he express it?

walking the way of love

Seeing with double vision

FOR READING AND MEDITATION – JOHN 1:29–42

'… You are Simon son of John. You will be called Cepha
(which, when translated is Peter).' (v. 42: NIV)

Love, says Paul, not only bears all things but believes all things. The Amplified
Bible puts it thus: 'Love … is ever ready to believe the best of every person …'
(1 Corinthians 13:7). What is it about *Agape* love that enables us to do this? I think it
is because love sees with a double vision – it sees things, not merely as they are, but
as they can be.

Our Lord, when he looked at Simon as he was, said: 'You are Simon son of John.'
What was Simon like before love changed him? He was bluff, impulsive, loud-
mouthed (and, on one occasion, foul-mouthed), a braggart, inconsiderate and so on.
That was Simon as he was. But what was Simon as he could be? Listen again to what
Jesus says: 'You shall be … Cephas' (rock). What a change! The unstable becoming
a rock. The impulsive blusterer could be clear in judgment and firm in will. The man
who could curse and swear and deny all knowledge of his Lord to save his own skin
would become a powerful spiritual leader with the privilege of opening the gates of
the Kingdom to the first converts after Pentecost.

Can this be the same man that we read about in the Gospels? Simon's friends
(perhaps you and I if we had been there) would not have seen it, but Jesus saw it.
And why? Because Christ sees with double vision. His love always looks beyond
what is to what can be. He looked on the unstable Simon and saw a rock. He looked
on Saul and saw Paul. He looked on Augustine the *roué* and saw Augustine the saint.
And that is what will happen to you and me when we allow our hearts to be invaded by *Agape* love. We will take on the same perspective as our Lord and see people,
not merely as they are, but as they can be.

*O Jesus, Lord and Master, help me to stand at your elbow and get the double vision. Fill me so full
of Agape love that I will become transformed in the way I look at people, and see then not as they
are, but as they can be. For your own name's sake. Amen.*

FOR FURTHER STUDY – John 21:1–22; Eph. 6:24; 1 Pet. 1:8–9
1. What was Jesus' question to Peter? / 2. What was Peter's response?

The influence of Agape love

FOR READING AND MEDITATION– ACTS 2:14–36

'Then Peter stood up … and addressed the crowd …' (v. 14: NIV)

We spend another day discussing what we touched on yesterday, namely, that love sees with a double vision. We said that our Lord saw two Simons. First, Simon as he was, and second, the Simon he could become. The two were so different that they required a different name. *Agape* love flowing through the heart of Christ toward Simon Peter took a while to bring about the change that Christ predicted (in fact, about three years), but, as we can see from the passage before us today, Peter became the fearless and unshakeable champion of a spiritual movement that shook the world.

In the same, but of course a lesser way, we too can come alongside men and women, as did our Lord, and look upon them as they can become. You may meet someone today who, at first glance, seems ineffective, inferior, frustrated, beaten by beastliness. Ask God to help you see them as they can become – saved, dependent, confident, effective, sanctified. I came across an interesting, though imperfect definition of democracy the other day, 'Democracy is the madness that believes about people that which isn't true, and yet without that belief they will never become what we believe them to be.'

A positive attitude tends to create the very thing it believes in. If this is true of democracy, then how much truer it is of love. Of course, it is important to recognise that simply believing the best of a person will not by itself bring that person into the Kingdom of God. Everyone needs to make their own personal commitment to Christ in order to be saved. Believing the best of a person, however – a function of *Agape* love – gives added influence to all the other ways God uses in bringing men and women to himself.

Jesus, my loving Lord and Master, help me also to see with a double vision – to view people, not just as they are but what they can become in you. For I know that the attitude of love adds untold strength and power to my words. In your name. Amen.

FOR FURTHER STUDY – 2 Cor. 8:1–9; Rom. 12:10; Phil. 2:4; 1 Cor. 10:32–33
1. What did Christ demonstrate? / 2. How did Paul's life echo this?

Hope – a powerful working force

FOR READING AND MEDITATION – 1 PETER 1:3–13

'... By his boundless mercy we have been born again to an ever-living hope ...'
(v. 3: Amplified)

Another characteristic of *Agape* love (God's love in us) is that it has at its heart a deathless hope. Love not only bears all things and believes all things but hopes all things (1 Corinthians 13:7: RSV). The only faith that uses hope as a working force is the Christian faith.

You may have seen a copy of the famous picture by G.F. Watts called *Hope*, which shows a blindfolded woman sitting with bowed head on a sphere and holding a lyre in her hand. Only one string of the instrument remains unbroken, only one star shines in the sky. The artist, reaching out for some meaning that those who do not think in symbols find difficult to grasp, called the picture *Hope*. Two charwomen were overheard talking about the picture early one morning and one said to the other, '*Hope*? Why is it called *Hope*?' The other charlady, gazing at the figure perched precariously on the sphere, replied, 'I suppose because she hopes she won't fall off.'

Many people think of hope as a poor, precarious thing, an illusion, a vanity, a disease of the mind. The cynic has said, 'He who lives on hope will die starving.' Cowley said, 'Hope is the most hopeless thing of all.' Schopenhauer, the distinguished German philosopher, looked upon hope as 'the bait by which nature gets her hook in our nose and makes us serve her interests rather than our own'. That is the common assessment of hope in our world – a poor, vain, unproductive thing. But hope is not so thought of in the New Testament. It is seen there for the buoyant thing that it is – a conviction that, no matter what, love, *Agape* love will ultimately bring all things to a good and glorious end.

My Father and my God, let my heart be so filled with your love that the things around me which seem hopeless may come alive with hope. For I sense that when I am alive with hope, everything around me will become alive with it. Thank you, dear Father. Amen.

FOR FURTHER STUDY – Rom. 15:1–4, 5:5; 1 Pet. 3:15
1. Where does our conviction spring from? / 2. What should we always be ready to do?

Anchored to eternity

FOR READING AND MEDITATION – HEBREWS 6:9–20

'… a hope that reaches farther and enters into the very certainty
of the Presence within the veil.' (v. 19: Amplified)

Yesterday we saw that the world views hope as something illusory and vain, while the New Testament looks upon it as a positive virtue. Today we ask ourselves: how did this sharp contrast arise? An illusion: a steadfast reality. A dream: a fact. Hope cannot be both. Is the world right, or is the New Testament right? The answer is not difficult, for they are talking of different things. There is a worldly and there is a spiritual hope. There is gilt and there is gold.

The world's view of hope is more easily understood if we call it by its rightful name – optimism. We cannot deny the value of optimism, of course – it is not the full cream but there is something to be said for skimmed milk. Optimism, we all know, is better than pessimism, but really it does not have a strong foundation to stand on. There are people facing problems today for which even the greatest optimism will prove inadequate. A minister tells of a man in the community whose wife was gravely ill. The man said to the minister, 'It's all right. She is bound to get better. I'm an optimist, you know. I always look on the bright side of things.' The minister buried his wife before the week was out.

Boisterous confidence which has no solid foundation in fact looks pitifully ludicrous when crushing disappointment comes. How different from the New Testament's description of hope which, in our text for today, is pictured as an anchor that is fixed in eternity. Optimism drops its anchor into the depths of trouble but cannot find the bottom. Hope drops its anchor into the depths of trouble and finds eternity.

O Father, what deep reassurance it gives me to know that whatever I am called upon to face today, my life is securely anchored to eternity. I have a hope that may be disturbed but cannot be destroyed. I am so deeply, deeply thankful. Amen.

FOR FURTHER STUDY – 1 Pet. 1:1–9; Prov. 14:32; Acts 24:15
1. How does Peter describe this hope? / 2. What effect does hope have on heaviness?

walking the way of love

God does not work our way

FOR READING AND MEDITATION – HEBREWS 1:1–14

'… Your throne, o God, is forever and ever …' (v. 8: NKJ)

Today we ask ourselves the question: what is it that makes the Christian hope so unique? It is based on two things – the indestructibility of truth and the permanence of God's eternal throne. We live in an age when scant respect is paid to truth. 'Truth', we are often told, 'is the very first casualty in war'. But truth is mighty. It may be nailed to a cross, taken down, hidden in a sepulchre and sealed with a great stone. But it rises again! The life principle in it cannot be killed. Truth partakes of the life of God and therefore of God's eternity. Its triumph is always sure.

The second ground of our confident hope is that God is on the throne. It may be difficult for many to believe that, especially when God appears to allow so much injustice in his world. The problem is a very old one; it puzzled the psalmists and perplexed the prophets. It even baffled Simon Peter as he stood and watched Christ being taken captive by the soldiers. The question must have hammered in his brain, 'Why? Why? Why?'

Let it be plainly said again, however simplistic it may sound to those who want answers they can clearly understand – God does not work our way. He allows things to happen that make it appear that he is uncaring and unconcerned. But that can never be, for his very nature is love. One thing is certain – even though we cannot understand why he allows us to go through many strange and difficult experiences, he will never forsake us in those experiences. The cross is the pledge of that. Our Lord will never forsake the world of his incarnation. Hallelujah! God is on the throne! This is why, when all the shallow hopes of the world are dead – we can hope on.

O Father, let me abound in love, for I see that when I do, I abound in hope. Help me to lay hold of these two facts – that truth is indestructible and that no one will ever unseat you from your throne. Father, my hope is eternally in you. Amen.

FOR FURTHER STUDY – Psa. 24:1–10; Isa. 9:1–7; Matt. 8:27; Eph. 1:22
1. What is the assurance of the believer? / 2. What did the disciples marvel at?

The loss of meaning

FOR READING AND MEDITATION – HEBREWS 12:1–13

'Looking unto Jesus … who for the joy that was set before him endured the cross, despising the shame …' (v. 2: NKJ)

We come now to the last of Paul's positives concerning love: 'Love endures all things.' Although the word 'endures' is similar to the earlier expression, 'bears', there is a slight difference. To *bear* has more to do with behaviour; to *endure* has more to do with the attitude that underlies behaviour.

Paul, when writing to Timothy, said: 'I am ready to … endure everything for the sake of the elect (God's chosen), so that they too may obtain the salvation which is in Christ Jesus …' (2 Timothy 2:10: Amplified). He was ready to 'endure' everything because he saw there was a point to his endurance: 'for the sake of the elect'. *Agape* love (God's love in us) strengthens and fortifies us to carry on right to the very end of everything God allows to come our way. And why? Because love would never let us go through what we have to go through unless there was a point and purpose to it. Convinced of this, we are able to face anything.

Creath Davies, in his book *How to Win in a Crisis*, says, 'The loss of meaning is perhaps the most devastating crisis we can experience.' He goes on to tell of the experience of Victor Frankl, who was interned by Hitler in one of his concentration camps. Frankl, now a famous psychiatrist, talks of how he observed that those who survived the horror of the Nazi concentration camps did so because they saw a point or a purpose for them being there. In other words, the concentration camps came to have some meaning for them. Without meaning, life becomes drained of its colour and bleached of all interest. Love, however, gives meaning to life. Believe me, it would never expose us to life's hardships unless there was a point and a purpose in doing so.

O Father, I see how much I need not only to hear this truth, but to absorb it into my being. Impress it so deeply within my spirit that I will never forget you love me too much to let me go through difficult situations unless they have meaning. Amen.

FOR FURTHER STUDY – Acts 20:17–24; James 5:11; Gal. 6:9
1. What did Paul declare to the Ephesian elders?
2. What does love bring about in due season?

He who has a why

FOR READING AND MEDITATION – 2 TIMOTHY 2:1–13
'Endure hardship with us like a good soldier of Christ Jesus.' (v. 3: NIV)

We touched yesterday on the experience of Victor Frankl in the Nazi concentration camps, who witnessed the fact that those who survived did so because they saw in their experience some deep meaning. When a man could no longer make sense of his suffering in those camps, he was finished.

Let Victor Frankl put what he discovered in his own words, 'Any attempt to restore a man's inner strength in the camp had first to succeed in showing him some future goal. "He who has a *why* to live for can bear with almost any *how*." Whenever there was an opportunity for it, one had to give them a *why* – an aim for their lives – in order to strengthen them to bear the terrible *how* of their existence. Woe to him who saw no more sense in his life, no aim, no purpose, and therefore no point in carrying on. He was soon lost.'

One of the components lying beneath non-organic depression is a sense of meaninglessness. Such despair often leads to suicide. Today, as you read these lines, many will bring their lives to an end simply because they do not have a *why* for living. The loss of meaning can be much less dramatic than the experience in the concentration camps. There is a type of depression called *Sunday Depression*, where people who have been active all the week in their work suddenly find themselves with nothing to do or no one to impress or please, whereupon the emptiness that is inside them becomes more apparent. The Christian whose heart is filled with *Agape* love will sense a meaning and a purpose in everything he or she is called to face. They can endure the *how* because they have a *why* – the *why* of eternal purpose and eternal meaning.

Gracious and loving Father, thank you for opening my eyes to see that endurance is not a chore, but a challenge. Love lets me go through things because love is at work, giving meaning to all things. I am so deeply grateful. Amen.

FOR FURTHER STUDY – Eph. 1:1–12, 3:10–11; Isa. 14:26–27
1. What is the purpose of God revealed in Ephesians? / 2. What did Isaiah prophesy?

Eros fails – Agape never fails

FOR READING AND MEDITATION – JEREMIAH 31:1–14
'… I have loved you with an everlasting love …' (v. 3: NKJ)

Paul now begins the section which Henry Drummond describes as the 'defence of love' with the words: 'Love never fails' (1 Corinthians 13:8: NKJ). The Amplified Bible puts it: 'Love never fails – never fades out or becomes obsolete or comes to an end.' How beautiful.

When Paul says: 'Love never fails', he is referring to *Agape* love which, as you know, is the highest form of love in the universe. Every other kind of love is prone to failure. At the centre of *Eros* love (as we saw) are the seeds of its own failure, for *Eros* love is self-seeking love. If you love people for what you can get out of them, then they give you back in kind – they love you for what they can get out of you. That is self-defeating. Each suspects the motive of the other, and in such an atmosphere – love dies.

I read recently of a wealthy businessman who came into contact with the love of God in such a way that it turned him inside out. He was an alcoholic, but one day he met a Christian who stopped and prayed for him and then just walked away. The man stood there all alone and suddenly felt God's healing presence come right into his being. He was immediately healed in mind, in soul and in body. His nerves became calmed and now, years later, he says that miraculously, the craving for alcohol dropped away and has never returned. He is now on fire with the love of God. Not all conversions are as dramatic as this, but here is my point – suppose someone had said to the man, 'Try to love God and you will be free of all craving for alcohol' – would that have helped? No, because in his own strength he could only have loved with *Eros* love. *Eros* love fails but *Agape* love never fails.

O Father, I am so grateful that your Agape love reached down to me and has lifted me to the highest heaven. It not only fills me with wonder and awe, but also with a passion to share it. May I share it liberally with all whom I meet this day. Amen.

FOR FURTHER STUDY –1 John 4:7–21; 2 Cor. 4:18; Heb. 12:27
1. Where does Agape love start? / 2. What important statement does John repeat twice?

walking the way of love

Either way you win

FOR READING AND MEDITATION – MATTHEW 10:1–16

'As you enter the home, give it your greeting. If the home is deserving,
let your peace rest on it; if it is not, let your peace return to you.' (vv. 12–13: NIV)

Today we face the thought that if our love has been failing, it is due to the fact that it is tainted with *Eros* and is lacking in *Agape*. For *Agape* love never fails. *Eros* has a hook in it – a hook of self-interest; *Agape* wants nothing – except to give itself. There are times, of course, when it may seem that *Agape* love does fail. It may be that you have been loving someone with true *Agape*, but up to this moment your love has not evoked a response in them. You must realise that I am not talking now about a romantic relationship, but a situation in which you may be continuing to express *Agape* love to someone who fails to respond and continues to show resentment and hostility.

Does this mean that *Agape* is failing? No, for the statement: 'Love never fails', does not mean that love will always succeed in gaining its immediate object. So what does it mean? It means (so I believe) that even though you may not succeed in a situation where you have expressed *Agape* love, nevertheless you have not failed, for you yourself are all the better for loving.

Look again at our text for today – Jesus is saying that if the people of a house to whom you give peace do not receive it, then let your peace return to you. So you see, you are more peaceful for having given the peace. Either way you win. If they take it, good; if they don't take it, then it is still good. The loving and peaceful person always wins, for he becomes more loving in the giving out of love, even if the other person doesn't receive that love. There is no failure in the lives of those who express *Agape* love.

O Father, how exciting and releasing is this thought – that because love is so victorious, I simply cannot fail when I love. For I become more loving in the giving of love. Continue to love in and through me this day and every day. Amen.

FOR FURTHER STUDY – Luke 6: 27–38; Matt. 10:8; Acts 20:35
1. What was Jesus' instruction to his disciples? / 2. What was his promise?

Love makes the world go round

FOR READING AND MEDITATION – COLOSSIANS 1:13–23

'For by him all things were created … all things were created by him and for him.'
(v. 16: NIV)

Today we ask ourselves: if it is true that 'love never fails' (for it never fails to enrich the giver of love), is it also true that those who are unloving cannot succeed? Yes, I believe it is. Those who succeed in carrying through an unloving attitude or deed do not really succeed, for the unloving attitude or deed registers itself in them in a way that brings about an inner loss and deprivation. The pay-off is in the person – they are demeaned by their unlovingness.

So you see, outer success can be an inner failure. If 'love never fails', then 'unlove' never succeeds. It can't by its very nature. I am persuaded that to love is the only way to live – and live effectively. To act in any other way than in love is to inject into any situation a disruptive tendency which will sooner or later complicate the situation and tie it up in knots. If there is one conclusion I have come to after many years of studying the Scriptures and talking to people about their problems, it is this – the world was made to work in love's way and in no other way. If we try to make it work in any other way than love, we work our own ruin.

A business organisation I know runs a seminar entitled *Putting People First*, in which businessmen and women are taught how to put others before themselves. This seminar is making a big impact on people even though it has a secular approach, for it is making the point that the loving attitude is the only thing that works – really works. Wouldn't it be wonderful if those who see this would go on to the next step and open up their beings to the Source of all love? Then they would find, not just an answer to living but *the* answer to living.

My Father, help me to love this day with your love. Then all ugliness will be turned to beauty, all littleness into greatness and all pettiness into significance. In Jesus' name I pray. Amen.

FOR FURTHER STUDY – John 1:1–13; 1 John 3:1–2, 4:7–8; Eph. 5:2
1. What are we called? / 2. What should our lifestyle reflect?

Transformed already

FOR READING AND MEDITATION – 2 CORINTHIANS 3:1–18

'But we all, with unveiled face, beholding as in a mirror the glory of the Lord,
are being transformed into the same image ...' (v. 18: NKJ)

We have been saying that even when love does not succeed in changing the object of one's love, it never fails to bring about changes in the one who expresses love. This thought, however, must not be allowed to turn our gaze away from the fact that love does have a powerful influence in bringing about changes in others, and to bring some perspective to our thinking, permit me to take up that thought and deal with it in more detail.

A woman who was bent on changing people but continually kept failing writes, 'The last morning of the conference I knew I was his, and knew that I had to stop trying to transform and change everyone. You didn't know it, but everything you said was a confirmation of what God had previously been trying to say to me. Suddenly I began to see people through the eyes of Jesus, and when I looked at them through his eyes they all looked so wonderful, so transformed already. I am not capable of transforming anyone. But to love them and help them find him is the answer. Thank you for showing me that.'

The letter was not written to me but to someone else, and I have quoted it because it makes a powerful point – the woman who had been trying to transform everyone was herself transformed by the love of Jesus within. Love does transform things, not into gold as did the touch of Midas, but into love, more precious than gold. If you are someone who likes changing people, then give it up now before you have a breakdown. It just won't work. Give out love and only love. For in the giving out of love, you not only transform yourself but there is a high chance that you will transform others. Hence – a double cure.

Father, help me to do just that – to give out love and only love. Show me that my task is not to transform people, but to love them. I fail only as I fail to love. Help me love as you love. In Jesus' name I ask it. Amen.

FOR FURTHER STUDY – Luke 10:25–37; Matt. 22:39; 1 Thess. 3:12
1. How did Jesus illustrate practical love? / 2. What was his conclusion?

Love – a conquering force

FOR READING AND MEDITATION – EPHESIANS 5:1–16

'… walk in love, as Christ also has loved us and given himself for us …' (v. 2: NKJ)

Today we look at a real-life situation to show that what we have been saying about the power of love to transform is not something intangible and vague but real and powerful. When I was in Singapore some years ago, I was told of a Chinese Christian who was saved from what looked like certain death through the expression of *Agape* love.

When the Communist portion of Chiang Kaishek's army took over Nanking (now Nanjing), they began to loot the city, and coming to a mission compound, entered some of the homes to seize whatever they could find. One of the Chinese Christians who was staying there, a professor of theology, decided that whatever happened, he would respond in love. When a soldier struck him on one side of the chest with the butt of his rifle, the professor pointed to his other side and said, 'This too, please.' The soldier dropped his gun in astonishment. The professor then found that some of the local people, who had followed the soldiers into the compound, were trying to get his brass bed down the stairs in order to take it away to their own home, when it got stuck. The professor said, 'Here, let me help you,' whereupon they blushed to the roots of their hair and fled.

At last the Communists decided to take him off and shoot him, so as he was being led away, he put his arm through the arm of the ringleader and said, 'You are my friend; I expect you to protect me.' Then he marched along arm in arm to his execution. When they got to the place where they intended to execute him, they let him go, saying, 'What can you do with a person like this?' Love may not always overcome evil in this way and save a person from death, but whether it does or not, you can be sure of this – it always has the last word.

Gracious Father, help me understand more deeply the truth that has been touched on today – that love always has the last word. It may sometimes seem that it has failed, but whether in death or in life, its power is always supreme. Thank you, Father. Amen.

FOR FURTHER STUDY – Matt. 5:33–42; Luke 19:18; 1 Pet. 3:9
1. What four practical demonstrations of love did Jesus mention?
2. What will result when we take these steps?

walking the way of love

More of Paul's lists

FOR READING AND MEDITATION – 1 CORINTHIANS 16:1–14
'Do everything in love.' (v. 14: NIV)

Following the statement: 'Love never fails', Paul gives us yet another of his marvellous lists in order to remind us of the supremacy of love. He tells us that the three things which men thought might last forever – prophecy, tongues and knowledge – would eventually pass away, but love and love alone would remain.

Let's consider the first of these three things – prophecy. We are told by Josephus and other first century writers that it was almost every Jewish mother's ambition for her son to become a prophet. Prior to the coming of Christ, it had been nearly four hundred years since God had spoken to Israel through a prophet, and the whole nation waited wistfully for another messenger to come. Undoubtedly, had one appeared, they would have hung upon his every word and given him their undivided attention. Of course, Paul was probably thinking more of the gift of prophecy which he had commented on earlier in the letter, but whether we think in terms of the role of a prophet as referred to in Ephesians 4:11, or the gift of prophecy mentioned in 1 Corinthians 12:10, the issue is still the same – one day prophecy will pass away and will have no further purpose. Not so with love – love goes on for ever.

It must be noted, of course, that Paul is not denouncing or denigrating prophecy and saying it is of no value. He is simply saying it is a temporary thing – a valuable gift but one that will eventually pass away. The message Paul wants us to get is that the Church must not stop desiring the best gifts; it must be careful, however, that it does not covet them more than love.

O God my Father, I am so thankful that you inspired Paul to hold to his line – the line of this supremacy of love. Help us in this, the Church of the 21st century, to sound that same note without hesitation or fear. In Jesus' name we pray. Amen.

FOR FURTHER STUDY – Mark 12:28–34; James 2:8; Gal. 5:6; Matt. 24:35
1. What is the royal law? / 2. In what way is love a law?

Love – the consistent motif

FOR READING AND MEDITATION – JOHN 21:15–25

'... Do you love me? ...' (v. 17: NKJ)

Yesterday we saw the supremacy of love over prophecy; today we see the same supremacy related to tongues. Here again, whether Paul had in mind the supernatural gift of tongues referred to in the previous chapter or simply languages in general, the principle is the same – they are all stamped with impermanence.

We have only to look around us to see that many languages are dying. Take the Welsh language, for example. Experts say that unless great efforts are made to revive it, it is in serious danger of lasting only for a few more generations. The same applies to the Irish language and the language of the Scottish Highlands (Gaelic). There are many other parts of the world where languages are dying – a fact which is a source of sorrow to many people. Take the Greek in which the New Testament was written – it is now just a language for study. The same applies to Latin. Love, however, will never die – it is guaranteed to last throughout all eternity.

Paul is putting things in this way, not simply to emphasise the impermanence of these things, but to show by contrast the supremacy of love. The great apostle has already told us that prophecy and tongues are nothing unless they are operated through love; now he is telling us that love will outlast them. In all other faiths, love is something that is touched on here and there – a chance note sounded among more dominant notes. Read the history of the world's religions, such as Islam, Buddhism, and so on, and you will see what I mean. In Christianity, however, love is not something that is put in and then cancelled out by other emphases. It is the whole motif – the supreme note.

O Father, thank you for striking one note as the supreme note – the note of love. Help me to decide right now that as love is the consistent motif of the Gospel, it shall be the consistent motif of my life also. In Jesus' name I ask it. Amen.

FOR FURTHER STUDY – Acts 2:1–13, 10:46–47; 1 Cor. 12:10

1. What happened on the Day of Pentecost? / 2. How did Peter explain it?

The transience of knowledge

FOR READING AND MEDITATION – 1 JOHN 2:15–29
'The world and its desires pass away, but the man who
does the will of God lives for ever.' (v. 17: NIV)

Having told us that love will outlast prophecy and tongues, Paul goes farther and with even greater boldness adds: 'As for knowledge, it will pass away' (1 Corinthians 13:8: RSV). Much of the knowledge of the ancients – where is it? It is largely gone. A schoolboy today knows more than Sir Isaac Newton knew, while his knowledge has vanished away. A schoolteacher told me a few years ago that although the same questions are used in some examination papers that were used twenty years ago, the answers are completely different.

Not so many years ago, a faculty at the University of Edinburgh was asked by the librarian of the University to send a member to the library to pick out the books on his subject which were no longer needed. The faculty member replied, 'This is something you can do yourself – just take every textbook that is more than ten years old and put it down the cellar.' Yesterday's knowledge is no good for today, and tomorrow's knowledge may change the following day. This is the kind of world we live in – a world where knowledge passes away.

Can you tell me anything that is going to last? I can think of things Paul did not condescend to mention, but they are facts nevertheless – money, fortune, fame and so on. I feel it necessary to remind you once again that Paul is not condemning these things and saying they are worthless. They are good things and some are great things, but they are not the supreme thing. Love is the supreme thing. There is a great deal in the world that is beautiful and good, but it will not last. An immortal soul must give itself to the thing that is immortal. And the only immortal thing is – love.

Father, help me to appreciate what is good and beautiful about the present, but help me to give myself only to that which is permanent. Just as you kept Paul's insight clear, keep mine clear too, I pray. In Jesus' name. Amen.

FOR FURTHER STUDY – Gal. 6:1–10, 5:13; 2 Cor. 9:6
1. What is the divine principle? / 2. How will you sow some love today?

Great – but not the greatest

FOR READING AND MEDITATION – GALATIANS 5:1–14

'… The only thing that counts is faith expressing itself through love.' (v. 6: NIV)

We spend one more day meditating on Paul's statement: 'As for prophecy … it will pass away; as for tongues, they will … cease; as for knowledge, it will pass away. For our knowledge … and our prophecy is fragmentary (incomplete and imperfect)' (1 Corinthians 13:8–9: Amplified).

I am convinced that if the men and women of today's church took these words to heart, it would revolutionise our approach to both our individual and corporate Christian living. Some Christians (thankfully, not all) are more interested in spectacular displays of prophecy, tongues and knowledge than they are in the demonstration of love. We are living in an age when tremendous things are happening in the church – things for which I continually thank God. Indeed, I am grateful to be alive to witness them. Miracles of great power are in evidence, especially in the Third World, and here in the West, the gifts of the Spirit are seen operating in churches and fellowships that once taught these things died out with the Early Church.

I want to make the point once again that I am not against the operation of the power gifts in the Church; I am one hundred per cent for it. I feel it necessary, however, to put this caution – that these things ought not to be allowed to occupy our attention to such a degree that we lose sight of the fact that they will all one day disappear and vanish. The thing that survives is – love. The greatest thing in the world is not exciting meetings, powerful conferences or informative seminars. They are great, but they are not the greatest thing. Let it never be forgotten: the greatest thing is – love.

My Father and my God, help me keep my perspective clear so that my initial focus is on the eternal and not the temporal. Continually keep before me, dear Lord, the fact that the only thing that will survive into eternity is love. In Jesus' name I pray. Amen.

FOR FURTHER STUDY – 1 John 3:14–24; 5:2–4; Eph. 5:1–2
1. How do we know we have passed from death to life?
2. How can we show the reality of our love?

When the perfect comes

FOR READING AND MEDITATION – PHILIPPIANS 3:7–21

'Not that I have already obtained all this or have already been made perfect,
but I press on …' (v. 12: NIV)

Paul, having made the point that tongues, prophecy and knowledge will pass away but that love remains for ever, completes the thought with this statement: 'But when the complete and perfect (total) comes, the incomplete and imperfect will vanish away – become antiquated, void and superseded' (1 Corinthians 13:10: Amplified).

Some think that the phrase 'when the perfect comes' has reference to the fact that when the early church had passed through its infancy and come to maturity, then the gifts of tongues, prophecy and so on would no longer be needed and disappear. This is a view that held great sway in the church until the past couple of decades. The interesting thing is that many of those who taught this interpretation have themselves experienced a deep encounter with the Spirit that has caused them to view things differently. 'When the perfect comes' does not have reference to the beginnings of the church and its passage through infancy to maturity; it has to do with the completion of the church when it arrives in eternity and is joined to Christ in perfect oneness.

One of the great Bible expositors of this century, Dr Martyn Lloyd-Jones, through his writings was responsible, perhaps more than anyone else, for showing thousands that the work of the Spirit in the early church was not a temporary thing but was intended to continue until Christ comes. The reason why the things that took place in the early church have not been seen in other centuries is not because God withdrew them, but because the church came not to expect them. In the church, both individually and corporately, we tend to get what we expect.

Father, I am grateful for this emphasis today, for I see that in seeking love I am not to neglect these other aspects also. Teach me to be a balanced Christian and to get my priorities in the right order. In Jesus' name. Amen.

FOR FURTHER STUDY – Isa. 26:1–9; Psa. 73:25; Matt. 7:7; 1 Cor. 12:7
1. What did the psalmist express? / 2. What did Jesus promise?

For God's sake – grow up!

FOR READING AND MEDITATION – EPHESIANS 4:1–16

'... speaking the truth in love, we will in all things grow up into him who is the Head, that is, Christ.' (v. 15: NIV)

We come now to the statement made by Paul which is probably one of the best-known and most quoted of all his sayings, both inside the Church and outside it: 'When I was a child, I talked like a child, I thought like a child, I reasoned like a child; now that I have become a man, I am done with childish ways and have put them aside' (1 Corinthians 13:11: Amplified). The verb used in the phrase 'done with childish ways' is a very strong one in the original Greek; the word is *katargeo*, which means 'to put away in a decisive act'. Paul is really saying (so I believe) that the way of love is the way of choice. In other words, one has to choose to abandon childlike (or childish) behaviour and grow up.

I once heard a preacher preach on this text under the title, *For God's sake – grow up*. When I heard him announce the title, I felt a little twinge of discomfort in my spirit (I thought his choice of words to be insensitive), but when he started speaking, it all made sense. He pointed out that if we are to become mature sons and daughters of God, then we must make a conscious decision to put behind us all childish behaviour and grow up. And we must do it, not just for our own sake, but for his sake: *For God's sake – grow up*.

Are you still a *baby* Christian – even though you have been on the way for a good number of years? Let me put it even more pointedly: do you regard the gifts of the Spirit as being more important than love? Do you hanker after supernatural manifestations more than the pursuit of holiness? You don't have to give up one in order to get the other – you just need to be mature enough to know which are the priorities.

Father, I see that maturity begins with a decision. So I make it today. I choose the way of love over every other way. Help me to let love be the arbiter of everything. In Jesus' name I ask it. Amen.

FOR FURTHER STUDY – 2 Peter 1:1–11, 3:18; Eph. 1:17; 1 Cor. 3:1
1. What did Paul say of the Corinthian church? / 2. How can we grow up into maturity?

walking the way of love

Unsatisfied now – but then?

FOR READING AND MEDITATION – PSALM 17:1–15
'… in righteousness I shall see your face; when I awake, I shall be satisfied
with seeing your likeness.' (v. 15: NIV)

Even the most casual reader of 1 Corinthians 13 cannot help but be impressed with
the fact that every verse is tightly packed with truth, beauty and inspiration. And the
verse before us now is no exception: 'For now we are looking in a mirror that gives
only a dim reflection … but then [when perfection comes] we shall see in reality
and face to face' (1 Corinthians 13:12: Amplified). If there was any doubt that the
'perfection' talked about in verse 10 had to do with seeing Christ at his coming, then
the matter is clearly settled here.

Many commentators believe that Paul's reference to a mirror comes out of the
fact that Corinth was known, indeed even famous for its mirrors of polished metal.
A Corinthian mirror was a prized possession, yet at best it reflected a somewhat
blurred and distorted image. The world 'dimly' (RSV) means it appears as a riddle
or an enigma, and Moffatt translates it as 'baffling reflections'. What Paul is saying
is this: our knowledge, which is just fragmentary, and our reasoning, which is often
faulty, produce only a distorted image of divine reality.

At Christ's coming however, we shall know with a knowledge which we do not
now have, and through that knowledge will come the full revelation of love. As long
as our spirits are confined by our human condition, our true comprehension of the
greatness of God's love will be only a dim perception, blurred by our partial blindness. But when the opaque veil of our humanity is torn away and the encroaching
cataracts of our partial blindness are removed, we shall love in the same degree with
which we are loved. Then imperfection will have put on perfection.

*O God my Father, when I sense the prospect that lies before me, my heart cries out: 'Even so, come,
Lord Jesus.' Help me live in the light of this expectation, not only today but every day. Amen.*

FOR FURTHER STUDY – John 17; Isa. 33:17; 1 John 3:2
1. What did Jesus say about his relationship with the Father? / 2. What was John's conviction?

Fully known, fully loved

FOR READING AND MEDITATION – PSALM 139:1–24

'How precious also are your thoughts to me, O God! How great is the sum of them!'
(v. 17: NKJ)

We continue meditating on the point we looked at yesterday, that our comprehension and understanding of love is at best limited. This does not stop us knowing or experiencing love, but what we know and experience is just a small part of what awaits us when we see our Lord face to face. The truth that we must hold on to, however, is this – although at this stage of our pilgrimage we do not fully know him – he fully knows us. I will never fully know or comprehend the divine love while in this earthly frame, and due to this limitation, I shall not be able fully to love God, but that does not stop God loving me.

I don't know about you, but I find this thought utterly compelling. Time and time again, when I have lamented the fact that my love for God is not as strong as I know it ought to be, I reflect on the wonder of his love for me – and invariably my heart becomes strangely warmed. Why should this be? I think it is because the greatest truth in the universe is not that I love God, but that he loves me. Follow me into this thought as I try to unfold it as best I can.

I am sure you will remember the story of Dietrich Bonhoeffer, the German pastor who was imprisoned by Hitler and later executed. He left us a number of writings, one of which was a short poem entitled, *Who am I?* The poem begins with the question, 'Who am I?' and ends, 'Whoever I am, thou knowest, o God, I am thine'. When he could not take solace in the fact that he knew God, the crucial thing that cut through his confusion and despair was that God knew him and loved him.

O my Father, help me to drop my anchor in the depths of this reassuring and encouraging revelation – that no matter how limited I am in knowing and loving you, no such limitation exists on your side. You fully know me and fully love me. I am eternally thankful. Amen.

FOR FURTHER STUDY – Matt. 28:11–20; Ex. 33:14; Isa. 43:1–2
1. What did God declare through Isaiah? / 2. What was Jesus' promise to his disciples?

The bottom line of faith

FOR READING AND MEDITATION – 1 JOHN 4:7–19

'In this is love, not that we loved God, but that he loved us ...' (v. 10: NKJ)

The fact that we are fully known and fully loved by God is one of the most encouraging and reassuring truths in the whole of the universe. We spoke yesterday of Dietrich Bonhoeffer's conclusions while in prison. Permit me to focus on them once more today, but this time in a little more detail. Listen to these lines taken from the poem: *Who am I?*

> Who am I? They often tell me
> I would step from my cell's confinement
> Calmly, cheerfully, firmly,
> Like a squire from his country house.
> Who am I? They often tell me
> I used to speak to my warders
> Freely, friendly and clearly
> As though it were mine to command ...
> Who am I? They mock me, these lonely questions,
> Whoever I am, thou knowest, o God, I am thine!

Nowhere in the poem (over 30 lines) does he say, 'My faith pulled me through.' He didn't even take solace in his knowledge of God. The truth that kept him going in that dark and depressing situation was the fact that God knew him. It is frightening for some people when they come face to face with the thought: God knows me through and through. Ah, but there's more. He not only knows us – he loves us. And the addition of those three simple words makes all the difference.

O Father, help me hold on to this truth, so that no matter what happens, I shall not lose touch with the fact that I am fully known and fully loved by you. In Christ's peerless and precious name I ask it. Amen.

FOR FURTHER STUDY – Rev. 1:1–8; Rom. 5:8; 1 Cor. 6:11
1. What was the extent of God's love? / 2. What did Jesus do before he washed us?

This incredible knowing

FOR READING AND MEDITATION – PSALM 103:1–22

'For He knows our frame, he earnestly remembers and imprints on
his heart that we are dust.' (v. 14: Amplified)

We spend another day meditating on the thought that we are fully known and fully loved by God. Let me introduce you to what Phillip Keller says on this point, 'God in Christ knows all the intricacies of my genetic make-up. He is fully aware of all the interrelated characteristics which were inherited from my grandparents and former forebears. He knows precisely why I am the unique, special person I am.'

He goes on to make the additional point that not even our parents know this much about us. God alone knows us in this intimate way. He understands exactly what goes on inside us, and for that reason, he and he alone can treat us with utter integrity, complete understanding and full compassion. You see, it is this infinite, incredible knowing that enables God to deal with us in dignity, forgiveness and love. He knows everything that has gone into the shaping of our personality, all the stresses, strains and pressures, and thus he alone can properly appraise the impact made upon us by our parents, peers, friends, schoolteachers, and so on.

This does not mean that he excuses us – he always holds us responsible for the decisions we make – but he looks upon us with a knowledge, an understanding and a compassion such as no other person in the universe could give to us. In the light of this, we can begin to see what underlies the cry from the cross: 'Father, forgive them, for they do not know what they do' (Luke 23:34: NKJ). It is this dimension of being known to the utmost depths of my being that conquers my heart's antipathies, and overcomes all my rebellion, all my suspicion and all my distrust. I am fully known and fully loved.

O Gracious Father, the knowledge that you fully know me and fully love me sends me to my knees in gratitude. I can hold on to this even when I can't hold on to myself. I am grateful more than any words of mine can tell. Thank you, dear Father. Amen.

FOR FURTHER STUDY – Matt. 10:22–31; Luke 10:20; Phil. 4:3
1. In what can we rejoice? / 2. How did Jesus express our value?

walking the way of love

Seeing God

FOR READING AND MEDITATION – PSALM 119:129–144

'The entrance of your words gives light; it gives understanding to the simple.'

(v. 130: NKJ)

Over the past few days we have been making much of the fact that in this life, we will not be able to love God fully and perfectly – that will come only when we see Christ face to face and we know as we are known. Paul, in the second part of 1 Corinthians 13:12, puts it more clearly still: 'Now I know in part (imperfectly); but then I shall know and understand fully and clearly, even in the same manner as I have been fully and clearly known and understood [by God]' (Amplified).

Does this mean that because we can never fully know God and his Son Jesus Christ until eternity, we sit back and give no further consideration to the matter of developing our knowledge and love for him? No, for despite the inner struggle we have to *see him* as he truly is, it is important to understand clearly the methods and means which God uses to reveal himself to us now. Although we are surrounded by imperfection, we can still *see God*, even though dimly or vaguely.

The primary means by which we come to *see God* is, of course, his Word, the Bible. It is not as good, of course, as seeing him face to face, but while we wait for that experience yet to come, we look into his Word and we *see him* in a way that nourishes our spirits and sets our hearts beating in eager anticipation of 'the appearing of our Lord Jesus Christ'. Those who try to know God without coming to the Bible end up with the strangest misconceptions and misunderstandings. In my youth, I had a friend who tried to do this and finished up spiritually beggared and bankrupt. He became subject to his own moods; self-centred instead of Scripture-centred – hence moody, irritable and off-centre.

Father, I see that it is only the entrance of your Word that gives light, and by implication, the neglecting of your Word gives darkness. Help me to take a daily look into your Word, for it is only in your light that I can walk with a sure and steady tread. Amen.

FOR FURTHER STUDY – 2 Pet. 1:16–21; Psa. 19:8, 119:105; Prov. 6:23

1. What was the basis of Peter's conviction? / 2. What do we have to guide us?

The Bible – self-correcting

FOR READING AND MEDITATION – 2 TIMOTHY 3:1–17

'All Scripture is given by inspiration of God, and is profitable …' (v. 16: NKJ)

We continue with the point that although we will never perfectly see or know God while in our human frame, we can come to see him and know him to a high degree through his inspired Word, the Bible. And, may I add, only through the Bible. We can know about God through such things as nature and providence, but we can only know God through the revelation contained in the Scriptures.

I have met many people in my time who have tried to come to God directly, that is, through the medium of their own thoughts and ideas. There comes to mind as I write a man I once knew who told me that he used to begin his day by focusing on God through meditation. It was not Biblical meditation, I hasten to add. What was the result? Did he get through to God? No, because the effort we make to *see God* through the medium of our own conceptions is doomed to failure. Human conceptions are man's ideas about God; the Bible is God's revelation of himself. Unless our thoughts are constantly corrected by God's thoughts, our thoughts invariably go off at a tangent and revolve around ourselves.

When the man I am talking about came to see this and surrendered his life to Jesus Christ, he began his day by looking into the Bible, and then – what a difference! After a few months of reading the Bible he said to me, 'I used to look into my own mind and all I saw is what I am – a sinner. I now look into the Bible and I see not only what I ought to be but what I can be – by the grace of God.' To attempt to come to know or *see God* without the Bible is like the captain of a large passenger liner setting out to sea without a compass.

O Father, how can I ever sufficiently thank you for giving me this most marvellous book, the Bible. I know it is inspired because it inspires me. Help me to draw daily strength and encouragement from its pages. In Jesus' name I ask it. Amen.

FOR FURTHER STUDY – 2 Tim. 2:7–15; 1 Pet. 1:25; Psa. 119:103; Jer. 15:16

1. What was Paul's word to Timothy? / 2. How did the psalmist describe God's word?

The silence of eternity – broken

FOR READING AND MEDITATION – 2 CORINTHIANS 9:1–15
'Thank God for his Son – his gift too wonderful for words.' (v. 15: TLB)

Today we ask ourselves: what is it about the Bible that makes it such a powerful force in helping us know and *see* God? That is a question to which there can be many answers. One thing, for example, is that it tells us all about what went wrong with mankind in the beginning and how we can be put back together again. The 66 books it contains are like 66 steps leading from the Garden of Eden in the book of Genesis to the New Jerusalem in the book of Revelation.

But the biggest single thing contributing to the unique power of the Scriptures is the revelation they bring to us concerning the nature and character of God. The Bible is the only book in the universe that has been specially inspired, protected and preserved to give us the truth about God and tell us exactly what he is like. So what is he like? The answer is – he is like Jesus.

Lao-tzu, the great Chinese philosopher, said, 'The Word that can be uttered is not the divine word; that word is Silence.' Many people have pondered that statement and wondered what he meant. I believe what he was saying was simply this: the truth about God is too great to go into words. But the alternative is not silence. Lao-tzu did not know Jesus, so for him, the word had to be silence. But the silence of eternity has been broken, broken by the appearance of Incarnate Love – Jesus. The Word became, not just words or printer's ink, but flesh. God appeared before us in human guise and the Bible has captured this revelation, bringing to us the thrilling reality that in Jesus, God is approachable, available, simplified, loveable. The Word has become flesh.

O Father, I am so thankful that when all other ways were inadequate, you opened a way to us that met our deepest need. When we couldn't come to you, you came to us. It is too wonderful for words. All honour and praise be to your name for ever. Amen.

FOR FURTHER STUDY – John 1:1–14; 1 John 1:1; Rev. 19:13
1. How does John describe the glory of 'the Word'?
2. List six things he says about 'the Word'.

Getting ready for eternity

FOR READING AND MEDITATION – 1 CORINTHIANS 3:1–17

'Each one's work will become manifest; for the Day will declare it,
because it will be revealed by fire …' (v. 13: NKJ)

We look now at the last of Paul's statements concerning *Agape* love (God's love in us): 'So faith, hope, love abide, these three; but the greatest of these is love' (1 Corinthians 13:13: RSV). A lot of debate has gone on (and still goes on) in relation to these words, for some interpret Paul as saying here: 'At the coming of the Lord, faith will disappear, hope will disappear and love alone will remain.' In other words, they give to the words of the apostle the meaning that when that which is perfect is come, two of these three things will pass away – faith into sight and hope into fruition.

But Paul is not saying that. He is saying that faith, hope and love, in contrast to the transitory gifts, remain even at the coming of the Lord. Those who might like to investigate this further should note that the Greek verb is singular although the subject is plural, indicating the indissoluble unity of the three virtues. They will all remain, but the greatest of them is love. We know little about the life that is to come, but it would appear from this that there will be a place for both faith and hope in eternity. If that is so, then the conclusion is that these are the only qualities which we will take with us into eternity.

Our passage for today shows us that on the threshold of eternity, there will be a review of our life's work and the only thing that will survive will be true character. And what forms character? Faith, hope and love. To the degree that these are present in us, to that degree are we building for eternity. If men or women invest their short lives on earth in anything else, then their days are spent without profit.

My Father and my God, help me to bind tightly together in my life the qualities of faith, hope and love, so that they will become a threefold cord that I will carry with me into eternity. In Jesus' name I ask it. Amen.

FOR FURTHER STUDY – 1 Pet. 1:15–25; 2 Cor. 4:18; Heb. 12:27
1. How have we been born again? / 2. What is our flesh like?

Three survivors

'… your work produced by faith, your labour prompted by love,
and your endurance inspired by hope …' (v. 3: NIV)

We said yesterday that faith, hope and love are the building materials which we send before us into eternity. The story is told of a man who died and went to heaven. Arriving at the Pearly Gates, he was asked his name and, after identifying him in the Book of Life, an angel escorted him through the streets of heaven. As they walked together down the different streets, the man said to the angel, 'Where are we going?' The angel replied, 'We are going to the dwelling place which has been prepared for you.'

As they walked, the man looked at the magnificent dwelling places that were all around, and wondered just which one had been prepared for him. Eventually they came to a small and tumbledown abode at which the angel stopped and said, 'Here is where you are to spend eternity.' The man was taken aback and said, 'Surely – not this. Why couldn't my home be like the beautiful mansions we have just passed by?' In solemn tones the angel said, 'I'm sorry, but we did the best we could out of the materials that you sent up.'

It is only a story, of course, and in some ways it has little Scriptural support except perhaps the passage we looked at yesterday. That showed us that the only materials that survive the refining fires we shall all have to pass through before entering into eternity are the gold, silver and precious stones of pure motive and character. Faith, hope and love have one thing in common – they are survivors; they last. They are, as one writer put it, 'a tightly intertwined three-strand cord, braided together to form the unbreakable line of Christ's character extended to us as our own lifeline of eternal duration'.

O Father, help me to accept responsibility for what I am expected to do this side of eternity. I see, as I look back on my life, that if I had decided differently I would have been different. From now on, I want all my decisions to be character-building ones. In Jesus' name I ask it. Amen.

FOR FURTHER STUDY – Rom. 5:1–9; Psa. 66:10; James 1:12; 1 Pet. 1:7
1. How does Paul show the outworking of faith, hope and love?
2. What is promised to the man who endures?

A woman in love

FOR READING AND MEDITATION – 1 PETER 1:1–9

'Whom having not seen you love. Though now you do not see him, yet believing,
you rejoice with joy inexpressible ...' (v. 8: NKJ)

If you have difficulty in accepting the fact that faith and hope, as well as love, will be a part of eternity, then listen to this illustration which Phillip Keller uses in his book, *A Layman Looks at the Love of God*. He tells of a young woman falling in love with a handsome young man in whom she puts enormous faith and hope. Eventually they are married, but she soon discovers that her *Prince Charming* is a deceiver and a rogue. All her dreams crash into rubble and she is broken-hearted. Why? Because she lacked faith in him? No. Because she lacked hope? No. Because she lacked love? No, she had invested her faith, hope and love in a person who had no character.

In time, the man dies and she tells herself that she will never have faith in any-one again, but one day a man comes into her life who is unpretentious, simple and transparently sincere. A tiny spark of faith is ignited within her. In due course the man asks her to marry him, and with faith no more than a grain of mustard seed, she sets out to begin another marriage. Things turn out well, for the man has impec-cable character and is extremely loving and kind. Her heart is healed. Her home is a little bit of heaven. Her happiness is complete.

Why? Was it just the faith she had? No. Was it just the hope? No. It was largely the character of the man. And it is just the same, says Keller, with Christ. His char-acter is impeccable, his integrity undeniable and his trustworthiness complete. It is for this reason that our faith, hope and love endure – they are rooted in him. His character validates our faith, honours our hope and confirms our love. They remain sure because he remains sure.

O Father, grant that my faith, my hope and my love shall be forever rooted in you. For I see that unless they are, they will come to nothing. Help me to keep my eyes firmly fixed on you, dear Father, so that your character will become my character. Amen.

FOR FURTHER STUDY – Isa. 6:1–8; Col. 1:15; 1 Tim. 1:17, 6:15–16
1. What aspect of God's character was revealed to Isaiah? / 2. How did God prepare him?

Faith, hope and love in heaven

FOR READING AND MEDITATION – REVELATION 5:1–14

'... in the midst of the throne ... stood a Lamb as though it had been slain ...'
(v. 6: NKJ)

Once we see the tremendous truth that faith, hope and love remain sure because Christ remains sure, then we will be delivered from self-concern and self-preoccupation. We will no longer fasten our attention on our own feeble faith, but instead lift up our gaze to the One who is totally reliable and trustworthy. Our hope, instead of being set upon those things which are seen, will be centred in the One who never fails. Our love, rather than focusing itself upon the trivial, will prefer to pour itself out in a continual love offering at his feet.

We simply must grasp the fact that unless Christ is the object of our faith, hope and love, then they are rooted in the wrong things. Change the word *faith* to *confidence* and you might begin to get a better idea of what I mean. Now ask yourself the question: in eternity, will my confidence be in Christ? What's the answer? It must be 'Yes'. Change the word *hope* to *expectancy* and ask yourself: in eternity, will my expectancy be in him? The answer again must be 'Yes'. There is no need to change the word *love* to anything else, mainly because there is no other word to which it can be changed.

Now tie all three things together. Will there be confidence in heaven? Yes – a never-ending confidence in the eternal value of Christ's sacrifice for us on the cross. Our text today gives us a beautiful picture of a Lamb on the throne 'as though it had been slain'. Why, in this vision of the future, do we see 'a Lamb as though it had been slain' – freshly slaughtered? It shows, so I believe, the tremendous immediacy of Christ's self-giving. He not only captures our faith, hope and love here on earth: he will continue to capture them in eternity.

O Father, I am so grateful that heaven will be, not only a different place, but a dynamic place where my confidence, expectancy and love can find endless and everlasting expression. Thank you, Father. Amen.

FOR FURTHER STUDY – John 1:29–36; 1 Pet. 1:19; Rev. 7:9–12
1. What did John declare? / 2. How do those around the throne respond to the Lamb?

How to love

FOR READING AND MEDITATION – 1 JOHN 4:19

'We love because he first loved us.' (NIV)

As we approach the end of our meditations on 1 Corinthians 13, one question remains. 'How do we go about the task of enriching and deepening our love for Christ on this side of eternity?' There are a number of ways by which we can increase in love, but by far the greatest is this – focus your gaze on how much he loves you. You see, when we concentrate our attention on how much he loves us, a tremendous spiritual law goes into operation – his love produces the same degree of love in us in return.

Look once again at what our text for today says: 'We love because he first loved us.' His love for us awakens within us a love for him, and thus the more we focus on how much he loves us, the more we will love him back. In the divine economy, love begets love. We cannot love until we are loved; we cannot serve until we are served. God, in his great love, has gone to the utmost lengths possible to let us know he loves us, and as we gaze at the greatest proof of that love – Calvary – the scales fall from our eyes and our love flames forth in response.

One writer says, 'We can love God only with *Eros* love and not with *Agape*. We can love others with *Agape*, but not God, because *Agape* is love regardless of the worthiness of the character concerned. We could not love God if God were not of good character. We love him because he is worthy. Hence our love for him is *Eros* and not *Agape*'. This writer fails to see one important thing – God's *Agape* produces *Agape* in me. This is what makes the Christian life so wonderful – the source of my love for him is his love for me. I do not love him with my love, I love him with his love – true *Agape*.

Father, I am so grateful that I do not have to love; I simply have to allow your Agape love to love me into loving. Keep ever before me that I am not the spring of love, but just the channel of it. Flow through me in Agape love this day and every day. Amen.

FOR FURTHER STUDY – Isa. 53; John 15:13; Gal. 3:13; 1 Pet. 2:24
1. What quality of love is revealed in Isaiah 53? / 2. How does John describe it?

No love – no identity

FOR READING AND MEDITATION – GALATIANS 5:16–26
'But the fruit of the Spirit is love …' (v. 22: NIV)

On this, the last day of our meditations in 1 Corinthians 13, we ask ourselves what our conclusions are concerning this vitally important matter of *Agape* love (God's love in us). Are they not these? No matter how spectacular, gifted or dedicated a person I might be, without love it is all ashes at God's feet. I may be able to prophesy and predict the future, speak eloquently with the tongues of men (or in supernatural tongues) and have enough knowledge to unravel the deepest mysteries of the universe, but if I do not have love, I am nothing.

The subtraction of love is the great subtraction. No matter how much else I have or do, no matter how energetic my efforts in promoting harmony and goodwill, it will all come to nothing without love. It is very much like multiplying by zero – no matter how large a number we take when we multiply by zero, the result is always zero. Paul points out three things that are true of the person who does not love: 'I am nothing', 'I gain nothing', and 'I just make a noise'.

What a picture of a lost identity. No philosophy of human nature can say anything more degrading about a man than that he does not have love. He is nothing, he achieves nothing, he is without purpose or meaning. He is just a loud nuisance. However, those in whom *Agape* love dwells remain for ever. A loving character is the universe's most precious value. It will survive all the ravages of time and go singing into eternity. Let the wonder of it grip you as you ponder in the days ahead. And keep ever before you the thrilling fact that both in time and in eternity, love holds the field.

O God, my Father and fountain of Agape *love, I am so glad that your love never wears thin – it is always* Agape. *Let me grow in the wonder of it, surrender to the call of it and live to be the channel of it. In Jesus' name I pray. Amen.*

FOR FURTHER STUDY – 1 Cor. 13; John 13:35; Eph. 2:4–5
1. Read 1 Corinthians 13, putting the name 'Jesus' in place of the word 'love'.
2. Read verses 4–6 again, putting your own name in place of 'love'. Does it fit?

God's blueprint for living

FOR READING AND MEDITATION – EXODUS 20:1–21

'… "Do not be afraid. God has come … so that the fear of God will be
with you to keep you from sinning."' (v. 20: NIV)

We begin today an in-depth study of the divine blueprint for living given several thousand years ago by the Almighty to Moses on the barren summit of a majestic peak in the Sinai peninsula. It seems to me that with the widespread moral breakdown going on all around us, we need to take a new look at these old principles and get it into our heads that the commandments are more than just ancient documents with a fascinating historical interest, but are as relevant today as the day on which they were first given.

Research conducted with over 20 000 churchgoers in a city in the United States found that only one in 100 could recite the Ten Commandments, and only 15 in a 100 could name the book of the Bible in which they are recorded. The Ten Commandments were one of the first things I was taught to memorise as a child, and although they did not give me a complete picture of God (that came later when I came to know Christ and began to understand the truths of the New Testament), they nevertheless generated within me a godly fear and a respect for moral law.

Many people – even some Christians – see the Ten Commandments as hard and as cold as the tablets of stone on which they were written and thus cannot imagine them to be the steps that lead to a happy and contented existence. A man once said to me, 'Keeping to the Ten Commandments gives people a jaundiced view of life.' I assure you that when properly understood, the Ten Commandments show us the way, not to jaundiced living, but to joyous living. And over the next eight weeks I hope to prove that point.

Gracious and loving Father, help me as I begin this quest for light and illumination on something that at first seems cold and forbidding. Enable me to see that not only do you set high standards – you also supply the power to reach up to them. Amen.

FOR FURTHER STUDY – Deut. 10:1–13; Josh. 24:11–15; Eccl. 12:13
1. What did the Lord ask of Israel? / 2. What choice did Joshua give to Israel?

Ten Words

God's blueprint for living

FOR READING AND MEDITATION – DEUTERONOMY 4:1–14
'Only be careful, and watch yourselves closely so that you do not forget …
or let them slip from your heart …' (v. 9: NIV)

Today we ask ourselves: what exactly are the Ten Commandments? They are, as someone described them, 'God's law for a lawless world – the principles and precepts by which the soul of man must be eternally judged'. Some commentators claim that some of the Commandments overlap and maintain that they should not be seen as ten distinct commands. But in Exodus 34:28 the Scripture very clearly says: 'And he wrote on the tablets the words of the covenant – the Ten Commandments.' In the Hebrew, the expression *the Ten Commandments* is literally, *the Ten Words* – *word* in this context meaning a royal edict, the mandate of a king. Hence, with reference to God it means a royal proclamation, a divine mandate, an authoritative statement which cannot be gainsaid. The Greek word for the Ten Commandments is *Decalogue* and this again reflects the idea of *Ten Words*.

To me, one of the greatest messages of the Ten Commandments is this – it is improper, from a biblical perspective, to separate morality (ethics) from true religion. The age through which we are passing is attempting to do this and I note with alarm the number of voices which argue that religion and ethics must be seen as two separate issues. The view that morality can be developed purely on the basis of its own presuppositions and does not need to be rooted in true religion is, in my judgment, the beginning of the end of a civilised and smooth-running society.

People may say that the Ten Commandments are out of date – but they are not out of the Bible. And if we, the Christians of this day, do not value them, hold fast to them and live by them, we will fail not only our own, but future generations also.

O God our Father, help us to hold fast to that which you have given, so that, as those who came before us have passed on a strong deposit to us, we may pass on a strong deposit to others. In Jesus' name we pray. Amen.

FOR FURTHER STUDY – Deut. 6; Jer. 3:21; Isa. 51:11–16
1. What did the children of Israel have to be careful about? / 2. What were they prone to?

Not merely ethics

FOR READING AND MEDITATION – ROMANS 3:19–31
'This righteousness from God comes through faith in
Jesus Christ to all who believe ...' (v. 22: NIV)

We continue with the thought we touched on yesterday that one of the greatest messages of the Ten Commandments is that it is improper to separate morality from true religion. The very structure of the Commandments forbids it. Of the Ten Words of Sinai, the first four deal with man's relationship to God and the remaining six with man's relationship to man.

Unfortunately, in so many discussions on the Ten Commandments, the first four are passed over and the emphasis falls on the last six. But this is a betrayal of the Decalogue. Why do people do this? The reason, in my opinion, is that in order to be truly moral, in the biblical sense of the word, one must be in a relationship with God. Can you see why non-Christians therefore skip over the first four of the Ten Commandments? They do so because it makes them feel uncomfortable to be faced with the challenge of surrendering their lives to the living God. And we all tend to avoid the things that make us feel uncomfortable.

As you work your way with me through these meditations on the Ten Words, keep this statement before you: the Ten Commandments are not simply a statement on ethics but are the terms of the covenant between man and God. You will never understand the deep meaning underlying the Ten Commandments until you see that they can only be kept in the context of a relationship with God. Therefore, how a man or woman thinks of God, and relates to God, is basic to biblical ethics. Morality without God, however good and beneficial it may be to society in general, is really a betrayal of what God intended when he gave us his ten famous Words.

My Father and my God, help me to see that you did not place me on this earth just to keep your law, but to enjoy your life. Deepen my understanding of the fact that the closer my relationship with you, the easier it is to keep your rules. In Jesus' name. Amen.

FOR FURTHER STUDY – Psa. 119:129–138, 48:1–11, 97:2
1. What is the foundation of God's throne? / 2. What was the psalmist's testimony?

All to be attempted

FOR READING AND MEDITATION – PSALM 119:137–142

'Your righteousness is everlasting and your law is true.' (v. 142: NIV)

Christians hold a surprising number of different views and attitudes on the Ten Commandments. One group of theologians says, 'They were relevant for the time in which they were given, but in today's culture we need a different set of moral principles and guidelines.' Others say, 'The Ten Commandments are not particularly useful for Christians because we are not under law, but under grace.' And there are some Christians (fortunately not many) who say, 'Once we are saved by grace we are free from all moral obligations and principles; we can then live as we choose.' A Church of England bishop, speaking to a school assembly said, 'The Ten Commandments should be treated like a school examination paper – "six only to be attempted"', the implication being that as long as you make an effort to obey some, then it won't matter too much if you don't keep them all.

The question, then, that we must come to grips with before we go any further is this: are the Ten Commandments obsolete – or absolute? Are they as true for today as they were for the day on which they were first given? As I have said, it is my belief that they are: God's expectations for human behaviour do not change from one generation to another. A librarian said, 'Knowledge is increasing at such a rate that titles of some subjects have to be replaced every few years. Some books written ten years ago are now out of date.' That is not how it is with the Ten Commandments.

God's words are never out of date. They apply with as much authority to the men and women of this 21st century as they did to the men and women of past centuries.

O Father, help me to measure up to your expectations and save me from attempting to bring them down to mine. Impress even more deeply into my spirit that the words you spoke at Sinai are not only unchanged, but unchanging. In Christ's name I pray. Amen.

FOR FURTHER STUDY – Psa. 19:1–11; Rom. 7:12–14; 1 Tim. 1:8
1. How did the psalmist sum up the law? / 2. How did Paul describe the law?

The timing of the Commandments

FOR READING AND MEDITATION – GALATIANS 5:16–26

'Since we live by the Spirit, let us keep in step with the Spirit.' (v. 25: NIV)

Before we examine in detail each of the Ten Commandments that were given at Sinai, we pause to consider some of the background features to the giving of the divine law. We ask ourselves: why were the Ten Words given to the children of Israel after they had left Egypt rather than before? I think one reason is that God wanted to emphasise that redemption comes first and morality second. The Exodus must come before the Commandments. Salvation leads, morality follows. To have morality precede salvation is salvation by works. And to mix salvation with works is the Galatian heresy of mixing law and grace.

Note, too, that the one – morality – must always follow the other – salvation. The God who redeems people expects them to be a moral people. Those who own up to Christ must own up to morality. Those who claim to be born of the Spirit must walk in the Spirit. When we are saved by grace, we come under the strongest moral mandate. Listen to how the apostle Paul puts it in one of his epistles: 'We died to sin; how can we live in it any longer?' (Romans 6:2: NIV). Further, it was with the giving of the law that the covenant made between God and his people was formally sealed (Exodus 24). The covenant was possible only when a moral God had informed a redeemed people that to enter into a relationship with him, they must be moral too.

Scripture has a profound doctrine of morality, just as it has a profound doctrine of salvation. And nowhere is the relationship between morality and salvation more clearly seen and more effectively illustrated than in the timing of the Ten Commandments.

Father, just as I own up to being Christ's, help me to own up to all that goes along with him – especially morality. Search me and see if there is any hidden sin in my heart. Bring it into the light and help me deal with it. In Jesus' name. Amen.

FOR FURTHER STUDY – Rom. 6; Psa. 27:1, 37:39; Isa. 12:2, 25:9

1. How does Paul relate law to grace? / 2. What was Isaiah's conviction?

The divine handwriting

FOR READING AND MEDITATION – 1 PETER 1:3–16

'But just as he who called you is holy, so be holy in all you do.' (v. 15: NIV)

The giving of the Ten Commandments established in the clearest possible manner that God is a righteous, holy and moral God. Although the idea of God as a God of indefectible morality had been implied in such expressions as 'Who is like you – majestic in holiness …?' (Exodus 15:11: NIV) it was not until the giving of the Ten Commandments that the righteous aspect of his character was most clearly seen.

Permit me now to pursue a thought with you that I hope will not in any way be offensive or irreverent. It concerns the subject of handwriting. Handwriting, it has been said, is an accurate indication of character. We cannot be absolutely sure about this, because graphology is not yet regarded as a science, but proceeding on the assumption that our handwriting does say something about us, let me suggest that at Sinai, God wrote to man in his own handwriting and an examination of that handwriting reveals an aspect of his character that hitherto had not been clearly seen. Out of the mists that mantled the top of Sinai came forth the hand of God and in his own handwriting, the Almighty inscribed on two tablets of stone the words of the Ten Commandments. Though there would be other occasions when God would write to mankind, this was the first evidence of his handwriting.

What does it reveal? Has it some vital secret to show us concerning his transcendent character? Most certainly it has! Above all else, it reveals that God is holy and righteous – an aspect of the Deity that needs restating and re-emphasising in the world of today. But there's more to it than that. God is holy: he requires that we be holy too.

O Father, in your presence I am made over and over again until I am transformed into your likeness. Help me to spend more time with you, then I will become more like you. I would emerge from every devotional moment more alive to you and more alive to others. Help me. In Jesus' name. Amen.

FOR FURTHER STUDY – Isa. 6:1–8; 1 Sam. 6:19–20; Psa. 99:9

1. What did Isaiah hear the angels declaring? / 2. What did the men of Beth Shemesh ask?

The God who is there

FOR READING AND MEDITATION – EXODUS 20:1–17
'I am the Lord you God, who brought you out of Egypt, out of the land of slavery.
You shall have no other gods before me.' (vv. 2–3: NIV)

We are ready now to begin the task of examining one by one each of the Ten Commandments. It is interesting to note that they begin, not with a prohibition – 'you shall not' – but with an affirmation: 'I am the Lord your God, who brought you out of Egypt …' Before we are given a single rule, God takes the time to tell us who he is. Therefore this first Commandment – that we are to have no other gods – is rooted in two great facts: first, who God is, and second, what God has done.

Let's look first at who God is: 'I am the Lord your God.' There is deep significance in the name by which God reveals himself here. The Hebrew word for *Lord* here is *Jehovah* and the Hebrew word for *God* is *Elohim*. The meaning behind the name *Jehovah* is: 'He that is, he that was, and he that will be.' Thus the very name brings us into the presence of the self-existent God who is because he is. Cast your minds back into the infinite labyrinths of the past. God says: 'I am he that was.' Stretch your mind into the infinite vistas of the future. God says: 'I am he that will be.' Focus your mind on all that is going on around you at this present moment. God says: 'I am he that is.' The word *Elohim* means 'the Creator, the Ruler of the universe, the supreme object of worship'.

Before the first prohibition is given, God gives us his name and says in effect: 'I am the ever-present One, the supreme object of your worship.' Just think of it – the God we worship is always there! At this moment, drop your anchor into this encouraging and reassuring revelation: what he is he was, and what he was he is, and what he is and was, he ever will be – world without end.

O Father, let the wonder of this thrilling truth take a firm hold on my spirit today. Others may fail me but you – never. You will always be there! I am eternally grateful. Amen.

FOR FURTHER STUDY – Psa. 96:1–9; Deut. 26:9–10; 1 Chron. 16:9; Psa. 95:6
1. What is worship? / 2. How does it relate to Lordship?

Salvation to precede service

'Therefore, I urge you, brothers, in view of God's mercy, to offer
your bodies as living sacrifices …' (v. 1: NIV)

We said yesterday that the first Commandment is rooted in two factors: who God is
and what he has done. Yesterday we looked at the first of those factors – who God is
(*Jehovah, Elohim*). Today we look at the second – what he has done: 'I am the Lord
your God, who brought you out of Egypt, out of the land of slavery.'

I referred earlier to the fact that the Ten Commandments were given to the children of Israel after their exodus from Egypt, not before it. The reason for this is that
(as we saw) we must be saved from something before we can be saved for something. This truth is portrayed everywhere in the Scriptures. Bible commentators
often point out that almost every scripture passage that contains laws or ethical
guidelines is preceded by a section on the doctrine of salvation and deliverance. The
book of Romans is a classic example of this. The first eleven chapters of Romans
explain and expound the plan of salvation and then in chapter twelve Paul urges us
to respond to this truth in sacrificial living. Why are we being urged? It is because
of the kind of God we have and what he has done for us. Then follow four chapters
of ethical rules and principles of conduct. In Romans, as in Exodus, God is saying:
'I am the Lord your God, who has brought you out of bondage … now live as I command you.'

I make the point again – understanding who God is and what he has done is
essential to comprehending the reason for the Ten Commandments. Because he is
who he is and has done what he has done, he has the right to demand our unqual-
ified worship, obedience and love.

O God, whenever I feel irked or challenged by the things you ask me to do, help me to remember
the things that you have done for me. May the inspiration of all you have done to procure my sal-
vation cause me to rise to new levels of living. In Jesus' name. Amen.

FOR FURTHER STUDY – 1 Chron. 29:1–5; Ex. 32:29; Prov. 23:6
1. What question did David ask concerning the building of the Temple?
2. What does *consecrate* mean?

All life is worship

FOR READING AND MEDITATION – EXODUS 34:1–14

'Do not worship any other god, for the Lord, whose name is Jealous, is a jealous God.'
(v. 14: NIV)

We continue looking at the fact that when giving the Ten Commandments, God first establishes his place in our lives: 'I am the Lord your God.' Then he gives the command: 'You shall have no other gods before me.' If it is true that he is *Jehovah Elohim* – the God who is there and the supreme object of worship – then the command is a very reasonable one. To put it another way – it is a very unreasonable thing to have any other God beside him.

Dr G. Campbell Morgan says of this first Commandment, 'Every man needs a god. There is no man who has not, somewhere in his heart, in his life, in the essentials of his being, a shrine in which is a deity whom he worships.' All life is worship. It is as impossible for a person to live without an object of worship as it is for a fish to exist out of water. There may be a false god at the centre of one's life but every activity of being, every energy of the personality, every devotion of our powers – all these things are worship. However worthy or unworthy, the thing to which an individual gives his or her ultimate devotion is the god of that person's life. In this sense, there is no such person as an atheist. The choice we have in life is not whether we will worship but which god we will worship – the true God or a substitute god.

In order to function on this earth, we must inevitably look to something beyond ourselves. And that *something* helps us make choices in life; it gives us a set of values or priorities that guide us and influence all our decisions. We have little choice as to whether or not we will worship, but we have a lot of choice about what or whom we will worship.

O God – invisible yet there – I see I have a choice as to which god I will worship. I choose you – the true and ever-present One. Establish yourself even more firmly at the centre of my being. In Jesus' name I pray. Amen.

FOR FURTHER STUDY – Lev. 26:1–13; Ex. 20:4; Deut. 7:25, 11:16–17
1. What are the rewards of obedience? / 2. What are the results of idolatry?

The dynamic behind idolatry

FOR READING AND MEDITATION – JEREMIAH 2:1–13

'… But my people have exchanged their Glory for worthless idols.' (v. 11: NIV)

We continue looking at the thought that man must worship something – either the one true God or a god of his own making. This incontrovertible fact reveals the dynamics that lie behind idolatry. When anyone refuses to relate to the living God or loses the vision of him who says, 'I am *Jehovah Elohim*,' then he or she puts something else in the place of the true God. What the first Commandment is really saying to us is this – let God be God.

Whenever I read the first epistle of John, an epistle in which John has been talking about some of the loftiest concepts in Christianity – 'God is love', 'Abide in him', 'We shall be like him' and so on – I am struck by the apparent anticlimax of the exhortation with which John ends: 'Dear children, keep yourselves from idols.' Did John end this great exposition of maturity with an immature ending? Or was it the very climax? I am convinced that John was never more guided of God than when he wrote those words. With profound insight he put his finger on the greatest single hindrance to spiritual maturity – idols.

We usually associate idols with pagan faiths but idols are an expression of a universal tendency – the tendency to put something else in the place of God. Anything that becomes a centre of love and attention – a love and attention greater than the love and attention we give to God – is an idol. Idolatry is really substitution – substitution of the unreal for the real. And idolatry does not have to be an outright resistance to God, or the result of a conscious hostility towards him; it can be demonstrated by simply relegating him to irrelevance.

O Father, help me to see the insidious nature of this enemy called idolatry. Guide me as in your presence I search my heart, and show me how to 'break down every idol and cast out every foe'. In Jesus' name I pray. Amen.

FOR FURTHER STUDY – Rom. 1:18–32; Acts 17:29; Jer. 10:5
1. What was the glory of God changed for? / 2. What was the result?

God has no plural

FOR READING AND MEDITATION – DEUTERONOMY 6:1–12
'Hear, o Israel: The Lord our God, the Lord is one.' (v. 4: NIV)

Today I want to put before you the idea that just as we have a need to worship built into our personalities, so also we have a built-in need for only one God. And we cannot come to health and fullness in our personalities unless we focus on and worship the one true God.

Elton Trueblood points out in one of his books that the number *one* is different from all the other numbers and this fact is caught up and reflected in our language. Singular means one and only one, while plural means more than just one; it means upwards of two. It can be two, three or three million. Thus the man who has one wife is fundamentally different from the man who has two wives, but the man who has two wives is in the same category as the man who has 400 wives. Whether a man has two or 200 wives, he is totally different from the man who has one wife, because he cannot say, 'I love only one.'

We Christians have only one God. The word *gods* is not the plural of the word *God*. That's why we spell it with a small *g*; God has no plural. We cannot love God with one part of our being and love some other god with another part of our being – and come to health and wholeness in our personalities. Idolatry, or divided loyalty in the soul, leads to disease in the inner being. Polytheism (many gods) in the heart leads to disintegration in the personality. We are built for a relationship with only one God and if we fragment our loyalty, we fragment our personalities. I myself am convinced that at the core of what psychiatrists call neurosis is a failure on the part of that person to give himself or herself in absolute surrender to the one true and living God.

O Father, I see that your command to have no other gods before you has within it a concern for my deepest welfare. For I can never wholly be what I am designed to be unless I give myself wholly to you. Help me understand this. In Jesus' name. Amen.

FOR FURTHER STUDY – James 1:1–18; Matt. 6:24, 12:25–30
1. What does double-mindedness bring? / 2. What did Jesus say?

Is a photograph a sin?

FOR READING AND MEDITATION – LEVITICUS 19:1–14

'Do not turn to idols or make gods of cast metal for yourselves.
I am the Lord your God.' (v. 4: NIV)

We move on now to examine the second of the Ten Commandments: 'You shall not make for yourself an idol in the form of anything in heaven above or on the earth beneath or in the waters below. You shall not bow down to them or worship them ...' (Exodus 20:4–5: NIV). At first this might look like a repetition of the first Commandment, but it is much more than that. It is the forbidding of a practice which becomes possible only when the one true God is no longer believed in or worshipped. The first Commandment forbids us to have any other gods besides the One who makes himself known by the name *Jehovah Elohim*, while the second, taking for granted that there is no god but the one true God, forbids the creation of anything which is supposed to be a representation of him designed to assist man in worship.

First, let's make clear what exactly is being forbidden here. I have known Christian people interpret this Commandment to mean that every form of art is idolatrous. Some who interpret it in this way believe that even having one's photograph taken is a sin and will not allow a picture or painting to be displayed in their home. Few people would hold to such an interpretation today, but in my own circle of friends and acquaintances I know of at least two.

This, however, could not have been the divine intention, for immediately after the giving of the Ten Commandments, God gave instructions for his people to make a tabernacle of worship, at the heart of which was to be an image of a cherubim and seraphim. It is not a sin to make a representation of something; it is a sin, however, to make that representation the focus of our worship.

O Father, show me in an even deeper way than ever before the art of true worship. I long to worship you in the way you long to be worshipped – in spirit and in truth. Help me, dear Father. In Jesus' name. Amen.

FOR FURTHER STUDY – 1 Cor. 8, 10:14–22, 12:2

1. What did Paul say to the Corinthians about idolatry?
2. How are we to show care for weaker brethren?

What about aids to worship?

FOR READING AND MEDITATION – PHILIPPIANS 3:1–11

'For it is we … who worship by the Spirit of God, who glory in Christ Jesus,
and who put no confidence in the flesh.' (v. 3: NIV)

Permit me to state once again what I think the second Commandment is saying: we are not forbidden to make a representation of things, but we are forbidden to make these things the focus of our worship. The force of the Commandment lies in these words: 'You shall not bow down to them or worship them.' Many years ago in Westminster Abbey, London, some of the statues were removed from the various niches around the building because people used to burn lamps before them and kneel down and worship them. This was a violation of the second Commandment and the ecclesiastical authorities moved in to stop it.

But what about the use of objects like pictures, paintings, crucifixes, as an aid to worship? Some say an object that has sacred associations, such as a painting or a crucifix, helps them to focus on God or Christ and thus assist them in the act of worship. They are at pains to point out that they do not worship the object but use it to help them think more deeply about spiritual things. I can understand how an object that has spiritual associations triggers off thoughts that lead towards God, but I have to say that reliance upon these aids can act as a snare to the soul.

Over the years I have talked to many who have told me that for them, meaningful worship depends on being in the right place, such as a church or cathedral, in the presence of the right objects, such as a painting or a crucifix. Can you see what has happened? They have become more dependent on their surroundings than on the Spirit. And God will have us dependent on no one but himself.

O Father, bring me into such a close relationship with you and the Holy Spirit that I will be less and less dependent on the material and more and more aware of the spiritual. In Christ's name I pray. Amen.

FOR FURTHER STUDY – John 4:1–26; Matt. 4:10; Rev. 14:7
1. What point was the Samaritan woman making when she asked about worship?
2. What did Jesus declare about true worship?

How more important than where

'… the true worshippers will worship the Father in spirit and truth …' (v. 23: NIV)

We spend another day discussing the issue we touched on yesterday – the relationship of things, such as sacred objects, ornate services, beautiful and aesthetic surroundings, ritualistic ceremonies and so on, to true worship. In the ancient tabernacle in the Wilderness, the worship centre of the children of Israel, there were three sections. First, the outer court where everyone could come; second, the inner court where only the priests could gather; third, the holy place into which only the high priest could enter.

Worship, it seems to me, can be related to three stages of our being: spirit, soul and body. We can worship God with our bodies (the outer court). We can worship him also in the soul (the inner court). We can worship him too with our spirits (the holy place). The most powerful worship takes place when we move beyond the realm of the soul (the senses) to where our spirit merges into God's spirit and we pour into his heart our thanksgiving, our adoration and our praise. Worship that reaches the deepest part of God's being is worship that flows from the deepest part of our being – the spirit.

We must watch that our love for the beautiful and the aesthetic does not entice us to stay in the realm of worship where our senses are being stirred (the soul) and we become more concerned about what we are getting out of the act of worship than about what God is getting. The woman at the well wanted to have a discussion with Jesus about where God should be worshipped, but our Lord was more concerned with pointing out the *how* of worship. As far as New Testament worship is concerned, the *how* is more important than the *where*.

O Father, help me in my worship to be more concerned about bringing glory to you than about having my own senses aroused or stirred. Teach me how to worship you in spirit and in truth. In Jesus' name I ask it. Amen.

FOR FURTHER STUDY – Luke 1:46–55; 1 Thess. 5:23; Heb. 4:12
1. How did Mary worship the Lord? / 2. What did Paul pray for the Thessalonians?

A God who brooks no rivals

FOR READING AND MEDITATION – DEUTERONOMY 4:15–24

'For the Lord your God is a consuming fire, a jealous God.' (v. 24: NIV)

We continue with our focus on the second Commandment and we come now to the words: '... for I, the Lord your God, am a jealous God'. Modern-day critics make a lot out of this statement. They say, 'I can understand a God who redeems and liberates and sets free but a God who is jealous? Isn't this going too far?'

People may be repelled by the idea of a jealous God, but that is only because they do not understand what the Scripture is saying here. The word *jealous* in the Old Testament has its roots in the same word as *zealous*. When we say that God is jealous, we are really saying that he is so full of concern for his redeemed people that he will tolerate no rivals. He knows that no one can do for them what he can do for them and he pursues their interests with all the zealousness and fervency of which he is capable. We must not import into the word any suggestion of the feelings we get when we are jealous – resentment, envy, distrust, suspicion, and so on. God has no sinful emotions and when the Bible says he is jealous, it means that he is filled with a white-hot zeal to maintain his good name, bring about the highest good in the lives of his children, and ensure that his people understand who he really is.

Think of it this way: God has given himself fully to us and in return he longs that we might give ourselves fully to him. He will not share the throne of our hearts with anyone else. He wants to look at us and say: 'You are my child; you are mine, you belong to me – totally.' This kind of jealousy does not deter me; it draws me. A God like this can have my heart any day.

O Father, how can I ever sufficiently thank you that your love is a jealous love. You love me so much that you will brook no rivals. This gives me constant hope and security. I am so deeply, deeply grateful. Thank you, dear Father. Amen.

FOR FURTHER STUDY – Josh. 24:16–27; 1 Kings 14:22; Deut. 29:20
1. How did Joshua describe the Lord? / 2. What was the response of the Israelites?

The most awful thing

FOR READING AND MEDITATION – DEUTERONOMY 7:1–16

'… he is the faithful God, keeping his covenant of love to a thousand generations of those who love him and keep his commands.' (v. 9: NIV)

We spend one more day on the second Commandment and we look now at the statement: 'I … am a jealous God, punishing the children for the sin of the fathers to the third and fourth generation of those who hate me, but showing love to a thousand generations of those who love me and keep my commandments.' These words contain both a warning and a promise and they are amongst the most misunderstood words in the Old Testament.

Take first the warning: '… punishing … for the sin of the fathers to the third and fourth generation …' Does this mean that if a man is sinful and impure, God will punish his child? No, that is not what it is saying. The plain meaning of these words in context is that if someone worships a representation of God and not the true God himself, then the iniquity of that action will have repercussions down throughout the generations. Anyone who worships something other than the true God sets up influences in his or her family that go on reverberating from generation to generation. Such people harm not only themselves but the children who follow them. Their idea of worship is transmitted to their children and their children's idea of worship will be transmitted to their children – and so on. To pass on to children a wrong concept of God is the most awful thing a parent can do.

But note the promise standing alongside the warning: '… showing love to a thousand generations'. Those who pass on to their children a worship that is strong and true are more likely to influence the thousandth generation for good, than the godless are likely to influence it for evil.

O Father, the understanding of how I may influence future generations strikes a sense of awe within my being. Help me to know you and worship you in such a way that others may see a true picture of you in everything I say and do. In Jesus' name I pray. Amen.

FOR FURTHER STUDY – Psa. 112, 145:1–7, 48:12–14

1. What will one generation declare to another? / 2. What does the psalmist do every day?

Damn is not God's last name

FOR READING AND MEDITATION – EXODUS 22:20–31
'Do not blaspheme God or curse the ruler of your people.' (v. 28: NIV)

We turn now to the third of the Ten Words given at Sinai: 'You shall not misuse the name of the Lord your God, for the Lord will not hold anyone guiltless who misuses his name' (Exodus 20:7: NIV). A popular view of this Commandment is that it forms a prohibition against using God's name as a swear word, but there is a lot more to it than that. However, let's begin there, because the Commandment certainly contains the thought that it deeply offends the Almighty when his name is profaned or blasphemed.

We are living in an age when people think their vocabulary is not rich enough unless they intersperse their sentences with blasphemous references to God or Christ. Some years ago I remember being slightly shocked by a sign I saw outside a church in Atlanta, USA, that said: 'Damn is not God's last name.' I thought about it for a few minutes and said to myself: it's not the kind of sign I would expect to see outside a church but it makes a point, nevertheless.

I don't know how you feel about the way in which the name of God is tossed around in today's novels, magazines, and television presentations, but every time I hear his name taken in vain, I am deeply disturbed. I wonder how God feels about it? I suspect the heart of the Deity is deeply wounded. Some of our popular comedians and television presenters talk as if they had been for a post-graduate course to hell with the devil as their speech instructor. Perhaps we ought to be doing more to point out to them, in letters and telephone calls, but as courteously as possible, that the Lord will not hold anyone guiltless who takes his name in vain.

O God, how it must pain you to hear your name so constantly and consistently blasphemed. You share so many of my pains; let me, as far as possible, share some of the pain you feel about this. In Jesus' name I pray. Amen.

FOR FURTHER STUDY – Rom. 2:17–24; Isa. 52:5; Ezek. 20:27
1. How can blasphemy be caused? / 2. How can it be avoided?

The dynamics of profanity

FOR READING AND MEDITATION – EZEKIEL 20:30–44

'… Go and serve your idols … But afterwards you will surely listen to me
and no longer profane my holy name …' (v. 39: NIV)

Today we ask ourselves: why do people use God's name as a common oath? Is it because they are familiar with him? No. In fact, the opposite is true. No one who communes deeply with God or is close to him falls into the habit of misusing his name.

Those who have studied what is called *the dynamics of profanity* say that people who sprinkle their conversations with blasphemies and oaths that relate to the Deity do so because of a deep insecurity in their personalities. They feel small on the inside and attempt to prop themselves up on the outside by linking their own puny personalities to a great and mighty power. But they do not do it in a humble way, but in an arrogant way. It is a kind of compensation that says: 'I feel small but I won't admit it and to show how much bigger I am than anyone else, I will bring the Deity down to my size.' What arrogance! A blasphemer is to be pitied as well as to be blamed.

The ancient Jews wouldn't even pronounce God's name – they held it in such awe. Even when writing it, a copyist would take endless pains to make sure he had it right. First, he would bathe and don full Jewish dress. Then he would proceed with the utmost caution, making sure that he had enough ink on his pen to finish writing, for it was regarded as irreverent to dip the pen back in the ink in the middle of writing the name of God. It was said that if a king addressed a copyist when he was writing God's name, the copyist would ignore him completely. This is legalism, of course, but a thousand times better than the libertarianism of this modern day.

O Father, help me to learn respect for your name. Give me a new vision of all that your name represents so that I may treat it with the respect and awe it deserves. In Jesus' name I ask it. Amen.

FOR FURTHER STUDY – Matt. 5:33–37; Lev. 19:12; James 5:9–12
1. What did Jesus teach? / 2. What should *not* be?

The meaning of 'profanity'

FOR READING AND MEDITATION – EZEKIEL 39:1–13

'I will make known my holy name among my people Israel.
I will no longer let my holy name be profaned ...' (v. 7: NIV)

We continue examining the third Commandment, and we look today at the meaning of the word *profanity*. It comes from the Latin *pro*, which means 'in front of', and *fane*, which means 'the temple'. Those who use profanities take the sacred out of the temple and allow their hearts, minds and thoughts to become a common market place. In other words, they reach up and take that which ought to be treated with awe and respect and drag it down to the level of the commonplace.

Charlton Heston, the famous film star, was once asked in an interview if any of the characters he had played in his religious films had changed his spiritual outlook. He thought for a moment and said, 'Well, you can't walk barefoot down Mount Sinai with the Ten Commandments in your hand and be the same person you were when you went up.' The same can be said of a true Christian; you can't spend time in the presence of God, talk to him in prayer, commune with him, read his word and then toss his name around lightly. I can never understand those Christians who refer to the Almighty in such phrases as 'the Man upstairs', 'the One above', 'the great Captain in the sky', and so on. You will never hear the men and women who truly know God talking in those terms.

Someone might say, 'Well what about Romans 8:15, where we are encouraged to call God not just "Father" but "Daddy"?' This verse says: '... And by him [the Holy Spirit] we cry, *Abba*' (literally 'Daddy') ... But I see no conflict, for although the term is familiar, it is not irreverent. The person who knows true reverence knows also that God's name is the doorway to the audience chamber of the Lord.

Grant, dear Father, that familiarity with your name may never breed in me irreverence or disrespect. It is a thin line between legalism and libertarianism, but help me walk it. In Jesus' name. Amen.

FOR FURTHER STUDY – Neh. 1:1–11; 2 Cor. 7:1; Rev. 11:18
1. What did Nehemiah delight in? / 2. What did Paul encourage the Corinthians to have?

God's blueprint for living

The worst profanity

FOR READING AND MEDITATION – ISAIAH 48:1–11

'Listen to this … you who take oaths in the name of the Lord …
but not in truth or righteousness.' (v. 1: NIV)

In Scripture, the name of God is always a revelation. In every new title by which God made himself known to man, he revealed some new aspect of the divine character. The names of Hebrew children were intended in every case to be a prayer or a prophecy and were based on the hope of the parents for that child's future. And something like the same principles holds true for the names of God. Men learned new facts concerning his nature with each new title by which God made himself known to them. Bearing this in mind, a new gleam of light falls on the Commandment: 'You shall not misuse the name of the Lord your God.' When we use the name of God, we must use it in a way that is true to its meaning and its intention, and when we fail to do this, we misuse his name and thus break the third Commandment.

This is what happened in the passage before us today – the people swore by the name of the Lord, but not in truth; they made mention of the name of God, but not in righteousness. They used the name of God, but their lives did not line up with the revelation contained in that name and thus they violated the command of the Lord. This, then, is the deep meaning behind the third Commandment – we misuse the name of God when we do not use it in the way God intended it should be used and when we ourselves are not true to the revelation of God which the name makes. When we say, 'Lord, Lord' and do not do the thing God asks of us, we profane his name.

If the truth be known, the profanity in the church is a far more insidious form of evil than the profanity of the world, the blasphemy of the sanctuary a far more serious issue than the blasphemy in the street.

O God, forgive us that we so easily take your name upon our lips, yet so often fail to live up to all that your name represents. Help us, dear Father, to bring our lives in line with your character. For Jesus' sake. Amen.

FOR FURTHER STUDY – Luke 6:43–49; Num. 30:1–2; Deut. 23:21; Eccl. 5:4
1. What does it mean to make a vow? / 2. How did Jesus illustrate the shallow vow?

Hallowing his name

FOR READING AND MEDITATION – MATTHEW 6:5–18

"'This, then, is how you should pray: ... hallowed be your name.'"(v. 9: NIV)

The words before us in our text for today are really a positive form of the third Commandment. The Old Testament states the Commandment negatively: 'Don't misuse the name of God'. In other words, 'Don't unhallow the name of God; don't besmirch it; don't defile it; don't drag it down.' We often hear the saying: 'What's in a name?' Everything – when it is God's name that is at stake. God's name is his character and when we take his name upon us, then we are expected, with the help of his Spirit, to live up to his character. If we don't, then we violate that third Commandment.

Reflect on your day-to-day living for a moment. Search your deepest motives, your attitudes towards God and others. Then ask yourself: can God sign his holy name to what is going on in my life? Look at your daily schedule, your routines, your list of priorities: can God sign his holy name to them? Examine your leisure time: can God sign his holy name to all that goes on in that area of your life? And what about your money? Can God sign his holy name on your cheque book? Does your life hallow or profane his name? This is what it means to pray *in his name*; it means he can sign his name to the thing we are praying for.

We said yesterday that there is a blasphemy of the sanctuary as well as a blasphemy of the street. What is the blasphemy of the sanctuary? I will tell you. It is the prayer that is denied by the life; the praise that is offered to God yet counteracted by inner rebellion; the activity and work seemingly done in his name yet done with a covert bid for attention. That is blasphemy, that is profanity, that is taking the name of God in vain.

Holy Spirit, I feel you probing deep within my heart and finding there the hidden infections of insincerity. Drain them to the last poisonous drop. Make me clean, make me whole and free from every hidden contradiction. In Jesus' name I ask it. Amen.

FOR FURTHER STUDY – Ezek. 36:22–32; Lev. 22:1–2; Isa. 29:23–24
1. What were the children of Israel guilty of? / 2. What did God promise?

Worship and work

FOR READING AND MEDITATION – ISAIAH 56:1–8

'Blessed is the man who does this ... who keeps the Sabbath
without desecrating it ...' (v. 2: NIV)

Today we focus on the fourth Commandment: 'Remember the Sabbath day by keeping it holy. Six days you shall labour and do all your work, but the seventh day is a Sabbath to the Lord your God' (Exodus 20:8–9: NIV). This Commandment is the last in the first section of the Decalogue – the section that deals with man in his relationship to God. A lot of confusion, dogmatism and misunderstanding surround this particular Commandment and so we must move very carefully and prayerfully over these next few days.

The Commandment in its original setting was given to the Hebrew people to establish the regular habit of making the seventh day a day of total rest. It is popularly believed that this fourth Commandment refers only to the Sabbath – but that is not so. Its full meaning can only be understood when we look at the second half, which has to do with the six days. The Commandment consists of two simple injunctions: first, 'Remember the Sabbath day by keeping it holy', and second, 'Six days you shall labour'.

It is the will of God for us that we should work, and it is also the will of God that on the seventh day we should cease from our labours and focus our whole attention on worship. Work and worship complement one another. The one who never works (accidents and illnesses excepted) is unfit for worship. The one who never pauses to worship is unfit for work. The two parts of the Commandment must not be separated; they must be seen as one. Obedience to the one creates the power to obey the other. Work makes for worship, and worship fits and tunes the whole being for work.

Father, I see you have made me for two important functions – worship and work. Help me understand the relationship of these two things so that I might get the best out of my worship and also out of my work. In Christ's name I ask it. Amen.

FOR FURTHER STUDY – Gen. 1; Heb. 4:1–11
1. On which day did God create Adam? / 2. What was the first day Adam experienced?

True re-creation

FOR READING AND MEDITATION – EXODUS 16:11–36

'This is what the Lord commanded: "Tomorrow is to be a day of rest,
a holy Sabbath to the Lord …"' (v. 23: NIV)

The idea of the Sabbath was not new to the children of Israel, for as we see in the passage before us today, God had introduced the Sabbath to them prior to the giving of the law on Sinai. And as you know, the principle of the Sabbath is rooted in the nature of God, for following the six days of creation we are told that 'on the seventh day he rested from all his work' (Genesis 2:2: NIV).

The idea of the Sabbath, or a one day rest in seven, is thought to be out of date in this high-tech age through which we are passing, but it was established by our Creator and thus must have a definite reason. Every part of our being – spirit, soul and body – is the result of careful consideration and forethought by our Maker and we are more likely to function at our maximum potential when we follow his instructions. Men and women are placed in a world which contains all that is necessary for their physical being, but to obtain it, they must work. To this side of the fourth Commandment the majority of human beings are obedient; most people realise that they cannot get their physical needs met unless they work.

There is another side, however. God decrees that every seventh day, men and women lay aside the tools of their trades and focus their minds on the worship of their Creator. To this side of the fourth Commandment, multitudes of human beings are disobedient. They focus on such things as rest and recreation and fail to realise that *re-creation* is not just a physical thing, but has spiritual elements also. None of us is really ready to face the challenge of six working days (or even five!) unless we have been spiritually prepared on the seventh by fully giving ourselves to the worship of God.

Loving heavenly Father, I see that you have established the Sabbath not merely as a holiday, but as a holy day. Help me to see the divine purpose running through this and to utilise it in my work and my worship. For your own dear name's sake. Amen.

FOR FURTHER STUDY – Isa. 58; Ex. 20:8, 34:21; Isa. 56:1–2
1. How is joy in the Lord equated to the Sabbath?
2. What is promised to the man who keeps the Sabbath?

God's blueprint for living

The Lord of the Sabbath

FOR READING AND MEDITATION – MATTHEW 12:1–14

'How much more valuable is a man than a sheep! Therefore it is
lawful to do good on the Sabbath.' (v. 12: NIV)

Although the principle of ceasing from all kinds of labour on the seventh day is
clearly established in the Old Testament, when we move to the New Testament, we
find that we are faced with several problems. Although it is quite clear that our Lord
affirmed the spirit of the law of the Sabbath, he appears at times to have broken the
letter of it. In other words, he did not hold to it legalistically. When his disciples were
criticised for picking some ears of corn and eating them on the Sabbath, Jesus
defended their action saying, 'For the Son of Man is Lord of the Sabbath.' Later he
himself healed on the Sabbath day and this so incensed the legalists that they went
out and plotted to kill him The healing at the Pool of Bethesda was, you remember,
done on the Sabbath day and John tells us quite plainly that as far as the letter of the
law was concerned, Jesus clearly broke the Sabbath (see John 5:18).

Another problem that occurs in relation to the Sabbath when we step into the
New Testament is that the fourth commandment is the only Commandment not to
be repeated there. All the other Old Testament Commandments are reiterated and
often tightened in the pages of the New Testament, but not the one concerning the
Sabbath. In all the list of New Testament sins, Sabbath breaking is never mentioned,
while in Galatians 4:10–11 and Colossians 2:16–17, Paul clearly warns against a
legalistic view of the Sabbath.

Does this mean that since New Testament times the keeping of the Sabbath is
no longer important? Is the fourth Commandment no longer applicable? We shall see.

*Father, I see now why there is so much confusion over this important matter of the Sabbath. Help
me to think this through with you so that I come out, not as a legalist, but as a loving and obedient
disciple. In Jesus' name I ask it. Amen.*

FOR FURTHER STUDY – John 7:14–24, 9:14; Mark 6:1–6
1. What did Jesus say of the Sabbath?
2. How did the people of Nazareth react to the teaching Jesus gave on the Sabbath?

From Saturday to Sunday

FOR READING AND MEDITATION – JOHN 20:1–19

'Early on the first day of the week ... Mary Magdalene went to the tomb
and saw that the stone had been removed ...' (v. 1: NIV)

Before answering the problems that we faced yesterday concerning the keeping of
the Sabbath, we must face the issue of why it is that most of the Christian church
keeps Sunday rather than Saturday as the Sabbath. The early church stopped cele-
brating Saturday Sabbath and instead began keeping the first day of the week (our
Sunday) because that was the day on which Christ rose from the dead. This was
done with the approval and authority of the apostles, Christ's appointed teachers. In
1 Corinthians 15 Paul talks about the great theme of the resurrection and then follows it in Chapter 16:2 with these words: 'On the first day of every week, each one of
you should set aside a sum of money in keeping with his income ...' In Revelation
1:10 John writes: 'On the Lord's Day I was in the Spirit, and I heard behind me a loud
voice ...' What a beautiful way to describe the day of rest – 'the Lord's Day'. Personally, I much prefer this to Sunday, or even to the word *Sabbath*.

In the action of changing the Sabbath from Saturday to Sunday in celebration
of the resurrection of our Lord, the early church swept aside the legalism that was
attached to it, while still keeping the principle that lay behind it. That principle –
that one day in seven be hallowed and set apart for worship – can never be repealed,
for it is grounded in the nature of God, in human nature and in the nature of the
universe itself. Animals can function without a day of rest, but not man.

So although the day has changed, the Sabbath principle has not. *The Lord's Day*
is still his gift to us – a day set apart, a day of rest and worship, a day of recupera-
tion, re-creation and joy.

Loving heavenly Father, whilst, in a sense, every day is your day, help me to understand and expe-
rience the specialness that you reserve for me in The Lord's Day. *This I ask in Christ's peerless and*
precious Name. Amen.

FOR FURTHER STUDY – Rom. 14; Eph. 2:11–16; Col. 2:13–14
1. What was Paul teaching in Romans 14?
2. What will each of us be required to do before God?

Remember

FOR READING AND MEDITATION – PSALM 105:1–11

'Remember the wonders he has done, his miracles,
and the judgments he pronounced.' (v. 5: NIV)

We saw yesterday that although the early church changed the day of rest from a
Saturday to a Sunday, they still kept to the principle of the Sabbath by refraining
from work and giving themselves to the corporate worship of God.

Two main principles underlie the Sabbath – rest and remembrance. The fact
that we need to rest one day in seven is a principle that has been shown to be physically and psychologically sound. A medical doctor by the name of Hagler says, 'A
weekly day of rest is necessary to restore the cumulative loss of oxygen from our six
days of labour.' Sir James C. Brown, a British physician, said, 'We doctors, in the treatment of nervous diseases, are now constantly compelled to prescribe periods of rest.
Some periods are, I think, only Sundays in arrears.'

But there is more to a biblical understanding of Sunday than just rest – there
must be remembrance. In Deuteronomy 5:15 God follows the command to observe
the Sabbath with these words: 'Remember that you were slaves in Egypt and that the
Lord your God brought you out of there with a mighty hand and an outstretched
arm.' In effect, he was saying: 'You were slaves but you have been delivered. Keep
one day in seven holy and remember.' Why remember? Because our sinful nature
makes it easy for us to forget. No Sunday ought to pass without our giving some time
to remembering how we have been saved from sin and brought out of the world.
Remembrance need not be the whole focus, but it ought to be given some focus. If
we forget that we were delivered from sin by the Saviour's efforts and not our own,
we might soon find ourselves being drawn back to it.

*Father, I see clearly now what Sunday means – rest and remembrance. Help me from this day for-
ward to carry these two principles with me into this coming Sunday and every Sunday. In Jesus'
name. Amen.*

FOR FURTHER STUDY – Jonah 2:2–9; Psa. 63:6; Eccl. 12:1; 1 Cor. 11:17–32
1. What jogged Jonah's memory? / 2. What is a focus for remembrance?

God's plan for the family

FOR READING AND MEDITATION – EPHESIANS 6:1–18
'"Honour your father and mother" – which is the first
commandment with a promise.' (v. 2: NIV)

The fifth Commandment, which we are about to examine, falls in the second section of the Decalogue – the section which focuses not so much on our relationship to God as on our relationship to each other. Differences of opinion have been expressed about the division of the Decalogue, some maintaining that the first four Commandments were written upon the first tablet of stone and the last six upon the second. We cannot be sure about this, but what we can be sure about is the fact that the six Commandments in this section reveal for all time the divine thinking on human relationships. First comes the family relationship: 'Honour your father and mother, so that you may live long in the land the Lord your God is giving you' (Exodus 20:12: NIV). Families are part of God's plan. Listen to how the Amplified Bible translates Psalm 68:6: 'God places the solitary in families and gives the desolate a home in which to dwell.'

The nature of life on this earth – human life, I mean – is that each new generation begins where the last one leaves off. That's not just an interesting theory; it is an indisputable fact. The blessings and sins of one generation have an impact on succeeding generations. This is true physiologically, psychologically and spiritually. And because this is the nature of human society, we need a Commandment that addresses that issue and gives us clear guidelines on how to behave.

No nation can rise higher than its homes and families. Indeed, I will go further – no nation can survive unless it gives attention to the principles of effective family living. We either heed the helm or we must heed the rocks.

Gracious and loving Father, help me to put in my home such a flame of pure living that the next generation may get from me and my family a torch that will never go out. In Jesus' name I ask it. Amen.

FOR FURTHER STUDY – Luke 2:39–52; Lev. 19:3; Prov. 4:1, 30:17; John 19:25–27
1. What did Luke say of the boy Jesus? / 2. How did Jesus show honour for his mother?

Lover, lawgiver and provider

FOR READING AND MEDITATION – PROVERBS 22:1–12

'Train a child in the way he should go, and when he is old he will not turn from it.'
(v. 6: NIV)

The fifth Commandment: 'Honour your father and mother' is closely linked in thought and intention to those that have preceded it, and although it is not directly stated, the implication is that the parent is in the place of God to the child.

In the early days of childhood development, when as yet the child is unable to grasp the most elementary ideas of God, the supreme facts concerning him are to be impressed upon the child by a revelation of them in his or her parents. Although, in the ultimate sense, God is the Creator of all life, in the procession of events, a child owes its being and existence to its parents. And from a vast amount of research it is clear that the attitude of a child towards its parents is quite different from its attitude towards others. What God is to the adult, the parent must be to the child – lover, lawgiver and provider.

The child's response to the parent-child relationship is the foundation on which that child will later relate to God. Someone has put it like this, 'Mother and Father are the skylight through which a child gets his or her first glimpse of God.' It is also a solemn fact that the children in the home catch the attitudes of the parents rather than their sayings. The child is like the subconscious mind – it learns by what it sees people acting on, rather than by what they say.

We wonder at the undisciplined young people of this generation, but do we not need to look back at the previous generation on whom rests a great deal of the responsibility?

O Father, help us to live in such a way that we will inspire in those younger than us, especially those in our families, a desire to move in the direction of the noblest and the best – because they see it in us. In Jesus' name we ask it. Amen.

FOR FURTHER STUDY – Deut. 6:1–7; Eph. 6:4; Isa. 38:19
1. When are parents to talk to children about the things of God? / 2. What are fathers to do?

Why didn't youth listen?

FOR READING AND MEDITATION – PSALM 127:1–5

'Sons are a heritage [assignment] from the Lord, children are a reward from him.'
(v. 3: NIV)

Before going into the reasons why God commands children to honour their parents, we spend another day reflecting on the importance of the parent-child relationship. We are doing this because, as we said yesterday, the fifth Commandment is closely linked to those that have preceded it. The implication is that a parent is in the place of God to the child. We also suggested yesterday that in the home children catch the attitudes of parents rather than their words or sayings.

This raised the question: why are there so many undisciplined young people in today's generation? There are many well-disciplined young people, of course, but it is clear that the numbers of the undisciplined are increasing year by year. This generation has been *put forward* by the parents of yesterday. Some parents are surprised at this and have said, 'But I repeated to them the claims of morality and religion that I myself was taught.' Why, then, didn't the youth listen? I think it is because so many people repeated the sanctions of morality and religion with less and less conviction.

It is attitudes, not just words, that make the deepest impact. My father put a torch in my hands when I was but a boy, though he did not know he had done so. The shadow of financial calamity was upon my home in Wales as a result of the miners' strike in the late thirties. Going upstairs one night, I heard a muffled voice. I stopped and heard my father in heart-breaking prayer. I saw through the little crack in the door more than just a person kneeling in prayer – I saw a flame of pure devotion. I took a wick from that lamp of devotion that night and it has lighted me down the years.

Gracious and loving heavenly Father, make us worthy of the heritage that has been passed on to us, and may we worthily give it to the age through which we are passing – an age so desperately in need of just this. In Jesus' name. Amen.

FOR FURTHER STUDY – Gen. 48; Prov. 20:11, 23:22

1. What are a parent's priorities? 2. What practical steps must be taken to accomplish these?

God's blueprint for living

What it means to 'honour'

FOR READING AND MEDITATION – COLOSSIANS 3:1–17

'... Forgive as the Lord forgave you.' (v. 13: NIV)

It is often taken for granted that the command: 'Honour your father and mother', is addressed only to young children. It is not. This false idea comes from confusing the word *honour* with *obey*. The word *honour* contains the thought of obedience, but is much wider in meaning. To *honour* means 'to attach weight to; to put in the place of high importance; to reverence and respect'.

For some children, the day may come – after they have married, for example – when they may have to disobey a wish of their parents because it is not in the best interests of their partner. But though the day may come when we are no longer required to obey our parents, the day never comes when we are no longer required to honour them. When we are young, we honour our parents by obeying them, but when we go out into life and are free to make our own decisions, then honour takes a new form – that of kindliness, courtesy and respect.

This is fine if we have been brought up with loving and considerate parents, but what if a parent has been cruel, difficult, indifferent or abusive? Then forgive them. 'Ah,' I hear you say, 'if you had been brought up with my parents you would not talk like that.' I can understand how some of you reading these lines might find it difficult to offer forgiveness to cruel and abusive parents – but on the strength of Scripture I have to say – it is not impossible.

Here are my suggestions. Reflect on how much God has forgiven you. Think of the hurt you brought to the heart of God – yet he has forgiven you. Think long about that. Then let the wonder of how much you have been forgiven flow out in forgiveness to your parents.

Lord Jesus Christ, you who hung upon a cross tortured in every way, yet prayed for those who tortured and abused you, help me now to forgive those who have wronged me and hurt me. For your own dear name's sake. Amen.

FOR FURTHER STUDY – Luke 17:1–6; Mark 11:25; Eph. 4:32
1. What did Jesus teach about forgiveness? / 2. Is there a family member you need to forgive?

Attitudes as well as arteries

FOR READING AND MEDITATION – DEUTERONOMY 11:8–21
'Observe therefore all the commands I am giving you today …
so that you may live long in the land …' (vv. 8–9: NIV)

We saw yesterday that the command: 'Honour your father and mother' has a twofold application: first, to the period of childhood, and second, to the period of adult life. We saw also that *to honour* means much more than *to obey*, although the thought of obedience is contained in the word *honour*.

Today we ask ourselves: why is the command to honour one's parents coupled with the promise of long life? I believe it is because the honouring of one's parents results in the accumulation of habits and character that contribute to the lengthening of one's days. Character moulded in the atmosphere of honour to one's parents has within it the elements of spiritual power that contribute to good physical health and longevity. On the other hand, character formed in the atmosphere of rebelliousness, disobedience, insubordination and disrespect has within it the elements of recklessness and fever which contribute to the shortening of life. Our attitudes, it must be remembered, are as important to our physical functioning as are our arteries. One commentator claims that the last six Commandments are all related to and included in the fifth: children who honour their parents will be slow to get involved in murder, impurity, theft, slander and covetousness.

Let every single one of us take this to heart today and pray and do what we can to preserve and practice the decree which God has given: 'Honour your father and mother.' And let every mother and father remember that in the plan and purpose of God, children get their first glimpse of him, not just through what their parents say, but through what they do.

O Father, as home and family life continue to be assailed from many directions, give me a new vision of what I can do to preserve and practise the truth of your Word. Hold me together, so that I may hold others together. In Jesus' name. Amen.

FOR FURTHER STUDY – 2 Tim. 1:1–7; Deut. 4:9, 31, 13; 2 Chron. 17:3, 26:4
1. What was Paul persuaded of? / 2. Why was the Lord with Jehoshaphat?

The gift of life

FOR READING AND MEDITATION – GENESIS 9:1–7

'Whoever sheds the blood of man, by man shall his blood be shed;
for in the image of God has God made man.' (v. 6: NIV)

We turn now to consider the sixth Commandment: 'You shall not murder' (Exodus 20:13: NIV). This brief Commandment contains a statement on the first principle of life: human existence is sacred. At the very foundation of the social fabric lies the truth of the sovereignty of God over every individual life. And if God regards human life as sacred – so must we. Life is God's gift and we must not tamper with it. It is only possible for a new human life to appear in this world because God has endowed upon men and women the ability to be mini-creators. Think of it this way – if today he were to take away our power to pass on life, then less than one year from now no new babies would be born.

Because God is the originator of life, we can say that human life is a divine creation, marvellous and magnificent in its origin and utterly beyond the comprehension of any human being. Thus life is not to be cut off at the hand of someone who does not know or understand all that it contains – its wonder, its meaning, its possibilities. God has a purpose for every individual who enters his world – a purpose stretching far beyond the present moment – and to terminate a single life is to set up the wit and wisdom of man as superior to the mind of the Eternal.

So immense are the issues relating to a person's death that there can be no sin against humanity greater than that of taking life. I say again, this sixth Word of the Decalogue contains a statement about the first principle of life, a statement so clear and so vital that it demands the closest attention – life is God's gift and we must not tamper with it.

O Father, I am so grateful that day by day your word is teaching me to look at life from your perspective. And when my point of view clashes with yours, help me to be willing to exchange my perspective for yours. In Jesus' name I ask it. Amen.

FOR FURTHER STUDY – Gen. 2:1–7; 1 Sam. 2:6; Job 27:3; Acts 17:24–26
1. What is it that sustains life? / 2. What did Paul declare to the Athenians?

A fiery law

FOR READING AND MEDITATION – JAMES 3:1–12

'With the tongue we praise our Lord and Father, and with it we curse men,
who have been made in God's likeness.' (v. 9: NIV)

We began to see yesterday that murder is such a heinous sin because man is God's offspring; he is a being made in God's image; he is what he is by divine power and volition. By bestowing the gift of life, God bestowed the gift of a most wonderful relationship of man to himself. It is important to see that all other relationships grow out of our relationship with God and are subservient to it. In other words, if we do not have a correct view of our relationship with God, we will not have a correct view of our relationship with one another. Just as night follows day, so those nations who lose their respect and awe of God will in turn lose their respect and awe of each other. Subsequent Commandments dealing with social, civic or blood relationships are binding upon us because they are included within this first and highest relationship of life – our relationship with God.

One Bible commentator says concerning this sixth Commandment, 'The sacredness of marriage, the right of property, the importance of reputation, the supremacy of character – all gain their force from the nature of life. They mark, in fact, the unfolding of life in all its varied possibilities. The giving of life includes all. The cessation of life ends all.' Every power of every individual on the face of the earth flows from the power that is God.

In four simple but stern words, the sixth Commandment flings a fiery law around the life of every human being and implies, if it doesn't state, that the right to end life lies in the hands of the One who first bestowed it.

O God, if only the men and women of this world could see that right relationships with others come only out of a right relationship with you. Help those of us who are your children to model this truth before their gaze. In Jesus' name. Amen.

FOR FURTHER STUDY – Eccl. 2:17–26, 3:1–14, 6:12
1. What did the Teacher say is meaningless? / 2. What is the gift of God?

God's blueprint for living

Cities of refuge

FOR READING AND MEDITATION – NUMBERS 35:6–29

'Six of the towns you give the Levites will be cities of refuge,
to which a person who has killed someone may flee …' (v. 6: NIV)

It is worth noting that although the Authorised Version of the Bible puts the sixth Commandment in this form: 'Thou shalt not kill,' almost every other translation uses the word *murder*. There is good reason for this. The Hebrew word *ratsach*, used in this verse, has a deeper meaning than just to kill; it means to kill in anger or with pre-meditation. All murder is, of course, killing but all killing is not necessarily murder.

The passage before us today brings out this point very clearly. God told Israel that they must appoint six cities of refuge to which anyone who had been guilty of killing could go and gain protection. The main purpose of these cities was to protect the killer from those who would take it upon themselves to avenge the death of a loved one. Note, however, the criteria which the Scripture gives for differentiating between a killing and a murder. Those who had killed someone but had not intended to do so were not to be seen as murderers. Those, however, who had killed 'with malice aforethought' (v. 20) were to be shown no mercy and to be put to death. The task of the 'assembly' (a jury) was to determine whether the killing was intentional or unintentional.

But notice that unintentional killing was not looked upon as a light offence. The man who took life in this way was denied his liberty for an indefinite term, having to remain in the city of refuge until the death of the high priest. If he ventured from the safety of the protecting walls, he could be slain by the avenger of the one whom he had killed. All this was to show that life is God's gift and the taking of it, even unintentionally, is a solemn thing.

Father, again I ask, impress deeply into my mind the sacredness and importance of human life. Help me see this whole issue from your point of view. For I realise that the way I see issues is the way I will relate to them. In Jesus' name. Amen.

FOR FURTHER STUDY – Deut. 17:11–13, 16:20; Isa. 56:1; James 2:12–13
1. What are we to maintain? / 2. What is linked to justice in the New Testament?

Judicial execution

FOR READING AND MEDITATION – 1 SAMUEL 15:24–35

'… And Samuel put Agag to death before the Lord at Gilgal.' (v. 33: NIV)

Once we have seen the clear distinction between the word *kill* and the word *murder* we have a key for resolving some, though not all, of the complex issues that we come up against when reading the Old Testament. It's interesting, for example, that the Hebrew word used in the sixth Commandment for murder is never used in the Bible when talking about someone being killed in a war, or of executing someone who has been condemned to death.

Murder is the ending of a human life, a prerogative belonging only to God, but in certain circumstances God does give to mankind the right to act on his behalf to bring about the death of another. This is what is known as *judicial execution* – the act of carrying out the death penalty, not out of personal pique, but in the interests of society.

In the history of the ancient Hebrew people, God delegated to mankind the right to take life for the purpose of maintaining a social order based upon righteousness. At his express command, certain forms of sin incurred the death penalty; and God also commanded the taking of human life in some clearly marked situations when the divine plan had been violated (the slaughter of the Amalekites, for example). Such killing was not murder but the carrying our of the divine will. Achan, who was stoned to death, did not lose his life by the will of men but by the will of God. The executioners were carrying out the express order of heaven. This may be terribly difficult for some to understand (I still struggle with it forty years after becoming a Christian) but I am convinced that when we 'know as we are known' (1 Corinthians 13:12) we shall not have any trouble accepting it.

Father, I am big enough to ask questions but not big enough to understand the answers. Until the day comes when I shall 'know as I am known', help me to trust your judgment – especially when it runs counter to mine. In Jesus' name. Amen.

FOR FURTHER STUDY – Josh. 7; Gen. 9:6; Ex. 21:14, 35:2; Deut. 17:5; 2 Kings 9:33
1. What was Achan's sin? / 2. What was God's judgment?

Are you a murderer?

FOR READING AND MEDITATION – MATTHEW 5:17–26

'But I tell you that anyone who is angry with his brother will be subject to judgment ...'
(v. 22: NIV)

We spend one more day looking at the sixth Commandment: 'You shall not murder.' The question is often asked: is suicide a form of murder? I believe it is. If God does not allow us to murder another human being, he is hardly likely to allow us to murder ourselves. What about abortion? Is abortion murder? Again, with some exceptions, such as the saving of the life of the mother, I believe it is. And what about euthanasia – is that murder? My answer is, 'Yes'.

But let's focus now on the passage before us today, in which Jesus restates the old Commandment: 'Do not murder,' but adds a new perspective. The Old Testament law forbids the outer blows that would bring about a person's death, but our Lord goes further and traces the emotion that produces murder down to its lair – unrestrained anger. I imagine that very few reading these lines have been involved in the physical act of murder, but how many of us, I wonder, are guilty of murder in the heart? We may not be able to stop anger arising in our hearts, but we can certainly take steps to bring it under control. If we don't, if we allow it to burn and boil within us, we violate the law of love, and in God's sight this makes us as guilty of murder as if we had stabbed someone with a dagger.

These are solemn words and difficult to accept, but the Scripture is clear. Let the apostle John have the last word: 'Anyone who hates his brother is a murderer, and you know that no murderer has eternal life in him' (1 John 3:15: NIV).

O Father, in the light of your word to me, I ask myself: am I allowing anger against another to abide within my heart? Am I a murderer? Father, I repent. Forgive me and this day help me to root out every vestige of anger from my heart. In Jesus' name. Amen.

FOR FURTHER STUDY – Psa. 37:1–8; Prov. 14:17; Eccl. 7:9; James 1:19
1. What should we be slow to do? / 2. When do we become foolish?

God's first circle

FOR READING AND MEDITATION – PROVERBS 14:22–35

'Righteousness exalts a nation, but sin is a disgrace to any people.' (v. 34: NIV)

We come now to what someone has described as 'the most unpopular Commandment of them all': 'You shall not commit adultery.' It is interesting that immediately following on from the Commandment which declares the sacredness of human life comes the one that declares the sacredness of marriage. We must always remember that within society, God's first circle is not the nation, not the community, but the family. And within the family circle, his purpose is that the sacred union between a man and women should remain inviolate.

Look again with me at the divine sequence that runs through the Ten Commandments. The first thing that is emphasised is our relationship with God. The second is our relationship with each other. Within this second realm, the relationship between man and wife is the type and origin of all subsequent relationships. Nothing can be more essential for the social order than the relationship upon which all subsequent ones are built. This means that it should be jealously guarded against every form of attack.

Any nation that does not uphold the sacredness of marriage and the unity of the family, and does not set its face against unchastity and adultery, is preparing the way for its own demise. The greatness of a people depends upon the purity and moral strength of the people, and every nation that believes the marriage relationship may be violated with impunity is sowing the seeds of its own destruction. 'An adulterer is an enemy of the state,' claims one Bible teacher. Strong words, but, in my opinion, true. Committing adultery is like dropping a stone in a pond; the ripples don't just stay in the centre – they spread.

O Father, help those who guide our nation to see the damaging effects of this sin upon the whole society. Raise up amongst us strong moral leaders who will give themselves to these concerns. In Jesus' name we ask it. Amen.

FOR FURTHER STUDY – Heb. 13:1–4; Prov. 18:22; Gen. 2:20–25

1. What do husband and wife become? / 2. Why is this sacred?

Why adultery is so heinous

FOR READING AND MEDITATION – PROVERBS 6:20–35

'Can a man walk on hot coals without his feet being scorched?
So is he who sleeps with another man's wife ...' (vv. 28–29: NIV)

Today we asked ourselves: why is the sin of adultery so heinous and repulsive in the sight of God? It is because it violates the unity of a husband and wife, which is unity designed to illustrate and express the divine image. The unity of husband and wife is not subject to human caprice, but is essential, for 'God created man in his own image... male and female he created them' (Genesis 1:27: NKJ). A man and a woman joined together in marriage reflect the divine image in a way that one person on his or her own is unable fully to do. Both male and female are necessary to give full expression to the divine. And the duality is the double expression of the most sacred and holy power of procreation.

We saw earlier, when we looked at the first and second Commandments, that God will allow nothing to interfere with his essential unity. And what he purposes for himself he also purposes for us; adultery disrupts and destroys the oneness which is designed to be an expression of the divine image. Can you see now why God is so set against this sin?

The words of the seventh Commandment are directed against the sin of un-faithfulness in marriage – the violating of the sacred rights of the marriage bond – but its spirit emphatically forbids all unchastity. Once the idea is accepted that marriage reflects the unity and oneness of the divine image, then it becomes evident that fornication (sexual intercourse prior to marriage) is a wrong done to the marriage that is to be. I know this sounds archaic and out of date to today's generation, but I remind you – it may seem out of date but it is not out of the Bible.

Father, help me to see the exceeding sinfulness of sin, for only then can I understand just what it does to your nature and your heart. Show me that amidst all the ways of men you too have a way – the Way. Help me walk it – faithfully and loyally. In Jesus' name. Amen.

FOR FURTHER STUDY – Matt. 5:27–32, 19:9; Rom. 7:3; 1 Cor. 6:9–10; Mark 7:20–21
1. How does Jesus define adultery? / 2. What is the consequence of saying 'YES' to adultery?

Where is the emphasis?

FOR READING AND MEDITATION – 2 TIMOTHY 2:1–15

'Keep reminding them of these things. Warn them before God …' (v. 14: NIV)

The subject we have been discussing over these past few days – unfaithfulness in marriage – is not just something that is being laughed at or ignored by modern-day society, but is under a direct philosophical and theological assault. One writer puts it like this, 'We are living in a sex-saturated society in which the media tells us in a thousand and one ways, "You shall lust, in thought and word and deed."' Within the Christian church itself some are saying of the seventh Commandment, 'This is a good ideal but one that is almost impossible to live up to.'

Of course it's impossible to live up to in one's own strength, but the emphasis ought to be not on how high God lifts the moral standards, but on the power he provides to enable us to reach up to them. If we fail, it is not because the standards are too high, but because we have not come to him in utter dependency and drawn from him the grace and power we need to do what he commands.

Another argument we often hear is this: 'Adultery is not the unpardonable sin – if someone lapses in this area there is always the hope of divine forgiveness. Yes, of course, adultery is a forgivable offence – I would be the first to affirm this. The problem, however, is that too many Christian teachers major on the aspect of forgiveness but do not spend as much time making clear the nature of the offence. We must not stop talking about forgiveness, but neither must we stop talking about the nature of the offence. If we took more time explaining just what is involved in the sin of adultery, maybe we might not have to spend so much time showing people how to find forgiveness for it.

O Father, help us to be as clear about the nature of sin as we are about the nature of forgiveness. Remind us, dear Lord, that the awful thing about sin is not that it breaks your law but that it breaks your heart. In Jesus' name I pray. Amen.

FOR FURTHER STUDY – 1 John 2:15–17; Gal. 5:7–15; Rom. 8:5

1. What are the marks of worldliness? / 2. Against what did Paul warn the Galatians?

A setback for society

FOR READING AND MEDITATION – 1 CORINTHIANS 13:1–13

'Love does not delight in evil but rejoices with the truth. It always protects,
always trusts, always hopes, always perseveres.' (vv. 6–7: NIV)

One of the evil things about the age through which we are passing is not that it
laughs at or ignores the seventh Commandment, but that it sets out to present a philosophy of life that is not only immoral but amoral. Not everyone takes this attitude,
of course, but many do. An amoral person is someone who is unconcerned about
morals and sees no point in them at all. Amorality took great strides forward in the
1960s with Hugh Heffner and his *Playboy* magazine. He was successful in launching
not just a popular magazine but also a philosophy of life which can be summarised
like this: sex is a function of the body, a drive we share with animals along with eating and drinking and sleeping. Sex is a physical demand that must be satisfied. If
we don't satisfy it, the repression will cause all sorts of neuroses and psychoses.

Then in the 1970s came the film *Love Story* in which Jennifer and Oliver changed
the word *marriage* to *agreement*. The film *Love Story* was, in my opinion, one of the
most socially disruptive films of our century. It helped to encourage the idea that a
man and woman who have established *a meaningful relationship* have a moral right
to sleep together. In God's sight they do not.

We Christians ought to wake up and realise that we are witnessing an all-out
attack on the Commandments given to us on Sinai, not least the seventh, and we
ought to do everything we can and use every influence possible – prayer, teaching
in our churches, pressure on governments – to let the world know that when they
leap God's moral fences, they imperil not only their own lives but the lives of many
others as well.

*O God, help me realise that the battle lines are being drawn between your truth and this 'sex-sat-
urated society'. You have placed me as one of your children right in the midst of this battle. Help
me to be a faithful witness to what is right. In Jesus' name. Amen.*

FOR FURTHER STUDY – 1 Thess. 4:1–8; Col. 3:5–6; Eph. 5:3–5
1. What are we to learn? / 2. What did Paul write to the Ephesians?

He puts the ladder in-between

FOR READING AND MEDITATION – MATTHEW 5:27–48

'… anyone who looks at a woman lustfully has already committed adultery
with her in his heart.' (v. 28: NIV)

When Jesus restated the seventh Commandment in the passage before us today, he
did with it what he did with the sixth Commandment: 'You shall not murder' – he
deepened it and set it in a wider perspective. Once again he traced the act to its lair
– a harboured thought.

Notice I say *harboured thought*, for there is a great difference between a thought
that pops into the head and one that is allowed to remain there. Many married men
and women (and single people too) suddenly find themselves possessed with the
thought of making love to someone to whom they are not married. Is the thought
sin? I have no hesitation in saying that at that stage it is not. It becomes sin when the
self welcomes it, adopts it, owns it and nurtures it. At that stage the thought passes
into lust and it is then that adultery is committed in the heart. A person's inability
or fearfulness to turn the will into a deed is irrelevant to the question of morality.
When someone identifies with the desire, that person has committed sin. It all happens in the mind and will. Thus, on Christ's view of morality, someone could keep
the seventh Commandment and still be a moral leper.

However, let me remind those of you who are often tempted in this way that
although our Lord carries the moral tests into the deep recesses of the soul, he gives
grace to pass them too. He shows us the evil embedded in our nature and yet does
not spurn us. He shows us what we are, then what we can be – and puts the ladder
in-between. If you are willing to climb it by turning your thoughts to him in the
moment you are tempted, then I promise you – to your willingness he will add his
power and bring you to a new plane of thinking.

*Father, I am so thankful for the reminder that in the moment of temptation you are there, not to
spurn me but to save me. Your promise is that my mind can be transformed. I give you my mind
for that process to begin. Help me. In Jesus' name. Amen.*

FOR FURTHER STUDY – James 1:12–15; Matt. 15:19; Titus 1:15–16; Phil. 4:8
1. Where is sin conceived? / 2. What are we to think about?

Inverting the order

FOR READING AND MEDITATION – ROMANS 2:17–29
'… You who preach against stealing, do you steal?' (v. 21: NIV)

We look now at the eighth Commandment: 'You shall not steal' (Exodus 20:15). In some ways this Commandment (as well as the two following it) is of lesser importance than the preceding ones, for these reasons: first, because, as Jesus said, life is more than possessions (Matthew 6:25) and up to this point the Commandments have focused on sins that interfere with our relationship to God or harm human life itself. Second, violation of the first seven Commandments incurred the death penalty and this was not so with regard to the last three. Be careful that you do not misunderstand what I am saying here. Though, for the reasons I have given, they are of lesser importance, that does not mean the last three Commandments are of no importance.

The thing that strikes me about modern-day society is the way it has inverted the order of importance of the Commandments. In almost every society in the world, the laws and principles governing stealing rank it higher in public opinion than laws and principles that govern our relationship to God. It would certainly be wrong for a man or woman to be punished for refusing to worship, or for worshipping gods other than the true God, but it is an indication of where our society has come to that the violation of a person's human rights should be of more importance than the violation of the divine rights. Ignoring God, misusing his name, defaming his character, denying his existence – public opinion, generally speaking, would not regard any of these as sins.

Nowhere is the rebellious nature of sin more clearly seen than in the way it has inverted the order of the Ten Commandments.

Father, help me always to keep in mind that worship and the relationship of the worshipper to yourself is not just a matter of importance but a matter of supreme importance. Give me grace to place the emphasis where you place it. In Jesus' name. Amen.

FOR FURTHER STUDY – Titus 2:9–15; Prov. 20:10; Eph. 4:28; 1 Pet. 4:12–17
1. What was Titus to teach the slaves? / 2. What are Christians to be known for?

Brunner's Law

FOR READING AND MEDITATION – ROMANS 7:14–25

'… Who will rescue me from this body of death? Thanks be to God –
through Jesus Christ our Lord! …' (vv. 24–25: NIV)

We ended yesterday with the thought that, generally speaking, public opinion is more concerned with the violation of human rights than with the violation of divine rights, and that stealing is seen to be a greater sin than rebellion against God. This indicates how society has inverted the Ten Commandments in terms of their order of importance.

A minister told me the other day that whenever he spoke out against such things as murder, adultery, impurity, theft or lying, he carried his audience with him, but whenever he focused their attention on the more subtle sins of godlessness (a failure to let God be God) he lost their attention. Why is this? I think it is because when we sit in church and hear about such sins as murder, lying, stealing, cheating and adultery, most of us can say to ourselves, 'I am not guilty of any of these.' But when the sin of godlessness is identified, who can stand up and say, 'In every area of my life I am letting God be God'? It is perilously easy to get worked up about the sins that other people are committing (and from which we know we are exempt) because it diverts attention from the unconscious sins (a failure to let God be God, for example) that may be going on deep down within our hearts.

Ever heard of Brunner's law? Brunner was a deep thinker and a student of human nature. After observing people for some time, he came up with this consideration, 'The more a decision will affect your way of life, the more your sinful carnal nature will enter into the debate.' It takes a battle to bring our rebellious natures under the control of Jesus Christ, but with God's help it is a battle we are well able to win.

O God, save me from the subterfuges and camouflages that are part of my carnal nature. Give me your perspective on all things and help me keep them in their correct order of importance. In Jesus' name I ask it. Amen.

FOR FURTHER STUDY – Matt. 23:13–18; 2 Tim. 3:5; James 1:26
1. What is Pharisaism? / 2. What is a danger for all of us?

Love and work

FOR READING AND MEDITATION – EPHESIANS 4:17–32

'He who has been stealing must steal no longer, but must work,
doing something useful with his own hands ...' (v. 28: NIV)

The Commandment: 'You shall not steal,' is probably one of the most clear-cut of all the Ten Commandments. To steal means to take something which rightfully belongs to someone else. Sociologists point out that this Commandment is probably the most universal of all the laws in the world. In even the most primitive cultures the prohibitions against stealing are of the highest importance. Just as the sixth Commandment ('You shall not murder') safeguards life, and the seventh Commandment ('You shall not commit adultery') safeguards marriage, this eighth Commandment safeguards a person's property and possessions.

It has been pointed out that there are only three ways we can come into possession of something: as a free gift from another person, by inheritance, for example; in payment for work done; and as the result of theft. The Scripture recognises the first two and forbids the third. The first two are based upon the essential laws of human interrelationships – love and work. The gift bestowed upon one person by another is an expression of love and becomes the property of the one to whom it is given. Property or possessions purchased from the rewards of toil and work have also been acquired legitimately. But theft violates these two important laws of love and work. The thief cannot love the person from whom he steals and thus he violates the law of love and he violates the law of work by attempting to possess without toil.

Thus the eighth Commandment recognises the true rights to property, and forbids the possession of anything save upon the condition of obedience to the laws of love and work.

Father, I see that your school is strict but the end is always our salvation. Your laws, however uncompromising, are our redemption. Help us not to chafe at them but to embrace them as friends. For all your laws are love. I am so thankful. Amen.

FOR FURTHER STUDY – 2 Thess. 3:6–14; Prov. 10:4, 13:4; Deut. 25:15
1. What rule did Paul give to the Thessalonians? / 2. What is the result of laziness?

Gaining a clear conscience

FOR READING AND MEDITATION – 1 TIMOTHY 1:12–20

'…. fight the good fight, holding on to faith and a good conscience …'

(vv. 18–19: NIV)

There can be little doubt, like so many of the other Commandments, that the eighth Commandment: 'You shall not steal,' is being widely broken in today's world. The drug problem has pushed up the crime figures enormously, as addicts intent on obtaining money to feed their habit indulge in breaking and entering, stealing, burglary and so on. But don't see this sin as confined to the lower levels of society. Almost daily our newspapers report on what is termed *white collar crime* – crime committed by those who work in the areas of high finance.

Perhaps you are saying at this moment, 'Well, this may be so, but Christians don't need to be lectured on this issue.' Well, just hold on a minute. Have you ever noticed how often the New Testament talks about the subject of stealing? Why do you think that is? Mainly it is because stealing is a form of temptation that many Christians fall into. Talk to any minister or counsellor who has had long experience of dealing with people, and you will find that this sin is high up on the list. One minister says, 'I find stealing an increasingly common sin to be confessed at the altar or in the counselling room.'

In a seminar I used to conduct on the subject *Gaining a Transparent Conscience*, one of the questions I asked people to face was this: have I stolen anything from anyone and not confessed it? I was amazed at how many Christians would confess to this. Permit me to ask you the same question now: have you violated this eighth Commandment? Expose your heart to the Holy Spirit, let him identify any possible violations, and then guide you to the steps you need to take to gain a transparent conscience.

O Father, I would be at my best and my best means having a conscience that is void of offence. Help me to be open and honest. Give me the courage to put right any violations that your Holy Spirit reveals to me. In Jesus' name I pray. Amen.

FOR FURTHER STUDY – Acts 24:10–16; Rom. 9:1; 2 Cor. 1:12; Heb. 9:14
1. What was Paul's testimony? / 2. Is your conscience clear?

Robbery in church

FOR READING AND MEDITATION – MALACHI 3:6–18

'Will a man rob God? Yet you rob me. But you ask, "How do we rob you?"
In tithes and offerings.' (v. 8: NIV)

It is surprising how easy it is to break the eighth Commandment: 'You shall not steal,' without realising it. We do it under euphemisms like *driving a hard bargain*, *business acumen* or *a good business deal*. We do it also when we borrow books and never return them, exploit an advantage (as did Esau) or fail to make an honest income tax return. The story of Zacchaeus (Luke 19:1–10) shows that we may never know the full joy of our sins being forgiven until we confess and right some wrongs in this area of our lives.

Gambling is also a form of stealing and a violation of the eighth Commandment. The human desire to take short cuts formed the basis of the three temptations of our Lord in the wilderness (Matthew 4:1–11). Moreover, many other things beside property and possessions can be stolen – a person's honour and good name, for example.

But what about stealing from God? We steal from him when we fail to fulfil our responsibilities as stewards of time, treasure and talent. Take the matter of treasure as an example – are we stealing from God by keeping for ourselves that which belongs to him? Listen again to what he said to ancient Israel: 'Will a man rob God?' The problem here was that the Israelites held back their tithes and offerings. Perhaps you might say, 'Tithing is an Old Testament principle; it does not apply today.' What does apply, however, is the principle of proportionate giving. And the amount some people give to God is a disgrace for which they will one day be held accountable. We know we are not to take that which belongs to another. So what about when that Other is God?

O Father, cause me to stand before you today with an open face and an open being. Save me from all rationalisations and help me take my medicine. If I am a robber and a thief – forgive me. Show me how to be a good steward of your property. In Jesus' name. Amen.

FOR FURTHER STUDY – Gen. 14:18–20, 28:22; Lev. 27:30; 2 Cor. 9:7
1. Who is Melchizedek a type of? / 2. What does the Lord love?

Character and reputation

FOR READING AND MEDITATION – PSALM 27:1–14

'… false witnesses rise up against me …' (v. 12: NIV)

We come now to the last but one of the Ten Commandments: 'You shall not give false testimony against your neighbour' (Exodus 20:16: NIV). The implications of this Commandment are wide and far reaching, but primarily it is designed to safeguard the reputation of another person. God knows that a reputation unsmirched by evil is a precious thing and it is his will and purpose that no man or woman's reputation be blackened by a false or evil report.

Reputation can be best understood by comparing it with the word *character*. Character is what a man or woman is within the depths of their being; reputation is the estimate that other people form of them. A person with a good character can have a bad reputation because of false reports that other people give about them.

Many a Christian has suffered from this and I would suspect that many reading these lines are in that position right now. If so, then let me bring you some words of encouragement. Our Lord Jesus Christ knows exactly how you feel for he was rushed to the cross on the basis of the very sin we are talking about at the moment – false witness. None knows more than he the weight and burden of this sin, for the Scripture says of him: 'He was despised and rejected by men, a man of sorrows, and familiar with suffering' (Isiah 53:3: NIV). So close does he come to tormented hearts in times when their reputations are besmirched that a new courage is created within their souls, enabling them to stand tall in the midst of their discouragement. And never forget, God's care for the reputation of his children is such that in time – his time – he will fully justify and vindicate them.

Father, help me to take care of my character and trust you to take care of my reputation. And when my reputation is unjustly besmirched, give me the grace to carry on, knowing that in the end truth will always be justified. In Jesus' name. Amen.

FOR FURTHER STUDY – Psa. 101; Ex. 23:1; Prov. 12:17, 25:18

1. What was the psalmist committed to? / 2. What is a false witness likened to?

As ... so

FOR READING AND MEDITATION – JOHN 1:43–51

'... "Here is a true Israelite, in whom there is nothing false."' (v. 47: NIV)

The words: 'You shall not give false testimony against your neighbour' demand that any statement made by one person to another, or by one person about another, be in harmony with the truth. As the third Commandment, which forbids the taking of the name of God in vain, lays down that the guidelines for man's relationship with God should be based on sincerity and truth, so the ninth Commandment demands that in their relationships with one another, men and women should be actuated by the same principles.

'God ever deals with man,' says one theologian, 'upon the basis of his full and accurate knowledge of what man is.' In other words, the divine attitude towards men and women is not governed or influenced by the appearances that they might like to keep up before others, nor by the opinions that others might have of them. God bases his dealings with us on his intimate and accurate knowledge, and that is the way he wants us to deal with others. Listen to these weighty and powerful words taken from the psalmist: 'O Lord, you have searched me and you know me ... you perceive my thoughts from afar' (Psalm 139:1–2: NIV).

Now when we step down from the divine level to the human level, we recognise that earthly knowledge is limited, but allowing for those limitations, God requires us as far as is possible to relate to one another in sincerity and in truth. Our whole social fabric rests on the testimony that one person bears in relation to another, and there can be no just society where this is not so. Beyond knowledge, no testimony must be borne, and in the giving of testimony, no facts are to be withheld.

Father, I see that you have fashioned me after yourself and any departure from that image demeans my whole being. Just as a train is made for the tracks, so I am designed to run on truth. Help me to stay on track – this day and every day. In Jesus' name. Amen.

FOR FURTHER STUDY – 1 Pet. 3:8–16; Psa. 34:13; 1 Tim. 5:11–13
1. How can others be made to feel ashamed of their slander?
2. Are you guilty of speaking ill of others?

The truth about lying

FOR READING AND MEDITATION – PSALM 141:1–10

'Set a guard over my mouth, O Lord; keep watch over the door of my lips.'
(v. 3: NIV)

The truth underlying the ninth Commandment is one that we Christians need to be so familiar with that it becomes part of the warp and woof of our beings. God wants us to relate to others in the way that he relates to us – in sincerity and in truth – and any departure from this is a violation of the divine will and purpose. No man or woman must be helped or harmed by statements made concerning them which are not in accordance with the facts as far as they are known.

A famous Bible teacher says: 'One of the greatest tests of character is this: when under pressure will this person tell a lie?' What is your attitude to a lie? It's surprising how many Christians wriggle on this hook. Some say, 'Well, there's nothing wrong with a *little* lie if it saves me from embarrassment.' Others say, 'There is nothing wrong with lying to save someone's life.' Be careful about these rationalisations – your attitude to a lie will reveal the kind of person you are. A lie is never justifiable – never! Evil means produce evil ends. If you tell a lie you become a lie. The deepest punishment of a lie is to be the one who tells the lie – the liar. He or she has to live with a person they cannot trust. That is an uneasy hell. In the Christian life there are to be no *white lies*, for they leave a black mark on the soul.

I was an inveterate liar before I was converted but divine grace cleaned me up and set me on the road of truth. It took a while for grace to overcome the old patterns, but after a while truth came out because truth had got in. Never forget, a lie is a sin against the God of truth.

Father, drive the truth deeply into my spirit that whenever I tell a lie, I become a lie. Then I have to live with a person I cannot trust. Keep my tongue from anything that would hurt you or hurt others. In Jesus' name I ask it. Amen.

FOR FURTHER STUDY – Col. 3:1–10; Psa. 63:11; Prov. 12:22, 19:5
1. What was Paul's admonition to the Colossians? / 2. Who does the Lord delight in?

Seven types of false witness

FOR READING AND MEDITATION – ZECHARIAH 8:1–17

'… Speak the truth to each other, and render true and sound judgment in your courts.'
(v. 16: NIV)

The first and simplest application of the ninth Commandment – 'You shall not give false testimony against your neighbour' – is, of course, to evidence in a court of justice. Justice is based upon truth, and when false testimony is given, then justice cannot be done. For this reason, perjury is made a punishable offence, and rightly so, for if perjury were allowed, many forms of crime might go unpunished and the innocent be made to suffer.

The ninth Commandment, however, has a broader application, and it is this wider perspective that I want to focus on now. It has been pointed out that there are seven clear ways in which this Commandment can be violated. The first is by libel and slander – lies which are written or spoken about someone and passed on with a malicious intention. It is hard to think of a worse form of bearing false witness than this.

A second form of bearing false witness is by tale-bearing. This is when someone repeats a story about someone else when there is no necessity to do so. How sad that scores of Christians who would never dream of committing murder, adultery or theft engage in this deadly sin of gossiping.

A third form of bearing false witness is through the giving of a false impression. A stigma has been cast upon many a person's reputation by such questions as, 'Have you heard about so and so?' 'No,' says the other person. 'Ah well, the least said the better.' Though the first speaker may be drawn no further, an unfavourable impression has been created and the innuendo has had all the deceiving effect of false witness. In the name of God, I say to the Christian church: such things ought not to be.

O God, help us repent of all the things that go on in the midst of the Church which dishonour and defile your name. I repent of any complicity that I may have in this. Help me to be a true and honest person. For your own dear name's sake. Amen.

FOR FURTHER STUDY – Titus 3:1–8; Eph. 4:31; James 4:11
1. What was Titus to remind the people?
2. What are we doing when we slander our brother?

No meaner form of rebellion

FOR READING AND MEDITATION – PROVERBS 13:1–9
'The righteous hate what is false …' (v. 5: NIV)

We continue looking at the seven ways in which we can bear false witness. The fourth way is by silence. If we hear someone being slandered and we know the words being said are not true, then if we keep silent, we are as guilty of the sin of false witness as the person who utters the slander.

A fifth way is by imputing to a person a wrong motive. 'Have you heard how well brother so and so is doing in business?' 'Ah, but how do you think he's got where he has? Don't you think he must have been involved in some shady business practices?' I have no hesitation in saying that to impute to another an ulterior, selfish or sordid motive is to bear false witness against that person.

A sixth way is flattery. To tell people things you do not believe to be true simply to please them, or to pander to their vanity, or win them over to your side in some issue, is a sin against those people, and a sin against God.

The seventh way the ninth Commandment can be broken is by an untrue testimonial. Whenever we utter unwarranted praise, give a testimonial to character that is untrue, or recommend an unsuitable person simply because he or she is our friend, we inflict injury upon the one requesting the testimonial.

Can you see now how subtle a danger false witness is? Every violation of truth is a desecration of the Decalogue and there is no meaner form of rebellion against God and one's fellow human beings than that of creating impressions in the minds of others that are simply not true.

Father, help me to see that the reason why you are straight with me is because you love me too much to let me get away with things that demean my character. Save me from telling a lie, spreading a lie, or living a lie. In Jesus' name I pray. Amen.

FOR FURTHER STUDY – 1 Tim. 4:1–12; Prov. 22:11; 2 Cor. 8:7; Eph. 4:15
1. What was Timothy to set an example in? / 2. What are we to do in love?

Desiring and coveting

FOR READING AND MEDITATION – ROMANS 13:1–14

'The commandments …"Do not murder," … "Do not covet," …
are summed up in this one rule: "Love your neighbour as yourself."' (v. 9: NIV)

The last word of the Decalogue is in one way radically different from those that have preceded it: 'You shall not covet your neighbour's house … his manservant or maidservant, his ox or donkey, or anything that belongs to your neighbour' (Exodus 20:17: NIV). All the preceding Commandments have forbidden overt acts; this one cuts right through to inner attitudes. Disobedience of any of the other nine Commandments will sooner or later be detected by others but the tenth Commandment may be broken without another person being aware of it at all.

The issue it deals with is that of covetousness. But what is covetousness? The word *covet* means 'desire to possess what belongs to another'. Does that mean that when I see a friend with a model of a car that I myself would like to possess, I am guilty of coveting? No. What about when I see a painting on the wall of a neighbour's house which I like so much that I make up my mind to get one like it? Is that coveting? No. In both these cases the desire is not the sin of coveting because it may be satisfied legitimately.

Covetousness occurs when the object desired is out of reach and I continue to desire it even though I know that to possess it would involve me in illegitimate action. The whole force of the Commandment lies in the words: 'your neighbour's'. Note the possessive – it indicates something that belongs to your neighbour and not to you. I repeat, it is not wrong to desire a wife, a manservant or maidservant, or an ox – it becomes wrong if one continues to desire them when circumstances have made it impossible to have them legitimately.

Father, let the truth sink deep within me that the penalties attached to evil are not just the signs of your wrath, but the signs of your love. Help me to work with that love – not against it. In Jesus' name. Amen.

FOR FURTHER STUDY – Jer. 6:1–13; Ezek. 33:30–31; Phil. 3:10–14
1. What was said of the priests and prophets?
2. What were the children of Israel doing to Ezekiel?

Much wants more ...

FOR READING AND MEDITATION – LUKE 12:13–21

'... Be on your guard against all kinds of greed; a man's life does not consist in
the abundance of his possessions.' (v. 15: NIV)

We touched yesterday on the fact that there is a great difference between desiring
something and coveting it. Without desire, human life would be impoverished. Our
desire for social approval makes us wash our face and comb our hair. Our desire for
respect leads us to be careful about the things we do and the way we behave.

Buddha taught that desire itself was the source of evil in the world and he
claimed that if we eliminated all desire we would eliminate all evil – Nirvana. But it
is not desire that is wrong – it is inordinate desire, the desiring of that which is
unlawful. As we said yesterday, it is not wrong to desire a house, a wife, a servant, a
painting, a car, but it is wrong to continue to hanker after the things our neighbour
possesses when there is just no way we can legitimately have those things for ourselves. Desire passes into covetousness when it runs rampant over our own reason
and the rights of others. It is desire directed to a wrong end. One Bible teacher
defines covetousness as 'desire that has run amuck'. You see, when desire passes into
covetousness, it then has within it the potential to kill, steal, or lie in order to get
what it wants. It is the attitude that says, 'I want what I want and I don't care what I
have to do to get it.'

One of Aesop's fables tells of a man who killed a goose that laid golden eggs.
The story concludes with this moral: 'Much wants more and loses all.' That is the evil
of covetousness – it stops at nothing to get what it wants and violates so many laws
of conscience on the way to getting it that it finishes up by not wanting what it gets.

O Father, I am so thankful that throughout the universe you have issued a yardstick against which
all life shall be measured. Forgive me for trying to live against that standard. Keep my life fully and
wholly to it from this hour. In Jesus' name. Amen.

FOR FURTHER STUDY – 2 Sam. 11; 1 Kings 21:1–16
1. What did David's covetousness lead to? / 2. What did Ahab's covetousness lead to?

The reason for the law

FOR READING AND MEDITATION – ROMANS 7:7–13

'… Indeed I would not have known what sin was except through the law …'

(v. 7: NIV)

We continue examining the nature of covetousness, which we have seen can best be described as the desire for what cannot lawfully be possessed – the desiring of things that circumstances have put out of reach. Desiring is not wrong, but when desire is directed to a wrong end, it can soon turn into covetousness.

The Commandment covering covetousness cuts more deeply into the conscience than perhaps many of the others. It identifies the presence of sin in our hearts in a way that is sharp and powerful. This is the point that Paul is making in the passage before us today when, in his great argument on the relationship of the law to sin, he says: 'I would not have known what sin was except through the law. I would not have known what coveting really was if the law had not said, "Do not covet."' Paul is showing us that sin is so deeply hidden within the recesses of our being that we would not be able to recognise it if God's law had not been brought to bear upon it. The fact that sin is present in every life is evidenced by the desire to possess unreachable things and this sin can only be discovered when before our eyes a law is displayed that says: 'You must not covet.'

I have often heard people say about the ninth Commandment: 'But it is impossible to prevent covetousness following on from desire.' This very point emphasises the fallen condition of humanity and shows why the law was given. Well will it be with men and women when they allow the searchlight of the divine requirement: 'You shall not covet,' so to astonish them that they are driven to him who alone is able to deal with the unexplored reaches of their nature.

Father, I am thankful for the law and I am thankful for grace. Both were needed to bring me to yourself. The law showed me how badly I needed saving and grace reached down and saved me. All praise and glory be to your precious name. Amen.

FOR FURTHER STUDY – Gal. 3; Rom. 3:20; 1 Tim. 1:9

1. Why were the Galatians foolish? / 2. What is the object of the law?

The impact of covetousness

FOR READING AND MEDITATION – EPHESIANS 5:1–21

'But among you there must not be even a hint of sexual immorality,
or of any kind of impurity, or of greed …' (v. 3: NIV)

Today we ask ourselves: was the command prohibiting covetousness kept to the last because it was the least of all the Commandments? I do not believe so. It is, in fact, the most far-reaching and comprehensive of them all. Covetousness affects all of our lives. It makes people greedy and acquisitive and causes them to steal. It drives people to ignore the needs of others and trample on their rights; in some cases covetousness will even kill in order to get what it wants. It gives rise to the unbridled lust that pushes people into fornication and adultery, and it breaks down trust between individuals, causing people to lie about themselves and each other.

Covetousness destroys the bloom and beauty of those characteristics which Paul calls the 'fruit of the Spirit', turning love to hate, joy to sorrow, peace to heartache, longsuffering to impatience, kindness to cruelty, generosity to miserliness, faithfulness to infidelity, meekness to arrogance and self-control to indiscipline and self-indulgence. The evil spirit that makes false witness possible is motivated by covetous aspiration far more often than is perhaps apparent at first.

The sin of covetousness proves not only that the soul is out of harmony with God, but that it is dissatisfied with him. Covetousness says, 'I can't trust God to give me what I need, therefore I shall reach out and obtain it myself.' The first Commandment and the last are closely linked and all those between are conditioned by them. If a man has no God but *Jehovah Elohim*, the God who is there, then he will desire nothing other than that which God supplies.

Father, perhaps the reason why I get so taken up with other things is because I am not taken up with you. May my desire for you be so strong and powerful that it will keep all other desires under control. In Jesus' name I pray. Amen.

FOR FURTHER STUDY – 1 Tim. 6:1–10; Prov. 15:27; Eccl. 5:10; Phil. 4:11–12
1. What did Paul say was great gain? / 2. What was Paul's testimony?

I want more grace!

FOR READING AND MEDITATION – ROMANS 5:12–21

'… But where sin increased, grace increased all the more.' (v. 20: NIV)

The last Word of the Decalogue: 'You shall not covet,' brings every man and woman who honestly faces it to the place of utter helplessness. It may be that as we have examined the other nine Commandments, we have a measure of self-respect still left, but in the light of this last searching Word, who can claim to be guiltless?

It was Paul who, after many years of Christian experience, could say when reviewing his old life as a Hebrew of the Hebrews: '… in regard to the law, a Pharisee … as for legalistic righteousness, faultless' (Philippians 3:5–6: NIV). Yet when he faced this last Commandment: 'You shall not covet,' Paul had to say that he found the Word brought not satisfaction but dissatisfaction. There are perhaps many reading these lines who can look at some of the Ten Commandments – Commandments like: 'You shall not murder' – and say, 'I am not guilty,' but is there anyone anywhere in the whole world who can say they have never desired forbidden things?

Christ is the only one who can deliver us from covetousness and he does it by focusing our desires on the right ends. Dr W.E. Sangster, in his book, *The Pure in Heart*, tells the story of the saintly John Fletcher who did so much for the community in which he lived that some of the officials arranged to give him a small financial gift. He thanked them for it but promptly handed it back and suggested it should be given to someone more needy. They then pressed him to tell them what he wanted most of all, saying that if it was within their power, they would collect and give it to him. Fletcher said, 'Well, there is one thing I want and I want it more than anything in the world – I want more grace!'

O God, these words echo how I feel. You have given me a clear understanding of your law and for that I am grateful – now give me more grace. In Jesus' name I ask it. Amen.

FOR FURTHER STUDY – 2 Cor. 12:1–12; 2 Tim. 2:1; Phil. 4:19

1. What was Paul able to boast? / 2. What was Paul's admonition to Timothy?

A travesty of the truth

FOR READING AND MEDITATION – HEBREWS 8:1–13

'… I will put my laws in their minds and write them on their hearts.
I will be their God, and they will be my people.' (v. 10: NIV)

Although we ended our examination of the Ten Commandments yesterday, our study on the subject has not yet been concluded. There are some other issues that now need to be brought into perspective and over the few final days we have left, I want to discuss these with you.

The first is this: what is the role of the Ten Commandments in the life of the Christian? If we say we are saved by grace, through faith, how does the law fit into the picture? As we saw at the beginning of our studies, there are many Christians in today's Church who claim that once we are saved, we are no longer under the judgment of the law of God and therefore the Ten Commandments have no meaning for a true believer. In my view, this *lawless* version of Christianity is a travesty of the truth – a misinterpretation of what the Bible is saying. Although it is true that we can never be saved by the law – for the simple reason that no one in their own strength can keep it – this does not mean that it no longer applies.

The passage before us today sums up what other parts of the New Testament teach us (for example, Romans 5:5; Galatians 4:6–7) – that when we are converted, the Holy Spirit writes God's law on our hearts and helps us to live by them. And he not only helps us to live by them, he helps us to do it lovingly and joyously. This is the new way of living that the New Testament holds out for us. It introduces us to the new and exciting truth that once the Holy Spirit abides within our hearts, obeying the law is no longer a daily duty but a daily delight. A true Christian does not rebel at the Ten Commandments; he or she rejoices in them.

My Father and my God, I see that when I became a Christian, I not only came into a new world but a new world came into me. Now I see the law in a different light – your light. What a difference this makes to daily living! Father, I am so thankful. Amen.

FOR FURTHER STUDY – 2 Cor. 3:1–15; Psa. 37:23–31; Heb. 10:15–16
1. What did Paul say of the Corinthians?
2. What is the result of having God's law in our hearts?

Fences along the road of grace

FOR READING AND MEDITATION – TITUS 2:1–15

'For the grace of God … teaches us to say "No" to ungodliness …' (vv. 11–12: NIV)

We continue nailing down the grave error that once we become Christians, we are free from any responsibility to obey the Ten Commandments. Before going any further, let me clarify my use of the word *law*. By *law* I mean the Ten Commandments. There were other laws in Israel – the ceremonial law, for example – that do not apply to us who live in New Testament times, for they were abrogated by the death of our Lord Jesus Christ. But the issues raised in the Ten Commandments are still absolutes today.

Let us focus on the text that is often repeated by those who advocate that once we are saved by grace, the law no longer applies: 'For sin shall not be your master, because you are not under law, but under grace' (Romans 6:14: NIV). What Paul is saying in the whole of the epistle to the Romans is that no Christian need depend on the keeping of the Ten Commandments as the means of his or her salvation. Paul does not mean that the law of God is abolished, but that the Christian does not look to the law for either justification or sanctification.

Forgive me for repeating the point I made yesterday, but I feel it is necessary. Once the Holy Spirit comes into our hearts at conversion, instead of rebelling against the law, we rejoice in it. And why? Because we sense within us a new power that enables us to do the things God asks of us. Ever noticed how the road of grace that has been opened up through the death of Christ has been fenced by so many prohibitions? The passage before us today is just one of many. We may be under a new law of love, but Scripture clearly teaches that love is the fulfilling, not the abolishing, of the law.

Father, help me to get this, for I see it is a deeply important issue. Show me even more clearly that being under grace does not mean I am no longer required to keep your law, but that grace is there to help me keep it. In Jesus' name. Amen.

FOR FURTHER STUDY – Rom. 7–8; Matt. 5:17–20
1. What conflict did Paul experience? / 2. Why did Jesus say he had come?

More don't's than do's

FOR READING AND MEDITATION – MATTHEW 23:15–28

'You blind men! Which is greater: the gift, or the altar that makes the gift sacred?'
(v. 19: NIV)

Now that we have nailed down the error that once we become Christians, we are no longer required to obey the Commandments of God, we look at another problem that arises in connection with this issue – the Christian who is saved but comes to depend for his or her salvation more on the keeping of the law than on divine grace. This is what is called *legalism*. The tragic thing about Christians who are legalists is that they have hardly any awareness of the fact that they are working to be saved, rather than working because they are saved.

The Pharisees of Jesus' day were a good example of legalism. They took the Ten Commandments and added a lot more of their own, so that by the time Jesus came they had a list of 365 *don't's* – one for every day of the year! And they meticulously observed all their rules. Legalists are not content unless they are surrounded by rules because they feel safe (or saved) only when they are keeping to them. And most legalists I have known add to the Ten Commandments every cultural and tradi-tional taboo they can lay their hands on. Since they are resting on their performance for their salvation rather than on the grace that God provides, the more rules they have to keep, the better they like it.

You can be sure that a legalist has a lot more *don't's* than *do's* and this kind of living makes life a daily grind rather than a joyous growth. I have seen legalism deprive so many of a joyous Christian experience that if God gave me one wish, it would be to blast legalism right out of the Church.

O Father, help me come to grips with this issue, for I see I can be a legalist without realising it. Help me get it straight that my dependence is on you and not on keeping the rules. I ask this in Jesus' all-powerful and saving name. Amen.

FOR FURTHER STUDY – Gal. 4:1–11; Isa. 29:13; Matt. 23:23
1. What was Paul's concern for the Galatians?
2. What was our Lord's complaint against the Pharisees?

No more warm baths

FOR READING AND MEDITATION – 1 CORINTHIANS 8:1–13

'… if what I eat causes my brother to fall into sin, I will never eat meat again,
so that I will not cause him to fall.' (v. 13: NIV)

We continue where we left off yesterday with our meditation on legalism. As we saw, the trouble with legalists is that they don't feel safe unless they have around them as many rules as possible. They thrive on rules – but not in the way that produces true Christian growth. And many of the rules they wrap around themselves are cultural and traditional rather than scriptural. But, you see, they like rules because they get their feelings of assurance from what they do rather than from what has been done for them in Christ.

A letter written in the second century, giving advice on how to live the Christian life, reads, 'Don't wear coloured clothes; get rid of everything in your house that is not white. Stop sleeping on soft pillows. Sell your musical instruments and don't take any more warm baths. Stop eating white bread and don't shave your beard – it is a lie against him who created us and an attempt to improve on his work.' Sounds very modern, doesn't it? Legalism takes relative matters and turns them into absolutes; it comes up with human ideas and claims that these have to be kept if a person is to be saved.

There is a way of dealing with matters that are non-absolutes – it is by the development of a sensitive conscience. Paul talks about it in the passage before us today. In one situation he would eat meat offered to idols, but in another situation he would not. Contradictory behaviour? No, he had developed a conscience that could detect the difference between what was relative and what was absolute. And it is this – a mature conscience – that prevents us from falling into the trap of legalism.

Father, I have prayed before for a clean conscience – now I pray for one that is neither under-sensitive nor over-sensitive, but is mature and balanced and always open to your Spirit. In Christ's name I ask it. Amen.

FOR FURTHER STUDY – Col. 2:13–23; Heb. 7:18, 8:13
1. What has God cancelled? / 2. What were the Colossians still doing?

So simple yet so sublime

FOR READING AND MEDITATION – ROMANS 13:8–14

'… Therefore love is the fulfilment of the law.' (v. 10: NIV)

We saw yesterday that every breach of the Decalogue is a violation of love and when love directs and controls our lives, there can be no such breach. So important is this simple but sublime principle that we must spend our last day together applying it to each of the Ten Commandments. If we love God supremely, then we will not be able to find room for another god and thus the first of the Ten Words is fulfilled. Supreme love for God also means that we will not suffer anything to stand between us and him, and so all graven images are broken to pieces. Out of love will spring the hallowing of his name and the drying-up of the springs of blasphemy. Love understands the principle behind the Sabbath and will not just cease from work but enter also into the restful activity of worship.

Passing to the second list of Commandments, love for God moves out towards others and provides us with the power to honour our parents. Again, loving God supremely supplies us with the power to quench all thoughts of hatred towards others. Unchastity of every description is burned up in the flame of love and theft also becomes impossible, because where love is, robbery is not. Love sits as a sentinel on the portal of one's lips and arrests the faintest whisper of false witness against one's neighbour. And it is love and love alone that, finding satisfaction in God, leaves no room in the heart for coveting anything but him.

When men and women learn to love, then Sinai, the mountain of fire, holds no terror. They stand erect before it, knowing that as Christ lives and loves in them, thoughts will be born, words will be spoken and deeds will be done – in love. Then in thought and word and deed, the law will be fulfilled.

O Father, from this hour forward, let the simple but sublime principle of love flood my life and fill my days. In Jesus' name I pray. Amen.

FOR FURTHER STUDY – 1 Cor. 13; Jude 21; 2 Thess. 3:5
1. What was Paul's desire for the Thessalonians?
2. How are the characteristics of love in 1 Corinthians also seen in the Ten Commandments?

To be, is to be in relationships

FOR READING AND MEDITATION – 2 PETER 1:1–9

'… enjoy other people and … like them, and finally you will grow to love them deeply.'
(v. 7: TLB)

For the next two months we will be looking at a theme of great spiritual significance – relationships. Of all the themes I have written on over the years, I can think of none as important as this. We begin by asking ourselves a penetrating question: how well do I relate to others? What am I like when I am in contact with other people – friends, family, workmates, acquaintances and strangers?

John Wesley said that he was 'a man sent from God to persuade people to put Christ at the centre of their relationships'. It would be difficult to give a better definition of our Christian task. I have no hesitation in saying that most of our problems in life arise from an inability to relate effectively to others. It is not an easy thing to adjust oneself to other people and their wills. But our Christian faith should teach us how to do it, for, as E.S. Jones puts it, 'Christianity is the science of living well together with others according to Jesus Christ.'

Many of our attempts to live with other people are haphazard and unscientific in the sense that they do not obey the laws of corporate living. There are principles or laws of corporate living as well-defined as those that underlie the world of nature. Since all of us have to live in relationship with others, we must attempt to discover these laws, and live by them, or else our Christian faith and testimony will be imperilled. Many try to handle their relationships without an understanding of these underlying laws and principles, and their relationships end in chaos. If we do not know how to relate, we do not know how to live, for, as someone has put it, 'To be, is to be in relationships.'

O God, in this delicate, difficult but delightful business of getting along with other people, help me gain the skill, insight, and patience I need. You relate so well to me, help me to relate well to others. In Christ's name I ask it. Amen.

FOR FURTHER STUDY – James 2:1–8; Matt. 22:37–39; John 13:34–35
1. What is the second commandment? / 2. What is the new commandment?

Our very first task

FOR READING AND MEDITATION – MARK 3:13–18

'He appointed twelve ... that they might be with him ...' (v. 14: NIV)

We ended yesterday with the words, 'To be, is to be in relationships.' I am not sure who first made this statement, but I am sure what it means – we come to know ourselves only as we know how to relate to others. A person who is known in a loving, trusting relationship by at least one other human being, is rich indeed and will have little fear about facing the world. Sydney Jourard in his book, *The Transparent Self* says, 'Every maladjusted person is someone who has not made himself known to another human being and in consequence he does not know himself. Nor can he be himself. More than that, he struggles actively to avoid becoming known by another human being. He works ceaselessly at it day and night. And it is work!'

Our text today shows that the Christian movement began in a relationship: 'He appointed twelve ... that they might be with him.' For the disciples, the very first part of their calling was to 'be with him' – in relationship. The first thing we Christians must focus on is not trying too hard to do good or be good – it is being 'with him'. When we come in contact with goodness, incarnate goodness, we begin to do good and be good. We touch the Life that gave birth to the universe, and within the depths of our being a new life bursts forth.

Our relationship with him is the fountain from which every good flows. Trying to be good without that relationship is like trying to get a stream without a spring, or sunlight without the sun. Anything that hinders the relationship with him blocks everything that flows from the relationship. Everything!

Father, I begin to see that your way is the way, not merely of theology but of life. You have set us in relationships, the most important of which is my relationship with you. Help me to know you better, this day and every day. In Christ's name I pray. Amen.

FOR FURTHER STUDY – 1 John 1; 1 Cor. 1:9; Rev. 3:14–20

1. What was John's experience? / 2. What was Christ's promise to the Laodiceans?

The dominant theme of Scripture

FOR READING AND MEDITATION – GENESIS 2:18–25

'The Lord God said, "It is not good for the man to be alone.
I will make a helper suitable for him." ' (v. 18: NIV)

The theme of relationships is not one of the side issues of the Bible; it is a theme that dominates Scripture from one end to the other. Psychologist Larry Crabb says, 'From Genesis to Revelation, the fabric of biblical truth is woven with the thread of relationships: perfect relationships in the Trinity, broken relationships in Eden, and restored relationships in Christ.'

The Bible is full of accounts and illustrations that reveal the different aspects of relationships: strained relationships between Cain and Abel, distant relationships between Abraham and Lot, ambivalent relationships between Moses and the Israelites, loving relationships between David and Jonathan, antagonistic relationships between Jezebel and Elijah, close relationships between Christ and his disciples, difficult relationships between Paul and John Mark, and so on.

Why is the theme of relationships so prominent in Scripture? It is because only in the context of relationships can the deepest longings of our beings be met and satisfied. As our text for today points out, we were created both for a relationship with God and with others. Note the phrase *and with others*, for some Christians are content just to relate to God and sense no responsibility to relate meaningfully to others. When God said: 'It is not good that man should be alone' (NKJ), he had far more in mind than marriage. The union of a man and woman became the starting point for the family, and the family would provide the basis for other legitimate relationships which lie outside the marriage bond.

Father, I see that I am designed in my inner being for relationships. Help me to bring to every relationship in which I find myself the full potential of what and who I am. In Christ's name I ask it. Amen.

FOR FURTHER STUDY – Psa. 102:1–7, 88:18; Heb. 13:5
1. How did the psalmist feel on occasion? / 2. What is God's promise?

Life: never meant to be solitary

FOR READING AND MEDITATION – PSALM 68:1–14
'God sets the lonely in families …' (v. 6: NIV)

We continue meditating on the point that we are designed in our inner being for relationships – a relationship with God and with others. Life was never meant to be a solitary existence. If we were totally cut off from personal relationships we would soon go insane. People can be isolated physically for a long period of time without becoming insane, but this is because they have experienced meaningful relationships in the past – they have known others who have awakened genuine selfhood within them. To know and be known by someone arouses something within us that sustains us in the darkest and most difficult situations.

Dr Bernard Steinzor in his book, *The Healing Partnership* says, 'The person who feels completely alone and has lost hope of a relationship will become a patient in the wards of a mental hospital or bring their life to an end through suicide.' Human life is incurably relational and those who ignore this simple empirical fact do so at their peril. 'Neglecting the truth that we have deep longings for relationship,' says one writer, 'is as foolish as pretending we can live without food.' He is right. Those who ignore their need for relationship and instead put their full focus on things like achievement, travel, the acquisition of knowledge, and so on, may find some degree of satisfaction but they will never know what it is to experience the health and wholeness that comes from relating effectively to others.

We all need to be close to someone, so never apologise for the longing that you find within you for a relationship. It was built into you by the Creator and is therefore part of a divine design.

O Father, as I am made and designed to connect with others, may all my relationships this day and every day be ones that will honour and glorify your name. For Jesus' sake. Amen.

FOR FURTHER STUDY – Psa. 119:49–63; Acts 2:37–44; 1 John 1:7
1. Who did David's friendship extend to?
2. What did the early disciples devote themselves to?

Total isolation: intolerable

FOR READING AND MEDITATION – ROMANS 12:9–21
'Be devoted to one another in brotherly love …' (v. 10: NIV)

It is clear from the teaching of Scripture that we need each other. Without a relationship, unhealthy and unhappy things go on inside us. Many studies suggest that individuals cannot function effectively without deep links to others. Two psychologists, Bernard Berelson and Gary Steiner, said, after examining more than one thousand social science studies on war, 'Total isolation is virtually always an intolerable situation for the human adult – even when physical needs are provided for.'

The medical consequences of loneliness are well known. In his book, *The Broken Heart*, James Lynch says, 'Most of the people I deal with have at the root of their physical problems the problem of loneliness. They may well be living with someone, or indeed in a busy, bustling family atmosphere but they do not know what it is like to experience a close relationship. The lonely are twice as likely to suffer physical problems as those who enjoy a warm relationship with at least one other person.'

What does this tell us? Relationships are good for us – physically as well as spiritually. Those reading these lines who are experiencing loneliness because of the death of a partner, a separation or a divorce, singleness, abnormal shyness or an inability to develop a close relationship with another person, need not despair, for later I shall be focusing on some of the principles that we can employ to build meaningful personal relationships. My purpose here is to reinforce the truth I introduced earlier: 'To be, is to be in relationships.' Whichever way we look at life, the bottom line is relationships. No relationships means no growth or development as a person. It is as simple as that.

My Father and my God, help me not to be discouraged by my failures in relationships or by my inability to relate well to others. I sense that soon you are going to show me your way in all this. Amen.

FOR FURTHER STUDY – 1 Thess. 3:1–13; 1 Peter 1:22; 1 John 4:7
1. What was Paul's prayer for the Thessalonians? / 2. How are we to love one another?

Unloved babies wither

FOR READING AND MEDITATION – 1 JOHN 4:1–12

'Dear friends, let us love one another, for love comes from God.' (v. 7: NIV)

We said yesterday that unhealthy and unhappy things go on inside us when we live in isolation from others and do not have at least one meaningful relationship. 'Continuous, meaningful and secure bonds are essential,' says Charles Swindoll, 'or we risk losing our humanity.' If an infant were physically cared for without knowing a loving relationship, he or she would be less than human. We pass on our humanity, good or bad, through our relationships. We are always just one generation away from regressing to barbarism. It is through relationships that cultural norms are passed on to succeeding generations, and only in that way do civilisations advance.

Many years ago, the helpers in orphanages who cared for abandoned babies found a wasting disease developing in these young children. They called it *Marasmus*. They researched the cause of this condition and discovered an amazing thing – the disease developed because the children were not being kissed or cuddled. When local mothers started coming into one orphanage to spend a short time each day feeding, cuddling and holding the babies close to their bosoms, the symptoms disappeared. The conclusion the authorities came to was this – unloved babies wither.

If we hesitate to put weight on the words of Laplace who said, 'Science is mere trifling – nothing is real but love,' we need not hesitate to say that science itself is discovering the power inherent in loving relationships. An international conference on mental health said, 'The taproot of most mental illness is lack of love.' Humanity is finding out through trial and error that in loving relationships people thrive; in unloving relationships they simply survive.

Father, I see more clearly day by day that your way is written into all our relationships. The universe was made for love – your love – and it will not run efficiently without it. Oh, when will humanity see it? Help them, dear Lord. In Jesus' name. Amen.

FOR FURTHER STUDY – John 15:1–17, 11:5, 35–36, 13:23

1. How is love demonstrated? / 2. What did Jesus call his disciples?

Who needs others?

FOR READING AND MEDITATION – ECCLESIASTES 4:1–12

'Two are better than one … If one falls down, his friend can help him up.'
(vv. 9–10: NIV)

We continue focusing on the thought that God has designed us to need each other. One of three alarming trends in today's society is the increasing emphasis on independence, isolationism and *doing your own thing*. Declaring a need is seen by many as a weakness, an open admission of failure, a flaw in one's character. Hence we see a spate of best sellers hitting the secular market with titles like *How To Be Your Own Best Friend*. Psychologists Newman and Berkowitz assert that in these books: 'We are accountable only to ourselves for what happens to us in our lives.'

The inevitable end of this *do your own thing* mentality is that people are held at a distance and sneeringly told, 'Who needs you?' Read the backgrounds of those who are involved in this kind of approach to life and you will soon discover how damaging isolationism can be. Not so long ago, here in Britain, the town of Hungerford witnessed a massacre when a disturbed young man went berserk and gunned down a number of innocent people. The reports that came out some time later showed him to be a man who spent most of his spare time in isolation from others.

This stress on isolation is completely opposite to the teaching of Scripture, where the emphasis is always on involvement. Don't buy into the selfish, ego-centric lifestyle being suggested by many of today's leading writers – the consequences are bitter and inescapable. That's why the simple, profound counsel of Solomon which appears in our text today remains so needed: 'Two are better than one.'

Father, I see so clearly that today's emphasis on isolationism has a way of eclipsing the contrasting light of Scripture. Help me to take your way in everything, no matter how plausible men's theories appear to be. In Jesus' name. Amen.

FOR FURTHER STUDY – Ex. 17:1–12; Judges 20:11; 1 Sam. 14:6–7
1. What happened when Moses' friends supported him?
2. What was Jonathan's experience?

The Gestalt Prayer

FOR READING AND MEDITATION – GALATIANS 6:1–10
'Share each other's troubles and problems, and so obey our Lord's command.'
(v. 2: TLB)

The philosophy of life that everyone should *do their own thing* ignores the fact the God has made us as inter-related and inter-dependent social beings. Fritz Perls, the founder of the Gestalt system of counselling, is famous for what is described as *The Gestalt Prayer*.

> I do my thing, and you do your thing.
> I am not in this world to live up to your expectations
> and you are not in the world to live up to mine.
> You are you and I am I.
> If by chance we find each other, it's beautiful.
> If not, it can't be helped.

These lines express very forcibly the human need for independence and self-expression. There is a sense in which I must have my own thoughts and feelings and I must have the right to express them freely. No doubt that was Perls' good purpose in writing those lines, but nevertheless the words are open to serious criticism. You see, I cannot do my own thing without affecting you. I am not free to swing my arm if it is likely to hit you on the nose. The subjectivism in Perls' lines ignores one of the deepest truths of human existence: for a person to be, is to be with others.

Human life, as we have been saying, is essentially relational. We cannot, indeed dare not, reflect the human need for independence without laying equal stress on the need for true and deep relationships.

Gracious and loving Father, the more I meditate on your Word, the more the conviction deepens within me that I live and move and have my being in relationships. Teach me more about the art of rightly relating to others. In Jesus' name I ask it. Amen.

FOR FURTHER STUDY – Phil. 1:1–6; Prov. 17:17; 1 Sam. 18:1
1. How did Paul describe his relationship to the Philippians?
2. How is David and Jonathan's relationship described?

Beyond Perls

FOR READING AND MEDITATION – EXODUS 17:8–16

'When Moses' hands grew tired … Aaron and Hur held his hands up –
one on one side, one on the other …' (v. 12: NIV)

We looked yesterday at what has been described as *The Gestalt Prayer*, written by Fritz Perls, and we observed some of its limitations. Walter Tubbs, a psychologist, has written an interesting supplement to this prayer which he entitled, *Beyond Perls*. This is how it reads:

> If I just do my thing and you do yours,
> we stand in danger of losing each other – and ourselves.
> I am not in this world to live up to your expectations
> but I am in this world to confirm you
> as a unique human being
> and to be confirmed by you.
> I must begin with myself, true;
> but I must not end with myself:
> The truth begins with two.

'The truth begins with two' – how beautiful. The Bible puts it even more beautifully in the verse we looked at two days ago: 'Two can accomplish more than twice as much as one, for the results can be much better' (Ecclesiastes 4:9: TLB).

The supplement offered by Walter Tubbs speaks for itself. It redresses the imbalance of thought uttered by Perls and gives a fuller view of the human condition. True human fulfilment is found only in relationships of love – with God and with others.

O Father, you have so clearly written the theme of relationships into your word and into human nature that to ignore it is to invite disaster. Help me to discover your mind in this matter and live according to it. Amen.

FOR FURTHER STUDY – Ruth 1; 2 Kings 2:2; Prov. 18:24
1. How did Ruth respond to Naomi? / 2. How did Elisha respond to Elijah?

No man is an island

FOR READING AND MEDITATION – 1 CORINTHIANS 12:14–26

'The eye cannot say to the hand, "I don't need you!" And the head cannot say to the feet,
"I don't need you!"' (v. 21: NIV)

We continue with the point we have been making: that God's purpose for our lives is not isolationism but loving involvement. Isolationism will not work. The seventeenth century writer, John Donne, wrote these gripping and arresting words just seven days before his death, 'No man is an island entire of itself; every man is a piece of a continent, a part of the main; if a clod be washed away by the sea, Europe is the less, as well as if a promontory were, as well as if a manor of thy friends or of thine own were; any man's death diminishes me, because I am involved in mankind; and therefore never send to know for whom the bell tolls; it tolls for thee.'

These beautiful words are eclipsed only by the inspired writing of the apostle Paul in the passage before us today, where he shows us the value of every single member in the body of Christ. Isn't it interesting (and also disturbing) that so many Christians are committed more to the pastor or the leaders of a church than they are to each other? If I understand the thrust of what Paul is saying in this passage, our allegiance ought to be the same to everyone.

Hero-worshipping Christians of our century have great difficulty believing these words of the apostle Paul, but not until we see the value of each member of Christ's body (rather than just those who are prominent in the church) will we catch the idea of what is meant by loving involvement. Putting people on pedestals is not what the church is all about. Everyone who belongs to Christ is expected to enter into loving involvement with everyone else who belongs to Christ – with no barriers or distinctions.

Father – I am so thankful for Scripture which enables me always to see things from your point of view. Help me to lean less on my own understanding and more on yours. In Christ's name I ask it. Amen.

FOR FURTHER STUDY – 1 Cor. 1:1–17; Luke 11:17
1. What problem did Paul address at Corinth?
2. What did Jesus say would happen to a divided kingdom?

I-can-do-it-all-myself

FOR READING AND MEDITATION – NUMBERS 11:10–17

'… I will take of the Spirit that is on you and put the Spirit on them …' (v. 17: NIV)

We must spend one more day focusing on the thought that we need one another. In the passage before us today, we see that Moses had become a target for the criticism and complaints of the people. Things had obviously gotten too much for him and he had begun to crack under the weight of responsibility. But God graciously relieved the pressure by bringing around him a group of seventy people to help him shoulder the burden he was carrying.

Strong leaders tend not to delegate responsibility as much as they should – a lesson I myself have had to learn. They often adopt an *I-can-do-it-all-myself* mentality and by so doing set themselves up for unnecessary stress. Add to this feelings of self-pity – feelings which often arise in the hearts of strong leaders, Elijah being only one example – and you have the breeding ground for extreme discouragement.

How does God help us when we find ourselves spiralling down the tube of over-commitment? He brings someone alongside us to help pull us out of our rapid descent. Life gets pretty grim when there is no one to help. Bruce Larson says, 'Life breaks down not so much because of the terrible things that happen to us, but because so few good things happen to us. A few words of encouragement, or a helping hand along the way can be like the little branches we cling to as we climb a mountain trail. No matter how steep the ascent, we can make it if from time to time someone gives us a helping hand.' Fix it clearly in your mind – however much you are able to do, you cannot do everything by yourself. Moses, the great leader of Israel, needed the help of others – so do we.

O Father, save me from this I-can-do-it-all-myself *mentality. For I see that when I adopt this attitude, I am going against the grain of the universe. You have made me not to be independent but inter-dependent. Help me to be willing to let others help me. Amen.*

FOR FURTHER STUDY – 2 Cor. 2:1–13; Phil. 2:25; 2 Tim. 1:16
1. Why did Paul leave Troas? / 2. How did Paul describe Epaphroditus?

No one is totally objective

FOR READING AND MEDITATION – ROMANS 12:1–8

'So in Christ we who are many form one body, and
each member belongs to all the others.' (v. 5: NIV)

Today we ask ourselves the question: what is a relationship? In *Children of a Lesser God*, the frustrated deaf bride anguishes out the sign for *relationship* by hooking her two thumbs and forefingers together. For her the finger chain spelled *connection*. She struggled to express it to her husband but could not *connect* with him.

A relationship can be described as one person connecting with another. On the level of acquaintanceship, it is the connection of mind with mind. On the level of friendship, it is the connection of both mind and feelings with the mind and feelings of another. On the level of marriage, it is the connection of mind, feelings and body. *Connection* means 'that which joins or relates, a bond, a link'. There is nothing sadder in the whole of life than someone who cannot make a connection, on the appropriate level, with another human being.

It has been said that non-relationship is non-being. This means that when a person is entirely out of touch with the thoughts and feelings of other people – a state of separateness – he enters a state of total subjectivity. He is in a world of his own. Of course, as C.S. Lewis said, 'No one can be totally objective.' Sometimes we hear people in the news media say, 'This is a totally objective report.' But such people are not only biased, they are blind. However, if we attempt to see things in a rounded and true way, we need the viewpoint of others, and above all, of God. Solomon touched on this when he said: 'The first to present his case seems right, till another comes forward and questions him' (Proverbs 18:17: NIV). From all directions, life presses in upon us with the clear and distinct message: we need one another.

Father, I see even more clearly that everything presses me towards relationships. As I move through life, may the vertical relationship I have with you enhance the horisontal relationships I have with others. In Jesus' Name I pray. Amen.

FOR FURTHER STUDY –Eph. 4:1–13; 1 Cor. 1:10; 2 Cor. 13:11

1. What four things did Paul urge? / 2. What are we to make every effort to do?

Voices from the past

'… We are asking God that you may see things, as it were, from his point of view …'
(vv. 9-10: J.B. Phillips)

We have defined a relationship as the ability to connect with another person. Now we must ask ourselves another important question: how do relationships begin? Obviously the first relationship experience we have is in the home. So crucial is this first relationship that what we learn from it stays with us through life, influencing our every attempt to *connect* with other people. The way we view ourselves as persons – our self-concept – is the result of our early home relationships. These first relationships powerfully shape the image we have of ourselves. Like mirrors on the wall, our primary relationships tell us what we look like, what we should look like and what others would like us to look like. The reflections we first receive from others make incredibly deep impressions on our minds and we conform unconsciously to the expectations we have received.

A 40 year-old woman, who was having difficulties in her marriage relationship, told me, 'I used to sit on the stairs at night and listen to my mother and father talking about me. They said such things as, "What a painful and pitiful child our daughter is; thank goodness she is out of the way."' This woman carried those voices that came out of that early relationship into her marriage and they gave her a view of herself which made it difficult for her to give herself to her husband or to have any optimism about her future. Her relationships shaped her life – until she learned how to see herself from God's point of view.

Like the life-giving atmosphere around the earth, relationships make it possible for people to live and grow. But no one thrives in a poisoned atmosphere.

Gracious Father, all my life I have been subjected to the views that others have of me, and perhaps I have been too influenced by their perspectives. Help me day by day to see myself from your point of view – the only true perspective. In Jesus' name. Amen.

FOR FURTHER STUDY – 1 Cor. 1:20–31; 2 Cor. 12:9, 13:4
1. What was Paul's testimony? / 2. What did the Lord assure him?

Home is not just a place

FOR READING AND MEDITATION – JOHN 14:15–31

'… My Father will love him, and we will come to him and make our home with him.'
(v. 23: NIV)

Yesterday we saw that our self-concept – the view we have of ourselves – grows out of the soil of our early relationships. Another thing that we learn from our primary relationships is the masculine and feminine roles. These are first learned by copying our mothers or fathers. Both mother and father play significant and much needed roles in a child's life. A small boy needs a masculine image which only a man can supply. A little girl needs a feminine image which only a woman can supply. When a boy gets into his teens, it is the mother who, by the way she relates to him, can communicate best what it means for him to be a man. In the case of a teenage girl, it is the father who can communicate best what it means for her to be a woman by the way he relates to her. There is an old saying that goes like this: 'A girl is not a woman until her father tells her so.' The alliance that allows her the most complete discovery of what it means to be male or female is a happy and successful marriage, where a man is a man and a woman is a woman.

Have you ever moved from home and felt the pangs of being separated from those who know you? Your relationships with people contribute more to making you feel comfortable than do your physical surroundings. You can be in a home without being at home. And you never feel at home until you are at home with someone – someone you love and enjoy. I was brought up in a mining village in South Wales in a closely-knit community. Now I live in a densely populated area. I still miss the village life I once knew, but the relationships I have with the people God has brought around me make me feel very much at home. Home is not just a place: home is people.

Father, help me to be at home with the people you have brought around me and teach me how to enjoy all my relationships. Show me how to give and how to take, when to speak and when to listen. In Jesus' name I pray. Amen.

FOR FURTHER STUDY – Jer. 9:1–14; 1 Kings 22:52; 2 Chron. 22:3; Prov. 22:6
1. In what ways can parents have a negative influence on their children?
2. What is the lesson from Proverbs?

At home in the universe

FOR READING AND MEDITATION – PROVERBS 22:6–16

'Folly is bound up in the heart of a child, but the rod of discipline
will drive it far from him.' (v. 15: NIV)

We are seeing that it is in the atmosphere of our early relationships that we develop our attitudes towards the basic realities of life. Our primary relationships are the proving ground or the testing laboratory of life. A child is a great tester. He or she tests different ways of behaving and of looking out at life. 'A child tries things,' says Dr David Seamands, 'but tests people.' It is in the home that a child learns either that rules don't matter, or that the universe is moral and orderly and it is necessary to grow up with a healthy respect for law and order. This is why limitations are a vital part of love and, as our text for today shows, why there has to be firmness and discipline at the heart of the family. A child tries to create his or her own universe. This produces conflict because we all have to live in a world which is already created and which has laws and regulations written into it.

The way discipline is applied in the home, however, greatly influences the way a child relates to himself and to others. If the discipline comes across as, 'You are bad,' the child develops a warped view of himself or herself or acquires a negative self image. If discipline is given with the clear message, 'You are loved, it's your behaviour that is bad,' then the child comes out with a much healthier self-concept and learns how to see himself in a clear light – worthwhile, but in need of loving discipline.

A great many emotional problems that arise in later life could be avoided if children were brought up in a relationship where they found out one of life's principles: you can't have your cake and eat it.

O God, open our eyes to see the importance of the influences that flow out of early relationships. But help us see also that our relationship with you can cancel out all the negative influences that come out of the past. We are so deeply thankful. Amen.

FOR FURTHER STUDY – 2 Chron. 26:1–4, 17:3; 2 Tim. 1:1–5
1. How important is parental influence? / 2. What did Paul recognise in Timothy?

Our first concept of God

FOR READING AND MEDITATION – JOHN 14:1–14

'… Anyone who has seen me has seen the Father …' (v. 9: NIV)

We continue examining the influences that come out of our early relationships. We said that a child gets his first picture of who he is from the way his parents relate to him. We said also that it is in the home that he gets his basic attitude towards the realities of life. A third and most important thing a child draws from his early relationships is his concept of God. Early relationships become the great window through which he gets his first glimpse of heavenly things.

A child gets his basic picture of God from the adults who dominate his world. He may get an intellectual idea about God from the Bible verses he is given in church or Sunday School, but these are all secondary to his basic feelings about God. The feelings he will develop about God come directly from the way his parents relate to him, and these feelings and emotions can sometimes colour his relationship with God for the rest of his life. When counselling, I can't begin to count the number of times that I have sat down with people and traced their problem to a wrong concept of God. And when I've probed to find out where this wrong concept has come from, nine times out of ten, I've discovered that it has come from their earliest relationships with their mother or father, because most of us will relate to God in the way we related to our parents – especially our fathers.

A great preacher of a past generation, F.B. Meyer, put it so well when he said, 'Christianity is not simply religion; it is religion saturated with family life until it means fatherhood, sonship, brotherhood and love.' How powerful and influential are our early relationships – for good or for bad.

Father, I come to you today and ask you to cleanse me from any negative influences I may have carried with me into adulthood – especially as they relate to my concept of you. Help me see you more clearly as you really are. In Jesus' name I pray. Amen.

FOR FURTHER STUDY – Isa. 40:12–28; Psa. 89:6; 1 Chron. 17:20

1. What question does Isaiah pose? / 2. How does he describe God?

Our relational style

FOR READING AND MEDITATION – COLOSSIANS 3:1–14

'… because of his deep love and concern for you, you should practice
tenderhearted mercy and kindness to others …' (v. 12: TLB)

Although there are many things on which psychologists and social scientists
disagree, there is one thing about which they have little or no disagreement – the
tremendous influence of the home on our ability to relate. 'We use our primary relationships,' says Karen Horney, 'as a mirror in which we check our progress and from
which we develop the ideas as to how best to relate to others.' It is from our early
relationships that we develop what might be called our *relational style* – a way of
relating to others that best suits us and with which we are most comfortable.

Generally speaking, there are three forms of relational style. We can move
towards people, we can move against them, or we can move away from them. Those
who move towards people are the ones who love relationships and find great delight
in getting involved with others. Those who move against people are anti-relation-
ship. In their past, they experienced difficult and unhappy relationships and now
their approach to others is based on the idea, 'If I let you come close to me you may
fail me, too, so I will act and behave in ways that will discourage you from wanting
to experience my closeness.' There is always a degree of hostility in such people – their
hostility being their defence. The third group, those who move away from others, are
rarely hostile – they just don't see themselves as worthy of a relationship. They were
never given a picture that their friendship meant something to somebody – a basic
cause of shyness.

Now take a moment to run a check on yourself and ask yourself: what is my
relational style? Then check with someone who knows you really well.

*Father, I want to be ready for the moment when you show me how to relate to others in the way
that you relate to me. Help me to get ready for that moment by being honest with you and myself
over the question I have been asked today. In Jesus' name I pray. Amen.*

FOR FURTHER STUDY – 1 Thess. 5:12–18; Eph. 4:2; Prov. 24:29
1. What does it mean to 'bear with one another'? / 2. What are we not to do?

As mature as our relationships

FOR READING AND MEDITATION – 1 JOHN 1:1–10

'But if we walk in the light, as he is in the light, we have fellowship with one another ...'
(v. 7: NIV)

We shall return later to discuss in greater detail the issue we raised yesterday, namely, our relational style, but now we turn to focus on the fact that our maturity as persons depends to a great degree on how effectively we relate to other people. Dr E. Stanley Jones, the famous missionary to India, said, 'We are as mature as our relationships. Show me someone who knows how to relate lovingly to others and I will show you someone who has a high degree of maturity. The immature person retreats on himself, withdraws from relationships, becomes self-preoccupied and is by virtue of the fact – immature.'

Strong words, but in my opinion, true. If I were to add anything to them I would add this – we are mature to the degree that we know how to relate to God, to ourselves and to others. One of the most awful things about sin is that it produces estrangement – estrangement form God, estrangement from ourselves and estrangement from others.

In the early days of my ministry I used to define sin as 'the breaking of God's law', but I have come to see that it is much more serious than that – it is the breaking of his heart. It is the severing of a relationship. The moment we sin there is a sense of orphanage, of being alone with our guilt, of being out of harmony. On the other hand, when we are redeemed and forgiven, there is the immediate sense of a restored relationship – we feel restored to God, to ourselves and to others. We are mature to the degree, and only to the degree, that we can establish a loving relationship with God, with ourselves and with others.

Gracious and loving heavenly Father, if it is true that I am as mature as my relationships, then help me to make my relationship with you the strongest and most powerful relationship in my life. For then I know that everything good will follow. Amen.

FOR FURTHER STUDY – Psa. 51, 23:3; Isa. 57:18
1. What was the heart cry of the psalmist? / 2. What is God's promise?

As I have loved you

FOR READING AND MEDITATION – JOHN 15:9–17

'My command is this: Love each other as I have loved you.' (v. 12: NIV)

We are focusing on the fact that we are as mature as our relationships. Let me define *maturity* so that there can be no misunderstanding about what I am saying. By *maturity* I mean 'mental and emotional wholeness, a well-adjusted and fully developed personality'. The point I am making is that no one can be a healthy, well-rounded personality until he or she knows how to develop good relationships.

The immature have withdrawn from relationships; they have retreated inside themselves; they are walled-in persons. They are immature because they are unable to relate well to others. When people are driven in on themselves by fears, resentments, inhibitions, self-preoccupations and guilt, then relationships are seriously impaired. The shut-in are shut out from maturity, for maturity is outgoingness. The problem is to get them out from behind closed doors and encourage them to be outgoing, able to give and receive fellowship and love.

Mature people are loosed from self-centred preoccupation and are free to have fellowship with God and with others. I would go as far as to say that the quality of the relationships we experience in Christianity, when properly understood and practised, are distinctive and unique. They are rooted in the fact that at the cross, God took the initiative and broke down all the barriers that were between him and us. The quality of the relationship he sets up with us is then (or should be) carried into our relationships with others. This is the way the Almighty purposes things to be. If we do not carry the quality of his relationship with us into our relationships with others, then where is the breakdown? We have to say it is in us!

Blessed Lord Jesus, you who broke down all barriers at the cross and showed us how to relate, help us carry the quality of your relationship with us into our relationships with others. For your own dear name's sake. Amen.

FOR FURTHER STUDY – 1 Peter 1:1–9; 1 John 3:16; John 16:27; Eph. 6:24
1. What is the fruit of a loving relationship?
2. How did Paul finish his epistle to the Ephesians?

The genius of Christianity

FOR READING AND MEDITATION – LUKE 15:1–7

'… This man welcomes sinners, and eats with them.' (v. 2: NIV)

We ended yesterday with the thought that the quality of the relationships found in Christianity is distinctive and unique. This new quality began with God's initiative towards us when he broke down the barriers that were between us at the cross, and continues as we carry it into our relationships with others.

My claim that the relationships in Christianity are unique might sound arrogant to some people, but let us examine the facts. In all other faiths barring none, a relationship with God is to be found, so they say, at the top of a long ladder. Step by step you purify yourself, and when you have reached the topmost rung you are then considered worthy of a relationship with God. It is thought that since you merit it, you relate to God on his level. In the Christian faith you do not relate to God at the top rung of the ladder but at the bottom. And why? Because we do not climb up to him; he comes down to us. We do not meet God at his level; he meets us at our level. 'This man receives sinners,' was the scandalised cry of the religious leaders of Christ's day. They thought that God loves only the righteous, but Jesus said he came not to call the righteous but sinners to repentance.

This reversed all the values of antiquity – and it reverses all the values of our present day. It is breathtaking and smashes all precedents. The genius of Christianity – a genius that is not found in any other religious faith – is that when we couldn't climb up to him, he climbed down to us. Hallelujah! As I sit here writing these words, the wonder of what I am saying makes me feel like throwing something high in the air. How about you?

O God, how can I thank you enough that at Calvary and with one stroke, you broke down every barrier that was between us. Only love could do it. I marvel and I wonder but I do more – I accept it with the deepest gratitude possible. Amen.

FOR FURTHER STUDY – Rom. 5:1–8; Gal. 4:4; Rev. 1:5
1. How did God demonstrate his love?
2. What comes before the cleansing and freeing from sin?

The saddest word

FOR READING AND MEDITATION – ISAIAH 2:1–5
'Come, o house of Jacob, let us walk in the light of the Lord.' (v. 5: NIV)

We continue exploring the thought that we are as mature as our relationships. The immature, we said, have retreated inside themselves, and are walled-in persons. How do they get out? The text we looked at three days ago is part of the answer: 'But if we walk in the light, as he is in the light, we have fellowship with one another, and the blood of Jesus, his Son, cleanses us from all sin' (1 John 1:7: NIV).

Some leading men were once asked to name the saddest word in the English language. One said *hopelessness*; another, *unloved*; another, *vacuum*. They still felt they hadn't found it until someone said, 'I've got it – the saddest word is *but*.' The group unanimously agreed.

The word *but* can be the saddest word – but it can also be the gladdest word, as in the text we have just quoted: 'But if we walk in the light ... we have fellowship...' Here the word *but* is not linked with loss, but gain; not with disintegration, but integration. It is God's redemptive *but* interposed into our estrangement – our estrangement from God, from ourselves and from others. That word *but* takes us by the hand to lead us from darkness to light, from ourselves to God, and thus it becomes the most hopeful word in the English language. You are immature – *but!* You are unable to relate well to others – *but!* You are just half a person – *but!* You are ineffective – *but!*

Maturity is not something you need to struggle to achieve. It is a gift before it is a growth. You give yourself to him and out of the relationship that develops flows a power that enables you to give yourself more fully and effectively to others.

O Father, I am so grateful that you make everything possible. I thought maturity was a long uphill struggle but now I see it grows out of my relationship with you. Help me open every pore of my being to your endless undying love. In Christ's name. Amen.

FOR FURTHER STUDY – Gen. 50, 8:1, 31:42
1. How important was *but* to Noah and Jacob? / 2. How significant was *but God* to Joseph?

Two sides of one coin

FOR READING AND MEDITATION – MARK 12:28–34

'... "Of all the commandments, which is the most important?" ' (v. 28: NIV)

One conviction keeps breaking in upon us as we move from day to day – a good relationship with others flows out of a good relationship with God. Nowhere is this more clearly unfolded than in the passage before us today. A lawyer stood up and asked Jesus: 'Teacher, which is the greatest commandment in the Law?' (Matthew 22:36: NIV). The angels in the heavens must have bent over to listen to the reply, for Jesus' answer would fix in the mind of humanity for ever the chief quality in the universe. A wrong step here and all the ages would go wrong with him. But Jesus did not go wrong.

Jesus unerringly picked out two commandments from the 3 600 which Jewish law contained: 'Love the Lord your God with all your heart ... love your neighbour as yourself.' That absolute commandment is as inevitable as the law of gravity, even more so, for when we obey it, life holds together; when we disobey it, life falls apart and goes to pieces. The whole of human history and the history of each individual are commentaries on that statement. If we do not love God and love others as we do ourselves, then we miss the purpose behind our existence.

Notice that although the lawyer asked what was the greatest commandment, the answer which Jesus gave contained two – to love God and to love our neighbour as ourselves. If Jesus had not gone on to give the second, then life would be left dangling with a loose end. We would be clear about how to relate to God but not clear about how to relate to each other. Jesus makes it clear – indeed, crystal clear – love for God is to be manifested in love to man.

Father, I see that the very first obligation you put upon me is to love. Somewhere inside me I hear a deep Amen. Teach this truth to me over and over again, for without love my soul will die. In Jesus' name I pray. Amen.

FOR FURTHER STUDY – Luke 10:25–37; Matt. 10:8; Luke 6:38; Acts 20:35
1. What is the message of the parable of the Good Samaritan?
2. Where do relationships begin?

Amazing love

FOR READING AND MEDITATION – 1 JOHN 4:13–21

'We love because he first loved us.' (v. 19: NIV)

We continue looking at the two highest commandments ever given to man anywhere, at any time: love God totally and love your neighbour as yourself. In Mark 12:31, Jesus added: 'There is no commandment greater than these.' These words closed the issue with absolute finality. Dare we reopen it? Of course not. To question these words of Jesus is to question our own sanity. Jesus' words are self-verifying and inescapable. We simply have to take them or leave them: and face the consequences if we leave them.

The question now arises: how do we go about loving God in the way we ought? There are different views of this in the Christian church. Some say we develop love for God when we obey him and do the things he commands us to do. The more we obey (they tell us) and the more we focus on doing what God wants, the more our feelings will change and eventually we will come to experience a rising tide of love for God.

There is no doubt that the principle of doing what God wants us to do – obedience – produces changes in our feelings, but that is not where love for God begins. We are indebted to the apostle John for the explanation of how love for God is created in our hearts: 'We love because he first loved us.' Note the *because*. Once we open ourselves to contemplating how much God loves us, we open ourselves to receiving that love, and then the inflow of divine love produces love in us in return. Before anyone can first experience love for God, he must see how much God loves him, and what God has done for him on the cross. Seeing his love, our own love flames in response.

O Divine Lover of my soul, your love has somehow kindled within me a love I could never create on my own. Seeing how much I am loved – I love. As you have loved me into love, help me to love others into love. In Christ's name. Amen.

FOR FURTHER STUDY – Eph. 2:1–10; Deut. 7:1–8; Jer. 31:3
1. What does the *but* of Ephesians 2:4 declare?
2. What did Moses and Jeremiah declare to the Israelites?

Love begins in contemplation

FOR READING AND MEDITATION – 2 CORINTHIANS 5:11–21

'For Christ's love compels us, because we are convinced that one died for all …'
(v. 14: NIV)

We are asking ourselves how we go about the task of fulfilling the greatest commandment, namely, that we should love God with all our heart and love our neighbours as ourselves. As we saw yesterday, love for God is certainly not the fruit of effort and labour. Once we become Christians, the principle of obedience works to strengthen the love that is in our hearts, but love for God begins, not in obedience, but in contemplation. God only knows the love of God and only God can reveal it.

And he has revealed it best at Calvary. Some words of Dr W.E. Sangster, a great preacher of a past generation, come to mind as I write, 'Attend to the cross! Sit before it, meditate upon it. Heaven knows no higher strategy for begetting love than to bring a person to the cross, hold him there, until they see in that bleeding sagging figure on the tree – just how much God loves them.' You cannot say to your heart, 'Come now, we are going to love God.' That strategy will not work. What does work, however, is to focus on how much he loves you and the more you contemplate that, the more love rises within you and floods your inner being. John Powell says, 'Before anyone can give his heart to God he must first know how much God has loved him, how much God has thought about him from eternity and what he has done on the cross to pay the price for his sin.'

Without a realisation of how much we are loved, we will try to bargain with God, and do little things for him in the hope that he will do something for us in return. Life and religion become, then, not a love affair but a chess game. No, there is only one way to love God, and that is first to let him love you.

O Father, I open my whole being to be invaded by your love. Come and love in me so that my human love will more and more take on the quality and character of divine love. Help me, dear Lord – I long to love like you. In Jesus' name I pray. Amen.

FOR FURTHER STUDY – Col. 1:15–23; John 3:16; Eph. 5:2; Phil 2:6–11
1. How does Paul depict God's love?
2. Spend time today contemplating the cross.

The royal law

FOR READING AND MEDITATION – JAMES 2:1–13

'If you really keep the royal law found in Scripture, "Love your neighbour as yourself,"
you are doing right.' (v. 8: NIV)

Having looked at the first of the two highest commandments: 'You shall love the
Lord your God with all your heart,' we turn now to examine the second: 'And you
shall love your neighbour as yourself.' Had Jesus responded to the questioner's
request for the greatest commandment with nothing more than the statement: 'You
shall love the Lord your God,' then we would have been left groping to understand
how we are supposed to relate to one another. We would be clear about how to relate
to God, but unclear about how to relate to man.

The phrase 'as yourself' is important. The love we have for others is not to be
more or less but as the love we have for ourself. This balances self-love and other-
love in exact proportion. I am talking here about self-love, not love of self. The
phrases might seem similar, but they are worlds apart in meaning. Self-love is
healthy; it is a sane and balanced estimate of oneself. Love of self is unhealthy; it is
a pompous and exaggerated view of oneself.

If you hold back from loving your neighbour, and don't love with your whole
self, you can't get along with your neighbour, for the parts of yourself that don't love
your neighbour are the parts of yourself that your neighbour doesn't love either.
Moreover, if you don't love your neighbour with your whole self, you can't get along
with yourself, for the parts of yourself that don't love others are unlovely. If you don't
love your neighbour, you can't live with yourself or your neighbour. James calls this
the 'royal law' because it is the supreme law that is in the source of all other laws governing human relationships. To understand it and apply it means that you have
mastered the art of living well with others.

*Gracious and loving Father, your words and my needs fit together like a hand into a glove. When
I follow your purposes I am not following the extraneous, but the intrinsic. You designed me to
function in a certain way. Help me follow it. In Jesus' name. Amen.*

FOR FURTHER STUDY – Rom. 12:1–10; Prov. 25:27; Matt. 23:12
1. How are we to think of ourselves? / 2. How are we to think of others?

The 'I-Thou' relationship

FOR READING AND MEDITATION – LEVITICUS 19:9–19

'… love your neighbour as yourself …' (v. 18: NIV)

The truth that we should love our neighbour as ourselves was first announced in Scripture in the passage that is before us today. But like so many Old Testament texts, it has to be seen in the light of the whole of Scripture to be properly interpreted and understood. Those who pick up one text of Scripture and build a doctrine around it, and it alone, rarely come out with a true understanding.

Many psychologists have taken a text of Scripture and used it to build a system of understanding that on the surface looks true and helpful, but because it is only part of the truth and not the whole truth, lacks final authority. An example of this can be seen in the way philosopher Martin Buber has taken the statement of Jesus: 'You shall love your neighbour as yourself,' and built from it an interesting and fascinating concept which he calls the *I-Thou* relationship. Buber says, 'Two mature people possessing the ability to meet one another on even footing relate to one another as I to Thou – as equals.' In a mature relationship, he claims, one should regard another person as one regards oneself. In other words, we must love our neighbour as we love ourselves. Each has his own sense of worth as a person and each values the other equally well. The *I-Thou* relationship is based on the ability of a person to enter into the life of another without losing his own identity or individuality. Out of the *I-Thou* relationship both people emerge as persons.

This is fine as far as it goes, but it does not go far enough. Can you see why? Think it through. I'll give you my answer tomorrow.

Father, I see that when men build on just a part of the truth, their conclusions may be interesting but not transforming. Help me never to be content with just a part of the truth; show me how to explore the whole truth. Amen.

FOR FURTHER STUDY – Rom. 15:1–13, 13:10

1. What ought we not to do? / 2. What should we do in order to bring praise to God?

The 'I-It' relationship

FOR READING AND MEDITATION – COLOSSIANS 3:1–14

'Most of all, let love guide your life …' (v. 14: TLB)

We ended yesterday with the assertion that Buber's concept of the *I-Thou* relationship, based on Jesus' words: 'You shall love your neighbour as yourself,' is good but does not go far enough. And why? Because it lays stress on the second commandment without recognising the importance of the first. Love of one's neighbour must flow out of love for God. If it doesn't, then the love of self and the love of one's neighbour is an egocentric love. It is the result of self-effort rather than divine infusion.

Martin Buber goes on to say that there is another kind of relationship as well as the *I-Thou* encounter and he calls this the *I-It* relationship. This is where a person treats another human being not as a person but as a thing. We do this, he says, when we use another person as a prop for our own ego, or when we seek to manipulate him for our own ends and purposes. Nothing damages or destroys a relationship between two people, he claims, more than when one treats the other as a thing and not as a person.

As far as they go, I find nothing wrong with these words. In fact, time and time again when counselling a troubled marriage, I have observed the great difficulties that arise when one partner relates to the other, not as a person, but as a thing. I can't count the number of times I have heard a woman tearfully exclaim, 'My husband treats me as an object and not as a person.' What we fail to realise is that when we treat another human being as an object and not as a person, then our relationship with ourselves is impaired. We demean others, and we end up demeaning ourselves.

Father, I come to you today to ask your forgiveness for the times I have treated people as objects rather than as persons. I see now why I have done this – I do not have enough respect for myself and hence little respect for others. Help me, dear Father. Amen.

FOR FURTHER STUDY – 1 Cor. 10:14–24; Matt. 16:25; Phil. 2:3–4

1. What is 'selfish ambition'? / 2. What should we seek?

'I-Thou' or 'I-It'?

FOR READING AND MEDITATION – 1 PETER 1:13–25

'Now you can have real love for everyone ... so see to it that
you really do love each other warmly ...' (v. 22: TLB)

We continue examining the dynamics of what Martin Buber calls the *I-It* relationship. When a child sets out on the journey of life, he begins by relating to things. The art of parenting is to teach him how to put things second and people first. Some children get stuck in their development as persons and go through their life loving things and using people. They manipulate and exploit others, often becoming frustrated and angry if their desires are not quickly responded to. Such people tend to become materialistic in their outlook and a slave to things.

This, however, is not the way life was designed to be – we were meant to love people and use things. 'Without an *I-It* relationship,' says Buber, 'man cannot live, but he who lives with an *I-It* alone is not a man.' He is saying that it is right to have a healthy regard for things and using them can be expression of one's creativity, but tragedy arises when we relate to other people as things. This becomes a form of suicide and murder – suicide for oneself as a person and murder for the one who is being used. In relating to others in an *I-It* relationship, we not only damage or destroy them, we damage or destroy ourselves.

It might be spiritually beneficial if at this stage every one of us paused and asked ourselves the question, 'What kind of relationship do I have with people, the *I-Thou* kind, or the *I-It* kind?' We must never forget that the way we relate to others says much about the way we relate to ourselves, and, may I add, the way we relate to God.

Father, your loving but relentless eyes see where we are ailing. But it is not enough that you see me – I must see myself as you see me. Show me where I am ailing and help me commit myself to change. In Jesus' name I ask it. Amen.

FOR FURTHER STUDY – 1 Cor. 13; Prov. 22:15; Eph. 4:14
1. What did Paul have to put away? / 2. What is found in the heart of a child?

Love – more than words

FOR READING AND MEDITATION – 1 CORINTHIANS 13:1–13

'If I … didn't love others … I would only be making a lot of noise.'
(v. 1: Living Bible)

We return now to focus on the *I-Thou* relationship and spend one final day considering it. In the *I-Thou* relationship, you will remember, one person sees that another is as significant as he is himself.

Dr Paul Tournier tells a moving story which most beautifully illustrates the power of the *I-Thou* relationship. When he was a small child, both his parents died and he went to live with an aunt and uncle. Unfortunately, his aunt was mentally ill and as a result, Paul grew up locked inside himself, not knowing how to relate to people. In school, a professor in Greek befriended him and used to take him home, sit him in front of the fireside and just chat. Paul's relationship with his professor broke the bonds of his repressed inner self and he became a completely different boy. Many years later, when Paul wrote the manuscript of his first book, he decided that the one person he most wanted to evaluate it was his professor. He took it to him and with some anxiety read the first chapter out to him. The professor listened and said, 'Please read on.' Hours later, after Paul had read the whole manuscript to him, the professor was silent for some time and then said, 'Paul, I feel we need to pray together.' Paul said, 'But I didn't know you were a Christian.' The professor said calmly, 'I am.' 'But since when?' 'As of this moment,' said the professor.

This is the power of the *I-Thou* relationship. It is never one way – both persons are affected by it. How wonderful it would be if our individual presentations of the gospel were more along this line, set in the context of warm relationships, rather than seeming like telegram deliveries.

Jesus, I long with all my soul to learn the art of loving relationships. I want to think love, feel love, and act love. I want to become love. For I see that only as I do, do I live. Help me, dear Father. In Jesus' name. Amen.

FOR FURTHER STUDY – John 20:19–23; Matt. 10:8
1. What was Jesus' message to the disciples? / 2. How are you carrying this out?

Love is to be lived

FOR READING AND MEDITATION – JOHN 13:31–38
'A new command I give you: Love one another. As I have loved you,
so you must love one another.' (v. 34: NIV)

We have been looking at the two highest commandments ever given to man any-where, at any time: 'You shall love the Lord your God with all your heart … and your neighbour as yourself.' These two commandments had been in existence from the very beginning, but no one fully understood how they could be put into practice until Jesus came. In Old Testament times, men and women loved God in the sha-dows, so to speak. They understood something of God's love from the way the cre-ation spoke to them or the way he acted towards them, but the full understanding of how much he loved them did not break in upon them until Jesus came.

Our Lord's entrance into humanity and his sinless life here on earth gave a focus for love which the Old Testament had not been able to do. This is why Jesus stood up towards the end of his ministry here on earth and gave us this new com-mandment: 'As I have loved you, so you must love one another.' The phrase, 'As I have loved you,' raised the commandment from the Old Testament to the New, from law to grace. Christ loved the disciples not as they loved themselves and each other, but with a different type and quality of love – a love that required a new word to express it: *Agape.*

By his coming into the world and his sacrificial death, our Lord put a content into the word *love* that it had never before seen. No one in the history of the universe had ever been able to say, 'Love as I have loved you.' No one else could utter the words, because before they could be uttered, they had to be lived. The content of the most beautiful life that has ever been lived has gone into these words. Thus this phrase is not merely verbal – it is vital.

Lord Jesus, I look at your life and see there the fullest meaning of the word love. Beside you, all other definitions fade into insignificance. I see love in you or I do not see it at all. For you are the Word of love become flesh. I am deeply, deeply thankful. Amen.

FOR FURTHER STUDY – Luke 10:25–37; Jer. 31:3; Matt. 9:36, 14:14
1. What did the Samaritan display? / 2. What moved Jesus?

Perfect standard and content

FOR READING AND MEDITATION – PHILIPPIANS 2:1–11
'Your attitude should be the same as that of Christ Jesus.' (v. 5: NIV)

We saw yesterday that the words of Jesus: 'As I have loved you, so you must love one another' (John 13:34: NIV) are the high-water mark in the history of mankind. What philosophers, thinkers and moralists have reached after through the ages, Jesus distilled in a sentence.

As we said, no one else could utter that sentence. Oh, of course they could speak the words, but when Jesus spoke, it was a good deal more than words – it was the Word become flesh. Someone has described the sentence, 'Love as I have loved you,' as vascular. 'Cut it and it will bleed – bleed with the life blood of the Son of God.' Thirty-three years of unstained living have gone into it. But more – the cross has also gone into it. And more still – the resurrection has gone into it. It is suffering love, but it is also triumphant love. It is a love that always wins out in the end. The love of Christ is the purest and most potent power in the universe.

Paul takes the words of Jesus and applies them to our hearts in the form of our text today. Listen to how Moffatt translates this text: 'Treat one another with the same spirit as you experience in Christ Jesus.' Treat one another as Christ treats you. Jesus made love central in his own life and in his relationships with others and he insists that we do the same. Don't see this as a harsh demand – it is the demand of love. And what love demands it also provides. You must love others as I love you, says our Lord, and if you have any difficulty doing that, come close to my heart, lay your head on my bosom and let me assure you how much you are loved. Then let my *Agape* inspire *Agape* in you.

Father, one thing is clear – without love in my relationships they just will not work right. My relationships cannot function without love any more than my lungs cannot function without air. Help me breathe in love – and breathe out love: your love. Amen.

FOR FURTHER STUDY – John 1:1–14; Col. 3:12–14; Eph. 5:2
1. What are we to put on above all virtues? / 2. What is Paul's exhortation to the Ephesians?

God's greatest word

FOR READING AND MEDITATION – JOHN 3:1–16

'For God so loved the world that he gave his one and only Son …' (v. 16: NIV)

We continue thinking about the fact of God's love and its relevance to effective Christian living. Many years ago, I sat down to prepare a sermon on the theme of God's love. I began to go through the Bible book by book in order to find references on the theme. You can imagine my surprise when I discovered that the first four books of the Bible have no mention of God's love at all, though of course it is quite clear from the passages that God really does love everybody. I relaxed when I came to Deuteronomy (what someone has called *The John of the Pentateuch*), for in this book there are several references to God's eternal love. The same is true of many of the other Old Testament books.

However, when I read through the first three Gospels I was again surprised – there are no clear references to God loving us in Matthew, Mark or Luke. There is an incidental reference to God's love in Luke 6:32–36, but no clear or direct statement. Once again, of course, it is evident from these three books also that God loves us, yet the statement is not directly made.

Then I came to John's Gospel and read in our text for today the first New Testament declaration of God's love. It was like a burst of sunlight in the darkness, and it simply overwhelmed my soul. The great preacher, C. H. Spurgeon, once said that if all of the Bible was lost to us and we had one text – John 3:16 – there is enough divine revelation in this one verse to present the gospel to the whole world. Let the words of this mighty text lie on your heart and mind as you travel through this day.

Gracious Father, it is as if your heart is uncovered in these matchless words of John 3:16. Help me meditate on this thought throughout this day. I would put my heart up against your heart, feel its beat and catch its rhythm. In Jesus' name I pray. Amen.

FURTHER STUDY – Eph. 3:14–21, 5:2; 1 John 3:1–16

1. Compare John 3:16 with 1 John 3:16. / 2. What does Paul pray that we will grasp?

Life's most inevitable question

FOR READING AND MEDITATION – ROMANS 13:8–14

'... love is the fulfilling of the law.' (v. 10: RSV)

I think we are ready now to answer one of life's greatest and most inevitable questions: what is the purpose of living? Throughout time, philosophers and thinkers have pondered this question and have answered it in different ways. The answer based on Scripture is this – the purpose of living is to love as we are loved. God has set up life so that when we relate to him and experience his love flowing into the core of our beings, we are able to relay to others the love with which we ourselves are loved. If we are not functioning in this way, then we are not living according to the divine design.

Here's a statement that might sound exaggerated, but I have reflected upon it deeply for many, many years – most of the problems we experience in our Christian life stem from the fact that we do not love as we are loved. Almost every spiritual and psychological problem brought to a counsellor can be identified at its core as a violation of the command of Jesus: 'Love as I have loved you.'

A girl said to me some time ago, 'Whenever I say or do anything loving for my father, he doesn't seem to appreciate it, and so I have given up trying. Now I just stay in my shell and let life go on around me anyway it wishes.' What was she saying? In my opinion, she was saying, 'I do not have the emotional resources to keep loving someone who doesn't seem to appreciate it.' But this is a violation of the law of love. She did have the resources to go out towards an unresponsive and unappreciative father in love – providing she assimilated them. The resources she needed are in Christ. She was not just blocked in giving; she was also blocked in receiving.

Father, I see that I fail in loving because I fail in receiving. Show me what is blocking my vertical relationship with you, and help me put my whole being under the great Niagara of your love. In Jesus' name I pray. Amen.

FOR FURTHER STUDY – 2 Cor. 5:12–21; Phil. 3:7–9; John 17:23
1. What message has Christ committed to us? / 2. How does this affect our relationships?

One ubiquitous fact

FOR READING AND MEDITATION – 1 THESSALONIANS 3:1–13

'May the Lord make your love increase and overflow for each other …' (v. 12: NIV)

We said yesterday that most of the problems we experience in the Christian life stem from the fact that we do not love as we are loved. Psychologist Larry Crabb says, 'I believe it can be successfully argued that every personal or behavioural problem one might wish to change (e.g. bad temper, perverted sexual desires, depression, anxiety, overeating) results ultimately from violations of the command to love.' A sweeping statement – but true. When we put the personal and behavioural problems with which people struggle under the spiritual microscope, we discover that underlying all of them is one ubiquitous fact – people do not know how to enter into a loving involvement with God and then with others.

I myself am convinced that every problem of living, both between people and within people, has within it a style of relating that violates God's standard of love. One of the things I have learned through many counselling sessions over the years is that there is nothing like a close relationship to bring the problems and difficulties that lie in the personality up to the surface. People can present a good front to the world, to their workmates, neighbours, acquaintances or even casual friends, but immediately they enter into a close relationship with someone, any deficiencies that are within will soon emerge. This is why a famous counsellor says, 'Relationships do not so much cause problems as reveal problems.'

We who are Christians must get this issue of relationships clearly sorted out in our minds, for we reflect our failures here not just to those who are around us, but through family life to the generations that are yet to come.

Gracious God and loving Heavenly Father, don't let me fumble at the place of relationships for I see that if I do, the effect is felt not only in the present, but in the future also. Help me, dear Father. My ideas are not good enough. I need yours. Amen.

FOR FURTHER STUDY – John 15:1–17; 1 John 2:6, 28

1. What does it mean to abide in the vine? / 2. With what love did Jesus love?

A transformed husband

FOR READING AND MEDITATION – ROMANS 8:28–39

'... we are more than conquerors through him who loved us.' (v. 37: NIV)

We continue reflecting on the idea that most of our problems in life arise from the fact that we do not love as we are loved. In one of my seminars, I tell the story of a man I once counselled who told me that when he was a boy of twelve, something happened to him that affected the course of his life. His father gave him a Christmas present which turned out not to be the train set he had expected – but a brick! As he looked at the *present* he had been given, the boy's father loomed over him and said, 'That's all you're worth. You've hardly done a thing I've asked you over this past year. Perhaps this will teach you how to behave.' From that traumatic experience the young boy made a decision: 'I will never again trust anyone or get close to them, for they may disappoint me and let me down.'

When he grew up and married, he found that after a few years his marriage got into serious trouble. It was clear that the strategy he had decided to follow, 'Don't trust anyone or get close to them because you might get hurt,' was destroying his marriage. I shared with him the truth that by holding on to the life strategy he had developed to prevent himself feeling pain, he was violating the command to love his wife as Christ loved the church (Ephesians 5:25).

Gradually he came to see that the reason why he feared rejection was because he did not feel deeply enough the strength and support of God's love. He repented of holding on to his wrong strategy, opened his being in a new way to receive God's love, and became a transformed person. And more – a transformed husband.

Father, I see how wonderfully your love can drive out all my fears. Forgive me for so often depending on my ideas about how to make my life work instead of trusting yours. This day, I open my being afresh to your love. Love in me – and through me. In Jesus' name. Amen.

FOR FURTHER STUDY – Eph. 5:22–33; 1 Peter 3:7; Col. 3:18–21
1. What are some of the characteristics of Christ's love for the Church?
2. What are fathers not to do to their children?

The sin of self-protection

FOR READING AND MEDITATION – GALATIANS 5:13–26

'The acts of the sinful nature are obvious … selfish ambition …' (vv. 19–20: NIV)

The man I referred to yesterday had developed a strategy that kept his life together, but it was a strategy that violated the law of love. He was depending on his strategy to make his life work, not on the fact that in Christ he was secure and worthwhile. Only as he came to see where his security lay – in Christ's love for him – and to assimilate that into his being, was he able to minister to his wife without the fear of rejection.

One of the main reasons why we are afraid to give ourselves to others is not, as many people think, because we are *shy by nature* but because we profoundly fear that others will withdraw from us and reject us. The fear of being hurt, let down, misunderstood, unappreciated or rejected, keeps many of us from getting involved with the people God has put us in touch with. It is probably the biggest 'relationship killer' in the universe.

At the heart of this fear is a desire for self-protection. We cannot trust God's love enough to see us through the pain of being misunderstood or rejected, and so instead of moving towards someone in love, we protect ourselves by holding back. We play safe, but at the same time violate the law of love. Larry Crabb says that self-protection is a category of sin that is not easily recognised in church life. Some have criticised him for coming up with a category of sin that is not mentioned in the Bible, but the term *self-protection* is simply a synonym for selfishness or self-centredness. When we fail to demonstrate love to others because we are afraid of their rejection, we are simply being selfish. We are depending on our own ideas about what works rather than his.

Father, I am so grateful that your Holy Spirit has been given me to overcome all the works of the flesh. Let your Spirit be at work in me today, helping me to resist the demands of my sinful nature and to receive the great inflow of your love. Amen.

FOR FURTHER STUDY – Luke 18:9–14; Prov. 28:26; 1 Cor. 10:12
1. What was the Pharisee's real problem? / 2. When are we foolish?

Self- versus other-centredness

'Nobody should seek his own good, but the good of others.' (v. 24: NIV)

We touched yesterday on the fact that self-protection (synonymous with selfishness) is a category of sin that is not often recognised in the Christian. When we are afraid to go towards others in loving involvement because we are afraid of the pain of possible rejection, in effect we are choosing to say to God, 'I know you've told me I am to love others as you have loved me, but I'm not going to do it because it might bring me some personal pain.' That is self-protection, which prefers withdrawal to involvement. And I have no hesitation in describing that as sin.

In Philippians 2:4 Paul exhorts us to look not only to our own interests, but also to the interests of others. One comment I have read on this verse says, 'Clearly the dividing line between a life lived in the flesh and one empowered by the Spirit is self- versus other-centredness. There is one source of energy behind every inter-personal act: either a priority interest in oneself, or a priority interest in others. The mark of the Christian is a quality of love that directs more energy towards others' concerns than towards one's own well-being.'

You will have noticed that many who are non-Christians are capable of great, even extraordinary, acts of kindness, but only a deeply committed Christian, who experiences in his being the sweep of God's love, can be concerned with another's interests more than his own. Very few Christians love like that. I certainly am very poor at it. Perhaps one of the chief reasons why we as Christians do not make the impact upon the world we should is because we love so poorly. We prefer the safety of self-protection to the risk of loving.

Father, help me, for I feel you calling me to challenges that I cannot climb up to in my own strength. Show me even more clearly that not only do you raise the standard high, but you also provide the power by which I can reach up to it. I am so thankful. Amen.

FOR FURTHER STUDY – John 13:31–38; Heb. 13:1–3; 1 Peter 4:8–9
1. How will the world know that we are disciples?
2. How is this worked out at a practical level?

The central issue

FOR READING AND MEDITATION – PROVERBS 3:1–10

'Trust in the Lord with all your heart and lean not on your own understanding.'
(v. 5: NIV)

We ended yesterday with the thought that far too often we prefer the safety of self-protection to the risk of loving. Let's face it, there are risks in loving others and becoming warmly involved in their lives. People can hurt. Their indifference, insensitivity, and sometimes their downright obnoxiousness, can cut deep into the human spirit.

I am convinced, however, that the reason why we hurt so much when those who we attempt to love reject us, is because the immediate hurt triggers off similar hurts from the past. Have you noticed that an unkind word from a friend, a snub by someone you respect, a sarcastic statement from a source you would least expect, can sometimes trigger off a reaction far more intense than the remark or action warrants? Why? Perhaps the words or action brought us close to the pain of profound disappointment that is deep within all of us – a pain that most of us desperately deny.

We have all been let down or hurt. There is not a person reading these lines who hasn't at some time been hurt or disappointed by others. Our usual response to these hurts is to make a commitment never to be hurt like that again. This commitment, if not faced and dealt with, becomes a barrier to a clear and open relationship with God and others. We try to love – but from a distance. We have to face the choice whether to run from the pain in self-protection or enter into the pain and trust God's love to carry us through. Self-protection or trust – this is the issue with which every one of us has to come to grips, not only in the matter of relationships, but in the entire field of Christian living.

My Father and my God, I see that my behaviour inevitably reflects one choice or the other – I either protect myself from further pain or trust your love to carry me through. Show me the way to trust you. In Jesus' name I ask it. Amen.

FOR FURTHER STUDY – Psa. 37, 118:8, 115:11
1. What are we able to do when we trust the Lord? / 2. What are we to refrain from?

An honest look

FOR READING AND MEDITATION – PSALM 26:1–12

'Test me, o Lord, and try me, examine my heart and my mind.' (v. 2: NIV)

We are touching upon one of the most important issues that could ever engage our attention – the choice between self-protection and trust. Those who are willing to take an honest look at their relationships can expect to make some surprising discoveries. One such discovery is that what motivates much of our behaviour towards one another is not genuine love, but self-protection.

One of the biggest shocks I ever received took place some years ago when I came to see that behind my own personal relational style was a whole lot of self-protection. I was helped to see this through the writings of a man whom I hold in personal regard – Lawrence Crabb. His penetrating words enabled me to see that I allowed people to come close enough to affirm me, but not close enough to hurt me. My relationship strategy was based on a commitment to keep the pain of past disappointments out of my awareness.

If someone had said to me at that time, 'Is there any sin in your life?', I would have said, 'Absolutely not.' I would have challenged anyone to find anything sinful about my lifestyle or behaviour, for I believed that in everything I was doing, I was manifesting a deep commitment to biblical principles. What I didn't realise was that my style of relating to others reflected a stubborn commitment to self-interest. And that is sin. I had chosen, albeit unconsciously, to develop a relational style designed to maintain a level of distance from others that guaranteed invulnerability to further hurt, and a level of contact with others that allowed them to come only as close as it felt good to me. I was putting my needs before the needs of others – a violation of the command to love.

My Father and my God, I want to be the very best for you. Help me examine my own relational style this day and help me discover those things that are going on inside me which prevent me from loving as I am loved. In Jesus' name. Amen.

FOR FURTHER STUDY – Psa. 51:1–6, 139:23–24
1. Where does God deserve truth? / 2. What was the psalmist's prayer?

Be nice to me

FOR READING AND MEDITATION – 1 CORINTHIANS 3:10–23

'… the Day will bring it to light. It will be revealed with fire, and
the fire will test the quality of each man's work.' (v. 13: NIV)

We continue examining the fact that behind our relational style can be a commitment to self-interest that violates the command to love as we are loved. We were created by a God who desires us to trust his love, so that we can freely love others and not protect ourselves from the pain of possible disappointment.

The reason we love so poorly is because we are afraid and unwilling to give up our commitment to self-protection. Behind a facade of friendliness can be a desire to please others, so that they in turn will be kind to us and make us feel good. A friend of mine tells how she discovered behind her sweet smile and approachable manner a strategy that said, 'Be nice to me because I can't stand being rejected.' The person who is always cracking jokes may be doing so in order to avoid isolation. I have heard many comedians say that their careers developed out of a desire to keep people away from the deep loneliness they experience in their hearts. 'A business efficiency,' says Lawrence Crabb, 'can keep people away from a tenderness that might be exploited. Shyness might be the means to keep us from ever looking foolish.'

All this must not be taken to mean that behind all friendliness and concern lies a commitment to self-protection – that would be taking things much too far. But a lot of it is – and we who are Christ's must be willing to examine ourselves and see whether our relational style is one that is designed to glorify God or glorify ourselves. In the final tribunal, when our lives are judged and the rewards given, the seemingly kind deeds we have done which were prompted by self-protection will be consigned to the flames, along with all other hypocrisies.

Father, your word tells me that if I judge myself I will not be judged. Give me the courage I need to look at the things that may be going on within me, and help me deal with these things in a way that glorifies you. In Jesus' name. Amen.

FOR FURTHER STUDY – 1 Chron. 28:1–9; Psa. 44:21; Jer. 17:9–10; Dan. 2:22
1. What advice did David give to Solomon? / 2. What does Jeremiah say about the heart?

The 'drain' factor

FOR READING AND MEDITATION – LUKE 6:27–36

'... do good to those who hate you, bless those who curse you ...' (vv. 27–28: NIV)

We said several weeks ago that it is out of our early relationships with others that we develop our relational style – the way of relating to others that best suits us and with which we are most comfortable. Generally speaking, we said, there are three forms of relational style – we can move towards people, we can move against people or we can move away from people.

You can probably see by now that the styles of moving against people, or away from people, are styles that reflect sinful self-protection – but what about the style of moving towards others? Surely there can be nothing wrong with that! But there is, if the motive is not true ministry, that is, the desire to give to others rather than to get for ourselves. A friend of mine says, 'We ought not to enter any relationship unless we go into it with the desire to bless others.'

Many people going through counselling are absolutely stunned to discover that behind their friendly approach to people there is a desire to manipulate others – to use others in order to satisfy their own needs – rather than a commitment to minister to others regardless of what they get out of it for themselves. This factor drains many marriages (as well as other relationships) of energy and power. In a marriage enrichment seminar I conducted, a woman said at the end, 'I can see now that because I was not drawing from God the nourishment I need to function as a person, I demanded it from my husband. My demandingness has put a great strain on our marriage. Now I shall be looking to give to my husband rather than get from him. I expect our marriage to be transformed as a result of this.' My comment on that was, 'It will.' For love never fails.

My Father and my God, I want to be at my very best for you. This business of being a Christian is serious and I need to reflect in my relationships with others the quality of your relationship with me. Help me, dear Father. Amen.

FOR FURTHER STUDY – 1 Cor. 13:8–13; Ex. 23:5; Prov. 25:21; Rom. 12:20
1. How does Paul describe his *growing up*? / 2. What militates against love?

Take another look

FOR READING AND MEDITATION – PSALM 139:17–24

'Search me, O God, and know my heart … See if there is any offensive way in me.'
(vv. 23–24: NIV)

We continue examining the relational style in which one person moves towards another with apparent friendliness and concern but where the real motivation is not to give but to get.

I am not drawing attention to this in order that you may begin to analyse everyone who approaches you in a friendly or loving manner, but to help you discover what may be the motivation behind your own relational style. Note my emphasis on the word *may*, for not all friendliness has self-interest behind it. My task here, as a servant of the Lord ministering daily to many people around the world, is to invite you to look at your life and see if there are hidden motivations that need to be discovered and brought to the Lord for him to deal with. Only God can help us discover this – hence my selection of the verse that is before us today.

Permit me to bring this home to you in the form of a question. Are you the kind of man whose confident, assertive, knowledgeable, 'let's-get-on-with-it' approach to people appears to reflect good adjustment and maturity? Take another look, for it may be the way you protect yourself from having to admit you can't resolve a problem. Are you the kind of woman who moves towards others with an agreeable and gracious manner that is regarded by those who know you as evidence of the fruit of the Spirit? Take another look, for it may be the fruit of the flesh – a desire to avoid criticism or rejection. Your relational style may reflect a fear that others could destroy you if you failed them. Ezekiel talks about flimsy walls that look strong because of whitewash (Ezekiel 13:10–12). It pays off spiritually to take another look.

Father, I realise that it is easier to look at others than it is to look at myself. I observe them with an open eye and then turn a blind eye on myself. So I look to you to help me. Show me my deficiencies and move me towards change. In Jesus' name. Amen.

FOR FURTHER STUDY –Ezek. 13:1–12; Matt. 7:24–28
1. What is the heart of Ezekiel's prophecy? / 2. What was Jesus saying in his parable?

The subtlety of sin

FOR READING AND MEDITATION – PROVERBS 16:1–19

'All a man's ways seem innocent to him, but motives are weighed by the Lord' (v. 2: NIV)

Self-protection is so subtle that we will not recognise its presence in our lives until we have some idea of what we are protecting ourselves against. We touched a little on this a week or so ago, but now I want to focus upon it in much more detail.

The reason why so much self-protection underlies our different relational styles is because of the deep pain we feel in our hearts whenever God is not allowed to be all-in-all to our souls. God has designed us for a relationship with himself and our souls can only function effectively when he resides within our beings and energises our personalities with his love. We were made for love and we can never function effectively until we are indwelt by love – *Agape* love. We experience spiritual and psychological pain to the degree that God's love is not touching us at the centre of our beings. We hurt when we feel we are not loved.

How do we deal with that pain? Because we have all been afflicted with the disease which Adam introduced into the universe – self-centredness and self-sufficiency – we attempt to alleviate that pain, or distance ourselves from it, by devices of our own making. And one of those devices can be our relational style. Rather than face the degree of pain within our beings that inevitably is there when God is not allowed to fill the core of our personalities with his love, we adopt a style of relating to others that protects us from our inner pain by keeping people at a safe distance. Our purpose is to maintain our comfort and not add to our pain – a subtle form of sin.

Father, hold me steady at this point. I sense I am touching something that, if I lay hold upon it, can mean the difference between success and failure, not only in my relationships but in every area of living. Help me, dear Father. In Jesus' name. Amen.

FOR FURTHER STUDY – Matt. 26:36–46; Psa. 40:8, 143:10
1. How did Jesus deal with pain when he faced it?
2. Find out what the word *Gethsemane* means.

Independence or helplessness

FOR READING AND MEDITATION – DEUTERONOMY 9:1–6

'After the Lord your God has driven them out … do not say to yourself,
"The Lord has brought me here … because of my righteousness"…' (v. 4: NIV)

So that there may be no misunderstanding, permit me to expand upon the point I was making yesterday, namely, that to the degree that we are not indwelt and motivated by divine love, to that degree we will experience spiritual or psychological pain. Whenever we feel pain, we set about trying to alleviate it. Often our relational style unconsciously reflects a commitment to defending ourselves against that pain more than a commitment to bless others with our lives.

The clear answer is to open the whole of our beings to the love of God, but here we come up against a problem – our stubborn and sinful desire to make our lives work by self-effort rather than by dependent trust. There is something in you and me – a legacy left over from Adam – which delights in finding our own answers to our problems. We would much prefer to work things out for ourselves than admit that we are helpless to make our lives work on our own. And it is this conflict – independence versus helplessness – that must be resolved if we are to communicate effectively with God and with others.

When we move towards others in order to get them to affirm us rather than to affirm them, our motivation may be to keep them at a distance so that they do not impinge upon our personal pain. What does that indicate about us? I believe it is saying that we are not secure enough to risk being vulnerable, and being hurt. We do not experience deeply enough the strength and security of God's love at the centre of our being. We are depending on a self-made strategy rather than the Saviour's love. And that, I say once again, is – sin.

Blessed Lord Jesus, your relentless love has once again cornered my soul. Don't let me wriggle and slip past your words today. Help me take my medicine – however bitter the taste. For I would be whole and not part sick. Help me, my Master. Amen.

FOR FURTHER STUDY – 2 Cor. 10:1–12; Prov. 12:15, 20:6; Jer. 2:35
1. When are we unwise? / 2. Where did Paul say the Corinthians were looking?

Facing our pains

FOR READING AND MEDITATION – PSALM 30:1–12

'… weeping may endure for a night, but joy comes in the morning.' (v. 5: NKJ)

I am moving carefully through this important stage of our meditations, because I am concerned not to leave one faltering soul behind. The point being made is this – to the degree that we do not experience God's love continuously sweeping into the core of our beings, to that degree we experience personal pain. The presence of divine love at the centre of our being spells out joy – the loss of that love spells out pain. Oftentimes (as we have said) our relationships reflect the presence of that pain – we are afraid to risk being hurt by others because it will increase the volume of pain we feel inside us and bring it to an unacceptable level. Thus we adopt a style of relating that protects us from the presence of further pain by keeping people safely distant. This is not the Christian way to relate.

One way of realising whether our relationships are self-protective is to ask whether we are willing to face and feel the pain that may be going on in our inner beings. This is not masochism, it is healthy spiritual adjustment. Facing and feeling the pain allows us to see just how much self-effort we put into making our lives work, and how much we depend on our own independent strategies rather than trusting the divine love. When we keep our distance from the pain by pretending it is not there, we set ourselves up for superficial living.

These next few days may be painful for many, but I want you to trust me as I walk you through them. Together, the Lord and I (forgive the arrogant-sounding phrase) will strike at the roots of your independence – not to demean you, but to develop you. Sometimes God has to make us feel worse on the way to making us feel better.

Lord Jesus, help me through these days of personal challenge. I want to be real – completely real. But there are many things to be faced and brought up. Help me to bring them up until nothing is left behind. Merge my life into a living whole – like yours. Amen.

FOR FURTHER STUDY – Rom. 8:18–39; Isa. 41:10; Psa. 40:17

1. What did Paul mean by 'groan inwardly' (v. 23)?
2. How does the Lord enable us to face our weakness?

The only true love

FOR READING AND MEDITATION – ROMANS 5:1–11

'But God demonstrates his own love for us in this: While we were still sinners,
Christ died for us.' (v. 8: NIV)

Today we face the question: how much denied and unresolved pain is there lying in our hearts? One way of discovering whether we are depending on God's love to hold our lives together or on our own self-centred strategies, is to explore the depth of disappointment within us which stems from failures in our past relationships. None of us likes to dwell on the disappointments we felt, and still feel, when those who ought to have loved us failed to come through for us. But why do the disappointments we experience in our relationships cause us so much pain? It is because everyone of us longs to be loved, and when we fail to experience this love, we hurt – and hurt badly. Because of this deep longing that is within us, we often deny the extent of our disappointment when those we have longed for have failed us. It hurts to face the fact that we were not loved, and so our minds try to push this knowledge aside.

Lawrence Crabb (on whom I am drawing heavily in connection with some of these ideas) says, 'Perhaps the most difficult thing for many people to admit is that they feel let down by their parents. Even victims of child abuse sometimes cling to the hope that the abusing parent really loved them but didn't know how to show it. It's hard to face the fact squarely that we have not been loved with the love we wanted so badly.'

The longing to be loved is so strong that it is easier to admit to our own failure to love others than acknowledge the profound disappointment that comes from admitting others did not love us. But facing that disappointment helps us to see that there is something in our hearts that no one, not even the most loving human being, can fully satisfy.

Father, I want to have done with the rationalisations and defences I have built into my life. They stop me from being a real person. I am through with explaining them away; I want them to be taken away. Help me, my Father. In Jesus' name. Amen.

FOR FURTHER STUDY – Jer. 31:1–14; Isa. 54:1–10; John 13:1
1. What is God's promise to us? / 2. Have you experienced the 'full extent' of Christ's love?

Love or self-protection

FOR READING AND MEDITATION – ISAIAH 49:8–16

'Can a mother forget the baby at her breast …? Though she may forget,
I will not forget you!' (v. 15: NIV)

We pick up from where we left off yesterday: it is only when we face the disappointment in our hearts – disappointment which would not be there had others loved us perfectly – that we can see how we ache for what no one has perfectly provided. Many Christians resist getting in touch with the disappointment that rankles deep inside them. They fear that to do so would stir up hatred and animosity towards those who had failed them: unloving parents, foster-parents, siblings, and so on. But the purpose is precisely the opposite. It is only when we face and feel the disappointment inside us that we can see how we wrongly demand that others always come through for us. When we see this, we are able to release them from that demand.

One of the reasons why it is so often difficult to forgive people who have let us down is that we expected too much of them. We relied on them, even demanded of them that they touch the core of our being with a love that only God can provide. Because we expected more than they could give, we became devastated when they failed to come through for us. It is when we depend on others to give us a love that only God can give that we feel devastated, perhaps even destroyed, when they let us down.

Only a deep awareness of the profound disappointment in our hearts can enable us to see how we protect ourselves by relating to people in a way that prevents us feeling any further discomfort. Self-protection and love are opposites. If love is the ultimate virtue, then self-protection comes close to being the ultimate problem.

O Father, I see that if only I can get hold of this truth and turn it from theory into practice, it will transform all my relationships. Help me do just that. I ask this in Christ's peerless and precious name. Amen.

FOR FURTHER STUDY – Psa. 136, 98:3; Phil. 1:6
1. What was the psalmist's testimony? / 2. What is the confidence we have?

Nothing!

FOR READING AND MEDITATION – JOHN 15:1–8
'... apart from me you can do nothing.' (v. 5: NIV)

The crux of what we are saying as we work our way through these important life principles is this: the more willing we are to face and feel our disappointment, the more clearly we can see how we manipulate others to give us what our souls ache for – the love that we should be seeking from God – and the more readily we will turn from self-protection to trusting God to meet the deep needs of our inner being. Only then will we engage in true ministry to others.

That's the theory – but what's the reality? The reality is that we can see all this and continue along our self-centred ways. Why? I take you back to something I said before – there resides deep within us a stubborn commitment to handle whatever pain there might be in our hearts through our own self-centred efforts. I sense within me (and I am sure you do also) a deep down desire to avoid the idea that I am powerless to make my life work on its own. For to admit to that idea puts me in a position of helplessness rather than control. I like being in control of my life – it makes me feel good. What I don't like is feeling helpless.

Yet it is only when I turn from attempting to relieve my inner pain through my own self-centred strategies, and trust God to fill me with a love that can overwhelm all my inner pain, that I know the deep joy about which the Scripture speaks and the peace the Saviour so graciously promises. I must come in helpless dependence on Christ and ask him to deal with all those things within me that I would love to resolve myself. I must confess the truth of the text that is before us today: 'Without me you can do nothing.' Nothing!

O Father, help me, for I desperately need your help. I cannot fight this terrifying desire that is within me, which prompts me to hold my life together independently of you. Show me how to deal with it – once and for all. In Jesus' name I ask it. Amen.

FOR FURTHER STUDY – Rom. 7–8; Eph. 3:16–21
1. How does Paul describe the inner struggle?
2. How does he sum it up from Roman 8:35 onwards?

The power of a pointed question

FOR READING AND MEDITATION – GENESIS 3:1–15
'Then the Lord God said … "What is this you have done?" …' (v. 13: NIV)

Without an awareness of the pain that reverberates with us, we will not be able to understand clearly why we resort to manipulation rather than ministry in our day to day relationships. Why should this be so? It is because being willing to face the pain is the first step along the road to full surrender. If we are blocked here, we may be blocked all along the line. Once we recognise that our self-protective patterns are a defence against our pain, then and only then can we set about dealing with the issue. The reason God asked Adam and Eve the questions in the passage before us today was not because he did not know the answers; the questions were more for their benefit than his. Only when problems are exposed can they really be dealt with. Whenever someone asks a question, the mind presses forward to answer it and sometimes illumination comes in the answering.

How do we deal with our defensiveness, our self-protection and our stubborn commitment to hold our lives together without God? There is only one way – we must repent. But what is repentance? The word means different things to different people. Some see repentance as a change in behaviour – a right about turn. It is that, but much more. Some see repentance as a change of heart. That gets closer to its meaning, but we would then need to ask, 'What do you mean by a change of heart?' Others define repentance as 'a verbal expression of sorrow over sin'. Then the question has to be asked, 'What exactly is meant by *sin*?'

Am I quibbling? No. I am raising these questions because it is only when we have a clear view of what has gone wrong inside us that we understand what it means to repent meaningfully.

Lord Jesus Christ, continue to probe and question me so that I am no longer able to hide behind my rationalisations and defences. There is something in my nature that resists the call to repentance. But hold me to it – it is my salvation. Amen.

FOR FURTHER STUDY – Luke 24:36–53; Matt. 3:2, 4:17; Luke 13:3; Mark 6:12
1. What was the primary message of John and Jesus?
2. What will be preached to all nations?

A declaration of independence

FOR READING AND MEDITATION – LUKE 19:11–26
' … "We don't want this man to be our king." ' (v. 14: NIV)

We ended yesterday with the statement, 'It is only when we have a clear view of what has gone wrong inside us that we understand what it means to repent meaningfully' In other words, a clear understanding of sin enables us to enter into a deep understanding of repentance.

So what is sin? Sin is much more than wrong actions, it is a wrong attitude. It is the attitude that proudly places the ego in the centre of our being, the part of us that God made for himself, and says, 'There now, I will run my life on my own terms.' Sin is God-displacement: pushing God out of the centre of our lives and replacing him with our egos. Over the years I have defined sin as 'a declaration of independence'. It is attempting to hold our lives together independently of God.

One of the places where we see sin in its ugliest form is in our relationships. Now don't leap up in protest and say, 'What about such things as child abuse, violence, murder, and other such sins? There we see sin in its ugliest form!'

I agree that sin is ugly when it manifests itself in physical hurt to others, but it is no less ugly when it inflicts a wound in a person's spirit. And that is precisely what we do when we fail to love as we are loved. I would imagine that most of my readers would be exempt from such sins as lying, stealing, cheating, adultery, and so on, but how many of us can plead exemption from relational sin? How many of us withdraw from loving involvement for fear that we might get hurt? When we do, we violate the command to love – the command, you remember, which Jesus identified as the first and greatest commandment!

God, help me track down this awful spirit of independence that is embedded deep within me. And not only track it down, but root it out. Until it is dealt with, I will continue to hurt you and others. Help me, my Father. In Jesus' name. Amen.

FOR FURTHER STUDY – Isa. 14:12–15, 30:15; Mark 10:17–31
1. What is the shortest definition of sin? / 2. What was at issue with the rich young ruler?

The path to life

FOR READING AND MEDITATION – MARK 8:27–38

'For whoever wants to save his life will lose it, but whoever loses his life for me …
will save it.' (v. 35: NIV)

We are suggesting that although there are many kinds of sins, one of the ugliest is relational sin. Its ugliness lies in the fact that it violates the command to love – the first and greatest commandment. Relational sin arises because we look to the wrong source in our attempt to relieve the deep longing for love at the core of our being. In consequence, we develop a style of relating that is designed to protect ourselves from fear and pain rather than the one which moves towards people with the aim of loving involvement. We cling to our right to protect ourselves, unaware that the demand underlying it is the very thing that keeps us from experiencing real life. We will never experience real life until that central independence is given up and replaced by dependent trust.

Once we understand the concept of relational sin, we can do something about it. We must repent of our commitment to self-protection. We must come before God in an act of genuine repentance and ask him to forgive us for choosing our own ideas about how to make our lives work, instead of his. We must also be willing to give up our dependence on defensive strategies that we have built around ourselves – strategies which we foolishly believe provide us with the energy to make our lives work.

However, we must expect a struggle at this point, for carnal nature will resist giving up its self-protective commitment and will fight it with all the strength and energy of a drowning man struggling for his life. To move into life without self-protection feels like an act of suicide. The desire to stay safe is strong. But the safety is an illusion. Only in Christ are we really safe.

O God, straighten out from my mind the quirks which distort and disrupt, leading me to think that the way to save my life is to hold on to it. Help me to see that although your way may be the less appealing way, it is always the best way. In Jesus' name. Amen.

FOR FURTHER STUDY – Phil. 3:1–11; John 12:24–26
1. What is the *grain of wheat* principle? / 2. How did Paul express the principle?

The steps of repentance

FOR READING AND MEDITATION – HOSEA 14:1–3

'Return ... to the Lord your God. Your sins have been your downfall!' (v. 1: NIV)

We have been seeing that once we understand how our self-protective patterns work, we can enter into a fuller and better appreciation of how God designed our lives to function and how we miss the mark. Today we ask ourselves: how do we repent of relational sin? Or, for that matter, any kind of sin?

The passage before us today shows us how it ought to be done. 'Return to the Lord your God'. We have chosen to look elsewhere for the energy to make our lives work; now we must choose again – to transfer our dependency to God.

'Take words with you': when we come to God we do not stutter and stammer, wondering why we are there. We must have a clear idea of what we are repenting of, and the clearer our understanding, the deeper our repentance. The Prodigal Son, you will remember, carefully rehearsed what he would say to his father when he returned home: 'I will arise ... and will say ... "Father, I have sinned against heaven and before you, and I am no longer worthy to be called your son"' (Luke 15:18–19: NKJ).

'Forgive all our sins': the change from wrongly relating to rightly relating begins in the forgiveness of God. We cannot rid ourselves of sin; it is something that has to be forgiven.

'Receive us graciously, that we may offer the fruit of our lips': repentance involves throwing ourselves on the mercy of God so that we may learn how to approach him in true worship. The thought here is: *Receive us so that we may rightly worship*. True worship flows out of an understanding that the power to make our lives work is to be found in God through Christ – and nowhere else.

Gracious Father, you have built into your word such clarity and direction. If I fail to follow it, it is not because it has not been made clear; it has to be because I don't want it to be clear. Help me to see – and follow. In Christ's name. Amen.

FOR FURTHER STUDY – Luke 15:11–32, 18:10–14; John 2:12

1. How did the Prodigal prepare himself? / 2. What was the Pharisee's approach?

Further steps to repentance

FOR READING AND MEDITATION – HOSEA 14:1–3
'Assyria cannot save us ...' (v. 3: NIV)

We continue looking at the passage in Hosea which spells out in detail the steps that are necessary to enter into a meaningful repentance: 'Assyria cannot save us; we will not mount war-horses.' When Israel was under threat from the surrounding nations, a pact with Assyria looked like a sensible precaution. But if Israel turned to Assyria for support, her dependency would not be fully on God. Assyria could not save Israel. If God failed to come through, Israel would be destroyed. Only when we see our lives in those terms can we understand what life is all about.

'We will never again say "Our gods" to what our own hands have made': only when we see that the real issue underlying sin is idolatry (that is, choosing a visible god instead of the invisible God), will we see how our self-sufficiency violates the divine scheme of things. Our foolish attempts to rely on our own strategies as we relate to others must be seen for what they are – idolatry.

'In you the fatherless find compassion': fatherless children are unprotected children, defenceless, and vulnerable to the point of helplessness. Repentance involves entering our disappointments and experiencing a sense of isolation and loneliness from which our souls would naturally shrink. Being willing to experience helplessness, however, enables us to see how desperately we need God and motivates us to turn to him in utter dependency, finding, as we do, the reality of his compassion entering deep into our souls. Repentance may seem like a path that leads to death, but in the divine scheme of things it is the path that leads to life.

O God my Father, as I solemnly and sincerely take these steps of repentance, let them become the burning glass that gathers everything into one focus of love. I want to love like you. Then and then alone can I kindle your love in others. Amen.

FOR FURTHER STUDY – Matt. 10:37–42; Mark 8:35; John 12:24; Phil. 3:8
1. How do we find life? / 2. What was Paul's testimony?

The benefits of repentance

FOR READING AND MEDITATION – HOSEA 14:4–9
'Who is wise? He will realise these things. Who is discerning?
He will understand them.' (v. 9: NIV)

Today we ask ourselves: what happens in the lives of those who know how to repent deeply? Repentance enables God to move into our lives with might and power. The first thing that happens is that our waywardness is healed (v. 4). The compulsive desire we have to go astray and do our own thing is checked and brought under his control. The second thing is that our lives become spiritually refreshed: 'I will be like the dew to Israel' (v. 5), and our roots go down further into the soil of God's love, giving us a deeper foundation and greater stability (v. 5). The third thing is that our lives gain an attractiveness that was not there before (v. 6). People sense we love them for their own sake, not for what they can do for us. Fourthly, this type of living encourages people to want to 'dwell … in [our] shade' (v. 7). They like to be near us for they become aware that in our company they are being ministered to – not manipulated. Fifthly, we learn that idolatry does not work and that the only fruitfulness that matters is the fruitfulness that comes from submission to God (v. 8).

'Who is wise?' asks Hosea. The answer is: the one who realises these things (v. 9). When we repent in the way Hosea describes in the first half of this chapter, we will experience the benefits he describes in the second half.

The challenge I have put before you over these past few days has been strong. I have walked this way myself and I know how disturbing it can be. But if repentance is to be deep enough to bring about changes at the core of our being, we must be willing to endure the challenge. No pain – no gain.

Father, let the steps I have taken over these past few days remain in my understanding so that whenever I find myself moving in a direction away from you, I know how to return. Grant it – in Jesus' name. Amen.

FOR FURTHER STUDY – Isa. 53:1–6; Jer. 50:6; Psa. 119:176
1. What is it our tendency to be like? / 2. What did David feel like?

He dwelt among us

FOR READING AND MEDITATION – JOHN 1:1–14

'He came to that which was his own, but his own did not receive him.' (v. 11: NIV)

The greatest demonstration the universe has ever seen of how to rightly relate to others was unfolded to this world when 'the Word became flesh and made his dwelling among us' (John 1:14: NIV).

Note again the phrase: 'and made his dwelling among us'. God did not make a momentary rift in the clouds and give us a fleeting glimpse of himself – a passing vision of his glory. No, he 'made his dwelling among us' – living with us from the cradle to the grave. It was not long – just over 33 years – but it was long enough to reveal God's character in operation amid the surroundings in which your character and mine are wrought. He met life as you and I meet it, but one of the main differences between Jesus and us is that he fully drew his security from his Father's love – we do it only falteringly and partially.

Over these past few weeks we have seen that love means going towards another person without self-protection, esteeming others more greatly than ourselves. This is precisely the kind of love which Jesus demonstrated when he came to earth to dwell among us. But, as we know, to involve oneself with others for the purpose of ministering to them is a risky business. Love can be rejected, as in the case of Jesus, but his love kept on loving still. Continued involvement at the point where people fail to receive our love is the measure of true ministry. Our Lord finally died for those who rejected him – for the soldiers who beat him and for the crowd who crucified him. The Scripture puts it thus: 'Having loved his own who were in the world, he loved them to the end' (John 13:1: NKJ).

Lord Jesus, love incarnate, I am thankful that when I seek the highest in love I find it in you. I could never have seen how to love unless I had seen it demonstrated through your life. And seeing is believing. I believe – help thou my unbelief. Amen.

FOR FURTHER STUDY – John 5:26–43; Matt. 8:34; Mark 6:1–3; Luke 4:28–29
1. What was Jesus' conviction? / 2. How did some respond to Jesus?

God's best gift!

FOR READING AND MEDITATION – 2 CORINTHIANS 9:6–15

'Thanks be to God for his indescribable gift!' (v. 15: NIV)

In the incarnation God relates to us in such a way that we in turn can relate to him. Imagine God trying to teach us the truth about relationships without giving us a demonstration of what it is all about. Suppose God had sat on a cloud, picked us up with a pair of celestial tongs and given us a lecture on relationships – what would it mean? Very little, I imagine.

Recently I heard of a father whose two small children used to plead with him every night just before they went to sleep to tell them the story of the three bears. The father said to himself, 'This is ridiculous. I'll record the story for them and let them play it for themselves.' The next day he made the recording and after showing them how to operate the tape recorder, he left them and settled down to read the evening paper. Soon the children appeared and climbed on to their father's lap. One of them said, 'We liked hearing your voice on the tape recorder but we missed you holding us in your arms. Please tell us it again – and this time hold us tight.'

How thankful we ought to be that our faith has within it an incarnation – God putting his arms around us and holding us tight. He held on to us all the way, even when we tried to shake him off at the cross. Think of it, he knew just how we would reject him, but still he came. What wondrous love! Too good to be true? Too good not to be true.

O Love divine, all loves excelling, we know you stooped to share. How deep that sharing is we cannot know, but we know enough to feel its impact in our beings. It is beyond us but deeply in us. Thank you, dear Lord Jesus. Amen.

FOR FURTHER STUDY – Phil. 2:1–11; Luke 2:1–7; Gal. 4:4
1. What does the manger speak to us of? / 2. Share Jesus with someone today.

The whole body aches

FOR READING AND MEDITATION – GALATIANS 5:1–15

'If you keep on biting and devouring each other,
watch out or you will be destroyed by each other.' (v. 15: NIV)

We turn now to focus on the question: what practical steps can we take to develop our relationships with one another in the church of our century? The first step, I believe, is to face up to reality and acknowledge that, generally speaking, as far as the area of relationships is concerned, the church is in a mess.

It is probably the greatest scandal in the universe that the church, which is designed by God to be the shop window through which the world can look and see what relationships are all about, reflects so poorly the principle of loving as we are loved. 'Parts of Christ's body,' says a Christian physician, 'are suffering from a disease called "relational conflictus" – caused by believers pulling against one another instead of alongside one another.' When relationships break down amongst Christians – and this happens all too often – those outside the faith become more convinced than ever that Christians lacks the very things they are in need of – love, affirmation and integrity.

In recent weeks (as I write this), I have heard of almost a dozen large Christian communities being split apart by relational conflicts – it was this fact that triggered me to write this present edition – and whenever this happens, it is inevitable that it is not just one section of the church that suffers – the whole body aches. You may not feel it in your own community, where relationships may be good, but believe me, when you see the big picture, it is a different state of affairs. And what's more, whenever those conflicts are made public, it gives the world the proof it is looking for that Christianity does not work.

O God, forgive us that we are such failures in the area of relationships. We come to you now in genuine and sincere repentance. We have much to learn. Help us, dear Lord, so that we will neither fail you nor the generation in which you have placed us. Amen.

FOR FURTHER STUDY – 1 Cor. 1:1–13, 3:3, 6:6; 2 Cor. 12:20
1. What did Paul write to the Corinthians about?
2. Could the same be written of your church?

The initiative is in heaven

FOR READING AND MEDITATION – REVELATION 1:1–8

'… To him who loves us … be glory and power for ever and ever! Amen.' (vv. 5–6: NIV)

Once we are prepared to face up to the fact that whatever else we, the people of God, do well, the thing we do least well is love as we are loved, then we are ready for the second step – to remind ourselves that love (*Agape* love) comes not as a result of pumped up effort but is our natural response to the awareness of how much we are loved. 'We love because he first loved us' (1 John 4:19: NIV).

This, in my opinion, is one of the most critical issues in the whole of the Christian life. I have dealt with it in detail in the earlier part of these meditations, but because it is such a crucial issue in living and loving effectively, I return to it in this summarised form. I often meet people who say to me, 'My problem is that I don't love the Lord as I ought to.' My usual answer to that statement is, 'That may be the problem as you see it, but I think the real issue is much deeper than that – it lies in the fact that you don't know how much the Lord loves you.'

The greatest and most effective Christians I know have one thing in common – they have a blinding realisation of how much they are loved by God. They have looked on the cross – for it is here that the heart of God is unveiled – until the scales have fallen from their eyes and they have seen that the heart of God is the heart of an aggressive lover. Those who take the time to focus continually on the fact that the initiative for love came entirely from heaven, and that the fount of true love is in the depth of God's own being, will, in the power of that revelation, move towards others with a love that doesn't want or need to bargain (love me and I will love you). They will love with a love that leaves every recipient free.

O Father, help me start every day by reflecting on the truth that only as your love flows into my heart can true ministry to others flow out of it. Drive this truth deeply into my spirit so that I never forget it. In Jesus' name. Amen.

FOR FURTHER STUDY – John 15:9–17; 2 Cor. 5:14–15; Gal. 2:20
1. How did Jesus describe the law of love? / 2. How did it affect the apostle Paul?

Proving your faith

FOR READING AND MEDITATION – JAMES 2:14–20

'… faith by itself, if it is not accompanied by action, is dead.' (v. 17: NIV)

Another step we need to take in order to develop a relational style that is truly loving and free from self-protection is deliberately to put ourselves in a position where we risk being hurt. I am not suggesting that we test our security in Christ by going up to people we don't know and seeing how we feel when they withdraw from us – that would be utterly foolish. But I am suggesting that in our day to day relationships amongst friends, neighbours, family and of course, our brothers and sisters in Christ, we put to the test our belief that we are deeply loved by Christ by moving more warmly towards others, even if it means risking rejection.

There are great risks in relationships, perhaps the biggest one being that when we move towards others, they may not respond. They may turn away, withdraw, or deliberately reject us. What do we do then? No one likes to be hurt, but if we are truly finding our life in God, then the hurt we receive from an unresponsive friend, spouse, son, daughter, or fellow Christian will be tempered by our knowledge of God's love for us. We will be hurt, but not destroyed.

It goes without saying, I hope, that this principle must be put into operation carefully and wisely. Don't begin by making a list of all the people you know who might not respond warmly to you and head in their direction. Wait for God to bring them across your path – and then put your belief to the test. Just as you will never know how strong a rope is until you are hanging on to it, so you will never know how secure you are in Christ until in love you move towards someone and then see them turn away.

Father, I see that I must be ready to put my faith in you to the test. Give me an opportunity this very day to demonstrate to someone the validity of your love to me – even though they may withdraw from me or reject me. In Jesus' name. Amen.

FOR FURTHER STUDY – Psa. 41; 2 Cor. 4:7–18; Prov. 18:24
1. How did the psalmist put it? / 2. How did Paul express it?

The power of a loving group

FOR READING AND MEDITATION – HEBREWS 3:12–19

'But encourage one another daily …' (v. 13: NIV)

Yet another step we can take in order to develop our relationships with one another in the Christian church is to meet together in small groups for the purpose of giving and receiving feedback. How do we know how we are doing in the area of relationships if no one reflects to us how we come across to others? John Stott, in his book *One People*, says, 'I do not think it is an exaggeration to say that small groups … are indispensable for our growth into spiritual maturity.'

One of the most transforming experiences in my life came after I sat for many hours with some fellow Christians, examining each other's relational styles. I learned that I would share an opinion with others only if I was sure it would not be disagreed with. I always had to be right. The group pointed out to me that this was defensive on my part – I was willing to give only those parts of myself that I thought others would be impressed with; thus they never saw the real *me* at all. I could have figured this out for myself, but it would have probably taken me years. The group lovingly brought this to my attention in hours.

We really do need the help of one another to see the subterfuges and camouflages that go on in our personalities. Someone might say, 'Why not trust the Holy Spirit or the word of God to bring to light the things within us that need to be changed?' This is my answer: the word of God shows us what we should be, the Holy Spirit shows us the work that has yet to be done, but our brothers and sisters in Christ can put their finger on the specific issues that need attention now.

O Father, I see how we, your people fail each other in not sharing with one another at a deeper level than we do. Lead me into a relationship such as the one I have read about today, so that I can become more mature in the way I relate to others. For Christ's sake. Amen.

FOR FURTHER STUDY – Mark 16:14–19; Acts 2:42–47; Heb. 10:19–25; Psa. 84:4; Micah 4:2
1. Where were the early disciples continually? / 2. What are we not to do?

Making God more real to others

'No-one has ever seen God; but if we love one another, God lives
in us and his love is made complete in us.' (v. 12: NIV)

My final suggestion for developing good relationships is this – focus on the fact that
when you rightly relate to others, you enable them to have a clearer and bigger
understanding of God. Every Christian knows that he or she is at all times wonderfully and deeply respected by God. This is an incontrovertible fact – nothing can be
added to it and nothing can be taken away. There is, however, a lot we can do for one
another to add to the feelings that underlie that fact.

Look at it like this: God is intangible and invisible. We, on the other hand, are
both tangible and visible. We are able to see each other, touch each other, and hear
each other. As physical beings we relate to one another in a way we do not relate to
God and in a way God cannot relate to us. When you are feeling spiritually low or
disconsolate and I move towards you with genuine care and concern, when I talk
with you, smile with you or cry with you, when my entire body language demonstrates to you that I care, then, although those things cannot add to the fact that God
loves you, they can greatly add to the feelings that go along with that fact.

God doesn't come to you and talk to you in an audible voice or put a warm hand
on yours when you are in need of support – but I can. He has made me as a physical being and he has made you in the same way, too. And when I need support – you
can give it to me. Together we can make the invisible God more real to each other
and bring about in each other's lives an experiential awareness of what it means to
be deeply loved by him. Seeing this clearly, and entering into it fully, makes the task
of rightly relating to others not just a duty but a delight.

O God, the fact that I can bring home to my brothers and sisters a deeper understanding and a
fuller enjoyment of what it means to be loved by you utterly overwhelms me. But I see it is true.
Help me make you more real to someone today. In Christ's name. Amen.

FOR FURTHER STUDY – James 2:1–9; John 13:35; 1 Pet. 1:22
1. What is the royal law? / 2. How do we sometimes commit sin?

Are you growing?

FOR READING AND MEDITATION – EPHESIANS 4:7–16

'… speaking the truth in love, we will in all things grow up
into him who is the Head, that is, Christ.' (v. 15: NIV)

Whilst every aspect of Christian living is important, the issue of whether or not we are growing in spiritual love is supremely important. If we are not growing in love for God and our neighbour, then we are not living – at least, we are not living abundantly.

Where do we begin? I suggest we start by looking at ourselves. Someone has said, 'Religion that does not begin with the individual does not begin.' The beginning must be within. We cannot point to the lack of spiritual growth in others and leave it at that, for that may turn out to be what psychologists call *projection* – projecting onto others the faults and lack we find in ourselves. It is an escape mechanism, a running away from responsibility. The first day of a new month is an appropriate time to engage in a spiritual check-up, so together let's face a few personal and probing questions: how well are we growing in God? What are the evidences that we are *taller* in God than we were this time last year? Are we conscious that there are things in our lives that greatly hinder our spiritual growth and development? Do we really want to grow?

We must be careful, of course, not to use these questions as a club with which to beat ourselves over the head. God does not bludgeon us into spiritual maturity; he beckons us into it. Where spiritual growth is concerned, we must feel the call – and the call to growth comes to us from above. God wills our growth and maturity. It is our destiny – and everything, except of course sin or evil, works towards it.

Gracious and loving Father, let this month be one of the greatest months I have yet known – especially in terms of my spiritual growth. I see that maturity is something you will for me; help me to will it, too. In Jesus' name I pray. Amen.

FOR FURTHER STUDY – Psa. 1; 2 Pet. 3:18; Psa. 92:12
1. What is a key to growth? / 2. What do the righteous grow like?

The stage is set for growth

FOR READING AND MEDITATION – MARK 4: 21–34

'All by itself the soil produces corn – first the stalk, then the ear,
then the full grain in the ear.' (v. 28: NIV)

We said yesterday that God does not to bludgeon us into spiritual maturity, but beckons us, and that the call to growth comes to us from above. What does this really mean? It means that God created the world of living things for growth and development. Everything works towards that end, everything, that is, except one thing – sin, or evil. Sin is an intrusion into God's universe and has thrown a monkey wrench into the machinery of human living. Except for this, all else – I repeat, all else – is made for growth and maturity.

Maturity is our destiny. Tagore, the great Indian poet and writer, sensed this when, in a moment of great inspiration and illumination, he exclaimed, 'Everything lifts up strong hands after perfection.' Of course, we can live against that destiny and hinder it, but it is our destiny, nevertheless, a destiny written into every nerve cell, every tissue and every organ.

Our passage today affirms the fact that God has set the principle of growth within the earth: 'All by itself the soil produces corn.' I suggest that God has not only put this principle of growth in the soil, but also in the soul. Once we are converted to Christ and have been redeemed from sin, then within our soul, 'Everything lifts up strong hands after perfection.' There is a drive within our being to grow up into the likeness of Jesus Christ. All we have to do in order to grow is clear away the hindrances and meet the conditions of growth. Then we grow – grow out of an inner necessity. When the conditions for growth are met, then nothing in earth or heaven can stop us from growing. The sky's the limit!

Father, I see that everything conspires to help me grow spiritually. I am in the grip of a divine intention. Help me yield and fulfil all the conditions that make a person grow. In Christ's name I pray. Amen.

FOR FURTHER STUDY – 2 Cor. 9:6–12; Col. 1:10–11; 2 Pet. 1:5–6
1. What are we to make every effort to do? / 2. What are we to increase in?

He died climbing

FOR READING AND MEDITATION – COLOSSIANS 1:15–29

'We proclaim him, admonishing and teaching everyone ... so that
we may present everyone perfect in Christ.' (v. 28: NIV)

It would not be going far wrong to affirm that the central thrust of all Paul's epistles
is his desire to produce mature Christians. If I were asked to put my finger on the
most pressing need in today's society, I would unhesitatingly state it to be the need
for spiritual maturity.

A Christian I spoke to some years ago who was struggling with a variety of
problems said, 'It's no use – I was never made for maturity.' I told him he was wrong
– in Christ we are all made for maturity. Introducing a Christian speaker at a meeting, a man used this beautiful compliment, 'I have known him for thirty years and
he has never changed – except upward. Many speakers lose their fire as they grow
older; this one never does. He is always growing.' Always growing – how wonderful.
Can this be said of you and me? On the tombstone of an old Alpine climber is this
inscription, 'He died climbing.' When the moment comes for you to be separated
from this world, will it find you still climbing?

Stretching before every one of us is still half a year. How are we to view all these
days ahead of us? As a daily grind – or a daily growth? If we allow God's word to
probe and penetrate our lives, then inevitably we will grow. If we pull back, resist
or prevaricate, then inevitably our growth will be retarded. So – reverently I say it –
for God's sake grow up.

*O Father, how I long for every one of the days that lie ahead of me to be days of dynamic spiritual
growth. Each day use your Word to show me my restrictions and then point me to your resources.
In Christ's name I ask it. Amen.*

FOR FURTHER STUDY – 1 Cor. 3:1–3; Eph. 4:14; 1 Cor. 14:20
1. What was Paul's indictment of the Corinthian church? / 2. What are we no longer to be?

We need never stop growing

FOR READING AND MEDITATION – PSALM 92:1–15

'The righteous will flourish like a palm tree, they will grow like a cedar of Lebanon.'
(v. 12: NIV)

Quietly the truth is taking hold of us – we are made to grow. The creative God has made us for creative growth; growth is the law of our being. When we violate that law, we violate ourselves. We feel unfulfilled, frustrated and unhappy.

The body, of course, ceases to grow after a certain time and begins to deteriorate. The process of decay can be minimised to some degree by the inner states of mind and spirit in oneself or in another. Of course, some people are afflicted with physical problems that affect the mind and the spirit, but in the end the body is destined for the dust. Unfortunately, many people are so closely linked to their bodies that deterioration of the body results in deterioration of the person. Some people spend their entire existence living only for the body and when the body begins to deteriorate – they deteriorate. Life's supreme tragedy is the triple decay of body, mind and spirit in oneself or in another. Of course, some people are afflicted with physical problems that affect the mind and spirit, but in my opinion they are by far the minority. Far too often, wrong mental attitudes take their toll on our physical frame and cause us to deteriorate more quickly than we should.

Recently I met a 72 year-old woman in a seminar on the subject of *Personal Growth*. She said to me, 'I am a little embarrassed at being in a seminar like this; am I too old to grow?' I said, 'My dear, you can keep growing until the day you die, and the more you grow, the more wonderful will be your later years.' She was overjoyed. A deteriorating body does not have to mean a deteriorating spirit. As long as we are on this earth, we need never stop growing.

O creative God and Father, help me to see the wonderful possibility of being a continuously growing and creative person. Show me that when my life is rooted in you, and not in the years, I am year-proof. I am always young in you. Amen.

FOR FURTHER STUDY – 1 Kings 4:26–34; Isa. 54:1–4; 1 Chron. 4:10
1. What did God give Solomon as well as wisdom? / 2. How did Isaiah put what?

The blessing of the by-product

FOR READING AND MEDITATION – 1 PETER 1:13–25
'But just as he who called you is holy, so be holy in all you do.' (v. 15: NIV)

It is difficult to think of any subject more important than spiritual growth. In my opinion, the decay of the person results in more unhappiness than all other causes of suffering combined. All other causes are marginal; this one is central. For a central and fundamental unhappiness descends upon the spirit if one knows or senses, consciously or unconsciously, that the central purpose of one's being – growth – is not being fulfilled. No amount of marginal happiness or adjustment can atone for this central dissatisfaction.

I would go as far as to say that if you are not a creative and growing person, you are an unhappy person. This central frustration spreads its dissatisfaction through all other satisfactions and makes them curdle and sour. On the other hand, when you are fulfilling the law of your nature by being a growing personality, then this spreads its central satisfaction through all the marginal happenings of life. Human happiness is a by-product of the creative, growing personality.

It is here that many people go wrong. They set out to find happiness instead of letting it find them – and thus it escapes them like a will-o'-the-wisp. If they gave up the chase for happiness and focused on the purpose of their existence, they would find happiness flowing in them as a by-product. Do you know that much of the iodine of the world is made as a by-product of nitrate in Chile? The manufacturers set out for saltpetre and incidentally found iodine. This is a parable. Set out to be a continuously growing person and incidentally, happiness will follow.

O Father, forgive me that I know so much about life except how to live it. I see that when I make happiness my goal, then it eludes me. But when I make growth into holiness my goal, then happiness comes as a by-product. Help me understand this – and live by it. In Jesus' name. Amen.

FOR FURTHER STUDY – 1 Tim. 4:1–16; Prov. 4:18; 2 Cor. 3:18
1. What was Paul's exhortation to Timothy? / 2. What would be the result?

I am the tadpole of an angel

FOR READING AND MEDITATION – ROMANS 8:28–39

'For those God foreknew he also predestined to be conformed
to the likeness of his Son ...' (v. 29: NIV)

Now that we are clear on the fact that we are made in the inner structure of our beings for growth and maturity, we ask ourselves: what kind of maturity does God have in mind for us? What is the goal of growth?

The passage before us today clearly shows that God's supreme goal for us is that we should become like Christ. *The Living Bible* paraphrase of today's text puts it thus: 'For from the very beginning God decided that those who came to him – and all along he knew who would – should become like his Son ...' As soon as we are converted God begins the process of making us more and more like Christ – a process which he finally completes when we get to heaven. I once heard an old Welsh preacher describe the glory that awaits the believer in heaven and the transformation that will take place when we see Christ. He ended his peroration with these words, 'Hallelujah! I am the tadpole of an angel.' Almost all the Christians who were present clapped their hands and shouted, 'Amen.' But I was disappointed – disappointed with the preacher's final statement and with my fellow Christians for agreeing with it. Our Christian experience will not end with us being turned into angels but transformed into the image of Jesus Christ.

Listen to how the apostle Paul put it: 'But we know that when he appears, we shall be like him, for we shall see him as he is' (1 John 3:2: NIV). God is so excited about his Son, the Lord Jesus Christ, that he wants everyone to become like him – not in physical or bodily appearance but in character. For it is character that the universe is all about.

Gracious God and loving heavenly Father, if it is true that character is what the universe is all about, then I see I am being made in the image of the world's most perfect character – Christ. I am eternally grateful. Amen.

FOR FURTHER STUDY – 2 Pet. 1:1–11; Gal. 2:20; Col. 1:27
1. Of what do we become partakers through God's Word? / 2. What was Paul's testimony?

Within an inch of quitting

FOR READING AND MEDITATION – MATTHEW 5:38–48

'Be perfect, therefore, as your heavenly Father is perfect.' (v. 48: NIV)

Today we ask ourselves: can we expect to be perfect in character this side of eternity? Is our text for today suggesting that this is what God expects of us? This utterance of Jesus in which he states that we are to be perfect on earth as God is in heaven is a verse over which many a Christian has stumbled. Yet however threatening and intimidating we may find this statement, it is a word which was uttered by our Lord, and so we must face it.

In the months following my conversion, these words were a great stumbling-block to me. I found them the most discouraging words in the Bible, and the more I read them, the more I thought to myself, 'It seems such an impossible project to live here on earth as perfectly as God lives in heaven that I might as well give up the Christian life right here and now.' The words of Matthew 5:48 brought me to within an inch of quitting the Christian life and over the years I have met hundreds of Christians who have told me a similar story.

But I discovered later that my problems with the text had arisen because I had misinterpreted it. I had thought it was perfection of character Jesus was imposing on me, but then I saw from the context that it was perfection of love: 'Love your enemies and pray for those who persecute you' (v. 44: NIV). What Jesus was saying was this: God's love is without discrimination; it is open to all, enemies as well as friends. When you love like that – without distinction or discrimination – then you are loving on earth as perfectly as your Father loves in heaven.

O Father, just as you have conquered my heart by your perfect love, help me to conquer everything and everyone by that same invincible power. Help me to love as I am loved. In Jesus' name I ask it. Amen.

FOR FURTHER STUDY – 1 John 2:1–6; Col. 1:28–29; Heb. 6:1

1. How is the love of God perfected in us? / 2. What did Paul strive for?

All-inclusive love

FOR READING AND MEDITATION – LUKE 23:26–43

'Then Jesus said, "Father, forgive them, for they do not know what they do" …'
(v. 34: NKJ)

We saw yesterday that when Jesus commands us to be perfect, he is not referring to a moralistic or a philosophical perfection but to the perfection of love. We must not forget that it is love which Jesus is talking about in the context of Matthew 5:43–48 – a love that is without distinction or discrimination. Listen to how the *Amplified Bible* translates Christ's command to be perfect: 'You, therefore, must be perfect, that is, growing into complete maturity of godliness in mind and character … as your heavenly Father is perfect.'

The Greek word for 'perfect' is *teleios*. It is an active word, a word which carries the meaning of moving towards a goal, of achieving a target. We were created in the image of God. Having perverted this image through sin, we are recreated in grace and predestined 'to be conformed to the image of his Son' (Romans 8:29: NKJ). The goal of the disciple is to live in this perfection, this *teleios*, this extension of the love of Christ. In context it means, as we have seen, that our love must be all-inclusive, as God's love is all-inclusive.

The way to understand this word *perfect* is to see that we can be *perfect* in embryo without being perfect in development. A bud, for example, may be perfect as a bud but not perfect as a flower. A five-year-old child may demonstrate a love that its parents and other members of the family would describe as *perfect*, but if by the time the child has reached 15 years, its love has not matured, then something is wrong. Love can also be *perfect* in intention even though its manifestation may be far from perfect.

Lord Jesus, you whose love was perfect not only in intention but also in manifestation, help me grow until my love is just like yours. For your own dear name's sake. Amen.

FOR FURTHER STUDY – 1 Thess. 3, 4:9–10; Eph. 3: 17–21
1. What was Paul's prayer for the Thessalonians?
2. What was his desire for the Ephesians?

It's the motive that matters

FOR READING AND MEDITATION – COLOSSIANS 3:1–17

'And whatever you do, whether in word or deed,
do it all in the name of the Lord Jesus …' (v. 17: NIV)

We ended yesterday with the statement: love can be *perfect* in intention even though its manifestation may be far from perfect. Perhaps an illustration might help clarify this point further. A father who had been away from home for several weeks returned to find his son so excited about his homecoming that the little boy could scarcely contain himself. He wanted to demonstrate how much he loved his father, so he said, 'Daddy, is there anything I can do for you?' 'Yes, son,' replied the father, 'you can bring me a glass of water.'

The little fellow ran pell mell into the kitchen, turned on the tap and poured some water into a glass. Then, grabbing the inside of the glass with his two dirty fingers, he brought it to his father. When the father took it from him, he saw two little muddy streams trickling down the inside of the glass. The father turned the glass around and drained it dry.

The little boy stood there rubbing his dirty hands on his jacket saying, 'Daddy, is there anything else I can do for you?' The father smiled and said, 'No, thank you, son, you've done enough for the moment.'

The little boy's love was perfect, even though the manifestation of that love was imperfect. It may be unrealistic to expect that while we are on the earth we can live perfectly, but it is not unrealistic to expect that while we are on the earth we can love perfectly. Since the perfection of which Jesus speaks is primarily a perfection of love, his command is not broken if that love is expressed imperfectly. It can be realised – and yet not realised; perfect as a bud, but not perfect as a flower.

Father, help me understand the great truth underlying spiritual growth: I have, yet I yearn to have; I realise, yet I do not realise; I am satisfied, yet I am not satisfied. I am the most satisfied, unsatisfied being on earth. Amen.

FOR FURTHER STUDY – John 15:1–13; 1 Pet. 1:22; 2 Cor. 5: 14–15
1. How can we be sure of abiding in God's love? / 2. What is the result?

Sinless perfection

FOR READING AND MEDITATION – 1 JOHN 1:1–10

'If we claim to be without sin, we deceive ourselves and the truth is not in us.' (v. 8: NIV)

We continue meditating on the thought that we should be *perfect* as our heavenly Father is perfect, but that we should not interpret the word perfect as a moralistic or philosophical perfection.

This is where many get into difficulties. They believe the statement to be saying, 'You are to live on earth as God lives in heaven, sinless, blameless and free from any stain of imperfection.' Such a command would be unrealistic. And I am not lowering the Christian standard when I say this. Over the centuries, a great debate has gone on within the Christian church over this issue. It has been summed up in the Latin words *non posse peccare* and *posse non peccare*, which mean, 'not possible to sin' and 'possible not to sin'. I do not believe that we will ever arrive at a stage in our spiritual pilgrimage here on earth where it is not possible to sin, but I do believe we can arrive at a place where it is possible not to sin.

It is possible, even in this evil world and with our infected natures, to act always with a perfect motive. We are only Christians-in-the-making but we can be perfect in love. And that is the maturity we must make it our goal to achieve – a maturity in love. We can love God with all our heart, all our mind, all our soul and all our strength and yet manifest that love imperfectly. For our actions are made up of intelligence and intentions. The intentions may be good, but the intelligence is less than perfect and therefore the action which is the offspring of these imperfect parents will be imperfect. Perfect character may not be ours until eternity; perfect love can be ours here and now.

Gracious and loving Father, I see that, although on this side of eternity I may never experience sinless perfection, I can experience perfection in love. May love, your love, be my guide in everything I do this day. In Jesus' name. Amen.

FOR FURTHER STUDY – 1 John 5; Heb. 3:13; Rom. 6:12

1. What controls the world? / 2. What are we to do daily?

Perfection vs perfectionism

FOR READING AND MEDITATION – PHILIPPIANS 3:1–14

'Not that I have already obtained all this, or have already been made perfect,
but I press on to take hold of that for which Christ Jesus took hold of me.' (v. 12: NIV)

The verse: 'Be perfect, therefore, as your Heavenly Father is perfect,' is so crucial to
the issue of our spiritual growth, that we must keep it before our gaze for a few more
days. I have mentioned already that over the years I have met many Christians who
have stumbled over this text. My own problems with it stemmed from the fact that,
being strongly perfectionist by temperament, I read into the word *perfect* the idea of
perfectionism. There is a great difference between the perfection spoken of by Jesus
and the personality problem known as perfectionism. Perfectionists always struggle with Matthew 5:48 because they look at it through the lens of their temperament
rather than through the lens of objective truth.

This leads to the question: what is perfectionism? A textbook definition is:
'Perfectionism is the morbid fear possessed by some people that others will not
accept them, nor will they be able to accept themselves, unless they do everything
perfectly.' It is a condition which afflicts multitudes of Christians and locks them
into what is often described as the *performance trap*. The perfectionist believes that
everything – his salvation and status with God, his relationship with himself, and
his relationship with others – depends on how well he performs.

There is nothing wrong, of course, with desiring to improve one's spiritual condition. but when one strives for improvement in order to be accepted rather than
because one is accepted, then the spiritual life soon gets into trouble and Matthew
5:48 becomes a threat rather than a thrill.

*O Father, if there is even the slightest degree of perfectionism in me, then show me how to root it
out – once and for all. Help me understand the difference between working to be saved and working because I am saved. In Jesus' name I pray. Amen.*

FOR FURTHER STUDY – Eph. 1:1–8; 2 Cor. 5:9; 1 Cor. 1:25–31
1. What does Paul declare to the Ephesians? / 2. What sort of people does God accept?

The tyranny of the oughts

FOR READING AND MEDITATION – 1 CORINTHIANS 15:1–11

'But by the grace of God I am what I am ...' (v. 10: NIV)

Perfectionism is one of the biggest hindrances to spiritual growth I know and one of the greatest contributors to discouragement, false guilt and inner stress. Perfectionists never feel they do enough for God to accept them. They live with the feeling that if they were to do a little better, then God would love them more. They cannot see that they are loved, not because of what they do, but because of who they are. Thus they get caught up in what Karen Horney describes as the 'tyranny of the *oughts*' – I ought to read more of the Bible, I ought to spend more time in prayer, I ought to do more for the church in which God has placed me, I ought to spend more time in sharing my faith.

There is nothing wrong with the desire to know more of God through his word and through prayer, or to share one's faith with others, but in the healthy personality this desire is the result of the divine beckoning, while in the perfectionist it is the result of an internal bludgeoning. Perfectionists are urged to improve their Christian lives from a self-centred motive: they feel more comfortable when they are doing something to alleviate their inner discomfort. It is a self-centred attempt to bring about spirituality: it is trying rather than trusting. Perfectionists equate perfection of performance with spirituality. Therefore they make every attempt to avoid appearing imperfect, as this, in their view, is tantamount to being unspiritual.

I make the point again that perfection, in the sense of flawlessness, is a human impossibility. The sooner we recognise this, the sooner we will grow.

Father, I am grateful for the way you corner me and constantly make me face the issue: are you the centre of my life or am I? Help me not to bow my knee to any idol – especially the idol of self. In Jesus' name I pray. Amen.

FOR FURTHER STUDY – Gen. 2:1–3; Heb. 4: 1–6; Matt. 11:29
1. What was the seventh day? / 2. What was Adam's first day?

Accepted in the beloved

FOR READING AND MEDITATION – EPHESIANS 1:1–14

'To the praise of his glorious grace, which he has freely given us in the One he loves.'
(v. 6: NIV)

After forty years in the Christian ministry, I am convinced that one of the root causes of spiritual and emotional conflicts is a failure to understand what it means to be, in the words of the King James version of today's text, 'accepted in the beloved'. Perfectionists (as well as many others) pay lip service to this text, but they have great difficulty in applying it to their lives because of their inner belief that God only accepts them when they are knocking themselves out, stretching themselves to the utmost limit, or working non-stop on the treadmill of spiritual performance.

This was a problem I struggled with in the early years of my Christian experience and it took many years for me to be completely free of it. Deep within me was a slave driver that kept on urging me forward, saying, 'Do more, preach more, achieve more.' When people talked about the joy of being 'accepted in the beloved', I agreed with them, then went right back to working as hard as I could to get God to accept me. I found release when someone said to me, 'If you were to lie down on this floor and never get up for a whole year, do you think that God would love you as much at the end of that year as he did at the beginning?'

'Of course not,' I said. 'How could he when I had spent a whole year not doing one single act of service for him?' As I spoke these words I saw how foolish they were, and in that moment I passed from dependence on performance to dependence on Christ. For the first time in my life, I understood what it meant to be accepted in heaven not for what I did, but for who I was.

O God, open up to me today what it means to be 'accepted in the beloved'. Help me understand the deep yet simple truth that in and through Christ, I am as precious to you, my Father, as your own dear Son. Amen.

FOR FURTHER STUDY – Job 42; Acts 10:34–35
1. What was the result of Job's humility and dependence on God?
2. Write out what it means to you to be 'accepted in the beloved'.

Symptoms of perfectionism

FOR READING AND MEDITATION – 1 JOHN 4:7–21

'… fear has to do with punishment. The one who fears is not made perfect in love.'
(v. 18: NIV)

This may surprise some, but after a lifetime of listening to people's problems and attempting to counsel them according to biblical principles, I have found that the one problem I have come across more than any other is the problem of perfectionism. And I am not alone in this discovery. The other day I came across the following statement by Doctor David Stoop, a Christian clinical psychologist in California, who, in his practice, counsels mostly Christians, 'It wasn't that I was looking for perfectionism to be a problem. It just seemed to keep cropping up as an issue with almost everyone who came to see me for counselling.' Dr David Seamands, author of a number of books on the subject of counselling, has said a similar thing.

What are the symptoms of perfectionism? There are many, but among the more significant are fear, hypocrisy and legalism. Perfectionists live with an inordinate fear. Fear is an anticipation of impending danger and the strong motivation underlying it is self-protection. The behavioural consequences of fear are avoidance and escape. Perfectionists expend considerable energy avoiding things that make them afraid, whether or not they are actually harmful. This fear can lead to a counterfeit spirituality. For example, perfectionists will avoid a difficult or painful situation out of what they believe to be a spiritual motive, when in reality the evasion stems from anxious self-protection.

Of course, not all fear is sin, but the fear that controls the perfectionist can soon lead to sin, because its grip upon his life will deter him from facing up to issues which would promote his spiritual growth.

O Father, take the shadows cast by fear from my face and from my heart. Let your love so invade me that no unhealthy fear will be able to live in me. I ask this in and through the peerless and all-powerful name of Jesus. Amen.

FOR FURTHER STUDY – Isa. 43:1–11; Gen. 26:24; Isa. 41:10; Matt. 10:26–31; Rev. 1:17–18
1. What was God's promise to Israel? / 2. Why are we not to fear?

Play-acting Christians

FOR READING AND MEDITATION – 1 PETER 2:1–12

'Therefore, rid yourselves of all malice and all deceit, hypocrisy, envy,
and slander of every kind.' (v. 1: NIV)

Today we look at the second symptom of perfectionism – hypocrisy. Hypocrisy is
pretending to a piety and virtue that do not actually exist. In the New Testament,
hypocrisy connotes either the idea of play-acting or of unprincipled action.

Perfectionists place a premium on flawless external behaviour and fail to dif-
ferentiate between motives and behaviour. Deceit occurs when the behaviour is
intended to disguise or misrepresent a person's true motives. Thus, two people can
engage in the same type of behaviour (like making a gift to a church or needy individual) but with different motives. A perfectionist oscillates between appearance
and reality and finally resolves the inner conflict by self-deception. He becomes, in
fact, an actor – the original meaning of the word *hypocrite* – but he lives the part he
is acting. He does not deny principles, but he admits exceptions.

The behavioural consequence of hypocrisy is inconsistency, and a major problem with all forms of inconsistency is that those who practise it are usually unaware
of it. Often an objective observer is needed to point out the inconsistency. If in a
church or group there is no one observant enough or aware enough to point this out
in a loving way and at an appropriate moment, then people can go on living stunted
Christian lives, never really growing, and missing out on true spirituality. One of the
reasons why perfectionism thrives amongst Christians is because so few are alert
enough to spot it. Thus a major preventative to growth thrives like a dark weed
amongst us. How sad. How very sad.

*O God, so often your finger goes unerringly to our problem. Forgive us that, generally speaking, we,
your church, offer no corporate challenge to the things that threaten to strangle our spiritual
growth. Forgive us and help us. In Jesus' name. Amen.*

FOR FURTHER STUDY – Acts 5:1–11; Matt. 7:3–5; Luke 6:46
1. What was exposed very early on in the New Testament church?
2. How did Jesus describe hypocrisy?

balancing the love scales

I almost took my life

FOR READING AND MEDITATION – GALATIANS 3:1–14

'Clearly no-one is justified before God by the law, because,
"The righteous will live by faith." ' (v. 11: NIV)

We look today at the third symptom that inevitably reveals itself in the life of a perfectionist – legalism. Legalism is an overly rigid adherence to the rules governing behaviour. The motivation behind it is the urgent need to win approval. Perfectionists view behaviour in black and white terms; no allowance is made for shades of grey. Anyone who deviates from the legalist's perfectionist standards is categorised as unspiritual.

The assumption underlying all legalism is that the person has within himself the capacity to gain God's approval. But perfectionism, with its accompanying legalism, is unable to achieve this approval. Legalism is unbiblical because God's approval is never predicted upon human performance. This is what Paul is saying in the verse before us today. Listen to how J.B. Philips translates this text: 'It is made still plainer that no one is justified in God's sight by obeying the law, for: "The righteous shall live by faith." '

The need to be perfect places a person in a destructive double bind. If the perfectionist fails to meet his own unrealistic expectations, he feels he has failed, but if he does meet them, he feels no glow of achievement because he thinks he has only done what was expected. Some perfectionists live in fear that they are going to make a mistake, and they go through life feeling that, no matter how hard they try, God is never pleased with them. A sad comment made by one perfectionist rings within my mind still, 'I really thought I had to earn God's love – and that almost caused me to take my life.'

Gracious God and loving Father, help me never to get into the dilemma of thinking I can do something to earn your love. And help me to help others who might be ensnared in this problem. In Jesus' name I ask it. Amen.

FOR FURTHER STUDY – Matt. 23:23–36; Isa. 29:13, 65:25
1. How did Jesus describe the Pharisees?
2. What was the Lord's complaint against the children of Israel?

Four life-determining concepts

FOR READING AND MEDITATION – DEUTERONOMY 6:1–12

'These commandments … are to be upon your hearts. Impress them on your children.
Talk about them when you sit at home …' (vv. 6–7: NIV)

Having looked at the symptoms of perfectionism, we turn now to consider the question: what are the causes? The problem arises mainly from faulty parent-child relationships. David Seamands suggests that four life-determining concepts grow out of the relationships we experience during our early years. The first is the way we see ourselves – our self-concept. The home is a mirror in which we see ourselves, and the way we evaluate ourselves will depend largely upon the worth or worthlessness reflected to us from the people who mean the most to us.

The second is our concept of God. We get our earliest feelings about God through our early relationships. And those feelings, as C.S. Lewis put it, '… are not just taught but also caught.' 'The home', says one writer, 'is the skylight through which we get our first understanding of the Deity.'

The third is our concept of others. However the family views others – as friends, competitors, antagonists, perhaps even enemies – that is the way a growing child will view them too. The home is a window through which we get a picture of others.

The fourth is our concept of reality. The family is the door to the world, and since doors open both ways, how a child experiences life depends on the parents' ideas of what comes in and what goes out of the home.

These are the four most important concepts in our lives and according to whether they are good or bad, positive or negative, they work either to help or hinder us in our growth into the kind of people God longs for us to be.

O Father, how thankful I am that any negative influences I may have picked up during my developmental years can be corrected in the relationship I now have with you. Now I am at home with you, teach me the way you want me to live. In Jesus' name. Amen.

FOR FURTHER STUDY – Prov. 22:1–6, 20:11; Matt. 21:15
1. What does the word 'train' mean (see Prov. 22:6)?
2. How did children respond to Jesus?

The cause of perfectionism

FOR READING AND MEDITATION – EPHESIANS 6:1–9
'Fathers, do not exasperate your children; instead, bring them up
in the training and instruction of the Lord.' (v. 4: NIV)

Now that we have looked at how powerful the influences are of our early relationships in the home, we are in a position to identify the root cause of perfectionism. The greatest contributory cause is being brought up by parents that were hard to please. When parents have high standards in the home and the child never seems to be able to reach up to them; when the love that is offered is conditional – 'Come up to our expectations and you will be loved'; when there is little or no affirmation but lots of criticism, then the child will often arrive in adult life feeling that his acceptance by others is determined by his performance. When he becomes a Christian, he then projects those feelings on to God and Scripture and comes out with a distorted view of both. And this projection (so I believe) is probably the number one reason why Christians fail to grow in the way they should.

It is important to remember that there is a difference between the perfectionist and the high achiever. The high achiever sets high goals for himself but is not devastated when he doesn't reach them – consequently, he is not dogged by constant feelings of failure. The perfectionist, on the other hand, is greatly upset when things are not the way he expects them to be, and he sees this as demeaning to himself as a person. He is unable to separate himself from his performance, and cannot live comfortably with his own failure or the failures of others.

I have said elsewhere that although God is perfect, he is not a perfectionist. How do I know that? It is because he has to live comfortably with you.

O Father, I see that if I am to grow, I must learn to live with my failures and not be devastated by them. Drive even more deeply into my spirit, dear Lord, the liberating truth that your love is unconditional. Amen.

FOR FURTHER STUDY – Col. 3:1–21; Titus 2:4; 2 Tim. 1:5
1. How do children get discouraged?
2. What did Paul observe about Timothy's faith?

Go with the flow

FOR READING AND MEDITATION – PHILIPPIANS 2:1–11

'Your attitude should be the same as that of Christ Jesus ...' (v. 5)

Having seen that Christ is both the starting point and finishing point for maturity, I would define spiritual maturity as the ability to respond to life and to any given situation in the same way that Jesus would.

If this definition is anywhere near being accurate, then it is obvious that many of us are not mature in practising spiritual love – myself included. How often do we demonstrate a Christlike spirit when our plans are crossed, or we find ourselves in difficult and confusing circumstances? It is so easy to be like Jesus when everything is going well; the test comes when the whole of our life suddenly seems to have been put into reverse. Maturity, it must be emphasised, is not a matter of age but of attitudes. I have known young believers, four or five years along in the Christian life, demonstrate more spiritual maturity than some who have been on the way for several decades. Thus maturity is not simply the result of an aging process. You can, in fact, age into infantilism. Maturity is getting hold of Jesus and his *Agape* love and letting him get hold of you, then walking with him into all that lies ahead.

Harnack, the great German theologian, said, 'Christianity does not provide solutions – it provides a goal and power to move toward that goal.' 'A goal and power to move toward that goal.' Profound words! The goal, the pattern, is, of course, Jesus, and the power we get to move towards that goal comes from the same source – Jesus. If Jesus is the goal, and if he provides the power to reach that goal, then, once we become Christians, we are in the grip of maturity.

Father, thank you for showing me that it is the intensity of the years, not their extensity, that measures maturity. By the years I may be a toddler, but by my longings after you I may be almost fully grown. I am so grateful. Amen.

FURTHER STUDY – Luke 2:25–40; Eph. 4:15; 1 Pet. 2:2
1. How did Jesus grow?
2. What characteristics accompanied this growth?

balancing the love scales

The first mark

FOR READING AND MEDITATION – JOSHUA 24:1–15

' …choose for yourselves this day whom you will serve …' (v. 15: NIV)

When is a Christian mature? In answering this question we must be careful not to give the impression that maturity is a destination when really it is a direction. Maturity is not so much having arrived at an end point, but moving through life with godly intent and purposes.

In recent years I have thought long and hard about maturity. As first and foremost mark of spiritual maturity I would like to suggest the following: it is the willingness to accept the responsibility for being what we are. There can be no denial of the fact that our surroundings, our upbringing, our environment, bring strong influences to bear upon us, but it is only those parts to which we respond that influence us. We do the responding. The choice is always ours. If we are half-persons with a half-output it is because, by a series of choices, we have consented to be that half-person. I have always thought it interesting that two people brought up in exactly the same circumstances and situations, with the same amount of pressures, difficulties and negative influences, can turn out quite differently. One focuses on the difficulties of the past and remains dwarfed and stunted, while the other focuses on turning those difficulties into stepping stones – and goes on to grow.

It has been said, 'We are what we respond to.' What is meant by this statement, I think, is that it is not so much what happens to us but how we respond to it that is important. We can't choose what happens to us, but we can choose how we respond.

Father, help me take the first step in maturity by accepting responsibility for what I am. This may challenge me, but drive this lesson deep into my spirit right away, for without challenge there is no change. Amen.

FOR FURTHER STUDY – 1 Cor. 13; Eph. 4:13; 1 Cor. 14:20
1. How did Paul grow up?
2. What is the relevance of 1 Cor. 13:11 to the rest of the chapter?

The answer to perfectionism

FOR READING AND MEDITATION – ROMANS 5:1–11

'… we have peace with God through our Lord Jesus Christ, through whom we have gained access by faith into this grace in which we now stand …' (vv. 1–2: NIV)

Previously, for a few days running, I delineated the evils of perfectionism because without doubt it is the prime preventative of spiritual growth. Perfectionism is counterfeit spirituality and a contradiction of authentic Christian living.

Now that we have looked long and hard at the problem, our next question must be: what is the answer to perfectionism? This can be given in one word – grace. I am referring here, of course, to God's grace – the unearned, unmerited favour which the Almighty delights to bestow on all those who are humble enough and willing enough to receive it. I have no hesitation in saying that if you do not understand the concept of grace – what it is and how it operates – you will never be able to understand the concept of growth. They are as inseparable as Siamese twins.

Here's how to understand the concept of grace. During the Napoleonic wars a young battle-weary French soldier fell asleep while on guard duty. He was court-martialled, found guilty and sentenced to death. His widowed mother somehow managed to get an audience with Napoleon himself and falling prostrate at his feet, she begged for her son's life to be spared. After listening to her for a while, the Emperor said coldly, 'Madam, your son does not deserve mercy; he deserves to die.' The mother hesitatingly replied, 'Of course, sir, you are right. That's why I am asking you to show mercy. If he were deserving of consideration, it would not be mercy.' Napoleon was so touched by the logic of the woman that he immediately arranged for the soldier to be pardoned. Keep this thought ever before you – if you deserved it, it would not be grace.

Father, how can I sufficiently thank you for the undeserved favour that reached down and lifted me from the deepest hell to the highest heaven? I didn't deserve it – yet you gave it. I shall be eternally grateful. Amen.

FOR FURTHER STUDY – 2 Cor. 8:1–9; Eph. 1:7, 2:7; 1 Tim. 1:14
1. How has God's grace been demonstrated?
2. What other word does Paul couple with grace?

A thing unheard of

FOR READING AND MEDITATION – ROMANS 3:21–31

'For all have sinned … and are justified freely by his grace through
the redemption that came by Christ Jesus.' (vv. 23–24: NIV)

We continue meditating on the subject of divine grace. The word *grace* comes from
the Latin word *gratia*, which was used to translate the Greek word *charis*. In ordinary Greek, *charis* meant gratefulness, graciousness, favour or kindness. Insurance
companies still use the word in this sense in relation to insurance claims. When, in
an appeal, they can find no legal reason to pay out, they may, out of the kindness of
their hearts, donate what is called *an act of grace*. The writer of the New Testament
used the word *charis* to mean the loving, unmerited kindness of God. The apostle
Paul used the word *grace* more than any other New Testament writer. Of the 155 New
Testament references to grace, 133 belong to him. No wonder he is often called *the
apostle of grace*.

Focus with me now on some of the essential features of divine grace. First it is
undeserved. Grace has nothing to do with our merit or demerit, our sinfulness or
worthiness. When the Bible says grace is free, it means that God freely bestows his
love and mercy upon us without the slightest limitation because of our sin. One
writer puts it like this, 'The moment you even bring up the question of unworthi-
ness and undeservedness, you cancel out the idea of grace.'

In the 2nd century, a critic of Christianity by the name of Celsus said the idea
of God loving sinners was 'a thing unheard of in any other religion'. He was absolutely right. Other religions say, 'Be good, straighten up your life, get things together
and then perhaps God will love you and accept you.' Christianity says, 'God already
loves you – come to him just as you are.'

*O Father, your grace is so overwhelming that I just can't take it in. Yet it is true. Help me to draw
heavily upon that grace, otherwise I am bankrupt. In Christ's name I pray. Amen.*

FOR FURTHER STUDY – Rom. 8:28–39; 1 Cor. 2:12; Matt. 10:8
1. How is God's grace given to us? / 2. What are we to do with God's grace?

The very last bastion

FOR READING AND MEDITATION – EPHESIANS 2:1–10

'For it is by grace you have been saved, through faith – and this not from
yourselves, it is the gift of God.' (v. 8: NIV)

Yesterday we said that one of the essential features of grace is that it is undeserved.
Another feature is that grace is unearnable. There is simply nothing we can do to
merit the grace of God. How often have I seen Christians start out on the highway
of underserved grace, saying, 'Hallelujah – I am saved by the grace of God!', only to
move away from that into believing that God's approval of them depends on how
well they perform. They are like the Christians in Galatia who started in grace but
then decided that the continuation of God's gift of grace depended on their own
input (Galatians 3).

Very many times I have counselled Christians who started the Christian life in
utter dependence on God, but then, albeit unintentionally, began to assume that
they could earn or win God's approval by works. Not *works* in the sense of good
deeds – they know better than that – but *works* in the sense of more Bible reading,
more prayer and more witnessing. There is nothing wrong with these things, of
course, indeed, they are essential to effective Christian living, but when we try to
change the grace base to a performance base then we set ourselves up for deep spiritual and emotional struggles.

In more recent years especially, one of the conclusions that I have come to is
that the very last bastion which the Holy Spirit has to conquer in our lives is our
refusal to admit that we are helpless to save ourselves. It seems it is easier to give up
any other thing than abandon the arrogant confidence that there is something we
can do to merit the grace of God. Yet that is the central sin.

*O God, I am so grateful that where sin abounds, grace does much more abound. Help me never to
forget it was my misery, not my merit, that drew you to me from above. I am so thankful. Amen.*

FOR FURTHER STUDY – Gal. 2:15–21; Matt. 7:22–23; Titus 3:4–5; 2 Tim. 1:9
1. What is the danger of works?
2. What did Paul underline to Timothy and Titus?

Salvation-by-promissory-note

FOR READING AND MEDITATION – MATTHEW 18:21–35

'The servant fell on his knees before him. "Be patient with me," he begged,
"and I will pay back everything." ' (v. 26: NIV)

Another essential feature of grace is that it is unrepayable. Some people try to turn the gift of grace into salvation-by-promissory-note. This is similar to the attempt to earn grace, but focuses more on the future – 'Lord, if you will forgive me, I promise to pay you back one day.'

Every time I read the passage before us today I wonder whether this was the servant's problem. Had he really received the king's forgiveness as an act of grace, or did he see it merely as an extension of time so that he could somehow earn enough to pay back the money? Frankly, I am at a loss to explain how he could have thrown the man who owed him a mere pittance into a debtor's prison unless it was that he had never really believed that he himself had been freely forgiven.

Thousands of Christians struggle with this problem today. They have been forgiven, but the full realisation of what it means has never really taken hold of them. Can you now see what I mean when I say that many spiritual and emotional struggles arise in the church when we do not have a clear theology of grace? One of the reasons why we find it difficult to forgive others is that we have never fully realised what it means to be forgiven ourselves. I have said elsewhere that when people say to me, 'My problem is I can't forgive,' I usually respond by saying, 'No, that's not your problem – your problem is you don't know how much you have been forgiven.' So let the thought grip you and take hold of you – grace is undeserved, unearnable and unrepayable.

O God, help me see once and for all how futile it is to try and repay the debts that by your Grace you have chosen to cancel. Give me the grace to receive what grace has given. In Jesus' name I ask it. Amen.

FOR FURTHER STUDY – Isa. 55:1–7, 43:25, 44:2–3; Micah 7:18
1. What does 'blot out' mean (Isa. 43:25)?
2. What does the Lord do when we return to him?

The self-sacrifice syndrome

FOR READING AND MEDITATION – ROMANS 11:1–10

'And if by grace, then it is no longer by works;
if it were, grace would no longer be grace.' (v. 6: NIV)

The issue we dealt with yesterday, namely, that grace is unrepayable, is so important that we must spend a few more days discussing it. When people do not have a clear understanding of what it means to be forgiven, and do not grasp that there is simply nothing they can do to repay God for his gift of grace, they make an attempt to repay him.

Sometimes they do this by self-atonement, that is, they refuse to forgive themselves for past sins or failures or they do not allow themselves to enjoy the legitimate pleasures of life. When counselling people who are concerned about their inability to enjoy themselves (on a fun-filled vacation, for example) I have many times traced the cause to the fact that they are inwardly seeking to punish themselves.

Other people attempt repayment through self-sacrifice. There is a legitimate place for self-sacrifice in the Christian life, of course, but I am thinking here of the type of spiritual asceticism in which a person becomes preoccupied with the idea that progress in the Christian life means constantly giving things up. A counsellor who worked in a Christian college tells how a young college student who was caught in the self-sacrifice syndrome came to him one day and said, 'Well, I finally gave it up.' 'Gave what up?' asked the counsellor. 'I finally threw my new stereo outfit into the college garbage bin,' said the student. The minister says that when the counselling session was over he rushed out to the garbage bin, but he was too late – someone had already retrieved the stereo. The next time he saw the student, still more things had been added to his ascetic list.

O Father, I see that unless I have a clear theology of grace, then I am open to all kinds of delusions and misinterpretations. Teach me all I need to know so that I can live a relaxed Christian life rather than a restless one. In Jesus' name. Amen.

FOR FURTHER STUDY – Gal. 2; Rom. 3:20; 2 Tim. 1–9
1. What can be wrong with doing all the right things?
2. How can we 'frustrate the grace of God' (Gal. 2:21)?

Heirs of grace

FOR READING AND MEDITATION – TITUS 3:1–11

'... whom he poured out on us generously ... so that, having been justified by his grace,
we might become heirs ...' (vv. 6–7: NIV)

Today we look at another way in which some people go about trying to repay God for his gift of grace – the way of sacrificial Christian service.

One of the most heartbreaking things I have had to endure as a counsellor is hearing so many ministers, missionaries and full-time Christian workers admit that repayment is the real motivation for their sacrificial service. I heard an American minister by the name of Stephen Brown say that a study done at Harvard University some years ago found that one of the major reasons why people went into full-time Christian service was out of a sense of guilt. They never felt fully forgiven and thus went into Christian service in order to try and work off their load of guilt. Some of John Wesley's biographers believe that it was this that motivated him to go to Georgia as a missionary. He is quoted as saying, 'I am going to Georgia to save the heathen, but, o God, who will save me?' Later, in Aldersgate Street, London, he came to know the grace of God in a deeply personal way and saw his debt as unrepayable.

Many missionaries have told me that in their quiet times their thoughts invariably focus on what they have given up in order to serve the Lord. People who have not been freed from this through a real understanding of grace know little joy and fulfilment in their lives. And in such people there is usually suppressed anger against God. They have done their best to repay him, but he does not keep his part of the deal by making them feel deeply rewarded.

Loving Heavenly Father, one thing is clear – unless I understand what it means to be saved by grace, then I will strive to be saved by works. Help me to stand forever on a grace base and not a performance base. In Jesus' name I pray. Amen.

FOR FURTHER STUDY – Rom. 8:1–8; Eph. 4:7; Heb. 12:28
1. What happens when we function in the energy of the flesh?
2. How are we to serve God?

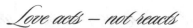

Love acts – not reacts

FOR READING AND MEDITATION – 1 JOHN 4:1–12
'This is love: not that we loved God, but that he loved us and sent
his Son as an atoning sacrifice for our sins.' (v. 10: NIV)

We spend one more day looking at yet another way in which some people try to repay God for his gift of grace – the way of scrupulosity. I am using this word in the sense of being meticulous or punctilious about the keeping of the divine laws.

But aren't we supposed to live up to God's commandments and the principles of his word? Aren't we expected to repay God with our service and our sacrifice? The answer is a firm and positive 'Yes'. We are to respond to God with obedience, but we are not to do these things in order to earn his grace or win his approval. If we go into the Christian life with the idea of balancing the credit-debit sheet, then we will create endless problems for ourselves, not the least being a slowing down of our spiritual growth. Keep in mind what I said earlier – you cannot understand growth until you understand grace. We are under an obligation to obey the laws of Christian living but we do not practise them in order to get God to accept us, but because we are already accepted. We do them, not in order to win his love, but out of gratitude for his love.

If God's love were conditional, that is to say, if it were caused by something in us, then it would also mean that there could be something in us that would stop God loving us. As the theologians put it: God's love is an action, not a reaction. His love depends not on what we are, but on what he is. He loves us because – he is love. We can reject his love and thus stop its inflow, but we can do nothing to stop its outflow. Nothing in us gave rise to his love and thus nothing in us can extinguish it. God loves us because he is love.

O God, help me see that my keeping of your commandments must always be the response to your love, not the reason for it. Show me how much I am loved, for then obedience flows more easily and more naturally. In Jesus' name I ask it. Amen.

FOR FURTHER STUDY – Gal. 4:1–11; Col. 2:20–22; Titus 1:16
1. What trap have some of the believers fallen into?
2. What are we no longer?

A good news, bad news story

FOR READING AND MEDITATION – ROMANS 5:12-21

'… But where sin increased, grace increased all the more.' (v. 20: NIV)

I don't know if you can feel these thoughts on grace taking hold of you as you read, but I can certainly feel them taking hold of me as I write. Nothing in heaven or earth is as wonderful as the message of divine grace. It is this which makes Christianity so different from all other religions. Other religions simply offer good views; Christianity offers good news – the good news that 'where sin abounded, grace did much more abound' (KJV).

I heard a story the other day that I must share with you. A farmer who had experienced several bad years went to see the manager of his bank. 'I've got some good news and some bad news,' the farmer said, 'which would you like to hear first?' The banker replied, 'Give me the bad news first and get it over with.' The farmer then spelt it out, 'With the bad drought and inflation I won't be able to pay anything on my loan this year and, as far as I can see, for a number of years to come.' 'My, that's very bad news,' said the banker. 'Now what is the good news?' 'The good news,' said the farmer with a smile, 'is this – I intend to keep on doing business with you.'

There is some very good theology in that story, providing we adapt it a little. The bad news is that sin has damaged the human personality to such a degree that even after we are converted, we still feel the *pull* of sin within our beings. And sometimes we fall or fail. However, the good news is that despite all our failures and imperfections, God still keeps on doing business with us. Can anything be more wonderful? The very thought of it makes me feel like throwing my hat in the air!

O God, help me to stretch out my hands and take all the grace I need to grow as you desire me to grow. Show me how to take with both hands and then give with both hands. For your own dear name's sake. Amen.

FOR FURTHER STUDY – Phil. 1:1-6; Jude 17-25; 2 Tim. 1:12
1. What was Paul's confidence? / 2. What is God able to do?

Grace is the soil

FOR READING AND MEDITATION – 2 PETER 3:10–18

'But grow in the grace and knowledge of our Lord and Saviour Jesus Christ …'

(v. 18: NIV)

I hope that by now the truth is crystal clear that there can be no real growth in the Christian life apart from grace. The grace of God is soil in which a Christian develops and grows. Where grace is not appreciated and understood, then growth will be dwarfed and stunted; where grace is absorbed and appropriated, then growth will be effortless and natural.

Our text today bids us 'grow in the grace and knowledge of our Lord and Saviour Jesus Christ'. Some of today's liberal theologians interpret this as meaning that you begin to grow in the grace and knowledge of Jesus Christ from where you are. In other words, you don't need to be converted, you simply decide you want to live like a Christian and begin to grow in Christian things. 'Moral progress,' they say, 'depends on how much effort you put into understanding and practising Christian principles. Put in little effort and there will be little growth. Put in lots of effort and there will be a lot of growth. This is what it means to be a Christian.' This is nonsense, of course, for the Scripture clearly tells us to grow *in* grace, not *into* it. You don't grow *into* being a Christian, you grow after you have become one.

The real question is, 'How do you get *in* grace?' It is by a new birth, a conversion, a changing of the centre of your life from self-interest to self-surrender. Planted in the soil of yourself, you simply cannot grow. You are not made to grow as a self-centred being. If you try by self-effort to grow in the soil of your own self, then you will grow only from tangle to tangle.

O God, I see I am doomed to sterility when I am planted in the soil of self, but I am destined for fertility when I am planted in you. I am the soul, grace is the soil, you are the Gardener. Therefore – I shall grow! Amen.

FOR FURTHER STUDY – Rom. 10:1–19; Psa. 27:1; Isa. 12:2; 2 Cor. 9:15
1. How does salvation come?
2. What does Paul say about salvation?

The way of transplantation

FOR READING AND MEDITATION – MICAH 7:1–14

'Shepherd your people with your staff, the flock of your inheritance,
which lives by itself in a forest …' (v. 14: NIV)

We ended yesterday with the thought that when we are planted in the soil of self, then the only growth we will experience is from tangle to tangle. The phrase *tangle to tangle* might take on more meaning if you read a different translation of the verse that is before us today. Listen to how Moffatt translates it: 'O shepherd, guide thy people, thine own flock, so lonely, lonely like a wild patch within a garden.' The universe is orderly because it obeys God – it is a garden. But if you obey yourself, then you are a wild patch of disorderliness within that garden of orderliness.

It is important to see that the first step in becoming a Christian is not the way of imitation, but the way of transplantation – shifting from a self-centred life to a God-centred life. This cuts across a good deal of modern-day teaching, which would find all the answers within the self. The big words being thrown around today are, 'Discover yourself'; 'Cultivate yourself'; 'Express yourself'. For a while this emphasis may work. It turns you away from negativism towards positivism. So far so good. But only *so far*. Beyond that initial boost, it cannot go. It exhausts its resources very quickly. So the aspirant in self-discovery, self-cultivation and self-expression turns to something else for inspiration.

The soil of self was never intended to be the seed bed of eternal values. The seed wrapped in itself will die. But when it is emptied into the earth, it lives again in the growing plant.

O Father, help me to see that I cannot begin to grow as a Christian until I have emptied my self into yourself. In my own hands I am a problem; in your hands I am a possibility. I want to be in your hands – now and forever. Amen.

FOR FURTHER STUDY – Luke 18:9–14; Prov. 28:26; 1 Cor. 10:12
1. What was Jesus teaching in the parable of the Pharisee and the tax collector?
2. What was Paul's warning to the Corinthians?

God himself obeys his own law

FOR READING AND MEDITATION – PHILIPPIANS 2:1–11

'Who, being in very nature God … made himself nothing …' (vv. 6–7: NIV)

So important is this issue that we grow *in* grace and not *into* it, that we dare not move on until all aspects have been made clear. Let me therefore make the point again – the Christian life begins with self-surrender. Our text shows that even God himself comes under this law. The central thing in the Incarnation is this: he 'emptied himself … Therefore God raised him high …' (vv.7,9: Moffatt). This is the inexorable law of life for God and man: lose your self and you find it again.

Recently I heard of a very sophisticated woman who faithfully went to church every Sunday, and considered herself very religious. One day she was in a business meeting in her church when she heard Christ say to her: 'This is not for you. Come outside, I want to talk to you.' She was hesitant to do what the voice suggested, as it meant disturbing two or three people, one of them her husband, and she thought it ill-mannered to push right past them. But the voice persisted, so she went. Outside, the Lord spoke to her in such a personal way that he seemed to pull out of her the buried resentments, the hurts, the hostility and the self-centredness that had filled her life for years. She was ashamed and said, 'What shall I do now?' The Lord said, 'What would you like to do?' She said, 'Let's have a funeral and bury everything.' She did, and she went back into the church having experienced for the first time in her life a personal encounter with Christ. A new birth had taken place. She was now in grace; free to grow.

God calls us in many different ways: it doesn't matter how we come to him as long as we end up at his feet – changed.

O Father, you emptied yourself for my sake, now show me how to empty myself for your sake. I know that grace is available to me to do anything you ask of me. Help me appropriate it. In Jesus' name. Amen.

FOR FURTHER STUDY – Luke 14:7–14; James 4:10; 1 Peter 5:5–6
1. What did Jesus teach in the parable of the guests at the wedding feast?
2. What are we to be clothed with?

A poor place for shelter

FOR READING AND MEDITATION – ACTS 27:3–12

'… the harbour was unsuitable to winter in …' (v. 12: NIV)

Our passage today tells us the story of how Paul on his voyage to Rome encountered some severe weather and found himself in a harbour which bore the name Fair Havens. Despite its beautiful and impressive name, however, Fair Havens was badly situated and couldn't protect the traveller against winter winds and storms. It was a fair weather harbour only, and was a poor place in which to spend the winter.

This story reminds me of those churches where everything is preached or discussed – except conversion. They are fair havens with lovely sounding names, but are not very secure in a storm. Many people are attempting to take refuge in churches that have lovely spiritual names but 'are badly placed to winter in' (Moffatt). They can't stand up against the rugged facts of sin, death and disaster.

Many years ago, when on holiday with my wife and family, I slipped into such a church and heard a man say, 'The great difference between a Christian and a non-Christian is that the Christian knows that he can sin and then find forgiveness for that sin.' I thought it unfortunate that he said *can*, rather that *if*, and I put it down to a slip of the tongue. However, it soon became clear that his words were part of a studied statement on spiritual laxity. He focused more on human helplessness against sin than on how sin can be overcome through the transcending grace of God. Churches that focus more on the power of sin than the power of transforming grace are like Fair Havens – 'badly placed for wintering in'.

Father, I am thankful that where sin abounded, grace did much more abound. And that grace is for me. Help me to absorb it and appropriate it, this day and every day. In Christ's name I ask it. Amen.

FOR FURTHER STUDY – Col. 2: 1–14; Job 11:14; Isa. 55:7; Eph. 4:22
1. How are we to deal with sin? / 2. How does God deal with sin?

My hands have corns on them

FOR READING AND MEDITATION – ROMANS 6:1–11

'If we have been united with him … in his death, we will certainly also be
united with him in his resurrection.' (v. 5: NIV)

If we focus on the transforming grace of God rather than on the power of sin, we
realise once more the importance of knowing Christ personally before we can move
on to become like him. Really the first step in spiritual growth is a step backwards,
for we have to get rid of our old values before we establish new ones. The verse
before us today shows us how we do this – we must go to the cross and there see
ourselves as dying with Christ. Each of us must die to the kind of people we are –
self-centred, proud, resentful – and then, when that happens we will find ourselves
rising to share the new life that Christ brought with him when he rose from the dead.
Listen to how the *Living Bible* paraphrases today's text: 'For you have become a part
of him, and so you died with him … and now you share his new life, and shall rise
as he did.'

A woman wrote to her minister, 'My hands have corns on them from working
and trying so hard to be good.' She was looking at her own hands instead of the nail-
pierced hands of Christ. In that condition, all she could hope for was self-salvation,
which of course, is no salvation at all.

The purpose of Christian redemption is to save us from ourselves. Prior to our
conversion, our biggest sin is the violation of the first commandment: 'You shall
have no other gods before me' (Ex. 20:3: NIV). The biggest and most persistent of
all rival gods is our self. If you have never moved from self-sufficiency through self-
surrender and put your life into the hands of the Saviour, then I urge you to do it
now. Pray this prayer with me and mean it:

*O God my Father, I turn to you now and repent of the fact that I have put myself, and not you, in
first place, and thus have made myself God. I surrender myself into your hands and take you now
to be my Lord and Saviour. Receive me and change me. In Jesus' name I pray. Amen.*

FOR FURTHER STUDY – Luke 13:1–3; Acts 3
1. What did Jesus teach in these verses? / 2. What did Peter declare to the people?

Activity – or receptivity?

FOR READING AND MEDITATION – PHILIPPIANS 2:12–24

'… continue to work out your salvation … for it is God who works in you
to will and to act according to his good purpose.' (vv. 12–13: NIV)

Now that we are clear on the issue that we do not grow into grace but we grow when we are in grace, our next question must be: what are the basic principles we must know and practise in order to grow in spiritual love, to mature into the likeness of Jesus Christ?

Over the centuries, preachers and teachers have tended to polarise on this. One group says that growth comes from obedience to the claims and commands of Christ, and their favourite text is: 'Work out your salvation with fear and trembling …' The other group says that growth is not so much the result of activity as of abiding in Christ, and their favourite text is: '… for it is God who works in you to will and to act according to his good purpose.' Activity or receptivity – which is right?

Both are correct, providing they are held together. You will notice that our passage today lays as much stress upon receptivity as it does upon activity. I believe that those who take a position on just one side of these two great truths fall into error. For, very often, error is truth out of balance.

But we must go further – those who accept these two great truths but put them in the wrong order, are equally in error. Activity must flow out of receptivity – reverse the order and growth will be impeded. Paul commands us to be obedient because God works in us to will and to act according to his good purpose. The secret of growing in Christ is thus very simple. All you have to do is take in and give out.

O Father, I see that there is a divine order in everything and when I get that order wrong, every-thing turns wrong. Help me never to forget that your inflow must precede my outflow. In Christ's name I ask it. Amen.

FOR FURTHER STUDY – Col. 3:1–17; Psa. 51:10; 2 Cor. 4:16; Titus 3:5
1. What are we 'renewed' in? / 2. What are we to allow to dwell in us?

Not in your own strength

FOR READING AND MEDITATION – HEBREWS 13:5–21

'May the God of peace … equip you with everything good for doing his will,
and may he work in us what is pleasing to him …' (vv. 20–21: NIV)

We pause to pick up on a phrase in yesterday's reading: '… work out your salvation with fear and trembling.' 'Fear and trembling' – is this how we are to live the Christian life? This is a phrase that legalists and perfectionists delight to fasten on. They say, 'Look, we are to strive hard at being Christians – the Bible says so.'

Let's look at this for a moment because it is an extremely important issue. The phrase 'fear and trembling' occurs three times elsewhere in Paul's letters (1 Corinthians 2:3; 2 Corinthians 7:15; and Ephesians 6:5: NKJ); it connotes distrust of self, its abilities and its resources. We are not to work out our salvation through human effort but through the divine enabling – 'not in your own strength' (Philippians 2:13: Amplified).

At a well-known national shrine in India a visitor was told, 'This is not a place of pilgrimage; this is a place of striving.' The atmosphere around the shrine spoke to the visitor of severe self-discipline. Salvation was to be attained by one's own disciplined efforts. It was a salvation by attainment. When I read that story and filed it away for future reference, I said to myself, 'I'm glad salvation isn't an attainment, but an obtainment – the gift of God.'

This, then, is the order. First: surrendering – becoming God-centred or God-loving instead of self-centred or self-loving. Second: receiving – accepting the gift of God's love and living by grace, instead of taking our own resources and living by groans. Third: overflowing – because we are linked to infinite resources. We take in God's love and we give out his love to our neigbours.

O Father, how can I thank you enough for showing me that growth in you comes not out of striving but surrendering. Teach me the secret of receptivity, for then I shall never be empty. In Jesus' name. Amen.

FOR FURTHER STUDY – Zech. 4:1–6; 1 Cor. 2:3; 2 Cor. 7:15; Eph. 6:5–10
1. What was the word of the Lord to Zerubbabel?
2. What does Paul link to 'fear and trembling'?

Humble enough to receive

FOR READING AND MEDITATION – JAMES 4:1–10

'That is why Scripture says: "God opposes the proud but gives
grace to the humble."' (v. 6: NIV)

We talked yesterday about a national shrine in India that was described by someone as 'a place of striving'. Such a place produces a strained piety, and where there
is strain, there is drain – strained souls become drained souls.

I heard a preacher tell a story about someone who died and went to heaven. As
he was about to enter in through the pearly gates, the man saw a pile of packages. 'What are all these packages?' he asked the Keeper of the Gate. 'These are blessings which were asked for but for some reason no one ever came to collect them,'
was the reply.

In the Bible, the invitation to receive is as definite as the command to renounce.
And when you learn the art and attitude of receiving, you soon go on to the next step
– rejoicing. This is the natural result, for a grateful heart cannot meditate long upon
the fact of grace without rejoicing. Listen to how J.B. Phillips translates some of the
verses before us today: 'You crave for something and don't get it; you are murder-
ously jealous of what you can't possess yourselves; you struggle and fight with one
another ... Do you imagine that this spirit of passionate jealousy is the Spirit he has
caused to live in us? No, he gives us grace potent enough to meet this and every other
evil spirit, if we are humble enough to receive it.'

'Humble enough to receive it.' That's it! Those who are humble enough to receive the gift of God's grace will soon sing about God's grace. The striving attitude
does not sing – all it does is sigh.

*Father, I am so glad that when my life is open to receive your grace, I can begin every day, not with
a sigh, but with a song. Help me to be humble enough to receive and grateful enough to pass on to
others. In Jesus' name. Amen.*

FOR FURTHER STUDY – Matt. 18:1–4; Prov. 22:4; Micah 6:8
1. How did Jesus draw attention to humility? / 2. How are we to walk?

Consider the lilies

FOR READING AND MEDITATION – MATTHEW 6:25–34

'And why do you worry about clothes? See how the lilies of the field grow.
They do not labour or spin, (v. 28: NIV)

We continue focusing on the fact that the first law of growth is receptivity. We must take in before we can give out; we must receive before we can offer.

One of the things I have noticed with reference to the text before us today (especially in the past, when people were more familiar with it in the Authorised Version) is that when quoting it, so many people refer just to the first part: 'Consider the lilies' – and leave the part: 'how they grow' unemphasised. But the latter part of the sentence is important. Our Lord is teaching men how to grow, and he points to a plant. How does it grow? By getting tense and anxious and striving to grow? Jesus rejected this: 'Who of you by worrying can add a single hour to his life?' (v.27). You can't grow by being anxious and tense about it – yet this is precisely what many Christians do.

The plant grows by its receptivity to earth and air and sun. It learns how to take, to receive. It keeps the channels of receptivity open and the earth and sun do the rest. This is the secret Jesus is teaching us through the illustration of the lilies. When we learn that, we have learned one of the most important lessons of the Christian life. Our life is described as a fight, but it is a fight of faith. Many set out to fight with their own resources and they finish up with weariness, fatigue and exhaustion. When we set out to fight the good fight of faith, that is, with God's resources, then the end is not exhaustion but exhilaration. We have enough and to spare for the next encounter. We are more than conquerors; we are conquerors who have conquered their own exhaustion.

My Father and my God, help me to learn the secret of living by relaxed receptivity – living by grace rather than by groans. Show me that everything I need in order to grow is available to me through grace. Help me assimilate your grace. In Jesus' name. Amen.

FOR FURTHER STUDY – Hosea 14; Psa. 84:7, 92:12
1. What does God promise to those who repent and receive?
2. What five things are evidenced?

Resting in his rest

FOR READING AND MEDITATION – COLOSSIANS 2:1–15

'So then, just as you received Christ Jesus as Lord, continue
to live in him, rooted and built up in him …'

(v. 6: NIV)

We pause a little longer on the attitude of receptivity. When we are planted in Christ by surrender, then the verse before us today is fulfilled: 'Grow out of him as a plant grows out of the soil it is planted in, becoming more and more sure of the faith as you were taught it, and your lives will overflow with joy and thankfulness' (J.B. Phillips). When we are rooted in Christ and see our effortless growth, we know that this is what we were made for. Out of the self-verifying assurance that Jesus is our *ground*, we begin to overflow with joy and thanksgiving; not a joy and thanksgiving over this or that event, but over the fact that our lives are planted in what can sustain us now and for ever. It is a life joy, not an event joy.

Another passage that points us in the right direction of relaxed receptivity is Hebrews 4:1, 3: '… the promise of entering his rest still stands … Now we who have believed enter that rest …' (NIV). When we surrender to God, and learn what it means to draw daily upon his grace, we have the inner assurance that we have entered into 'his rest'. It is the rest of adjustment to reality, of feeling that this is the right way to live, that we have cosmic approval for our way of life, that the sum total of reality is behind us, is approving of us, is furthering us. We enter into the same rest as God.

Recently I came across this choice verse: 'Spiritual stability depends on the grace of God, and not on rules of diet' (Heb. 13:9: J.B. Phillips). Spiritual stability depends on what God does for us, not on what we do for him.

O God, I am so thankful that through the door of faith I can enter into rest – your rest. Help me to rest in your rest, with all my restlessness dissolved. In Jesus' name. Amen.

FOR FURTHER STUDY – Matt. 13:1–8, 19–23; Rom. 11:16; Eph. 3:16–17

1. What is Jesus teaching in the parable of the sower? / 2. What does the root need to be?

The 'try harder' syndrome

FOR READING AND MEDITATION – ISAIAH 26:1–12

'You will keep in perfect peace him whose mind is steadfast,
because he trusts in you.' (v. 3: NIV)

We continue focusing on the fact that spiritual growth first of all involves depending on God to work inside us, enabling us by his strength to desire and carry out his will, and then means working out our salvation with awe and responsibility. But if the truth that we must depend on God to flood our lives with his grace and power is to be more than just inspired rhetoric, how do we go about it? Several years ago a man came up to me after I had spoken at a meeting in Leicester Cathedral and said, 'You told me what I should do – be receptive to the grace of God – but you didn't tell me how.' I don't want to make the same mistake here, so let's focus now on the *how*. How do we learn the art of dependence on God?

I will answer this question as best I can, but I have to say that while the answer is simple, it is more elusive than first appears. Perhaps that's why so much teaching on the subject of spiritual growth gives as the single answer: determined and disciplined effort. Someone has described it as the 'try harder syndrome'. I know Christian teachers and counsellors whose answer to all the problems of the Christian life is just that – 'Try harder.' It doesn't matter whether the problem is that we are doing something we should not be doing, or not doing something we should be doing, the answer is always the same – 'Try harder.'

But that is only part of the answer; to grow spiritually does involve effort (as we shall see) but unless we understand what it means to trust deeply, we will become what someone has described as 'rocking horse Christians' – plenty of motion but no progress.

My Father and my God, help me understand this important issue of what it means to trust deeply. For I see that if I am to grow, it must be more than a fine idea, it must be a living reality in my life and experience. Help me, dear Lord. In Jesus' name. Amen.

FOR FURTHER STUDY – Phil 4:1–7; 1 Pet. 5:7; Eph. 2:14

1. What are we not to be anxious about? / 2. What is the result?

More than obedience

FOR READING AND MEDITATION – PSALM 84:1–12
'O Lord Almighty, blessed is the man who trusts in you.' (v. 12: NIV)

We said yesterday that the strategy for growth that is based on effort is more easily defined than the strategy that is rooted in dependence on God. This is why sermons and books about growth usually involve instructions about learning biblical principles and then living consistently with them. Some church leaders view spiritual growth solely in terms of how well church members perform their Christian duties. Our spirituality is then judged by how often we go to church, how regularly we give money to the church, and how meticulously we observe the rules and regulations drawn up by our church leaders.

Don't hear me deriding this – there can be no real growth in the Christian life unless we choose to obey the principles of Christian living which are detailed for us in the Scriptures. But the point I am making is that there is more to spiritual growth than just obedience.

Our Lord has strong, indeed harsh, criticism for those who simply focused on obedience as the hallmark of spirituality. In his rebuke to the Pharisees, our Lord declared a principle that must guide our thinking in relation to spirituality – visible conformity to external expectations is to be commended but true spirituality involves more than that. The Pharisees performed well, their level of conformity was high, but listen to our Lord's remarks when he spoke to them: 'You clean the outside of the cup and dish, but inside they are full of greed and self-indulgence' (Matthew 23:25: NIV). Little wonder that our Lord was not a favourite speaker at their conventions!

Gracious and loving Father, I want to be a balanced Christian, growing in spiritual love, one who knows the relationship between performance and dependence. Unfold to me more deeply the meaning of both. In Jesus' name I ask it. Amen.

FOR FURTHER STUDY – 2 Cor. 10:1–12; Prov. 20:6; Matt. 6:1–18
1. What is not wise? / 2. What is the tendency of the human heart?

This 'terrible tendency'

FOR READING AND MEDITATION – ROMANS 7:7–25

'So I find this law at work: When I want to do good,
evil is right there with me.' (v. 21: NIV)

Today we ask ourselves: why is it so difficult to trust? I have no hesitation in saying that throughout my Christian life – a period spanning more than forty years – the most difficult thing for me has been trust. I still struggle with this – not as deeply as I once did – but I am nevertheless conscious of a problem in this direction. I am much more able to turn to a passage of the Bible, meditate on it, expound it and write about it than I am to trust it. Performance comes easily to me. I fall on my knees and pray, or get up and preach, at the drop of a hat. But trust – that's different!

I have thought long and hard about this and with the help of other Christian writers and thinkers, I have come to see that the reason why we find it so difficult to trust is that there is something in our nature that hates to be dependent. Ever since Adam and Eve violated the covenant God made with them in the Garden of Eden, everyone who has been born into this world (with the single exception of Jesus Christ) has a nature that is committed to independence. I have often described the original sin in the Garden of Eden as a 'declaration of independence' – a collision of a human will with the will of the Creator. All Adam's descendants struggle with the grim reminder of the Fall, for within every single one of us there functions a desire to make our lives work through self-sufficiency and self-determination.

But doesn't conversion sweep away this terrible tendency? Not entirely. And what is more, unless it is recognised and acknowledged, then it will work insidiously at the core of our beings to hinder our growth in Christ.

My Father and my God, I see I have inherited a legacy from Adam which can be called Do it your-self. Help me be aware of its insidious nature and of how it can hinder my growth and development in you. In Jesus' name. Amen.

FOR FURTHER STUDY – Rom. 8; Gal. 2:20
1. How many times is the word 'I' mentioned in Romans 7:14–25?
2. What law does Paul mention in Romans 8?

Still enjoying freedom

FOR READING AND MEDITATION – 1 CORINTHIANS 1:18–31

'… Let him who boasts boast in the Lord.' (v. 31: NIV)

We ended yesterday with the thought that unless we recognise the terrible tendency within us that moves us towards self-sufficiency and self-determination, it will work insidiously at the core of our beings to hinder our spiritual growth.

How is this? Let me illustrate. Some years ago I was involved in counselling a young man whose years of struggle to overcome sexual sin had brought him to the edge of a breakdown. Previous counsellors had tried to help him by encouraging him to spend more time in prayer, in deeper study of the Scriptures, in greater church involvement and so on, but although he had given himself rigorously to all these things, none of them seemed to help. There was nothing wrong with the advice his previous counsellors had given him, but they had failed to get to grips with one thing – the 'terrible tendency' towards self-sufficiency. I gently brought him face to face with his desire to find release from sexual bondage through self-effort and self-determination. 'Can it be,' I said, 'that for your release you are depending more on your spiritual exercises than on God? Do you see the solution to your problem as revolving around the amount of effort you are putting into the task of bringing about your spiritual freedom?' For a moment he appeared thunderstruck. Then he said, 'That's it! I see it all so clearly now. I have been relying on my efforts, my disciplines, my exercises, rather than on God.' There and then he fell on his knees, repented of his self-sufficiency, and rose to a new sense of freedom.

That was ten years ago. I spoke to him on the telephone just a few days ago. He is still enjoying spiritual freedom.

O God, it is clear that if I am to discover how to grow, then I need to be aware of how self-serving motives can stain even the noblest deeds. Help me see, dear Lord – see to the deepest parts of my being. In Jesus' name. Amen.

FOR FURTHER STUDY – Gal. 5:1–18; John 8:36; 2 Cor. 3:17
1. What is the 'yoke of slavery' (Gal. 5:1) that Paul says we can fall into?
2. What does Jesus mean by 'free indeed'?

Nothing more humbling

FOR READING AND MEDITATION – PSALM 51:1–13

'Surely you desire truth in the inner parts; you teach me
wisdom in the inmost place.' (v. 6: NIV)

We have been saying that one of the reasons why we find it difficult to trust is
because there is something within our nature that hates to be dependent. And unless we recognise the fact that within us there is a depth of corruption that stains
everything we do – even our efforts to improve – with selfishness, we will never
come to know the joy and freedom that flows from dependent trust.

We are ready now, I think, to face a sentence I have been wanting to write for
several days: spiritual growth comes out less because of what we try and do and how
we try and do it, and more because of our willingness to face our stubborn commitment to independence. I find that many Christians overlook (or even deny) this
fact. And it is easy to see why. There is, as we said the other day, something terribly
attractive about knowing what to do to add a cubit to our spiritual stature. Nothing
is more humbling than the recognition that we are entirely dependent on someone
else to make our lives work. But unless we face that fact, our spiritual obedience may
work towards strengthening our self-sufficiency.

Do you see the difficulty we come up against here? Facing realistically the fact
that we are utterly helpless to make our lives work without God, puts us in touch
with a level of helplessness to which our carnal nature does not want to admit. None
of us likes to feel helpless, but that is precisely the position we must come to if we
are to know what it means to trust deeply. The greater our sense of helplessness, the
more we will be able to trust.

*O God, you know how instinctively I fight any feeling of helplessness that rises within me. Yet I see
that unless I admit my spiritual helplessness I can never know what it means to trust deeply. If ever
I needed your help I need it now. Help me. In Jesus' name. Amen.*

FOR FURTHER STUDY – Psa. 37:1–7; John 3:27; Jer. 10:23; Psa. 127:1–2
1. What has God promised to those who trust in him?
2. When is our 'labour in vain' (Psa. 127:1)?

The need to see things clearly

FOR READING AND MEDITATION – PSALM 139:17–24

'Search me, o God, and know my heart … See if there is any offensive way in me …'
(vv. 23–24: NIV)

Perhaps one of the greatest difficulties we face as we move along the path to spiritual growth is the difficulty of coming face to face with our basic helplessness. Nothing is more humbling than the recognition that we are entirely dependent upon someone else to make our lives work, but this is the helpless position we must not only recognise but admit to if we are to learn what it means to trust.

So deeply ingrained in our nature is the spirit of independence that we have no hope of ever seeing ourselves clearly unless God comes to our aid. The thing that has often amazed me as a counsellor is the ease with which I can go straight to the roots of other people's problems whilst struggling for years to identify the basic causes of my own. It is this fact (quite apart from the direct teaching of Scripture) that has convinced me of the need for close relationships with others. Over the years, friends have pointed out things to me about myself that I might never have seen had I indulged in hours or days of self-examination. I have said before (though it is not an original statement of mine) that God has three ways of opening up our lives – the Word of God, the Spirit of God and the people of God. Sometimes, and especially in relation to this matter of admitting our helplessness, we might need the operation of all three.

We simply must see clearly on this matter, but for this we need help, and I warn you that help, when it comes, will often hurt. The searching work of the word of God, the Spirit of God and the people of God often make us feel extremely uncomfortable.

Tender and skillful Invader of my soul, help me face everything that would hinder my growth in you. I give You the freedom to use any of your resources – your Word, your Spirit or your people – to nudge me towards Christlikeness day by day. In Jesus' name. Amen.

FOR FURTHER STUDY – Jer. 17:1–10, 23:24; 1 Chron. 28:9
1. What is the condition of the heart? / 2. What was David's fatherly word to Solomon?

FOR READING AND MEDITATION – JEREMIAH 25:1–14
'And though the Lord has sent all his servants the prophets to you again and again,
you have not listened …' (v. 4: NIV)

I referred the other day to a man I once talked to who, when he was confronted with
the idea that his problem was rooted in self-sufficiency, immediately fell upon his
knees and repented. Honesty compels me to admit that that reaction is more the
exception than the rule. As we have seen, usually Christians (myself included) have
great difficulty facing the fact that they are deeply committed to their independence; it sometimes takes a ton of spiritual TNT to move them from that position.

Just recently I talked to a man who insisted that the problem in his marriage
was due to the fact that his wife did not understand and practice the truth of biblical submission. It was clear to me that whilst this was a problem in their marriage,
there was an even greater problem – his inability to demonstrate loving leadership
to his wife. In my judgment, the husband was using his wife's unsubmissive attitude
as a smokescreen to avoid facing his own failure to love his wife as Christ loves the
church. I felt it necessary to draw his attention to this, but no matter what I said, he
just would not face the truth. His one concern was that I would see his wife and
teach her how to be submissive. Sadly, after an hour I had to let him go, knowing
that there was little I could do to help.

The diagnosis that deep down we are committed to independence is not pleasant, and we tend to resist it whenever we can. In the same way, it's easier to accept a
doctor's diagnosis that we have the 'flu than it is that we have cancer. But the truth
must be faced, no matter how unpleasant or uncomfortable it may be.

*O God, help me to face up to your diagnosis of my condition, however uncomfortable and unpleas-
ant it may be. This stubborn nature of mine needs more than a sedative, it needs spiritual surgery.
I am willing – help me. In Jesus' name. Amen.*

FOR FURTHER STUDY – Ex. 32:1–9; 2 Chron. 24:19; Jer. 32:33
1. How did God describe the children of Israel? / 2. Could that be said of you?

Remember – and repent!

FOR READING AND MEDITATION – REVELATION 2:1–7
'Remember the height from which you have fallen!
Repent and do the things you did at first ...' (v. 5: NIV)

We must spend another day focusing on the fact that the diagnosis of our independence is not pleasant, and our tendency is to resist it or deny it. Admitting that deep down we are committed to self-sufficiency is never easy, not even for the most mature. But we must face up to it, even though it may cause us considerable spiritual pain and discomfort. Growth almost always brings pain and discomfort – this is as true in the spiritual as it is in the natural realm.

The Spirit was not given just to comfort but also to convict (John 16:8). If, as Jeremiah tells us, our heart is the problem and we manage to hide its ugly contents beneath a covering of self-deceit (Jeremiah 17:9), then the truth that God can see into the depths of our heart is something we must not only believe but apply. We must be willing to let God look into our hearts, and believe him when, through the Holy Spirit, he tells us what he sees.

What does God see when he looks into your heart? I know what he sees in mine – self-sufficiency, self-dependence and self-concern. What ought I to do when I pause in a moment of self-examination like this and become aware of how much self-sufficiency is within? Turn to my Bible and start meditating? Listen to a tape of some well-known Bible teacher? Fall on my knees and pray for an hour or two? These things might well be part of the answer, but I must watch that I do not turn to spiritual activity and busyness as an excuse for avoiding the primary thing, and the only thing, that can sever me from my self-sufficiency – that is, sincerely and meaningfully to repent.

O Father, help me see self-sufficiency in its proper light – as idolatry. Forgive me for the arrogant assumption that I can make life work on my own. How this attitude must hurt you. I turn from it now in deep repentance. In Jesus' name. Amen.

FOR FURTHER STUDY – Acts 7:1–53; Isa. 28:12, 30:15
1. What was Stephen's indictment of the High Priest?
2. To what point must we come to hear God speak?

Nothing!

FOR READING AND MEDITATION – JOHN 15:1–17

'… apart from me you can do nothing.' (v. 5: NIV)

We spend one final day on this important subject of dependent trust. Earlier we asked ourselves the question: why do we find it so difficult to trust? The answer, we saw, is that deeply ingrained in our nature is a disease that has been passed on to us from Adam which can be described as *Do it yourself*.

Everyone of us, whether we realise it or not, has within our nature a stubborn commitment to independence. Trusting one another is one of the most difficult requirements of the Christian life. We hate to be dependent because we have learned to trust no one fully. Everyone in whom we have placed our confidence has in some way disappointed us. To trust fully, we conclude, is suicide. Nothing is more humbling than the recognition that we are entirely dependent upon someone else to make our lives work, and admitting to this fact puts us in touch with a level of helplessness which our carnal nature does not acknowledge. Unconsciously, to save face, the mechanisms of our personality work to keep this fact out of our awareness. Once the issue is recognised and dealt with by committing ourselves daily to depending upon the sufficiency of Christ, rather than our own sufficiency, then there is less likelihood of the stain of self-interest appearing in our works of Christian obedience.

None of us likes to feel helpless, but this is the position we must learn to live with if we are to grow spiritually. We must remind ourselves over and over again that we are dependent beings standing before a uniquely sufficient God, and if he does not come through for us, then no matter how hard we try – we are sunk.

O Father, now I see what is involved in trusting you, help me never to forget. Let me begin every day in dependent trust, realising that no matter how hard I try, without you I can do nothing. In Jesus' name I pray. Amen.

FOR FURTHER STUDY – 2 Cor. 2:1–6, 9:8; Phil. 4:13
1. What does Paul admit? / 2. What does he affirm?

balancing the love scales

Destined to obey

FOR READING AND MEDITATION – 1 PETER 1:1–12

'We have been chosen according to the foreknowledge of God the Father ...
for obedience to Jesus Christ ...' (v. 2: NIV)

Now that we have some idea of what it means to trust deeply, we move on to consider the matter of Christian obedience. Some may be feeling that the strong emphasis I have placed so far upon trust and grace may weaken any emphasis I may now want to place upon obedience. I think that by the time we finish this edition, that fear will be dissolved.

Our text for today tells us that we are predestined to obey Jesus Christ. What does that mean? It means (so I believe) that the way of Christ is written into the fibre of our being, our nervous system, our blood, and our tissues. In other words, the way of Christ is the way to live. In Acts 9:2 we read of those 'who belonged to the Way'; in Acts 19:9 of maligning 'the Way'; in Acts 19:23 that there arose 'a great disturbance about the Way'; in Acts 24:22 of one who was 'well acquainted with the Way'. What does the 'Way' with a capital *W* mean? We usually interpret it as the way of salvation but it is much more than that; it is the way to live – period. It is the way to do everything: the way to think, the way to feel and the way to act in every conceivable circumstance and relationship.

The Scriptures not only say God redeemed the world through Christ, but created it through him: 'Through him all things were made; without him nothing was made ...' (John 1:3). This means that everything that has been created has the stamp of Christ upon it. His will is wrought into the very structure of things. They work in his way or they do not work at all. We are predestined to obey his Way; we can live against that destiny and get hurt, or live with it and be fulfilled.

O Father, clearly you have fashioned me in my inmost and outmost being for your will. I am destined to live Christianly. Help me to fulfil my destiny, this day and every day. In Jesus' name I ask it. Amen.

FOR FURTHER STUDY – Col. 1:10–29; Eph 1:15–23; Heb. 1:1–2
1. What does Paul say about 'all things'? / 2. What dwells in Christ?

The daily Quiet Time

FOR READING AND MEDITATION – MARK 1:29–39

'Very early in the morning, while it was still dark, Jesus got up, left the house
and went off to a solitary place, where he prayed.' (v. 35: NIV)

We touched yesterday on the fact that obedience to Jesus Christ is our destiny. We
must accept this fact and live with it – or get hurt. Today we ask ourselves: what are
some of the things we need to do in order to contribute to our growth in Christ? What
are the major principles to which we ought to give our obedience if we are to
become strong and mature Christians?

The first is – establish a daily devotional time with God. *By devotional* I mean
a time before God when we expose ourselves to his resources, meditate on his Word,
remind ourselves that without him we can do nothing, and drink in fresh inspiration and power to meet the day. Twenty-five years ago I set out to encourage people
to establish a daily Quiet Time in which a portion of the Word of God was read, a
comment made, and a prayer suggested. Over the years thousands upon thousands
have written to me saying how this daily devotional aid which you are now reading
has contributed to their spiritual growth.

What is the secret? Those who have analysed the books say that it is the way
the notes focus on opening up all parts of the personality – spiritual, intellectual,
emotional and volitional. They help open up the spirit by focusing on God; they help
open up the intellect by stirring the mind to think; they help open up the emotions
through the stories of real life situations with which people can identify; they help
open up the will by challenging the reader to act.

It is not enough just to grow – we must be sure that we are growing totally, not
lopsidedly. I am deeply humbled to think that right now I have a little part to play in
helping you to grow.

Father, help me to see that just as I need to take time out of the day to feed myself physically, else I
will die, so I need to take time out to feed myself spiritually. Help me not just to say it, but to do it.
In Christ's name I pray. Amen.

FOR FURTHER STUDY – John 15:1–17, 14:31; Rom. 5:19
1. What was the testimony of Jesus? / 2. What are we the beneficiaries of?

In the morning

FOR READING AND MEDITATION – PSALM 5:1–12

'In the morning, O Lord, you hear my voice; in the morning I lay
my requests before you and wait in expectation.' (v. 3: NIV)

We continue where we left off yesterday, emphasising the need to establish a daily devotional time with God. If I were asked to reduce the disciplines of the Christian life to an irreducible minimum, I would say it is to keep in union with God. Only when union with God is intact do we experience any of God's blessings. And I know of no one thing that cultivates union with God more surely and constantly than the regular practice (emergencies apart) of starting the day with the Quiet Time. Some condemn this approach, saying it encourages legalism, but as I have dealt with that problem earlier, I need say no more.

This is how, I suggest, a devotional time with God should be set up. First we should find a solitary place where we will not be disturbed. This is not so easy for busy housewives and mothers, but, as the saying goes, necessity is the mother of invention. Next, we should read a short passage of the Scriptures. Nothing primes our spirit for reaching out to God like the reading of his Word. Then we should pause to give God's word time to drop into the centre of our being. We should meditate on it for a few moments and see what God brings out of it and how he wants to relate it to our lives. After this, we should talk to God in prayer and, as prayer is conversation, we should also listen, and let God talk to us.

I shall talk later about deeper prayer and a deeper study of the word, but a daily devotional time with God – preferably in the morning – is, in my view, one of the biggest catalysts to spiritual growth there is. If you are too busy to begin the day with God, then you are busier than God intends you to be.

O Father, show me the importance of spending time with you. For it is natural and inevitable that if I spend all my time with the world and none with you, then the world will seem more real to me than you. Help me begin every day with your perspectives. Amen.

FOR FURTHER STUDY – Luke 6:1–12; Mark 1:35, 6:46–47; Luke 5:15–16
1. What example did Jesus set? / 2. Have you got a solitary place?

Can I cry with you?

FOR READING AND MEDITATION – MATTHEW 6:1–14

'… Then your Father, who sees what is done in secret, will reward you.' (v. 6: NIV)

Today we look at yet another thing we ought to do in order to cultivate spiritual growth – learn the art of intercessory prayer. We have already talked about the need to spend some time at the beginning of the day talking to God, but now I am thinking of more intense times of prayer when we come before God, not in order to focus on our own needs, but on the needs of others.

In a church I pastored many years ago there was a lady who, in addition to her daily Quiet Time, spent an hour a day praying for the needs of others. When she came from the place of prayer to go out and do her shopping, remarkable things would take place. On one occasion a woman came up to her in the local market and said, 'Excuse me, my dear, you look so approachable. My husband has just died and I haven't got anyone to cry with. Do you mind if I cry with you?' I happened to be walking behind her down the street one day when she was singing softly to herself, and I heard one workman say to the other, 'I just heard that lady singing to herself; the world must be getting better.' I thought to myself, 'It is – as long as there are people who are transmitters of light and life through prayer.'

One of the most interesting things about praying for others is that sometimes the first changes to be seen are not in others but in us. A man I know spent half an hour a day praying for the conversion of his neighbour. One day the neighbour said to him, 'You are a much more friendly person now than you used to be. I'd like to come to your church with you next Sunday.' He did, and was gloriously converted. In praying for others, we ourselves grow more like him.

O Father, what endless possibilities a deeper prayer life throws open to me – not just for my growth but for the benefit of others. Help me to accept this challenge and give more time to prayer this year that I have ever done before. In Jesus' name. Amen.

FOR FURTHER STUDY – John 17; Luke 22:32, 23:34; John 14:16
1. What are some of the ingredients of Christ's intercessory prayer?
2. What three groups did Jesus pray for?

God's spiritual generator

FOR READING AND MEDITATION – ISAIAH 65:7–25

'Before they call I will answer; while they are still speaking I will hear.' (v. 24: NIV)

Has the idea ever occurred to you that prayer is not just communion but also commission? Let me explain: out of the time we spend with God in prayer, asking him to reach out and bless others, a power is generated that turns the spiritual machinery of the world. The more time you spend in prayer, the more conscious you will be that when you go into the world you are a person who is sent.

Just recently I heard of a woman who, although she had been a Christian just six months, decided to give God an hour a day in prayer. One day, while she was praying for her neighbours, an idea came to her. She went to her pastor and said, 'The people in my area won't come to church but they will come to my house. Would you be willing to lead an *abundant living* group in my home if I got them together?' The pastor agreed and on the first evening 75 people turned up. There was not enough room for more than 25 so, much to the pastor's consternation, she hastily arranged to have three sessions: one from 19:00 to 20:00, one from 20:00 to 21:00, and the third from 21:00 to 22:00. In the next week it settled down to two separate evenings, each with a group of 25 people. In six months that woman saw over 30 of her neighbours receive Christ and join the local church.

A Christian of six months had a sense of commission when she turned aside to give herself to deeper and more intensive prayer. And a living movement of the Holy Spirit came out of that prayer time. The more we pray, the more we grow – grow not only in spiritual stature but in influence and power in the world around.

O God, wake me up to the possibilities there are in prayer. Give me the passion that Jesus had for both prayer and people. May my needs drive me to you and may the needs of others drive me to them. For your own dear name's sake. Amen.

FOR FURTHER STUDY – John 20:19–23, 17:15–18
1. What is the divine equation? / 2. What is the result?

The inexhaustible book

FOR READING AND MEDITATION – PSALM 119:81–96
'Your laws endure to this day, for all things serve you.' (v. 91: NIV)

We have looked at two things we must do in order to grow in God: establish a daily devotional time and learn the art of praying for others. Today we look at a third pre-requisite for spiritual growth – taking time to explore God's Word.

This devotional booklet you are now reading will help you establish a daily devotional time and thus act as a catalyst to growth, but you will still need to spend time exploring the Scriptures in a deeper and wider way if you are to grow strong and healthy in God. I have often said that I expect the comments I make in any devotional to be exhausted of meaning once they have been read, but that is not true of the Scriptures. You can never exhaust the Bible, for it contains the Word that is bigger than men's words. One of the Pilgrim Fathers is recorded as saying, 'God has much more light to break out of his Word.' I find that to be true – do you? After studying the Bible for over forty years, I sometimes feel I am standing on the edge of a great ocean – and still paddling.

If you do not already attend a Bible study class where the Scriptures are opened up, then if one is available, enrol right away. If this is not possible, write to a Bible college and ask them to introduce you to a correspondence course that will guide you through the Scriptures in an in-depth way. The Moffatt translation of Acts 1:3 says: 'Revealing himself to them for forty days.' The passage suggests that Christ did not just reveal himself to his followers physically, but also revealed his spirit and purpose and meaning. He has been revealing himself ever since – and the meanings are inexhaustible.

Father, the entrance of your Word brings light and the neglect of your book brings darkness. Help me to open myself more and more to that light. Then I shall walk with a sure and steady tread. In Jesus' name I pray. Amen.

FOR FURTHER STUDY – 2 Tim. 1:1–15; Rom. 15:4; Acts 17:11; John 5:39
1. What was Paul's commission to Timothy? / 2. What do the Scriptures bring?

Working at God's Word

FOR READING AND MEDITATION – PSALM 130:1–8

'I wait for the Lord, my soul waits, and in his word I put my hope.' (v. 5: NIV)

Today I want to talk about how to get the best out of studying the Scriptures. When Jesus stood up in the synagogue at Nazareth and read the passage from Isaiah, the account says: 'Then he shut the book ... and he began to tell them, "This very day this Scripture has been fulfilled ..."' (Luke 4:20–21: J.B. Phillips). At that moment revelation passed from precepts to Person. Now the Person gives meaning to the precepts. So when studying the Bible, first: always look for the person of Christ. Sometimes he is hidden in types and shadows – but nevertheless he is there.

Second: come to the Word expectantly. The book is alive with meanings: 'For the word of God is living and active. Sharper than any double-edged sword ...' (Hebrews 4:12: NIV). Expect it to speak and penetrate right into your inner being, and it will. After all, faith is expectancy: 'According to your faith will it be done to you' (Matthew 9:29: NIV).

Third: come surrendering to the truths that are revealed. 'If anyone chooses to do God's will, he will find out ...' (John 7:17: NIV). In a moral universe, the key to moral knowledge is response. The moment we cease to obey, that moment the revelation ceases to reveal.

Fourth: come expecting to use the truths that are revealed. Not only receive the truths, but make yourself the channel of those truths to others.

Fifth: come even if nothing seems to result from your coming. To have exposed yourself to the Word is itself infinitely worthwhile. For where love is, silence may be the only language. To be with him, though unseen and unheard, is the reward.

Father, help me to come to your Word with quiet expectancy – expectancy that here my weakness shall become strength, my doubt become faith, and that I shall become an instrument of your peace. In Christ's name I ask it. Amen.

FOR FURTHER STUDY – Col. 3:1–16; 2 Pet. 1:19; Jer. 23:29
1. What was Paul's exhortation to the Colossians? / 2. What is God's word like?

Resentment can kill

FOR READING AND MEDITATION – EPHESIANS 4:17–32
'Get rid of all bitterness, rage and anger, brawling and slander,
along with every form of malice.' (v. 31: NIV)

We look now at another principle of spiritual growth which, if not obediently practised, blocks and chokes the life of God within us – the regular emptying out of the
soul of all hates and resentments. A minister friend of mine once grasped my hand
and said, 'Show me how to overcome resentment, for it is quietly bringing me down
to my grave.' His face showed the tension he was under and it was clear that resentment was draining him mentally, spiritually – and physically.

A verse I have used hundreds of times in counselling sessions is this: 'Be careful that none of you fails to respond to the grace which God gives, for if he does there
can very easily spring up in him a bitter spirit which is not only bad in itself but can
also poison the lives of many others' (Heb 12:15: J.B. Phillips). When we cease to
avail ourselves of the grace of God which flows down to us every moment of the day,
then the roots of bitterness can soon begin to grow in us. And of all the things that
choke and poison spiritual growth, bitterness and resentment are the most devas-
tatingly effective. I heard of a missionary who was so resentful of his mission board
and his colleagues that it caused a nervous breakdown and he was sent home, a broken and dispirited man. No one was able to help him, for he regarded his resentment
as righteous indignation.

Resentment can kill you – literally. I knew a church deacon who carried so
much resentment inside him that it brought on a heart attack. He attempted to tell
another deacon what he thought of him and died before he could get the words out.
His doctor said, 'I warned him. He died as he lived – an angry man.'

*O God, help me live with grace, not with grudges. Save me from the things that would destroy me.
If I am nourishing in my bosom any cobras of bitterness and hate, then help me fling them from
me this very moment. In Christ's name I pray. Amen.*

FOR FURTHER STUDY – James 3:1–16; Heb. 12:15; Eph. 4:29–32
1. What happens when we fail to respond to God's grace?
2. How does bitterness usually show itself?

balancing the love scales

Here are your orders

FOR READING AND MEDITATION – PROVERBS 19:1–20

'A man's wisdom gives him patience; it is to his glory to overlook an offence.' (v. 11: NIV)

Bitterness and resentment are not just wrong because they have a devastating effect upon us physically and emotionally – they are wrong according to the teaching of the Christian faith. If you are a Christian, here are your orders: 'So if you are offering your gift at the altar, and there remember that your brother has something against you, leave your gift there in front of the altar and go. First be reconciled to your brother, then come and offer your gift' (Matthew 5:23–24: RSV). Stop all religious observance, says Jesus; it is useless if you are not attempting to be reconciled to your brother. For shutting out your brother shuts out your Father – automatically. This scripture, of course, refers to someone who has a grievance against you, but now look at the other side of the coin – when you have something against your brother: 'If your brother sins against you, go and tell him his fault, between him and you alone' (Matthew 18:15: RSV).

In either case, you are under an obligation to settle the disagreement – to settle it as far as you are concerned. The other person may not respond, but you have cleared your own soul. A woman wrote a stinging letter to her husband, left it, and drove away, intending to burn her bridges behind her and leave her husband. But she was convicted by the Spirit, drove 40 miles through the rain, arrived home just before her husband and tore up the letter. They there and then settled matters and have lived happily ever since.

Bitterness and resentment must have no place in our hearts – those are our orders. Like good soldiers, soldiers of the cross, let's be sure we obey them.

O God, I know your grace is available to help me relinquish all resentment. You have done everything you needed to do – now help me do everything I need to do. I give over to you every resentment that is in my heart. Bury them at the foot of the cross. In Christ's name. Amen.

FOR FURTHER STUDY – Mark 11:12–26; Luke 11:4, 17:1–4; Eph. 4:32
1. On what basis do we forgive others? / 2. How often?

True virtue

FOR READING AND MEDITATION – PSALM 40:1-17
'I desire to do your will, o my God ...' (v. 8: NIV)

The motive which underlies the obedience of those who are truly mature: not duty, but delight. The truly virtuous in terms of obedience are those whose very heart is given to doing the will of God. The immature may be kept on the path of obedience by the influence of others, or as a matter of *safety first*, or even as a matter of duty. The mature, however, say from the heart, 'I desire (or delight) to do your will, o my God.' But how is this delight obtained? What is the secret?

As I write, I am thinking of a home I know where a devoted daughter is tenderly caring for her aged mother and wants to make her life as bearable as possible despite the prostration of old age. If you were to ask this daughter why she does it, what sort of answer do you think you would get? 'Because I was brought up to be like this'? 'Because I am impelled with a sense of duty'? 'Because I am concerned what others will think of me if I don't'? No. I think she would say something like this, 'I delight to do it; it's all an outcome of the love I have for my mother.'

Delight in service is explained by personal love. The daughter I am thinking of operates neither from fear or duty; she loves. And those who love delight to serve. That is the secret of obedience. Those who delight to do the will of God have seen God in Jesus, and behind the dictate of conscience stands a loved and loving Person. Obedience, to the mature, is not merely a duty done well – it is a direct and deliberate service to Christ, the Beloved. To be strong in obedience, simply love Jesus; then obedience will cease to be a burden and become a delight.

O Father, if delighting in obedience is explained by personal love, then help me to fall deeper in love with you and your Son than I have ever been before. This I ask in Christ's peerless and wondrous name. Amen.

FURTHER STUDY – John 13:1-17; Luke 22:24-27; Matt. 20:28; Phil. 2:7
1. What did Jesus display? / 2. Do others see this characteristic in you?

balancing the love scales

Spiritual contagion

FOR READING AND MEDITATION – JOHN 4:11–30

'Come, see a man who told me everything I ever did. Could this be the Christ?'
(v. 29: NIV)

We look now at yet another law of growing in spiritual love – sharing our faith with others. 'Christianity is catching,' said someone, 'and if people don't catch it from us, then perhaps it's because we don't have a valid case of it ourselves.' Slightly over-stated perhaps, but worth thinking about, nevertheless. Christianity is not merely a conception, it is a contagion. By that I mean it is something that must not be kept to ourselves. When the contagion is lost, then the conception suffers. A member of the Evangelical Council of Britain once said to me, 'How long can we remain evangeli-cal if we are not evangelistic?' It is a law of the mind that that which is not expressed is no longer impressed, for, as I have said many times before, all expression deepens impression. Nothing is really ours until we share it. Whenever we share our faith with someone and that someone responds to our faith, then the faith we have shared comes to mean just that much more to us.

Listen to what Paul said to the Philippians: '… you have contributed to the gospel from the very first day down to this moment; of this I am confident, that he who has begun the good work in you will go on completing it until the day of Jesus Christ' (Philippians 1:5–6: Moffatt). From the very day they took the love of God into their hearts and stepped into the kingdom of God, they began to contribute to it – to spread it. This was not something they learned; it was instinctive.

A Jewish Rabbi said on television, 'All religions are glad to have inquirers come to them, but Christianity is different – it goes looking for people.' When I heard him say that, I said to myself, 'Thank God it does – or else I would never have come to faith.' Would you?

Father, I see that it is not enough to have an experience of you – that experience must become an expression. Help me share my faith with someone in a loving, sensitive and appropriate way. In Christ's name I ask it. Amen.

FOR FURTHER STUDY – Jer. 20:1–9; Psa. 66:16; Isa. 63:7; 2 Cor. 4:13
1. What was Jeremiah's testimony? / 2. What motivates us to share our faith?

The heartbeat of the faith

FOR READING AND MEDITATION – ACTS 5:17–41

'We are witnesses of these things, and so is the Holy Spirit,
whom God has given to those who obey him.' (v. 32: NIV)

The four great commands of the Christian gospel are these: 'Come, see, go, tell' (Matthew 28:6–7). First, we come to Christ and get a firsthand knowledge – we 'come and see'. Then the instinctive impulse is to 'go and tell'. If there is no 'go and tell' impulse, then it would suggest that the 'come and see' experience has not really gripped us. Or, if it has gripped us, perhaps it is not gripping us any more. The expression of our faith is the essence of our faith. The more we share our faith, the more we grow, and the more we grow, the more of our faith we want to share. In a church in the United States, I saw a motto that said, 'To know him, to help others know him'. This sums up the heartbeat of the Christian faith: to know him ourselves as personal Saviour and Lord, and then to help others know him as personal Saviour and Lord.

These two concepts have been described as 'the alternate beats of the Christian heart': the intake and the outgiving, receptivity and response. And if both sides are not in operation, the Christian heart may soon cease to beat. Then we settle down to dead forms, dead ceremonies, dead rituals, dead attitudes and dead prayers. 'What do you say when you kneel in the pew at your church?' asked a friend of a regular churchgoer. 'Nothing,' was the reply, 'I just count to 40.' How sad.

A verse I have recently come across reads: 'He who gives the seed to the sower' (2 Corinthians 9:10: J.B. Phillips). He gives seed to the one who uses it; it seems to suggest that he gives it only to the sower. If you don't use the seed, you won't get it.

Gracious and loving Master, give me the heart that cares and shares and dares. Help me to sow beside all waters and help me also never to be ashamed of you – no matter who I am talking to. Amen.

FOR FURTHER STUDY – Matt. 9:35–38; Psa. 126:6; Luke 10:2; John 4:35–36; Gal. 6:9
1. What did Jesus ask his disciples to pray for? / 2. What are we not to do?

'Them' and 'him'

FOR READING AND MEDITATION – HEBREWS 10:19–31

'Let us not give up meeting together, as some are in the habit of doing,
but let us encourage one another …' (v. 25: NIV)

We look at just one more important principle of spiritual growth – fellowship with other Christians. Jesus said: 'Where two or three are gathered together in my name, I am there in the midst of them' (Matthew 18:20: NKJ). To the two or three there is added Another – a divine plus is given. The spiritual awareness of each is heightened by the Other. Those who refuse the fellowship of others find that their faith is diminished – a minus appears.

When I was a young Christian, the thing that used to draw me like a magnet to regular fellowship with other Christians was the realisation that in meeting with my fellow believers, I was also meeting with Christ. I can remember coming home from my work in the engineering shop where I was apprenticed, having a quick wash and a change of clothes, and literally running to join my fellow Christians in a Bible study or prayer meeting. The fact that Christ would be there in our midst filled me with a sense of wonder; I was thrilled by the knowledge that in meeting with them, I would be meeting with him.

When we link ourselves with 'them' and 'him' we are in touch with one of the greatest of all sources of spiritual growth. As I look back now to the early days of my Christian experience, I realise that one of the most encouraging outcomes of meeting with my fellow Christians was that I grew in leaps and bounds. 'My, how you are growing,' my pastor, David Thomas, often used to say to me when he saw me in the house of God. I didn't fully realise it then, but being with my fellow believers was one of the ways in which my growth was stimulated.

Gracious and loving Heavenly Father, I cannot fully understand it, but clearly there is something very important about meeting together with my fellow Christians. Help me to get out of every meeting all that you put into it for me. For your own dear name's sake. Amen.

FOR FURTHER STUDY – Acts 2:1–47; Psa. 119:63; Phil. 1:3–5
1. What was one hallmark of the early church?
2. Why did Paul give thanks for the Philippians?

Spiritual nuclear fission

FOR READING AND MEDITATION – ACTS 2:42–47

'They devoted themselves to the apostles' teaching and to the fellowship ...' (v. 42: NIV)

Speaking of the well-known verse in James 5:16: 'Confess your sins to each other and pray for each other,' someone has said that today the situation is often reversed and the words made to mean: 'Confess your sins for each other and pray to one another!'

In the early Church, as our passage for today shows, *koinonia* – a sharing, giving fellowship – was placed on a par with doctrine, prayer, worship and the Lord's Supper. Since the first Christians did not have church buildings, they met mostly in small groups in homes and other convenient places. Very often, open sharing and confession was made to the group and the group members then supported the struggling person with their love and prayers. After the first few centuries, this approach to worship almost disappeared, but it re-emerged during the great Evangelical Revival in Britain under the Wesleys. John Wesley and his workers organised *class meetings* which were small groups of five to ten people under the leadership of a converted layman, who met to study the Scriptures, share and pray together. It was the incredible power of these groups which brought about such tremendous spiritual growth in the people and 'spread scriptural holiness which helped to reform the nation'.

There is amazing power in a small group of believers who are committed to sharing Christ and the Scriptures with one another. If you cannot find such a group, then find at least one other person – a true Christian – and open your life to that person. Then let the group grow. Transparent openness and agreed praying (Matthew 18:19) sets off a kind of spiritual nuclear fission which generates tremendous growth and power.

Father, thank you for reminding me of the strength and power that comes from fellowshipping with other Christians and with you. In company with some two or three may I meet with you in that unique way today. Amen.

FOR FURTHER STUDY – 1 John 1:1–7; Rom. 1:11–12; 1 Pet. 3:8

1. What is the basis of fellowship? / 2. What is the result of fellowship?

Jesus – 'the Big Tree'

FOR READING AND MEDITATION – REVELATION 22:12–21

'The grace of the Lord Jesus be with God's people.' (v. 21: NIV)

We end our meditations on the theme of *Balancing the love scales* by reminding ourselves that from the very first moment we come to know Jesus Christ in a personal way, an inward drive takes hold of us that pushes us towards conformity to his character. And this conformity should manifest itself also in a maturing love for our neighbour. A visitor to Japan tells how he saw a number of ropes going out from big trees in the forests, and asked what it meant. He was told, 'The big trees pull the little ones that are crooked into straightness.' Jesus is the Big Tree planted in eternity. I am bound to him by cords of love, and he is pulling me into straightness. And as long as I walk in his Way, the Way will lead me to his likeness. Can anything be more wonderful on earth or in heaven? If there is, then I do not know it.

We need also to keep constantly before us the truth that the soil in which we grow is that of grace – God's free and unmerited favour. Unless we understand this, we will focus only on obedience and grow lopsidedly. The final and finished formula for spiritual growth is quite simple – receptivity and activity. And in that order! The old hymn, which is still sung in many sections of the Church, puts the truth even more effectively when it says:

> Trust and obey, for there's no other way
> To be happy in Jesus, but to trust and obey.

Trust and obey – there you have it in a nutshell. We trust God for the power to make our lives work, and we demonstrate our love for him in glad and willing obedience and in reaching out to others. Go on growing in God – it's what life in Christ is all about.

O Jesus, my Saviour and my Lord, I love your Way for many reasons, not the least because your Way is leading me to your likeness. May the days that lie ahead of me be days of real spiritual growth. For your own dear name's sake. Amen.

FOR FURTHER STUDY – Psa. 1, 52:8; Isa. 61:3
1. What kind of tree does God want us to be? / 2. How deep are your roots?

David – the giant-killer

FOR READING AND MEDITATION – 1 SAMUEL 17:1–58
'The Lord … will deliver me from the hand of this Philistine.' (v. 37: NIV)

For the next two months we will be looking closely at some of the things which may still be standing in our way as we seek to move on with God and enter into all the fullness of Christ. I have chosen in this edition to refer to matters that impede our spiritual progress as *giants* because of the way in which they loom over us and intimidate us. Giants can be tough and threatening and strike terror into the hearts of those who have to confront them. Take, for instance, the well-known story of David's encounter with the giant Goliath, which we have read today.

Day after day Goliath paraded along the slopes of the Valley of Elah, bellowing out challenges to the Israelites. Over nine feet tall and clad in armour that weighed about 125 pounds, he must have presented a fearsome figure. His war cries boomed across the valley with alarming regularity – every morning and evening for forty days – but no one in the camp of Israel felt able or equipped to accept his challenge. However, onto the scene came a young shepherd boy by the name of David. He could not believe the way his fellow Israelites – God's chosen people – allowed themselves to be intimidated by Goliath. You know the outcome. With a sling, a small stone and a mighty confidence in God, the young shepherd boy ended the giant's reign of terror once and for all.

Are there any *giants* looming large on the horizon right now? The chances are some are threatening your life at this very moment. Together let's set out to slay and behead them. Giants don't seem nearly so threatening when they are prostrate.

My Father and my God, with the sling of faith, the stone of truth and the power that lies in your mighty name, I set out today to do battle with all the giants that loom large in my life. May I end the year in glorious victory. For Jesus' sake. Amen.

FOR FURTHER STUDY – 2 Sam. 21: 15–22; 1 Chron. 20:1–8; Num. 13–33
1. What were the Israelites often troubled by? / 2. What was one of the things that kept the children of Israel from entering the Promised Land?

The Spirit's expertise

FOR READING AND MEDITATION – 2 CORINTHIANS 10:1–18

'The weapons we fight with are not the weapons of the world.' (v. 4: NIV)

One thing must be clear before we set out to identify some of the *giants* that stand on the horizon of our lives and eclipse the Son. And that one thing is this: victory comes not through any special formulas or techniques but by trusting in the name of the living God and by focusing on his *Agape* love.

We live in a day when Christians seem to be turning more and more to literature on psychology for methods of dealing with the problems that invade their lives. I am not against psychology per se; I simply believe it is a poor substitute for the truths contained in Scripture. King Saul, you remember from the passage we read yesterday, set out to dress David in his armour. How ridiculous the young shepherd boy must have looked in Saul's coat of mail and helmet. He wasn't used to moving around like this. It just didn't feel right. He was far more comfortable with a sling, a stone and a steadfast trust in God. David's greatest defence was his inner shield of faith. It kept him cool and composed in the midst of the greatest danger.

But don't run away with the idea that because David slew Goliath with just one stone set in a sling, slaying a giant is a simple matter. It requires great skill, great dedication and great discipline. The weapons of our warfare, as Scripture says, may not be carnal, but they are weapons nevertheless and are effective only in the hands of dedicated and disciplined operators. Using the sling of faith and the stone of truth is less cumbersome than wielding a sword, a club or a spear, but it requires just as much expertise. That expertise, however, is born not of the flesh but of the Spirit.

O God, drive this truth that I have been confronted with today deep into my heart, namely that the weapons of the Spirit are weapons nevertheless, and must be handled with precision and expertise. Give me that expertise. In Jesus' name. Amen.

FOR FURTHER STUDY – Deut. 20:1–20; Ex. 23:27; 2 Chron. 16:9; Psa. 34:7; Deut. 9:1–3
1. What was God's word of encouragement?
2. What was God's promise as they faced the battle with giants?

The Spectre on the Brocken

FOR READING AND MEDITATION – MARK 11:20–33

' "Have faith in God," Jesus answered.' (v. 22: NIV)

Today I want to pull out the files and look at the *mugshot* of the first *giant* that intimidates so many of us – fear. Is this *giant* looming large on the horizon of your life at the moment? Is its frightening appearance making your life a misery? Do your ears ache from its constant threats? Don't run. And don't dress up in Saul's armour either. Instead, learn with me some of the spiritual principles that must be put into operation if the *giant* of fear is to be slain.

Before we look at these principles, however, consider this: some fears have no basis in reality. They are as unsubstantial as the *The Spectre on the Brocken*. The Brocken is the highest peak of the Hartz mountains in Germany. For centuries it was rumoured by people who lived in the valley below that a giant lived on the summit. Credible witnesses swore they had seen him. But with the advance of learning, people grew sceptical and began a careful investigation. They found that the *giant* was seen only at sunrise or sunset (when the sun's rays are almost horisontal), and when the Brocken itself was free of cloud but the neighbouring peaks were covered with mist. Before long they realised what was happening. The ghostly and terrifying spectre which people saw on the peak was nothing but a magnified and distorted image of themselves. They trembled at their own reflection.

Some of our terrors are like that. They are not real. They are the result of a diseased imagination. So look over your fears and separate the real from the imaginary. You will find that most fears – yes, most fears – exist only in the imagination.

Father, I am so grateful that I need not live in bondage. I can be free from fear – even imaginary fears. Help me sweep all litter from my mind that it may be your dwelling place. And yours alone. In Jesus' name I pray. Amen.

FOR FURTHER STUDY – Matt. 14:22–36; 17:1–8

1. Why was the disciples' fear unrealistic? / 2. Why was there no basis for fear on the mount?

No false remedies

FOR READING AND MEDITATION – ISAIAH 31:1–9

'Woe to those who go down to Egypt for help ... but do not look
to the Holy One of Israel ...' (v. 1: NIV)

Fear has many faces: fear of failure, fear of rejection, fear of meeting new people, fear of heights, fear of enclosed spaces, fear of thunder and lightning, fear of unemployment, fear of financial reversal, fear of the future, fear of dying, and many more. Fear, we must understand, is quite different from anxiety. Often we equate the two but strictly speaking they are quite different emotions. Anxiety is a vague and unspecified apprehension; fear always has a specific object.

We saw yesterday that the first step in dealing with fear is to look over your fears and separate the real from the imaginary. Next we must decide to reject all unbiblical routes taken to get rid of fear. No dressing up in Saul's armour. What are some of the wrong routes people go down in an attempt to rid themselves of their fears? One is alcohol. They get drunk to a greater or lesser degree to forget or run away from their fears. But the following morning, when the effects of the alcohol have worn off, the fears are all back. Another false route taken to escape fear is overeating. Food can be exceedingly comforting and induces pleasant physical sensations that override the unpleasant psychological effects which fear brings.

However, every diversion, whether it is drink, overeating, illicit sex, gambling or entertainment, are *cul-de-sacs* – dead ends. They lead only to deeper difficulty. So make up your mind not to take any false routes to escape fear. No subterfuge can ever be a refuge. We need to close all wrong doors so that the right one is more obvious. When we see the right door – Jesus – we can then walk boldly through it into release.

Father, help me not to take a road with a dead end when trying to get rid of my fears. May I decide also that I will have no crutches, for I'm not a lame duck; I'm a Christian. I need no false remedies. I need you, Father. And only you. Amen.

FOR FURTHER STUDY – Mark 4:35–41; 5:25–34

1. What caused the disciples' fear? / 2. Why was the woman trembling with fear?

Open-eyed honesty

FOR READING AND MEDITATION – 1 PETER 4:1–11

'... be clear minded and self-controlled so that you can pray.' (v. 7: NIV)

Having separated the real fears from the imaginary ones, and having decided to avoid all false routes to ridding oneself of fear, the next step is this: look the real fears straight in the face. The Christian way is the way of complete honesty. There must be no attempt to deceive the mind, to entice it into entering a fool's paradise. 'No one can play tricks on the universe and get away with it,' says one Christian writer, 'least of all the universe of the mind.' The verse that most clearly expresses the need to face things rather than evade them is Matthew 24:6: 'You will hear of wars ... but see to it that you are not alarmed' (NIV). In other words, confront fears and don't be scared. Our Lord is the One who is speaking here. His way is the way of open-eyed honesty.

A further step we must take in dealing with fear is this: learn the art of prayer, for fears dissolve in its powerful atmosphere. Samuel Chadwick, one-time principal of Cliff College in Derbyshire, England, said, 'The one concern of the devil is to keep the saints from praying. He fears nothing from prayerless study, prayerless work, prayerless religion ... but he trembles when we pray.' One woman I knew was troubled by fear concerning the future. Whenever it loomed before her, she would get down on her knees, pray and repeat the Lord's Prayer. She told me that after doing that a number of times, the fear went away and never disturbed her again.

In fact, one of the greatest fears that prayer destroys is the fear of the future. And it destroys it by assuring us that though we do not know what the future holds, we are held by the One who knows the future.

Father, I see that in the atmosphere of prayer my fears are not so much solved as dissolved. Forgive me that often I make prayer the last instead of the first resort. Help me become a more prayerful person. In Jesus' name I ask it. Amen.

FOR FURTHER STUDY – Psa. 118:1–9; Isa. 12:2; Psa. 3:6; Isa. 26:3
1. What did the psalmist declare? / 2. What choice did Isaiah make?

The three omni's

FOR READING AND MEDITATION – PSALM 91:1-16

'I will say of the Lord, "He is my refuge and my fortress, my God, in whom I trust."'
(v. 2: NIV)

The next requirement for overcoming fear is one that I have struggled to define, so I am going to call it attachment to God. Attachment to God suggests a relationship with God in which one does not use prayer merely as a defence but moves on to the kind of prayer which welds us to him. Henri Nouwen says that all of our lives may be freed from fear if we are content to glory in his presence. What does he mean? He means, I think, living in the knowledge that we are always in God's presence, that we are all attached to a God who is omnipotent, omniscient and omnipresent. The three *omni's*, as they are called by theologians, capture such wonderful truths that I want to spend a little time exploring them with you today.

Look with me at the first of these *omni's* – omnipotence. This means God is all-powerful. And he makes his strength available for our needs. We only have to attach ourselves to God (as our text for today makes clear) for him to become our fortress. Take next his omniscience. This means that he is all-knowing. As we gain strength to face our fears by leaning on the all-powerful God, so we also gain strength from his wisdom. James counsels us: 'If any of you lacks wisdom, he should ask God, who gives generously to all without finding fault' (James 1:5: NIV). Then third, omnipresence. This means God is present everywhere. I cannot go where he is not. Because I am in Christ nothing about my life can be Christ-less. He is with me both in the present and in the future.

When we see God as he is and our attachment to him deepens, then fears are reduced to their proper size. They grow large only when God grows small.

Gracious and loving God, I see that life is attachment – attachment to you. Help me use prayer not merely as a defence against fear but to develop my knowledge and experience of your omnipotence, omniscience and omnipresence. In Jesus' name. Amen.

FOR FURTHER STUDY – Psa. 31:1-24; 32:10; 125:1
1. How did the psalmist describe his plight? / 2. What did he affirm about God?

Fear – not from God

FOR READING AND MEDITATION – 2 TIMOTHY 1:1–12

'For God did not give us a spirit of timidity, but a spirit of power,
of love and of self-discipline.' (v. 7: NIV)

Before we leave the subject of fear, it is necessary to point out that some fears are healthy and work positively in our lives. Fear of getting hurt or killed, for example, is one of the best policemen on our traffic-infested streets. The fears I have been talking about over the past few days are those which are harmful and debilitating. This kind of fear, we must bear in mind, is prompted by Satan.

Now let me make myself clear: I do not believe that every fear is a demon but I do believe that all crippling and debilitating fear has Satan behind it. The devil wears many masks while attempting to thwart our Christian lives, and fear is one of his most convincing. You who live in the Valley of Elah and daily have to contend with Satan stomping into your life shouting, 'I defy you,' must take your stand like David and retort: 'You come against me with sword and spear and javelin, but I come against you in the name of the Lord ...' (1 Samuel 17:45: NIV). So now, without going overboard on this matter of rebuking the devil (as some Christians appear to do), be aware that the Holy Spirit indwells you and his strong voice will overcome your weakness and defeat Satan's work in your life. Calmly and confidently stand up to that devilish fear in the authority which is yours in Christ.

Remember your resistance must come from an inward trust based on your personal relationship with Christ. It wasn't just the sling and the stone that caused Goliath to fall. It was the sling, the stone and the mighty name of Jehovah. Take your stand now against every crippling fear in your life and resist the work of Satan in Christ's mighty and powerful name.

O Father, may your Spirit reinforce my spirit this very hour so that I will rise up as did David and in your mighty and victorious name see every crippling fear crashing to the ground. May my rebuke be your rebuke. Amen.

FOR FURTHER STUDY – Eph. 6:10–18; Job 11:15; 1 Cor. 15:58; Gal. 5:1
1. What action are we to take after we have done everything to stand?
2. What darts will the shield of faith enable us to withstand?

Fear not!

FOR READING AND MEDITATION – 1 JOHN 4:7–21

'There is no fear in love. But perfect love drives out fear …' (v. 18: NIV)

No one lived a life so completely free of every foolish fear as did our Lord Jesus Christ. When we look at his peerless life we see him demonstrating the truth of today's text: perfect love casts out all fear. We must never forget that the Lord Jesus lived in our world, and one of the reasons God became flesh was that we should learn what the God of love is like and how to live the life of God here on earth. It was a world then (as it is now) of accident, earthquake, famine, treachery, corruption, lust and war. Lunacy was common in the world where Jesus moved and death was frequently brutal. Crucifixion was a regular occurrence in those days, and Jesus must have often seen a man dying in slow agony on a Roman cross.

Our Lord taught his disciples that fear (properly understood) has only one object – God. 'I will show you whom you should fear,' he said to his disciples on one occasion. 'Fear him who … has power to throw you into hell' (Luke 12:5: NIV). The fear of which Jesus spoke is not a fear 'that has torment'. Rather, it is what someone has described as 'the awed and fitting fear of a mortal for his God'. It is filial and trusting. When we fear God – fear him in the most positive sense of that word – then we will fear nothing else.

One of our Lord's favourite phrases was 'Fear not'. Again and again it rang out: 'Fear not.' How was it that Christ was so free of fear? Because of his complete confidence in his Father who was on the throne, and knowledge that all his purposes were wise and good. Assured of this his mind had no crevices in which fear could hide. Have this mind in you which was also in Christ Jesus.

Lord Jesus Christ, give me your mind I pray – a mind in which there are no crevices where fear can hide. Drive this truth deep within me – that God sits on the throne and thus all is well. For your own dear name's sake. Amen.

FOR FURTHER STUDY – Prov. 14:27; Psa. 111:1–10; Prov. 1:7, 9:10; Isa. 11:1–3
1. What is the fountain of life? / 2. How are we to be like Jesus?

It is good for me!

FOR READING AND MEDITATION – MATTHEW 26:36–46

'My soul is overwhelmed with sorrow to the point of death.' (v. 38: NIV)

We spend another day meditating on why our Lord, when he was here on earth, lived a life that was free from every foolish fear. 'But what about Gethsemane?' someone might say. 'Didn't he demonstrate there a certain degree of fear?' The incident in the Garden of Gethsemane needs special study to discover the true meaning of what went on there in our Lord's heart, but I do not believe the emotion he exhibited was fear. Whether dealing with an angry mob, a madman or a storm at sea our Lord seemed never to be afraid.

We found one reason for that in yesterday's meditation – his complete confidence in his Father on the throne and belief that all his purposes were wise and good. Here is another reason: his faith in his Father's ability to bring good out of all that happened. Jesus accepted everything with the assurance that whatever God allowed, he did so because it could be used to advance his eternal purposes. In the face of the most awful thing that could befall him, Jesus probably told himself something like this: 'If My Father allows this then it is good for me!' We see that most clearly in Gethsemane. 'Shall I not drink the cup the Father has given me?' Jesus asked (John 18:11: NIV). Note the words 'the Father has given me'. Men were about to lift him up on a cross but he saw that his Father had a purpose even in that.

Jesus knew that his Father who was great in creation was mighty in transformation also. These two facts alone were enough to keep Jesus free from fear. They are enough for us too.

O Father, just as your Son was free of all tormenting fear so may my life be also. Help me inwardly digest the two truths I have looked at over these past couple of days until they are absorbed into my whole being. In Jesus' name. Amen.

FOR FURTHER STUDY – Mark 14:32–42; Luke 22:39–46; John 6:38
1. What did Jesus pray three times? / 2. What had he declared?

Two kinds of jealousy

FOR READING AND MEDITATION – PROVERBS 27:1–11

'Anger is cruel and fury overwhelming, but who can stand before jealousy?' (v. 4: NIV)

We continue pulling out the *mugshots* of some of the *giants* that threaten our lives, and we look now at one of the most formidable of them all – jealousy. If there was ever a time to plunge your hand into the stream, grab a few stones, load up your sling and in the name of the Lord take aim, it is when this Titan is around. Perhaps you are under threat from this very giant at the moment. Let me see if I can help.

The word *jealousy* is used in the Bible in two senses: good jealousy and bad jealousy. The teaching of the Bible concerning jealousy cannot be properly understood unless this fact is kept in mind. It's a pity we have the same word for both but there it is. An instance of good jealousy is found in the words: 'I, the Lord your God, am a jealous God' (Exodus 20:5: NIV). Because God loved his people with an abounding and pure love he was jealous for them. He was not jealous for himself but jealous for them – for their highest good. His interest was not primarily in himself but in the good of his people. But this is not the way in which the word *jealousy* is usually used. The more common form of jealousy is as hateful as the other is praiseworthy.

'Jealousy is envy born of some deep love of self,' says one writer. This is how it works. You love something or someone very much and desire to possess it or them completely. But the thing or person you love slips out of your hands into the possession of another. You then begin to experience the gnawing pangs of jealousy. And in some cases love quickly turns to hate – deep, dark, abiding hate. 'Who can stand before jealousy?' asks our text for today. Who indeed!

O God, help me bring down the giant of jealousy once and for all so that it might never again plague my life. Remove the shadows cast by jealousy from my face and also from my heart. In the name of Christ my Saviour and Deliverer I pray. Amen.

FOR FURTHER STUDY – Ex. 20:1–17, 34:14; Deut. 4:23–24
1. What is one of the names of the Lord? / 2. What did Moses link God's jealousy to?

Jealousy's peculiarity

FOR READING AND MEDITATION – PROVERBS 6:20–35

'… for jealousy arouses a husband's fury, and he will show no
mercy when he takes revenge.' (v. 34: NIV)

Yesterday we noted that jealousy has been defined as 'envy born of some deep love of self'. It is the feeling of coldness and resentment that stirs in your heart when something or someone you wanted is about to be, or is being, possessed by another. In some people's hearts, jealousy arises when they hear somebody else being praised, somebody with whom they had compared themselves in thought and to whom they had fancied themselves superior. Jealousy is also the dislike that turns to bitterness when someone attracts more attention than you, or has sipped the waters of success more deeply than you have.

The peculiarity of this vice is that it is not usually directed against those who might seem most likely to provoke it – the people who far outstrip us in attainment. Often it is focused on those in our immediate circle, those who are similar to us. 'Doctors are rarely jealous of people who come from another group,' says one psychologist, 'such as schoolteachers, businessmen, and so on. They are jealous of their peers – the people who are most like them, someone with whom they match themselves in thought.'

Some distinguish between envy and jealousy and point out that though the words are frequently used interchangeably, there is a difference. Charles Swindoll puts it like this, 'Envy begins with empty hands mourning for what it doesn't have. Jealousy begins with full hands but is threatened by the loss. It is the pain of losing what I have to someone else, in spite of all my efforts to keep it.'

One thing is sure – the *giant* of jealousy is a killer. You must make up your mind in God's name to kill it. If you don't, it will eventually kill you.

O God, I come to you for freedom. I do not want to be in bondage to a giant; I want to be in bondage to Jesus. If jealousy is threatening the peace of God in my life then together let us bring it down. I know you will do your part. Help me to do mine. Amen.

FOR FURTHER STUDY – Gen. 37:1–36; 1 Sam.18:1–30
1. What lengths can jealousy take us to? / 2. What was its result in Sauls' life?

A mental cancer

FOR READING AND MEDITATION – GENESIS 4:1–16

'… on Cain and his offering he did not look with favour. So Cain was very angry,
and his face was downcast.' (v. 5: NIV)

We have all seen logs caught on rocks in midstream and prevented from being carried any further by the current. Likewise many Christians are hung up on the rocks of jealousy and life flows past them.

Jealousy was Cain's sin, as outlined in today's passage. I realise Scripture mentions Cain's anger rather than his jealousy, but the anger was doubtless the consequence of his jealousy. Interestingly the Hebrew word for jealousy is *quanah*, which means literally 'to be intensely red'. The term is descriptive of someone whose face is flushed as a sudden rush of blood indicates the surge of a strong negative emotion. Cain was jealous of Abel because Abel's offering had been accepted while his own was rejected. No doubt his face was red with emotion as he saw God smile on Abel's sacrifice, and not until Abel's blood had been poured out into the earth did his jealousy and anger subside.

This account brings to mind the story of another two brothers, as told by Jesus in the parable we call *The Prodigal Son*. The younger brother squandered the money given to him by his father in riotous living. His sin could be described as a sin of the flesh. The elder brother had a different kind of problem. His sin was jealousy – a sin of the spirit. And when the curtain comes down on that immortal story, we see the man who sinned in the flesh being forgiven and inside the father's house, while the man who sinned in the spirit is holding on to his jealousy and remains outside.

Jealousy distorts and throws everything out of focus. A woman who was delivered from jealousy said, 'I've been healed of a mental cancer.' She called it by its right name.

O Father, I want no cancer eating at the heart of my relationships. Show me the steps I need to take in order to be freed from its paralysing and hellish grip. I ask this in Christ's name. Amen.

FOR FURTHER STUDY – Luke 15:11–32; Matt. 20:1–16
1. What was the basis of the brother's envy? / 2. What was the basis of the workers' envy?

Jealous? Me?

FOR READING AND MEDITATION – 2 CORINTHIANS 12:11–21

'I fear that there may be quarrelling, jealousy, outbursts of anger…' (v. 20: NIV)

Over the past few days we have seen something of how debilitating and soul-destroying jealousy can be. It can decimate friendships, dissolve a romance, destroy a marriage and disrupt family unity. I have even seen it ruin a whole church and separate preachers from one another.

There is a fable that tells how one day the devil came across some minor fiends trying to tempt a holy hermit. They experimented with the seductions of the flesh but it got them nowhere. 'Your methods are too crude,' said the devil. 'Watch this.' Going up to the hermit he asked, 'Have you heard the news? Your brother has been made bishop of Alexandria.' A scowl of malignant jealousy clouded the face of the holy man.

How can the giant of jealousy be slain? First we have to admit that it exists. This might seem to be stating the obvious but I have known many who were loath to admit that their souls were plagued with jealousy. If they suspected it, they shrunk from it. Of course it can be humiliating to admit to things in our lives that we wish were not there. And pride can play its part in this too. Pride rebels at the idea that we can be jealous of another person, especially when we perceive them as being unworthy of comparison with ourselves. Jealous? Me? Of her? Of him? So we brush aside the fact that we may be jealous and go on for a few more years denying the deadly thing which is ruining our lives.

For 40 days Goliath intimidated the camp of Israel. But then came the forty-first day which heralded the end for the giant from Gath. I hope that this day marks the end of the giant of jealousy that looms over your life.

O God my Father, indeed let this day mark the end of any jealous attitudes that may be overshadowing my life. Give me the faith of David to believe that as I do the possible, you will do the impossible. In Jesus' name. Amen.

FOR FURTHER STUDY – Rom. 13:8–14; 1 Cor. 3:1–9
1. What are we to do in the face of jealousy?
2. How was jealousy exhibiting itself in the Corinthian church?

Organs of one another

FOR READING AND MEDITATION – 1 CORINTHIANS 12:12–31

'Now you are the body of Christ, and each one of you is a part of it.' (v. 27: NIV)

Once we have admitted that jealousy is a problem in our lives, what should we then do? Look on jealousy as self-centredness. Jealousy, we noted earlier, is 'envy born of some deep love of self', so you must realise that if you are a jealous person, you are a self-centred person. Go to the root of the problem by self-surrender and jealousy will drop away – rootless.

What a different climate there would be in the church if everyone could see and accept this. The church is a fellowship where we are *organs* of one another. A good worship leader is my organ of worship. A good singer is my organ of song. A good church officer, such as a church secretary for example, is my *organ* of secretarial ability. There is no need for jealousy because that other person is the organ of me.

I am convinced that most of our problems in the Christian life have their roots in an unsurrendered ego. We can be saved but not yet fully surrendered. It took me years after I had committed my life to Christ to enter into a full surrender. In the book, *Masks of Mercy*, by Robert Frost, one of the characters, Jonah, brings the subject around to the life of another character, Jessie. She counters, 'Let's change the subject. It makes me nervous.' And Jonah replies, 'That's all the great questions ever make you.' It makes us nervous, too, to get close to the root of our problems – self-centredness. But deal with it we must.

I say again: jealous people are self-centred people. If jealousy is a problem in your life, repent of holding on to self-centredness for so long, and make a complete surrender to God.

O Father, help me see that when I let go of my resistance to self-surrender, then all other problems go too. I repent of my self-centredness and surrender my whole being into your hands today. In Christ's name. Amen.

FOR FURTHER STUDY – Prov. 27:4; Gal. 5:16–22

1. What question does the writer of Proverbs ask? / 2. What did Paul describe jealousy as?

Right comparisons

FOR READING AND MEDITATION – JOHN 21:15–25

'When Peter saw him, he asked, "Lord, what about him?" ' (v. 21: NIV)

We continue considering what action we can take, with the help of the Lord, to bring down the giant of jealousy. Another thing we need to do is this: stop looking around to see what is happening to this, that, and the other person. Your approval and joy comes from God. In the passage before us today we find Peter saying to Jesus: 'Lord, what about him?' Did Peter have a little lingering jealousy of John? We can't tell for sure. Some commentators seem to think so. One says, 'Peter was jealous of John as Pentecost had not yet burned it out.' Whether or not he was jealous, it seems pretty clear that his gaze at that moment was John-ward instead of Jesus-ward.

The tendency to compare ourselves with others is strong in us all – more so in those who have a jealous nature. Constantly comparing ourselves with others can do us a great deal of harm spiritually. If we conclude we are better than those with whom we compare ourselves, we can be trapped into pride. If we conclude we are inferior to them, we can be trapped into envy. Christ draws near to us and says: 'Don't compare yourself with others. Compare yourself with me. Accept me as your standard. Claim the help I offer and work to this end.' That comparison becomes spiritually fruitful and the stumbling block is made a stepping stone.

To compare ourselves with Jesus is a healthy spiritual discipline, and one that has been practised throughout the centuries by those who have known the Lord intimately. So keep your eyes fixed on Jesus and satisfy this impulse to make comparisons in a way that will yield spiritual gain for your life.

O God, help me I pray, to adjust this tendency I have to make comparisons so that those I make are directed towards you, not others. Forgive me that so often I have compared myself with others instead of you. Now, by your grace, it will be different. Amen.

FOR FURTHER STUDY – Phil. 2:1–4; 1 Cor. 10:24, 13:4–6

1. What does Paul exhort the Philippians to do? / 2. What is the antidote to jealousy?

Gaze on him alone

FOR READING AND MEDITATION – JOHN 3:22–36

'… that man who was with you … is baptising, and everyone is going to him.'
(v. 26: NIV)

We spend one more day reflecting on how to bring down the giant of jealousy. When we are rightly related to God and fully surrendered to him we become conscious that each one of us has a place in the plan of God – and that his plan is best. Being convinced of that, we envy no one. We see from the passage before us today that when the disciples of John discovered Jesus was attracting large numbers of followers they said: 'Rabbi … everyone is going to him' (v.26). John replied that he was a friend of 'the bridegroom', and added: 'He must become greater; I must become less' (v.30). In other words, 'I know my place and I'm happy in it.'

Once we are rightly related to God, and we are caught up in the fact that Infinite Love and Infinite Wisdom are guiding our course, how can we want to change places with others? In his will is our peace. When we have established the right *Agape* love relationship with God (the key to it all) then he takes from us the eagerness for human praise, which is the cause of so much jealousy. It is the intense longing for admiration which leads many people into this sin. They want the applause, the flattery – this is how they come to envy the people who get it. Christ would have us live independent of human praise. He would have us fix our gaze on him and him alone, to be overjoyed at his smile though all the world hate us, and be heartsore at his frown though all the world think us great.

So now, take out your sling. Put in it the stone of truth (the thoughts we have been reflecting on over the past few days) and tell the Lord how anxious you are for him to win the victory. Not the giant, and not you. Him!

Loving heavenly Father, I have lost many battles in my Christian life because I wanted to experience the feelings of victory more than the joy of bringing glory to you. Now it's different. I shall aim the stone but the victory will be yours. In Jesus' name. Amen.

FOR FURTHER STUDY – Job 42: 2; Eph. 1:11; Jer. 29:11
1. What was Job's conviction? / 2. What was Paul's conviction?

Runaway desires

FOR READING AND MEDITATION – MARK 7:14–23

'For from within … come evil thoughts … greed, malice, deceit, lewdness…'
(vv. 21–22: NIV)

Another giant that overshadows the life of many a Christian is that of lewd desires. Those afflicted in this way say that all other giants are as nothing in comparison. By lewd desires I mean lust, lasciviousness and carnality. Many will admit to having an occasional lustful or lascivious desire, but the condition I am describing here is that in which the life is not merely visited by lewd desires but dominated by them. One man whose life was governed by lewd longings put it like this, 'My mind is a merry-go-round of lustful images.' This problem seems to afflict men more than women, but I have been amazed at how many women have confessed to me in counselling sessions that they burn with lust towards men who are not their husbands.

Desire, as such, is one of the God-given forces of the personality. Without it, life would be dull and sluggish. But when desire becomes our master rather than our servant, then something has to be done about it. Buddha tried to help people over-come desire by cutting the root of desire itself. But you cannot cure the ills of life by eliminating an integral part of life. You can get rid of a headache by cutting off your head, but it is a drastic remedy!

There is a way of living which is exemplified by the horse that lies down in harness and won't move. There is another way which may be likened to the horse that runs away, breaks the harness and smashes everything. What is necessary is to find the balance between lying down and running away. We can't stop lustful thoughts arising in our minds, but with God's help we can stop them residing there.

O God, I have now got to grips with the raw material of human living. This raw material is recalcitrant and needs a master. Be thou my Master – the Master of my desires. I give the reins into your hands. Control them for me. In Jesus' name. Amen.

FOR FURTHER STUDY – Rom. 1:18–31; 2 Cor. 12:11–21
1. What was the result when man didn't give God his rightful place?
2. What caused Paul grief?

A judge's downfall

FOR READING AND MEDITATION – JUDGES 14:1–20

'His father and mother replied, ... "Must you go to the uncircumcised
Philistines to get a wife?"' (v. 3: NIV)

One preacher I heard described Samson as a 'he-man with a she-weakness'. It is interesting that the very first words we hear him utter in the Scriptures are these: 'I have seen a Philistine woman ... now get her for me as my wife' (v.2). Samson was born of godly parents and set apart from his birth to be a Nazarite (see Numbers 6), but as soon as he was a man he became bent on taking an attractive Philistine woman to be his wife. Was this natural desire or lust? Though natural desire was obviously present, I think it was about to cross the line and become lust.

Several things said about Samson in the book of Judges suggest that though he was appointed to be one of Israel's judges, he was unable to conquer the giant of lust. In chapter 14 we find that his desire for the Philistine woman was so great that he married her – even though the Philistines were the longstanding enemy of Israel and worshippers of idols. And God had decreed that no Israelite should take an idol-worshipper as his wife (Deuteronomy 7:3–4). In chapter 16 we discover Samson spending a night with a prostitute, and later setting up home with another Philistine woman by the name of Delilah. He became so preoccupied with his lustful desires that the time came when he didn't even know the Lord had departed from him (16:20). The result of Samson's lustful affairs is known to us all. The strong man was taken captive, had his eyes gouged out, his hair shaved and finished up as a grinder in a Philistine prison. His eyes would never wander again.

What can we conclude from all this? Sin binds, sin blinds and sin grinds. Lust is a flame no one dare fan. You'll get burned if you do.

Father, since sexual desire is a part of me – a creative part of me – show me how to prevent it becoming chaotic. Sin has affected the whole of me, but I know that through your blood I can be cleansed. Cleanse me my Father. Every part of me. In Jesus' name. Amen.

FOR FURTHER STUDY – Prov. 5:1–23, 6:20–29, 7:1–27
1. What can we die from a lack of? / 2. What happens when a man scoops fire into his lap?

No respecter of persons

FOR READING AND MEDITATION – 1 THESSALONIANS 4:1–12

'For God did not call us to be impure, but to live a holy life.' (v. 7: NIV)

Yesterday we looked at the downfall of a judge who was brought low through lust. A few years ago a chill ran down the spines of many Christians when satellite television reported the fall of a number of well-known spiritual leaders who similarly were toppled from their roles in the church through inordinate sexual desires. I mention this not to be judgmental but to show that no one is immune from sexual temptation. You are not, and I am not. Lust is no respecter of persons. Its alluring voice can inveigle the most intelligent minds and persuade its victims to believe a lie.

I once spent hours counselling an academic with a string of letters after his name who was brought to court for a sexual offence. He could see the foolishness of his act but said, 'My feelings overwhelm my intelligence.' It made me think of the silver-tongued orator of Rome, Mark Anthony. Of him it was said that in his youth he was so consumed with lust that his tutor once shouted in disgust, 'O Marcus! O colossal child … able to conquer the world but unable to resist a temptation!'

Some years ago, in Bexhill-on-Sea – a town on the south coast of England – people discovered that the trees in a lovely leafy avenue were dying. They investigated and found that a gas main running underneath them was leaking. Everything above the ground appeared fine but the trees were being poisoned from beneath. Men and women reading these lines today are in a similar position. Their lives are being poisoned from beneath – by lust. Who can save them from this condition? Let them hear the good news – Jesus can.

My Creator and my God, take me by the hand lest I be lost in the jungle of sensual desire. For if I get off the track here, I find myself in a jungle which grows more and more dense every moment. Master me so that I shall not be mastered by anything else. Amen.

FOR FURTHER STUDY – 2 Sam. 11:1–27; Job 31:1; Matt. 5:28
1. What does the lust of the eye lead to? / 2. What covenant did Job make?

The law of the sex life

'… a man is a slave to whatever has mastered him.' (v. 19: NIV)

We ended yesterday by asking: when life is being poisoned from beneath by lust who can help us? And we answered by saying, of course, that Jesus can. He is able and willing to come to our aid in every struggle, no matter how much of a stranglehold it has upon us. But just how does a person go about being set free from lust?

I suggest that first we recognise sexual desire for what it is – a God-given desire. It is neither moral nor immoral in itself but moral or immoral according to its use. This takes the shame out of sexual desire and puts it where it belongs – in the illicit use of sex. Sexual desire is divine in origin and comes to us as a powerful instinct. If it ceased then the human race would vanish from the earth. God did few things more wonderful when he made us, than to share with us the joy of creation. But though he gave us life which is pervaded by great instincts, God never said that every instinct has to be satisfied, that to want a thing is reason enough for taking it. Sexual desire is not an appetite (as some argue) on the same level as the desire for food or water. We can live without sex but we cannot live without food or water.

So bring the fact of sex into the open in your thinking and at the same time invite Christ to guide your thoughts on this issue. Settle it once and for all that sex is not your master – Christ is. If you put sex first, it will corrupt your whole life. If you put Jesus first he will co-ordinate your whole life. Sex will then be your servant and not your master. The law of the sex life is this: he that saves his sex life – puts it first – shall lose his life. There are no exceptions and no exemptions.

O God, I see that if sex takes your place and rules me, then I shall be the servant of a desire. And that desire will drive me to the hell of self-loathing. Once again I confess you are my Lord. May no other be my master. In Jesus' name. Amen.

FOR FURTHER STUDY – 1 Cor. 7:1–40; 1 Thess. 4:3–6; 2 Tim. 2:22
1. What was Paul's view of sex? / 2. What was Paul's advice to Timothy?

Our reply to lust

FOR READING AND MEDITATION – ROMANS 6:1–14

'… sin shall not be your master, because you are not under law, but under grace.'
(v. 14: NIV)

There are those who claim that sexual lust relates to the body and is thus a physical problem. Their remedies therefore run along this line: eat the right foods, have plenty of physical exercise and keep your body under control. Now it would be foolish to say that lust has no physical aspects, but it is more a mental problem than a physical one. No sharp distinction can be drawn between mind and body. The mind does not live within the body as a kernel exists within the shell of a nut. Mind and body interrelate in a mysterious way. What affects the mind can affect the body, and what affects the body can affect the mind. But I repeat: lust is more a problem of the mind than the body.

In fact I can go further and indicate which part of the mind is involved. It is the imagination. This is the battleground where much of the fighting that lust provokes takes place. A picture, a word, a story, an advertisement, a glance, an odour – almost anything can trigger a thought in the mind and in a passionate nature, and the whole being then becomes hot with desire.

Lay hold of this: victory or defeat depends on the skill and speed with which a sensual thought is managed in the mind. If men or women turn their thoughts to Christ, think about him, talk to him and make this a firm routine whenever tempted, it will save their vagrant thoughts from escalating into lust. One writer puts it like this, 'When Lust suggests a rendezvous, send Jesus Christ as your representative.' Remind yourself of the verse before us today, which tells us that we are united with Christ. You are no longer a slave to a giant. You have a new Master.

O Father, help me establish the firm routine of disciplined thinking so that when unacceptable ideas invade my mind, I turn my thoughts immediately to you. I supply the willingness but you must supply the power. Help me Lord Jesus. Amen.

FOR FURTHER STUDY – Gen. 6:1–22; Rom. 8:6
1. What caused God to bring judgment? / 2. What does the sinful mind produce?

One law for Christians

FOR READING AND MEDITATION – MARK 12:28–34

'Love the Lord your God with all your heart and with all your soul
and with all your mind ...' (v. 30: NIV)

The point we made yesterday – of gaining victory at the place of your thinking – is an important one and I want to say a little more about it before we move on. Emerson stated, 'The ancestor of every action is a thought.' This being so, then we can stop the action at the place of the thought. Don't dally with the thought saying, 'I won't dismiss the thought, but I'll stop before I do anything about it.' You won't, for in any battle between the imagination and the will the imagination always wins. Mind-adultery soon expresses itself (if it has the opportunity) in body-adultery.

But there is more to this problem than simple mind-control or the exercise of the will, and if I were to leave the matter there, I would be failing you both as a Bible teacher and a counsellor. The ideas I have suggested are only the fences along the sides of an open road – the open road which leads to being passionately taken up with Jesus Christ. You can expel one desire only by a higher desire, one passion by a stronger passion. Let the love of Christ, therefore, be the love that consumes all lesser loves. All the prohibitions against the wrong use of sexual desire will not save you unless the love of Christ is at the centre. There are thousands of laws on the statute books designed to make people good. The Christian has just one: thou shalt love. And love becomes the fulfilling of the law.

George MacDonald, the Scottish novelist and poet, said, 'When a man knocks at the door of a brothel, he is looking for God.' What did he mean? This: God has placed a thirst for himself deep in every heart, and unless that thirst is quenched by him, then we will look for other ways to satisfy it – sensual satisfaction being one of them.

Lord Jesus Christ, I would so fall in love with you that all lesser loves become unnecessary. Help me to lose myself in you so that I can find myself. Blessed Saviour, I love you. Amen.

FOR FURTHER STUDY – Gal. 5:1–6; 1 Cor. 13:13; Eph. 3:17–19
1. How should faith express itself? / 2. What was Paul's prayer for the Ephesians?

Sublimated desires

FOR READING AND MEDITATION – 1 CORINTHIANS 6:12–20

'Do you not know that your body is a temple of the Holy Spirit, who is in you …'
(v. 19: NIV)

We spend one more day looking at spiritual ways by which we can defeat the giant of lust. It is more (we said) than a matter of mind control or the exercise of the will. The heart of the issue is the matter of the heart. Is our heart taken up with Christ and fully occupied with him? If so, then his love brings all other love under his control.

But what about those who are not married, and thus are denied by Scripture the ordinary outlets of sexual expression? Are they doomed to a life of repression? No, in them the sex drive can be sublimated. The sex drive, as you know, is the creative urge, and physical creation is not the only way in which it can be fulfilled. It can produce creativity in other areas of life. Blocked on one level, it can express itself on another. It can find expression in ways such as the creation of new systems of thought and new methods of helping and ministering to others. The strongly sexed are those who strongly serve. Some of the greatest work in the world has been done by those who, denied voluntarily or otherwise the normal outlets for the sex drive, turned this strange tide of power into other forms of creativity. Their urges were not so much suppressed as expressed – but in a different sphere. Those who are single or bereft of a spouse need not despair because of their sexual desires. Let God lead you into new areas of creative activity that will benefit his kingdom.

Remember, the God who delivered Goliath into the hands of David is just the same today. Take aim in his strength and even this giant will fall.

Lord Jesus, because you were human, sexual desire must have been in you as it is in me – yet without sin. Teach me the art of sublimation so that what is blocked on one level can be released on another. For your own dear name's sake. Amen.

FOR FURTHER STUDY – 2 Peter 1:1–9; Rom. 6:12, 8:1–4
1. What is linked to self-control? / 2. What had Paul discovered?

Memories of the past

FOR READING AND MEDITATION – ISAIAH 43: 14–28

'Forget the former things; do not dwell on the past.' (v. 18: NIV)

We continue dipping into God's files of *most wanted* villains in order to identify some of the devilishly inspired giants which threaten us. The one I select now may not be easily recognisable, but believe me, he is active in the lives of countless Christians, nevertheless.

It is difficult to put a name to this intimidator, but he is best described as the giant of shame. Part of his work is to revive memories of things that are best forgotten. He picks on those who have committed some grievous sin in the past – a sin which has been brought to the cross and forgiven – and works to make sure they will not forget it. Whenever they feel they have left the failure of the past far behind, his voice booms across the valley of their soul, reminding them that even though God has forgotten their sin, he will make sure they never forget it. 'How could you have committed such a terrible sin as that?' he jeers. 'Shame on you. What if people knew the kind of person you really are? How can you expect ever to be given a position of trust after what you have done?'

I have been amazed at the number of people I have met who have told me that even though they knew God had forgiven them for some ugly sin of the past, memories and feelings of sorrow and remorse remained to such a degree that a dark shadow was cast over their lives. The giant who keeps alive memories that ought to be forgotten makes sure of that. Those tormented by him are filled with feelings of self-contempt that hinder them from moving on in the work of God. Turn the giant over to Jehovah. He's the best giant-killer there is.

O Father, I want to be rid of this devilishly-inspired giant undermining my life with reminders of sins or mistakes that you have forgiven. You defeated Satan once and for all on Calvary. Now apply that victory to my life here in the present. In Jesus' name. Amen.

FOR FURTHER STUDY – John 3:16–18, 5:24; Rom. 8:1–17
1. What did Jesus promise to those who believe in him? / 2. What did Paul affirm?

Just holding the coats

FOR READING AND MEDITATION – ACTS 7: 54–60

'Meanwhile, the witnesses laid their clothes at the feet
of a young man named Saul.' (v. 58: NIV)

We continue looking at the problem of those who have received the forgiveness of
God for some wicked sin of the past but whose memories continue to be lacerated
by feelings of shame. Paul the apostle had a *past*. The first time his name is mentioned in the New Testament is in connection with a judicial murder.

Paul is without doubt the greatest figure in the church next to Jesus, but when
we first meet him, he is implicated in a dreadful crime. Stephen had defended himself with great skill before the Sanhedrin, but no sooner had his speech finished
than they set upon him and dragged him out of the city to stone him to death.
Historians say that it was a form of execution that came very close in brutality to
crucifixion. Flung against a wall, the victim was pounded with stones until all life
had gone out of him. Despite his agony, Stephen died victoriously. He followed the
Saviour's example by praying in his last moments: 'Lord, do not hold this sin against
them' (v.60). And Paul was there. No wound on the martyr's body could be attrib-
uted to him. He had simply been looking after the coats of those who murdered him.
But in the language of today, he was an accessory before and after the fact. Though
he might have left the scene saying to himself, 'I had nothing to do with it,' the blood
of the first martyr was on his hands.

Yet Paul found forgiveness. And years later, when he faced the future, he said:
'Forgetting what is behind and straining towards what is ahead, I press on towards
the goal …' (Phil. 3:13–14). No giant was allowed to intimidate him. He was not glad
about what he had done but he did not allow the past to determine his future. That
is the way it must be with us also.

*O God, help me forget the bad things of the past. May I be like Paul who, having been forgiven, did
not allow his past to intimidate him. In Jesus' name. Amen.*

FOR FURTHER STUDY – John 8: 1–11; Rom. 8:34; 1 John 3:21
1. What did Jesus say to the woman? / 2. What question did Paul ask?

What it means to 'forget'

FOR READING AND MEDITATION – 2 PETER 1:1–11

'… he is short-sighted and blind, and has forgotten that he has
been cleansed from his past sins.' (v. 9: NIV)

The question facing us now is this: how do we go about annihilating this giant which seeks to paralyse us by reviving memories of past sins that have been forgiven? But first let's be clear about what we are saying, as a wrong understanding can lead to unrealistic expectations and dampening disappointment.

Some psychologists tell us that it is impossible to forget anything. All our thoughts (they claim) are stored up inside us, and though they may be beyond the reach of recollection, they are not outside our mental make-up. We may not be able to recall them at will, but they are not forgotten. Sometimes, of course, an accident or a trauma will produce what is known as amnesia (loss of memory), but with this condition, memories are not so much lost as unable to be recalled. I do not believe it is part of God's purpose to expunge unpleasant memories from our memory banks. Instead, he takes the sharp edge off them and helps us avoid an emotional overload.

As I sit here at my computer, I can see on the top of my thumb an ugly scar. And I remember, albeit dimly, what caused it. Once, when I was using a sharp blade to cut some paper, it slipped and the blade penetrated my thumb. A few unpleasant hours followed, but now the memory of the accident is all but forgotten. The pain has gone and the memory is faint. There are things in our past that can be remembered as dimly as that. Give God the chance and he will make you forget anything that it would be harmful to remember. Not the event, but the acute recollection of it.

My Father and my God, I see that forgetting does not mean all my memories are obliterated, but that by your grace, the sharp edge is taken off them. If I am in need of this special ministry, let grace flow into my open wounds. In Jesus' name. Amen.

FOR FURTHER STUDY – Phil. 3:1–14; Rev. 12:10; 1 John 3:20
1. Where do accusations come from? / 2. What is God greater than?

Repenting by 'repentance'

FOR READING AND MEDITATION – 2 CORINTHIANS 7:1–16
'Godly sorrow brings repentance that leads to salvation and leaves no regret …'
(v. 10: NIV)

How do we work with God to annihilate the giant who seeks to paralyse our Christian lives by replaying memories of things that are best forgotten? First, we need to be sure that we have properly repented of our sin. I am aware that I am continually drawing attention to this subject of repentance in my writings, but I do so because I believe it is seriously misunderstood in some church circles. The path to God (as you know) is the path of repentance. Yet so often our repentance is not what it should be. Wasn't it George Whitefield who said, 'Our repentance needs to be repented of, and our tears washed in the blood of Christ'? Why should he say that? Because often our repentance is not really repentance at all. It is only remorse or fear. We can be sad, even in tears, not because of the wrong we have done but because we have been found out or may yet be found out.

When I was a pastor, more than once I went to court with a young man who had gotten himself into trouble and who appeared to be repentant. I would speak on his behalf and then, when he was let off, all the distress would instantly disappear. He wasn't sorry for his sin at all. He was only sorry about the price he feared he would have to pay. What I thought was repentance was nothing more than apprehension and passing remorse – a shabby counterfeit.

Many have no sense of forgiveness because they have not really repented. So if you have not truly repented, I suggest you do so now. Remember, repentance is not only being sorry for sin but being sorry for the self-centredness that prompted the sin in the first place. Sin is self in the place God ought to be.

O God, forgive me that so often I am not sorry for sin but sorry for the trouble that my sin causes me. My repentance needs to be repented of and my tears washed in the blood of Christ. Help me repent – truly repent. In Christ's name I ask it. Amen.

FOR FURTHER STUDY – 1 John 1:1–10; Psa. 103: 1–12; Isa. 43:25
1. What has God promised through confession of sin? / 2. How did the psalmist express it?

Remembering to forget

FOR READING AND MEDITATION – JEREMIAH 31:31–37

'For I will forgive their wickedness and will remember their sins no more.' (v. 34: NIV)

We continue examining the nature of true repentance. On more than one occasion while I was a pastor, I was consulted by an unmarried young girl who was in anguish because she thought she was pregnant. I would help her find forgiveness and do all I could to assist her to plan for her future. And then she would discover she was not pregnant after all. So often in cases like that the distress would depart and the girl would appear bright and happy. There was nothing wrong with that of course, but the real tragedy lay in the fact that her sin was now seen in a new light – not as sin at all, just an unfortunate mistake. Her repentance was not real repentance – just remorse and passing fear.

Now let every one of us be on our guard against feeling superior about this. Hasn't our repentance been spurious at times? Haven't we been sorry not because we have offended God and broken his holy laws but because we have lost our inner peace? Haven't we been cast down not by genuine sorrow over sin but because we have suffered some personal deprivation? What does God say to a truly repentant people? He gives the message of our text today: 'I will ... remember their sins no more.' Note the words 'I will remember no more'. Whether or not God can forget is a moot point. I am not sure myself that God forgets in the sense that his memory of events is expunged. The reality, I think, is that he remembers to forget. This might seem to be playing with words but the truth we all ought to exult in today is this: when we repent of our sin – truly repent – then the forgiveness that God gives is absolute and eternal.

O God, may the sense of forgiveness permeate my soul. I know that when I truly repent you truly forgive. Help me move forward with the light and steady step of someone who has been forgiven by God. In Jesus' name. Amen.

FOR FURTHER STUDY – Acts 3:1–19; Ezek. 18:31; Hosea 14:2; Acts 17:30
1. What was at the heart of Peter's message? / 2. What has God commanded?

Righting wrongs

FOR READING AND MEDITATION – LUKE 19:1–9

'… if I have cheated anybody out of anything, I will pay back
four times the amount.' (v. 8: NIV)

Another matter we must consider if we are to understand repentance is that of restitution. Nowadays we don't hear much about this in sermons. Yet though restitution
may not be mentioned in modern-day sermons, it is certainly mentioned in the
Bible. Restitution is the attempt to make reparation for the damage we may have
caused by our sin. Of course restitution isn't always possible, but it is something that
we should always aim for nevertheless. And we must be clear also that it isn't restitution that wipes out the sin; it is the forgiving grace of Christ.

Once I had to deal with a man who had sexually abused a neighbour's child. It
was a terrible situation. The law took its course and he was imprisoned. But in
prison he genuinely repented, and when he came out he told me he felt God had spoken to him about the matter of restitution. But how could restitution be made in a
case such as this? We didn't know, so I went with him to the home of the parents
concerned and listened as he humbly sought their forgiveness. After they forgave
him, he asked if there was something he could do to help the young girl he had
abused. They were reluctant to talk at first, but eventually it emerged that because
the father had been off work, due to the trauma they had gone through as a family,
he did not have the financial resources to put his daughter through college. Immediately the man said, 'I'll take care of that.' It cost him his life savings – a matter of
over £1 000 – but he did so cheerfully and willingly.

No one can forget the wrong he has done until he has done whatever he can to
put the wrong right.

*Father, I recognise that it is not restitution that cleanses from sin, but I see also that making
amends, whenever possible, helps misdeeds to fall into oblivion. May I be divinely led in this, and
not allow my inability to make restitution create false shame. Amen.*

FOR FURTHER STUDY – Ex. 22: 1–15; Lev. 6:1–7; Prov. 6:30–31
1. What was an important element of the statutes God gave?
2. Do you need to make restitution to anyone?

On forgiving yourself

FOR READING AND MEDITATION – ROMANS 8:28–39
'Who will bring any charge against those whom God has chosen?
It is God who justifies.' (v. 33: NIV)

Probably right now someone reading my words is being confronted by the giant of shame. A sin for which you have been forgiven by God is being drawn to your attention by the terrible Titan. These devotionals might be read by a number of men and women who are in prison as a consequence of some crime they have committed. To such I want to say today: if you have genuinely repented of what you did, then although the law still has to take its course, God has eternally and absolutely forgiven you.

Others reading these lines may not be in a physical prison but in a mental one. The giant of shame threatens to bring some forgiven sin out from your past and ruin your reputation. Before you surrender your case as hopeless and abandon the fight, go over the things I have said during these past few days. Understand what it means to genuinely repent. Consider restitution. But talk that matter over with a minister or counsellor before doing anything about it, as sometimes restitution can be a very complex issue, requiring great thought and care. Then ask yourself this: God has forgiven me; have I forgiven myself?

When a sense of shame remains after having been forgiven by God, one ought to suspect the presence of pride. What you may be saying to yourself at some deep level of your emotional life is this, 'How could I have ever done that? Me, of all people?' Hear the pride? Self-hate and self-contempt is rooted in pride, so recognise what is going on and repent even of that. Now, just as you forgive others, forgive yourself. God has forgiven you. Who are you to have superior values to the Almighty?

Father, forgive me if by my pride I make the job of the giant of shame so much easier. May I put in my sling the smooth stone of truth that I have learned these past days and bring down this Titan once and for all. In Jesus' name. Amen.

FOR FURTHER STUDY – Psa. 51: 1–19; Isa. 57:16–18; Jer. 3:22; 30:17–22
1. What does God promise? / 2. How did the people respond?

Under the broom tree

FOR READING AND MEDITATION – 1 KINGS 19:1–21

'[Elijah] came to a broom tree, sat down under it and prayed that he might die.'
(v. 4: NIV)

The next face we come across as we work our way through the files of God's *most wanted* villains is that of the giant of despair. Fortunate are those who have never been intimidated by this Titan, bellowing out threats with a *basso-profundo* voice that sounds like a dozen out-of-tune tubas.

Elijah, the great prophet of Israel, knew what it was to have an encounter with the giant of despair. Sit with me for a moment in the shade of the broom tree and watch how this devout man of God falls prey to the deepest form of melancholy. The prophet has just experienced a tremendous victory over Ahab and the Baal-worshippers, but then the giant of despair is ushered in by Ahab's wife Jezebel. She predicts that Elijah's life will be over within twenty-four hours. Though this mighty man of God has overcome all previous threats, somehow Jezebel's statement finds its mark. Elijah runs for his life. Finally he sinks in utter despair beneath the broom tree and says: 'I've had enough, Lord. Take my life' (v. 4). Did God rebuke him? Or tell him how disappointed he was with him? No, he ministered to him by allowing him to take a long rest and providing a meal or two. Later he gave him a close friend by the name of Elisha to encourage him. Gently he prodded the prophet to get a new perspective on things.

Elijah came back from despair. And so can you. The good news is that this giant too can be defeated. I know, for at one time I had an encounter with him myself.

My Father and my God, help me in the hour of pressure and crisis to remember what you did for Elijah. The last word is always with you. And that last word is deliverance. I am so grateful. Thank you my Father. Amen.

FOR FURTHER STUDY – Josh. 7:1–10; Psa. 42:6; Luke 24:17
1. How did Joshua feel? / 2. What did God say to him?

Spiritual highs and lows

FOR READING AND MEDITATION – 2 CORINTHIANS 1:1–11

'We were under great pressure …so that we despaired even of life.' (v. 8: NIV)

It's strange how periods of depression can follow times of great spiritual elation and victory. We saw Elijah affected in this way yesterday. Fresh from a stunning victory on Mount Carmel, the prophet became vulnerable and frightened. He cried out to God beneath the broom tree, not words of praise but a plea that his life might end. Surely no despair can be greater than that.

Baffling as it may be, it is not unusual to find oneself at a low ebb following a period of great vision or victory. Some time ago, I ministered at a conference in Adelaide, Australia, along with an American Bible teacher by the name of Bob Mumford. Bob warned the congregation about what he called *post-convention depression*, which he described as the low feelings we get following a spiritual high. This dejection is not clinical depression that needs medical treatment, but it must be guarded against nevertheless, for the giant of despair will step in and take advantage of our vulnerability.

The apostle Paul appears to have become despondent during his great missionary journey into Asia. They were under such great pressure, he says, that they despaired even of life. Paul's despair and Elijah's despair took quite different forms, of course. The prophet's despair was of such a nature that he wanted his life to end. The apostle's despair was because his life might end. But they were both affected by despair, nevertheless. Why did God allow such a thing to happen to the great apostle? This is how Paul understood it: 'That we might not rely on ourselves but on God' (v. 9). God can use even despair to advance his purposes for us.

O Father, give me the confidence that no matter what happens in my life you are standing by ready, willing and able to turn everything to my spiritual profit. I may sink into despair but I need not stay in it. Amen.

FOR FURTHER STUDY – Eccles. 2:1–26; Gen. 27:46; Job 7:16
1. Why did the writer of Ecclesiastes hate life? / 2. What point did Rebekah come to?

It can be done

FOR READING AND MEDITATION – JOB 1:1–22
'The Lord gave and the Lord has taken away; may the name of
the Lord be praised.' (v. 21: NIV)

If we are to overcome despair whenever it hits our lives we must understand something of its dynamics. By *dynamics* I mean the elements that go to make it the debilitating power it is. Top of the list is a sense of loss. Whenever I talk to a person who is in the grip of despair, the first thing I try to identify is their perceived sense of loss. Loss comes in two general categories: the loss of those we love, and the loss of things we love.

When I was a young boy, I was once present in the home of a man whose wife had just died. As soon as he saw the spark of life fade from her eyes, he picked up a knife and attempted to kill himself. Fortunately, another family member was able to intervene before he did himself great harm. Despair can set in very quickly and sometimes have serious consequences when a loved one dies. The other kind of loss is the loss of things we love – the loss of one's job, the loss of an object desired, the loss of a goal, the loss of wealth, and so on.

Job was a man who experienced both the loss of those he loved and the things he loved. Three times in the chapter we have read today, we find the phrase 'while he was still speaking'. Did you sense as you read those words the rapid succession of events described in the account? One after another the calamities struck. Job lost those he loved – his ten sons and daughters – and the things he loved – the herds which made him wealthy. How did he respond? He was devastated but not in despair. He didn't blame God and he didn't sin. He worshipped. Imagine that! It's difficult not to fall victim to the giant of despair in such circumstances, but as Job shows, it can be done.

O Father, forgive me if, when calamities strike, my tendency is not to worship but to whine. How I long to have the deep inward trust that your servant Job so wonderfully demonstrated. Draw closer to me, Lord, as I draw closer to you. In Christ's name. Amen.

FOR FURTHER STUDY – Psa. 42:1–11, 62:5, 31:24
1. What did David ask of himself? / 2. What did he say to himself?

Three cardinal virtues

FOR READING AND MEDITATION – 1 CORINTHIANS 13:1–13
'And now these three remain: faith, hope and love.' (v. 13: NIV)

We saw yesterday that the chief element underlying despair is a sense of loss. And loss, we said, comes in two general categories: loss of those we love, and loss of things we love. But as we probe deeper into the dynamics of despair, we find that the greatest loss is the loss of hope. I turned to my dictionary a few moments ago to see how it defined despair. This is what it said: 'a complete loss or absence of hope; thing that causes this whether by badness or unapproachable excellence'.

Throughout time writers and artists have been divided on the subject of hope. You may have seen a print of the famous picture by G.F. Watts called *Hope* which shows a blindfolded woman sitting with bowed head on a sphere and holding in her hand a lyre. Only one string of the instrument remains unbroken, only one star shines in the dark sky. There is a story that when it was first shown in an art gallery in London, two tramps who had crept into the building to get out of the cold were overheard discussing it. 'Hope,' said one, 'why is it called *Hope*? To which the other replied, gazing at the figure perched precariously on the sphere, 'I suppose because she hopes she won't fall off.' Many think of hope like that – as being precarious, an illusion, a vanity, a dream. 'Hope is the most hopeless thing of all,' said one cynic.

How different is Scripture's view of hope. Paul tells us in today's passage that it is one of the three cardinal virtues of the Christian faith. But for hope to be real hope, it must be linked to Christ. All other hopes are illusions. Only in Christ can hope be spelled with a capital *H*.

Gracious Father, I see that all is not lost while I have hope. And in you hope is more than an illusion, more than a mere pipe-dream. I may lose things and I may lose loved ones but I will never lose you. Thus I can go on – no matter what happens. Thank you my Father. Amen.

FOR FURTHER STUDY – Eph. 2:1–13; Heb. 6:18–19; 1 Pet. 1:3
1. What does Paul exhort us to remember? / 2. What does hope provide?

Tied to God's ends

FOR READING AND MEDITATION – LAMENTATIONS 3:19–33

'Yet this I call to mind and therefore I have hope.' (v. 21: NIV)

You do not have to be widely read in secular literature to notice how the world's view of hope is quite different from that of Scripture. Schopenhauer, the distinguished German philosopher, looked upon hope as the bait by which nature makes us serve her interests rather than our own. Indeed, most secular writers seem to regard hope as vain, poor and deceptive.

But hope, as we saw yesterday, is not so thought of in the Scriptures. Paul speaks of the patience or endurance of hope (1 Thessalonians 1:3), and hope that does not disappoint us (Romans 5:5). The author of the epistle to the Hebrews makes what seems a paradoxical statement when he likens hope to an anchor for the soul that is firm and secure (Hebrews 6:19).

Why this contrast between the view of the world and the view of Scripture? The answer is not difficult. They are talking about different things. There is genuine hope and there is counterfeit hope. There is gold and there is gilt. What the world means by hope (with a few exceptions) is optimism. Of course optimism is much better than pessimism. Every doctor knows that. But optimism is not enough to hold us when our expectations are not realised. 'It's all right,' an optimist told me when I visited his wife in hospital because she was seriously ill. 'She's going to get better.' But I conducted her funeral before the week was out. Optimism alone is not enough to save us from despair. We must have Christian hope: hope that is tied to good ends – God's ends.

Father, I see that my hope is only as good as that to which it is tied. How thankful I am that my hope is in you. Help me always to see past earthly issues to heavenly ones. And remind me that nothing will ever cause you to vacate your throne. Amen.

FOR FURTHER STUDY – Rom. 15:1–6, 8:24–25; 1 John 3:3

1. Where do we draw hope from? / 2. What does hope result in?

The larger story

FOR READING AND MEDITATION – DANIEL 3:1–30

'... the God we serve is able to save us ... But even if he does not ...' (vv. 17–18: NIV)

How different is Christian hope from the optimism displayed by the world. It is as different as the proven results of scientific research are from the gambler's dice. The Christian moves into life not inflated with foolish optimism (which seems to give needed buoyancy to those who do not know Christ) but with a quiet and unquenchably hope drawn from the depths of our faith. And the language which comes easily to optimists is avoided by us.

Rather, we take the attitude of the three young men whose story is recorded in the passage before us today. They were confident that God could deliver them from the burning fiery furnace, but if not, they said, they would still take their stand on his principles. Confident boasting of a victory or wishful anticipation that things will go the way we think they should is not what Christian living is all about. It is based not on what we think is best but what God thinks is best.

The ground of our hope is that God is writing what Dr Larry Crabb calls a 'larger story'. By 'larger story' he means the purposes of God for our lives which often are quite different from our purposes. So perverse is our human nature (even though we may have been Christians for decades) that we prefer not only to write our own story but to direct it, produce it and star in it also. The three young men in today's passage sensed that God was writing a bigger story than they could compose and wanted to be part of it. They were ready for their own plans to be crossed if his plans could be advanced. That is the hope that holds us and helps us rise from the depths of despair. Often things don't go our way because they are going his way.

O Father, forgive me that I so easily forget my life is part of a larger story. And forgive me also that often I am more concerned about how you can fit into my story than how I can fit into yours. Cleanse me and help me, dear Father. In Jesus' name. Amen.

FOR FURTHER STUDY – 1 Pet. 3:8–15; Col. 1:5; Prov. 14:32
1. How are we to explain our hope to others? / 2. What springs from hope?

Beating a hasty retreat

FOR READING AND MEDITATION – 2 CORINTHIANS 4:1–18

'We are hard pressed on every side, but not crushed; perplexed,
but not in despair … (v. 8: NIV)'

Having looked over the past few days at the dynamics of despair, today we ask ourselves: how do we go about actually defeating this fearsome giant? Like David we
must have a stone to put in our sling that, coupled with confidence in God, will bring
down the giant of despair. What is that stone? It is the stone of truth. But what particular truth? This: that despite all appearances to the contrary, God is at work and
he is good.

It has been said that these twin truths are the most difficult to believe, especially for the victims of some great loss. I can vouch for that, both from my own
experience and my experience with others. So how can we hold on to these truths
when we are in the midst of circumstances that bring us almost to the point of
despair? We retreat to the cross. The cross symbolises for us God's power, wisdom
and love. From one perspective Calvary appears to have all the elements that spell
out despair. But from another it spells out hope – hope that no matter how dark
things look, a divine purpose sweeps through everything. Everything!

When life falls to pieces all around you, it is not easy to believe that God is active.
And it is certainly difficult to believe that God is good. But as we have just
said, the cross gives the lie to that. Though circumstances may appear desperate, in
reality that can never be so. Take your stand at the cross and hold on to that. Hope,
remember, is more than optimism. When the shallow hopes of the world are dead,
hope on in God. Then, like the apostle Paul, you will be able to say: 'We are perplexed,
but not in despair.'

*O Father, how thankful I am for the cross – the one luminous point in a dark and mysterious uni-
verse. May the truth it symbolises be the stone in my sling that brings down the giant of despair.
In Christ's name. Amen.*

FOR FURTHER STUDY – John 14:1–14; Rom. 8:28–29; Isa. 43:2
1. What larger story did Jesus encourage his disciples with?
2. What promise did God make to Israel?

The tallest Titan

FOR READING AND MEDITATION – PROVERBS 16:9–20

'Pride goes before destruction, a haughty spirit before a fall.' (v. 18: NIV)

Giants are tall, tough and terrifying. Of that there can be little doubt. We now meet the tallest of the Titans, and one with which almost every Christian has to do battle at some time or another – pride. This (in my opinion) is the most dangerous of the giants we have considered so far. For pride, theologians conclude, is the most deadly sin of all.

When I have made this point publicly – that pride is the greatest evil – someone has usually come up to me afterwards and said something like this, 'I can think of sins that are worse than pride. Murder, for example. Or lust. Or envy. All these are more deadly than the sin of pride.' Notwithstanding this argument, I believe the theologians are right. St Augustine, one of the greatest Christian thinkers, held that view. So did Thomas Aquinas. Dante did too. And, if it were necessary, I could add a hundred more famous names. In the Bible, pride is portrayed as the primal sin. This is what turned an angel into a devil and, in turn, emptied heaven of a host of angels (see Jude v. 6).

But how can pride be defined? Pride is the ego in the place God wants to be. This is the essence of this awful soul disease. It puts self in the centre. It struts and shouts and brags. It has the attitude, 'I … I … I.' It dethrones the Almighty in the human heart and instates the puffed-up ego. Can you see now why it is regarded as the ugliest and deadliest of all sins? It gives self, not God, the supreme position. Such is its ruinous nature that William Law said of it, 'Pride must die in you or Christ will not be able to live in you.' Strong words but true.

Lord Jesus Christ, I see that you and pride are incompatible. May the giant of pride be dealt a death blow in my life over these next few days so that he will never be able to intimidate me again. For your own dear name's sake. Amen.

FOR FURTHER STUDY – Isa. 14:12–15; Gen. 11:4; Luke 22:24
1. Why did they want to build a city and high tower?
2. Why did the disciples end up in dispute?

The devil's handiwork

FOR READING AND MEDITATION – PSALM 8:1–9

'When I consider your heavens … what is man that you are mindful of him?'
(vv. 3–4: NIV)

Before we begin to do battle with pride, we must be clear as to the foulness of its nature and see it for the enemy that it is. Pride, we said yesterday, is self in the place of God. Spiritually-minded people echo the words of the psalmist: 'The Lord is God. It is he who made us, and we are his; we are his people, the sheep of his pasture' (Psa. 100:3). But pride rebels against that. William Henley, the poet, spoke for the rebellious when he declared blatantly:

> I am the master of my fate,
> I am the captain of my soul.

When men and women claim to be the measure of all things, to be able to run their own world (how did it become theirs?), to solve their own problems, secure their own salvation and manage their own destinies, they push God aside and take over his role in the universe. Indeed, as one person has put it, 'The principle of pride, when taken to its *nth* degree, is capable, in intention at least, of pushing God out of the very universe he made.'

Dr A.C. Craig, a 20th century theologian, made this point plain by changing the words of today's Psalm so that part of it reads thus: 'O Man, how excellent is thy name in all the earth! Who has set thy glory above the heavens? When I consider thy inventions, the work of thy fingers, the aeroplanes and atomic bombs which thou hast made, what is God that I should be mindful of him, or the Son of God that I should reverence him?' Pride is not a half-harmless sin. It is the devil's finished handiwork.

Gracious Father, the more I see the evil nature of pride and what it has done to your universe, the more I want to be rid of it. Out of all the deliverances you have given me, this could be the greatest. I wait with eager anticipation. Amen.

FOR FURTHER STUDY – Rev. 3:14–22; Prov. 11:2, 16:18, 21:4
1. What was the tragedy of the Laodicean church?
2. How does the Bible describe pride?

Shallow thinking

FOR READING AND MEDITATION – PROVERBS 1:1–11

'When pride comes, then comes disgrace, but with humility comes wisdom.' (v. 2: NIV)

The word *pride*, like *jealousy*, can be used in two different ways. There is a good form of pride as well as a bad one. It is good for men and women to have pride in their work, their appearance, their achievements, their families, and so on. A person without pride, in this sense, would lack self-respect. It is only unworldly doctrinaires who would look upon this kind of pride as sin. So remember that when I speak of pride, I mean its sinful aspect.

Pride not only denies that God is the Creator and Upholder of the universe, but relegates every other person to a minor role in it. The really proud man or woman never sees other persons as equal but as inferior, as minor actors in a play in which he or she is the leading character. One writer tells of a valet who spoke of his master in these terms, 'He had to be the central figure in everything. If he went to a christening he wanted to be the baby. If he went to a wedding he wanted to be the bridegroom. If he went to a funeral he wanted to be the corpse.' You may have heard of the nurse who was so conceited that when she took the pulse of one of the men in her ward, she always knocked off a few degrees to allow for the impact of her personality on the patient!

However, before we laugh, we ought to take a look inside our own hearts to see how much pride lingers there. When we really understand what pride is, we realise it is the greatest sin of all. One commentator says of it, 'It can even make virtues vicious and the other vices more vicious than they were.' It is shallow thinking that dismisses pride as half-harmless, a thing to be brushed aside with a tolerant smile.

O God, give me clear insight to see pride for what it really is and the courage to face the fact that it may have a deeper hold on me than I have realised. I would harbour no dangerous parasites in my soul. Help me my Father. In Jesus' name. Amen.

FOR FURTHER STUDY – Dan. 4:1–5:31; 2 Chron. 26:16; Prov. 3:7
1. How did God deal with Nebuchadnezzar's pride?
2. How did God deal with Belshazzar's pride?

One great snare left

FOR READING AND MEDITATION – LUKE 18:9–14

'For everyone who exalts himself will be humbled, and he who humbles
himself will be exalted.' (v. 14: NIV)

Yesterday we made reference to the quotation, [Pride] can even make virtue vicious
and the other vices more vicious than they were. How can this be so? The other vices
grow in the soil of vice: stealing out of covetousness; fornication and adultery out of
lewd desire; murder out of hate and the desire for revenge; lying out of a heart filled
with deceit. But pride is more subtle. It propagates itself in the soil of virtue also.

How easy it is, for example, for good people to convince themselves that they
are the author of their own goodness. Readers who have been Christians for some
time and have developed a strong devotional life, have regular prayer times, put
aside their tithes in an orderly way and spend time studying the Scriptures, can still
be trapped by one great snare – the temptation to believe that they have done it all
by themselves.

The Pharisee stood in the Temple, looked up to heaven and said: 'God, I thank
you that I am not like other men – robbers, evildoers, adulterers – or even like this
tax collector. I fast twice a week and give a tenth of all I get' (vv. 11–12). And it was
all true. He was not lying. He was not an extortioner. And certainly he could not be
accused of committing adultery. He did fast twice a week. He did give tithes of all he
possessed. So why did Jesus single him out for condemnation? Because of his pride.
He did not trace his advance in his spiritual life to the grace of God. He thought he
had achieved it. The tax collector was different. He cried out: 'God, have mercy on
me, a sinner' (v. 13), and went back to his home justified. One individual had God at
the centre of his life; the other had ... himself.

*O Father, I accept that it is easy to attribute my growth in spiritual matters to my own efforts.
Forgive me if I have done this. I am what I am by the grace of God. Help me never to forget that.
In Christ's name I ask it. Amen.*

FOR FURTHER STUDY – 2 Cor. 10:1–12; Prov. 12:15, 30:11–14
1. When are we not wise?
2. Ask God to help you to see if you are being unwise.

One hell ... one heaven

FOR READING AND MEDITATION – PROVERBS 21:20–31

'The proud and arrogant man – "Mocker" is his name; he behaves
with overweening pride.' (v. 24: NIV)

Yesterday we looked at the Pharisee who appeared to be within hailing distance of the summit of sanctity but tobogganed to the bottom because of pride. Nothing is more hateful to God than self-righteousness, because it treats the blood of Christ as worthless and thus regards Calvary as unnecessary. Pride can even trap us by causing us to feel superior to those it has ensnared. Like the old lady who, after listening approvingly to the story of the Pharisee and the tax collector, commented to her friends on the way out of church, 'Well, thank God I'm not like them Pharisees!'

By now I hope you are convinced that pride is the deadliest sin and the most formidable of all the giants on God's *most wanted* list. But how do we combat pride? Once again, we can do so by resorting to the stone of truth and aiming it at the giant with the assurance that the battle is God's. And the truth that seems to have most helped people overcome pride is the truth about Christ, as recorded in the four Gospels. Read through them again with this question in mind: How did our Lord walk through this world? Gaze upon him. Compare yourself with him. See how he embodies that great quality, humility, which, of course, is the very opposite of pride.

Pride takes various forms and often is not easily noticed. But in Christ's light, evidences of pride that are hidden in the dark crevices of the soul are revealed and seen as abhorrent. William Law who, as we noted earlier, stated, 'Pride must die in you or Christ will not be able to live in you,' also said, 'Look not on pride only as an unbecoming temper, nor at humility only as a decent virtue ... One is all hell and the other all heaven!'

O God, only when I look into your Word can I see how deeply pride has stiffened my spirit. Help me spend more time looking at that source of light. In Jesus' name. Amen.

FOR FURTHER STUDY – Isa. 57:1–15; Prov. 16:19, 29:23
1. Who does God dwell with? / 2. How can we gain honour?

The marks of pride

FOR READING AND MEDITATION – PHILIPPIANS 2:1–11

'Who, being in very nature God … made himself nothing ...' (vv. 6–7: NIV)

We are saying that the best way in which to fell the giant of pride is to consider our Lord and look at ourselves in the light of his life. It is wrong to compare ourselves with others; it is right to compare ourselves with him. What are some of the evidences of this thing called pride? One is remembering insults long after you have forgotten sorrows. Another is staying upset when someone has treated you with contempt. Yet another is being touchy about your background. To these we can add being over-sensitive or unduly concerned about such matters as your present status, abilities, power to get your own way, and lack of education. There are, of course, many more.

Bring your life now to Christ and measure yourself against him. And don't forget, I am using the word *pride* or *proud* in its bad sense, not its good sense. Is status all-important to you? Is that what you are proud of? He who was God laid it all aside and confined himself to a virgin's womb. Are you proud of your birth and your family? He grew up in a poor home in Nazareth. Are you proud of your profession? He was a carpenter. Are you proud of the social circle in which you move? He moved mainly among tax collectors and sinners. Are you proud of your abilities? He said: 'By myself I can do nothing' (John 5:30: NIV). Are you proud because you can intimidate people and get your own way? He said: 'I seek not to please myself but him who sent me' (John 5:30: NIV). Are you proud of your position? He said: 'I am among you as one who serves' (Luke 22:27: NIV).

How do you appear to yourself in the light of such amazing humility? I am not afraid to tell you that as that light falls on me, I feel ashamed.

O God, the more I compare myself with your Son, the more clearly I see how deeply pride has become entrenched in my soul. My hope is now in you. I know you will not fail. Amen.

FOR FURTHER STUDY – John 13:1–17; Matt. 20:28; Luke 22:27
1. How did Jesus demonstrate humility? / 2. What sort of heart did Jesus display?

What an amazing sight!

FOR READING AND MEDITATION – JOHN 13:1–17

'I have set you an example that you should do as I have done for you.' (v. 15: NIV)

Look with me finally at our Lord on the last night of his incarnate life. As it is time for the Feast of the Passover, Jesus has borrowed a room to celebrate the feast, and now all is ready – not just the meal but the water jugs and basins and towels. During the meal Jesus gets up from the table and proceeds to wash the disciples' feet. This menial task would normally be performed by a servant, but as no servant is present, our Lord undertakes the task himself.

Let your imagination dwell on this amazing sight. He who is God stoops to wash the disciples' feet. Why did he do it? Was it mere acting? No, it was his answer to their pride. It was an act done deliberately to emphasise the point that greatness lies not in being served but in serving. In dramatic terms it sets forth the need for selfless service which would later be exemplified by our Lord's death upon the cross. One Gospel tells of the disciples arguing among themselves during this meal (Luke 22:24–27), and by washing their feet our Lord in one stroke sweeps from their minds the idea that the great are those who lord it over others and remain 'uncontaminated' by menial tasks.

I ask you to look into our Lord's lowly mind because it is only there that we can see our pride for what it really is. That's the stone of truth that brings down the giant of pride. But as you hurl that stone at your adversary and see him fall, remember not to have pride in your conquest. The victory is God's, not yours. We must not claim to be the architect of any virtue or victory. If we do, the giant may fall but will not be beheaded. He will rise again.

Father, let me live so closely to your Son and know him so intimately that his humility replaces all my pride. And help me see that every virtue and every victory is due not to my power but to his power flowing through me. For his honour and glory I pray. Amen.

FOR FURTHER STUDY – Luke 7:36-50; Matt. 15:30; Mark 5:22, 7:25; Luke 10:39
1. Where is the best place to sit for pride to be dealt with?
2. What contrast is seen in the Luke 7 account?

The invasion of revenge

FOR READING AND MEDITATION – LEVITICUS 19:1–19

'Do not seek revenge or bear a grudge against one of your people ...' (v. 18: NIV)

Another giant we have to confront and annihilate if we are to experience the freedom and joy which characterises those who are moving on with God is the *giant* of revenge. The passion for revenge is grounded deep in our fallen human nature. Psychologists describe it as a compound of self-regard and anger. Through the long history of the human race, the desire to *get even* has disrupted families, provoked wars, and is one of the chief reasons for the institution of systems of public justice.

Everyone who comes into the world receives at some time a *hard knock*. But hard knocks are of different kinds. Some arise from circumstances such as an accident, for which no one is to blame. Others arise from situations where, because of a person's foolhardiness rather than intent, we find ourselves on the receiving end of some trauma or tragedy. But there is a great dissimilarity between those knocks where no ill-will was intended and those caused because someone deliberately set out to hurt. Counsellors know that the most difficult wounds to heal are those inflicted intentionally. The stab that was meant to injure; the hurt that was cruelly and consciously planned. These are the wounds which fester, and in some people generate a passion for vengeance that can remain in their hearts until the day they die. I have known people who have gone to their graves well before their time, consumed by anger and bitterness.

If you are having a battle with the giant of revenge, then make up your mind that the battle must come to an end. The Titan must be slain – and without delay.

Gracious Father, I see that from the beginning you have urged your people to get rid of the desire for revenge. Forgive us that we allow our lives to be controlled by wrong passions rather than by right ones. Help us be free of all corrupting passion. In Christ's name. Amen.

FOR FURTHER STUDY – 1 Pet. 3:1–9; Lev. 19:18; Prov. 20:22
1. How are we to deal with insults? / 2. What will be the result?

A germ in the mind

FOR READING AND MEDITATION – ROMANS 12:9–21

'Do not take revenge, my friends, but leave room for God's wrath …' (v. 19: NIV)

The passion for revenge is like an evil germ in the mind. It breeds bitterness, depression and disease. Sometimes (though certainly not always) it is a factor behind mental unbalance and nervous breakdowns. The longing to *get even* can do more harm to a person harbouring that desire than the one or ones who caused the desire for revenge in the first place.

Once, in a church I pastored, I watched a man become consumed with bitterness because one of his children was killed by a careless motorist. Everyone in the church sympathised with him and shared his sorrow, and when he referred to the careless motorist as a murderer, no one disagreed with him. But when the initial shock had passed and his grief lessened in intensity, he showed such a desire for revenge that people became concerned, and I felt it necessary to speak to him about it. 'My anger and bitterness are justified,' he argued. 'That murderer took away one of my beautiful children, and I will never let go of my bitterness until I know he too is lying in his grave.' I tried to show him that such an attitude would ruin not only him but also his relationship with his family. But to no avail. He continued to burn with concentrated hate. I stood by helplessly as his family grew afraid of him and the atmosphere in the home became darker and darker. Eventually he lost not only a child, but his whole family too – alienated not by the accident but by his own resentment.

Bitterness and the desire for revenge may be a compensation to a mind overcome with sorrow, but not to those with whom they live. To cultivate the germ of resentment in the mind is as harmful as cultivating a germ or virus in the body.

Father, you are always urging us to get rid of our desire for revenge, for you see the harm that resentment wreaks upon the whole person. Help us see it too – and be rid of it. In Christ's name. Amen.

FOR FURTHER STUDY – Gen. 27:1–46; Heb. 12:15; Prov. 10:12
1. What are we to make sure we don't miss? / 2. What happens when we do?

Sand in the machinery

FOR READING AND MEDITATION – HEBREWS 12:14–29

'See to it ... no bitter root grows up to cause trouble and defile many.' (v. 15: NIV)

There can be little doubt that to cultivate the desire for revenge fills one's heart with bitterness and resentment and injures both body and soul. If the desire for revenge is not dealt with, it will soon turn a vengeful person into a morose, sour, embittered individual. One doctor says, 'Resentments and the passion for revenge put the whole physical and mental system on a war footing all the time and then the person concerned becomes a drained personality.' He adds, 'I once saw a man kill himself inch by inch simply by thinking of nothing but hatred of a relative who had sued him. Within a year or two he was dead.'

Once I observed an experiment in which a strong person was asked to think about someone he liked and to have good thoughts about that person, at the same time holding one arm outstretched. As he did, the individual conducting the experiment tried to pull down the outstretched arm, but failed. Then the person was asked to think of someone he disliked and have bad thoughts about them, still holding out his arm. The other individual was then able to pull down the outstretched arm with ease. Why? The answer given was that our whole being – body, soul and spirit – will not function at its best when we harbour bitterness and resentment.

We are not created for hate; we are created for love. When we hate, we violate the design which God built into us. We are less than we were meant to be. When we say of another, 'He burns me up,' that's true. Though you want to burn him or her up, all you succeed in doing is burning yourself up. The desire for revenge is sand in the machinery of living. It fouls it up.

O God, we see that you have made us for love. Forgive us for having introduced into the delicate fabric of our being the havoc of hate. We are made for you and your way is love. Help us live that way. In Jesus' name. Amen.

FOR FURTHER STUDY – 1 Kings 22:1–53; Esth. 3:6; Lev. 19:18
1. Why did Ahab hate Micaiah? / 2. What revenge did he take?

The havoc of hate

FOR READING AND MEDITATION – EPHESIANS 4:17–32

'Get rid of all bitterness, rage and anger, brawling and slander,
along with every form of malice.' (v. 31: NIV)

By now I hope you are convinced (if you needed convincing) that to cultivate a passion for revenge is to nurture ill health. Hate plays strange tricks with the memory. It exaggerates injuries and militates against time's healing touch. To use Shakespeare's phrase, it curdles 'the milk of human kindness' and stunts the development of the soul.

I heard of a farmer whose crops were threatened by a flock of crows. He caught one of them and tied a small stick of dynamite to it, lit the fuse, then turned it loose, expecting it to blow itself up in mid-air and thus frighten the other birds. Instead the crow flew into his barn and the explosion wrecked the barn. Our hates and resentments are always more destructive to us than they are to the objects of our hate.

How can we be delivered from this consuming passion? Who can help us bring down the giant of revenge? Christ can! When he was here on earth he said: 'Love your enemies, do good to those who hate you, bless those who curse you, pray for those who ill-treat you' (Luke 6:27–28: NIV). Did our Master set an unattainable standard and make an impossible demand? There are some who claim normal people cannot be free of the desire for revenge. They are probably right, so far as those who do not know the grace of God are concerned. But they are quite wrong when it comes to those who do. Throughout time, Christ has entered the lives of men and women who have been consumed with hatred and has eradicated all their desire for revenge. He can do it for you now.

O Father, how patient and persistent is your love. You love me as I am but too much to let me stay as I am. Help me overcome the hurts I harbour, for I see that when I cherish them, they hurt me even further. In Christ's name I ask it. Amen.

FOR FURTHER STUDY – Mark 6:14–29; Luke 9:54; Acts 23:12
1. What did Herodias nurse? / 2. What was the end result?

The spirit of the cross

FOR READING AND MEDITATION – LUKE 23:43

'Jesus said, "Father, forgive them, for they do not know what they are doing."' (v. 34: NIV)

So how do we overcome the desire to *get even*? How do we fell the great giant of revenge? Our weapon is the smooth stone of forgiveness. 'Ah, easier said than done,' I hear you say. 'Jesus may have been able to do that, but I am not Jesus.' My answer is this: if Jesus lives in you then he can also love in you.

The first person ever to die for Christ (as we saw the other day) was Stephen. He was unjustly murdered. But Christ lived in him and loved in him. As the stones pounded the life out of his body, his last words were a prayer. A prayer, you remember, that was similar to that uttered by Christ after they hammered him to a cross: 'Lord, do not hold this sin against them' (Acts 7:60).

So let me say again, if Christ lives in you, then he can also love in you. The crucial factor is how much you are prepared to relinquish control of your life. Some give the Lord little space in their lives and wonder why they cannot put into operation the more demanding Christian principles, such as forgiveness of others, reconciliation, and so on. Here, then, is the simple principle that I have found explains much of the mystery as to why some Christians are able to achieve much more than others: the more territory Christ occupies in our heart, the more effective will be his influence on what we say or do. The spirit of forgiveness expressed in the first words Christ spoke from the cross: 'Father, forgive them' can be found in your heart if you allow Christ to have full sway in your life. In his strength you too can forgive injuries, pray for your enemies, and love them to the end.

O God, is this really possible? Can I respond to those who hurt me in the same way that Jesus did? If your Son lives in me, it must be so. Occupy the whole of my heart, dear Lord, so that there is room for nothing but you. Amen.

FOR FURTHER STUDY – Eph. 1:1–7; Psa. 130:4, 103:3
1. What have we received in Christ? / 2. What does Paul link forgiveness to?

The right thing to do

FOR READING AND MEDITATION – COLOSSIANS 3:1–17
'Forgive as the Lord forgave you.' (v. 13: NIV)

The only way to slay the giant of revenge, we are saying, is by the smooth stone of forgiveness. But is forgiveness always effective? I have heard it argued (where a criminal act is concerned) that to forgive the perpetrator of a crime is to ignore the consequences of crime and thus encourage criminals to act with impunity. Punishment, they say, is necessary, if society is not to be undermined, and simple forgiveness is counter-productive if it does not deter people from doing wrong.

But punishment is quite different from revenge; the two are not synonymous. In the case of revenge, a man insists on being the judge in his own quarrel. Where punishment is concerned, the injured party hands the matter over to society for someone else to be the judge. I have known many people forgive a criminal for the offence he or she committed against them, but society has decreed, 'You may have forgiven him, but in order that justice is seen to be done, we will now take over and ensure he is punished.'

We must accept the fact also that sometimes forgiveness seems not to beget a moral response in the one forgiven. But that is no reason not to forgive. Jesus' prayer of forgiveness after the soldiers had hammered him to the cross: 'Father, forgive them' does not appear to have broken the stony hearts of these men. Was it then a useless prayer? No, for the attitude of forgiveness was the right attitude to exhibit. They could hammer the life out of him but they could not hammer the love out of him. It was the Godlike response to evil. Forgiveness, whether it is received or not, is always the right response.

Father, help me not to see forgiveness as a means of changing people but as the right response at all times. In my own strength I cannot forgive. But I am ready to be made willing. Take my willingness and then empower me. In Jesus' name. Amen.

FOR FURTHER STUDY – Mark 11:20–25; Luke 11:4, 17:1–5
1. What was the disciples' response to Jesus' challenge? / 2. Make it your prayer today.

Free!

FOR READING AND MEDITATION – 1 PETER 2:13–25

'When they hurled their insults at him, he did not retaliate.' (v. 23: NIV)

We spend one more day considering this matter of forgiveness. I heard Dr W.E. Sangster preach a sermon once in which he outlined the three basic elements of forgiveness as demonstrated by Christ on the cross.

First (he said), Christ forgave them. He cried to God not for vengeance but for forgiveness. He handed the responsibility for judgment over to his Father. Second, he prayed for them. There is nothing like prayer to scour hate out of the heart. Of course I hasten to add there was no hate in Jesus' heart. But that does not make his example the less impressive. Praying for someone who has hurt you will dissolve any seeds of resentment there may be in your heart. Third, he served them. Their wickedness and sin could not deter him from loving. He was as free to escape from the cross as he was to walk away from the cliff-top at Nazareth when the people wanted to hurl him off. He accepted death on the cross because he knew there was no other way that sin's power could be broken and reconciliation brought about between God and humankind. Had he drawn back sin would have won. Those for whom Jesus prayed did not know he was dying for them but that made no difference. He served them.

To those who say they cannot follow these principles, my reply is this: it's hard but not impossible. Put your hand in the stream of God's provision and you will find the stone you need to defeat the giant of revenge once and for all. It is the stone of forgiveness. Forgiveness is not guaranteed to rid you of your enemies but it is guaranteed to rid you of your enmity. You are free.

Lord Jesus Christ, you who prayed for your enemies on the cross, help me whenever I am wronged to forgive my enemies too. And also to pray for them. In Christ's peerless and precious name I ask it. Amen.

FOR FURTHER STUDY – Eph. 4:17–32; Col. 3:13; Titus 3:5
1. What does Paul set as the benchmark for forgiveness?
2. What is also a part of forgiveness?

The 'poor me' syndrome

FOR READING AND MEDITATION – LUKE 22:39–46
'Pray that you will not fall into temptation.' (v. 40: NIV)

We have one final giant to encounter before we bring these meditations to a close – the giant of self-pity. Let me expose the strategy of this cunning colossus.

Like all the giants we have looked at previously, he relies upon threats and intimidations to make his conquests. He is particularly successful with those who feel life has never given them a chance, those who have been hampered from the start by some difficult circumstances. He urges, 'Give up. You never had a chance. How can you expect to get on when so much is against you? You poor thing – quit now and take refuge in self-pity.' Self-pity, you see, acts as an anodyne (a pain-killer) to the soul. It is often called the *poor me* syndrome, as it causes people to focus on themselves and their own feelings rather than facing the issues of life with courage.

While I was in New Zealand a few months ago, a woman came up to me during a break in the seminar I was conducting and told me that something I had said had made her realise she was wallowing in self-pity. She had sought forgiveness for it and came to tell me of her release. 'What caused the self-pity?' I asked. 'I got caught on the rebound,' she said, 'and then lapsed into self-pity. In that mood I became involved in something sinful that has since blighted my life. Tonight, however, I have found forgiveness and I'm free.' Her life had been marred by a sin to which she became susceptible in a mood of self-pity. When our misfortunes dominate our thoughts, then temptation has even greater power.

My Father and my God, I wonder how many sins have gained access into my life when I have lapsed into a mood of self-pity. I am dealing here with a force that is bigger than I. But you are my Deliverer. Free me from the power of this giant. For Jesus' sake. Amen.

FOR FURTHER STUDY – Luke 24:13–35; 2 Sam. 22:29; Micah 7:8
1. What did the disciples seek to draw Jesus into? / 2. How did he turn their feelings around?

No bed of roses

FOR READING AND MEDITATION – 1 PETER 5:1–11

'Your enemy the devil prowls around like a roaring lion looking for
someone to devour.' (v. 8: NIV)

It would be hard to exaggerate the dangers of self-pity. It steals a person's courage and filches the will to win. It disregards the fact that 'life is more tragic than orderly', as Oswald Chambers put it. Nothing can be more foolish than thinking that because we are Christians, we should spend our days on a bed of roses. We live in a fallen world – never forget that.

Self-pity is a solvent that dissolves faith and pushes people deep into doubt, where they find constant reasons for thinking that God does not keep his promises and that he forgets, at times, to be gracious. Self-pity also makes one entirely self-centred (as opposed to other-centred) so that one's own petty problems become of greater concern than the tragedies affecting the lives of others. But perhaps the worst thing about self-pity is that it exposes a person to temptation. When faith ebbs, it is easy to become careless and I know of many, who having lapsed into self-pity, made shipwreck of their lives.

Admittedly, many people find themselves in circumstances which easily give rise to complaint. Some bemoan their inherited problems, for instance some mental weakness that means it is hard for them to get on in the world. Or perhaps they were orphaned at an early age and brought up in a children's home without much love. Maybe the trouble is quite different. It may be something purely physical – some malformation of the body that makes it difficult to be accepted by the rest of society. But remember, no matter how hard life is, self-pity is not the answer. Though it may bring temporary relief, it is not a permanent solution.

O Father, prevent me from settling for temporary relief when I can find a permanent solution. Help me go to the roots of my problems and find release there. Save me from lapsing into self-pity. In Jesus' name I ask it. Amen.

FOR FURTHER STUDY – Num. 11:1–15; Job 10:1; Psa. 69:1–18
1. How did Moses express self-pity? / 2. What did David do in the midst of self-pity?

Be happy and renewed – it's springtime

FOR READING AND MEDITATION – ISAIAH 53:1–12

'Surely he took up our infirmities and carried our sorrows …' (v. 4: NIV)

It may seem strange that I should choose to discuss the subject of self-pity in these springtime days, where everything seems renewed and everyone should also feel happy and renewed. Well, it's because not everyone shares the same feeling of being renewed outwardly, let alone inwardly. For that matter, many feel worse than at any other time of the year. Even in Spring many people suffer from depression, a condition that could even affect suicide rates, as statistics could probably report.

What is the reason for this? It is that people are expected to feel happy and renewed in Spring. 'Why have you got such a long face?' people say. 'Be happy, look, everything is looking fresh and new.' The pressure to be happy and look happy is more than some people can take and thus they lapse easily into self-pity and depression. Every faithful minister will know something of the dismal thoughts people carry in their hearts, which seem even darker when set against the bright sunshine and budding blooms which characterise this time of the year. The knowledge that one was an unwanted child, that there is some mental instability in the family, the depressing feeling that one's intelligence is below the average, and so on.

If these or similar dark thoughts fill your mind, remember that God in Jesus took upon himself the heaped-up sorrows of the whole human race and, however unfriendly the world may seem to you today, he knows and cares. Do you need courage to face the next few days? He can give it to you. All he asks is that you acknowledge your need of him and he will help and sustain you. Just kneel in prayer before him now and ask for his help. He cares, this Man of Galilee.

My Father and my God, as I face the usual demands and expectations of this time of year, I come to you to find the grace and power that I need. I know you will not let me down. I draw from your resources in Jesus' name. Amen.

FOR FURTHER STUDY – Prov. 15:15–30, 17:22, 12:25
1. What should Spring herald in your life?
2. Share an encouraging word with someone today.

Some unfamiliar aspects

FOR READING AND MEDITATION – LUKE 2:1–10

'… Mary … was pledged to be married to him and was expecting a child.' (v. 5: NIV)

Allow me to draw your attention to certain unfamiliar aspects of a familiar story, to which you might relate should you be ridden with self-pity in these days. The circumstances of our Lord's birth were unusual in many ways. It was obvious to all who knew Mary that she had conceived before she was married, and the tongue of scandal would soon have been busy. The evil-minded always love to direct their darts at those who have a reputation for purity. And none was more pure than Mary. Does it require a vivid imagination to picture our Lord's life in Nazareth in the years he was growing up? As he played with his brothers and sisters some gossiping creature might have pointed to him and told the ugly and lying story once again.

Consider also our Lord's genealogy. He had a tainted lineage. Jesus' family tree was nothing to boast about. Included on it are some famous names, but there are some infamous ones as well. David is there, but so is Bathsheba. Ruth is there, but so is Rahab the harlot. Does your ancestry give you concern? Then no one understands you better than Jesus. Perhaps you feel you have always been at a disadvantage because you lost a parent early in life. There is a tradition in the church that Joseph died while Jesus was still young. The years in Nazareth would not have been easy for him. He busied himself at the bench as a carpenter and was thirty before his ministry began.

All our difficulties and problems are known to Jesus. Is he not worthy of your confidence? Draw therefore close to him now and let him kill all inclination to feel sorry for yourself. In the presence of one who had so much against him, dare you say 'I never had a chance'?

Father, thank you for reminding me of these aspects of your life here on earth that are often overlooked. You have worn my flesh, measured its frailty and know just how I feel. All honour and glory be unto your peerless and precious name. Amen.

FOR FURTHER STUDY – Matt. 1:1–25, 13:55–57; John 9:34

1. What did the Pharisees imply? / 2. What is the glorious truth we rejoice in?

Truly worth remembering

FOR READING AND MEDITATION – 2 CORINTHIANS 12:1–10

' ... for Christ's sake, I delight in weaknesses, in insults, in hardships,
in persecutions, in difficulties.' (v. 10: NIV)

It occurs to me that you may be saying to yourself at this stage of our meditations, 'Jesus had reserves of strength to draw upon that are not available to me. He was the incarnate Son of God. I cannot be expected to live as he did.' Well, let's look at how one of his most famous followers – the apostle Paul – was able to make it through life without feeling sorry for himself.

More than once in his letters Paul talks about some great difficulty he was facing. Some think the trouble was ophthalmia. Others reckon it was recurring malaria. And some consider it was epilepsy. No one knows for sure. What we do know is that he sought the Lord three times for it to be taken away. Yet we never read of Paul being caught up in self-pity as a result of his problem. He prayed about it and accepted it as God's discipline in his life.

Perhaps you are now saying, 'But Paul was an exceptional man. I am just an ordinary person with no great advantages.' Then listen to the testimony of Dr Robert C. Barnes, professor of counselling at Hardin-Simmons University in the USA. When he was thirteen he was struck down with polio – just two years before the polio vaccine became available. Did he sit back and say, 'I've got no chance now'? No, drawing strength and courage from God, he went on to make something of his life. I listened to him make what I consider to be one of the most significant statements I have heard with the exception of those recorded in the Bible, 'I knew that no disease, no accident, could take anything away from me that I needed in order to fulfil the purposes the Creator had for my life.' If that's not worth remembering then I don't know what is.

My God and Father, I belong to you in the same way that Paul did – and Robert Barnes does. Let that same courageous and creative spirit that supported them also support me. Instead of sighing, help me to sing. In Jesus' name. Amen.

FOR FURTHER STUDY – 2 Cor. 11:16–33; Phil. 4:11–12; 2 Cor. 4:9
1. List some of the experiences of the apostle Paul. / 2. What was he able to say?

Wanted at a wedding

FOR READING AND MEDITATION – JOHN 2:1–11

'… and Jesus and his disciples had also been invited to the wedding.' (v. 2: NIV)

Comb the Gospel records and not once will you ever find a trace of self-pity in Jesus Christ. He is described as 'a man of sorrows' (Isaiah 53:3: NIV) but he was never sorry for himself. Nobody with self-pity in his heart could have inspired strong men to give up all to follow him. Who would follow a whiner? Nobody wants a whiner at a wedding either. But they wanted Jesus at the wedding in Cana, as today's text tells us. And later, when he told a would-be disciple that he himself had no place to lay his head (Matthew 8:20), it was not to evoke his sympathy, but a frank intimation of what the young man would be taking on.

I have heard some argue that Jesus showed self-pity when he cried out on the cross 'I am thirsty' (John 19:28: NIV). None but the unbelievably callous would find signs of self-pity in that statement. Surely the dying can ask for a drink without being accused of complaining.

Our Lord's freedom from self-pity is all the more wonderful when we delve into the details of his life. We do not know at what point the awareness came to him that he was the Son of God and had a mission to save the world, but it is clear that once he was aware of it, he knew what it would entail: alienation from his friends and loved ones, the implacable hate of his enemies, the need to travel throughout the length and breadth of Israel, and finally an ignominious death upon a cross. The temptation to indulge in self-pity would have been enormous. But he moved forward resolutely, doggedly, courageously. His courage came from knowledge of the fact that nothing could happen to him without God permitting it, and that everything God permitted he would use. Hold on to that and you too will be invincible.

O God, you permit only that which you can use, so how can I ever descend into self-pity? Help me not merely to consider this truth but lay hold of it. In Jesus' name. Amen.

FOR FURTHER STUDY – 1 Pet. 5:1–10; Matt. 10:39; 2 Cor. 4:11
1. What is God's promise? / 2. How did Paul view the constant trial of his faith?

A great teacher

FOR READING AND MEDITATION – PHILIPPIANS 4:10–20
'I can do everything through him who gives me strength.' (v. 13: NIV)

Do you feel you have a lot to complain about? A physical disability perhaps? A physical disability can have strange effects upon a person. It can create an inferiority complex, as many psychologists would agree. In fact Alfred Adler, the man who coined the term *inferiority complex*, said that because of a physical weakness in his life he was plagued by a sense of insignificance and inferiority. But even adverse physical factors can be used by the Holy Spirit to bring glory to God. Think of Helen Keller for example – deprived of hearing and sight but yet radiant in spirit.

But perhaps you struggle not so much with a physical disability as a psychological one. Were the circumstances of your birth shadowed in shame? Born out of wedlock perhaps? I know this does not carry the stigma it once did but there are many, nevertheless, who can't get over this fact. If you struggle with this then let me introduce you to Dr Alexander Whyte, one-time minister of a church in Edinburgh, Scotland. He too was an illegitimate child. Yet he rose to become one of the finest preachers and saintliest men Scotland has ever seen.

No physical or psychological difficulty can prevent God using us – as long as we yield ourselves to him. Remember a day is coming when you will stand before God and be expected to give account. Will you plead a physical disability with Helen Keller standing at your side? Will you come up to the throne and whisper 'Illegitimate' with Alexander Whyte standing there? With God, difficulties can be made to yield a spiritual profit. Adversity is one of our greatest teachers. And God uses it to polish his jewels.

Gracious God, keep watch over my spirit and keep me sound there. Save me from all self-pity, and let me be outgoing and positive, taking on myself the problems of others. In Jesus' name. Amen.

FOR FURTHER STUDY – 1 Cor. 1:26–30; John 15:16
1. What sort of people does God use? / 2. What did Jesus assure the disciples?

All is not lost

FOR READING AND MEDITATION – 2 CORINTHIANS 9:6–15
'And God is able to make all grace abound to you …' (v. 8: NIV)

Are you ready now to slay the giant of self-pity that may be towering over you? And slay him once and for all? You have already been given the stone which you need to put in your sling. Feel its smoothness once again: no disease, no sickness, no infirmity can take from you whatever you need to fulfil the purposes of God for your life. So when this cunning giant stands over you and demoralises you with words such as, 'You never had a chance … give up … console yourself with self-pity,' put your trust in God and hurl this stone at him with all your force.

The ablest man I have ever known was struck down with a disease that could have put him out of action for the rest of his life. But he didn't moan or complain about this major setback. He slew the giant of self-pity and went on to make a contribution to life that was quite astonishing. Don't be so foolish as to envy those who seemingly have every advantage in life; the absence of advantage is sometimes the greatest advantage of all. Many will never get anywhere because they have not been provoked by awkward circumstances. Dr G. Campbell Morgan said of a certain young preacher, 'He is a good preacher, but when he has struggled a bit and overcome he will be a great preacher.'

Let everything spur you on towards God and his grace. Go forward in hope. God is above you, Christ and the Holy Spirit are within you, the angels of God are around you – what more do you need? Life may not have given you much of a chance, but in God you have every chance. All is not lost while you have courage. And Christ excels in giving that.

Lord Jesus Christ, you who overcome every difficulty in life, live your life so fully and powerfully in me that I too will be able to overcome every difficulty in my life. For your own dear name's sake I ask it. Amen.

FOR FURTHER STUDY – Ex. 3:1–22; Judg. 6:15; 1 Kings 3:7; Jer. 1:6; Isa. 6:5
1. How did some of God's servants respond to his call?
2. What was the end result?

overcoming giants

The sword of Goliath

FOR READING AND MEDITATION – 1 SAMUEL 21:1–9
'David said, "There is none like it; give it to me."' (v. 9: NIV)

In the passage before us today we come across an intriguing though somewhat sad incident in David's life. Having incurred the wrath of King Saul, and parted from his friend Jonathan, he makes his way to Nob. There he deceives Ahimelech the priest by telling him he is on a mission for the king which demanded the utmost secrecy. Why David should lie we cannot say, but clearly he is a long way from being the David of the psalms now!

When David asks for food the priest tells him that only the bread which has been consecrated to God is available and, according to the law of Moses, could be eaten only by those who were ritually clean. However, men who were engaged in active military service and were not in contact with their wives were regarded as clean. So Ahimelech, believing this to be true of David, offers him the consecrated bread. Having been given the bread, David then asks Ahimelech if there is a sword he can have and is told that lying behind the ephod is the sword of Goliath. 'There is none like it,' says David, 'give it to me.' The sword that was once used against him in an attempt to secure his destruction is now about to be used by him in his own defence.

This incident suggests a thought, namely that the very weapons which the devil intends to bring about our defeat can, through divine ingenuity, be put to our use. That same truth can be put this way: in every obstacle there is an opportunity, in every difficulty a door, and in every stumbling block a stepping stone. In God's service everything can be used – everything: the good, the bad and the indifferent.

My Father and my God, many years ago through the prophet Isaiah you said: 'No weapon forged against you will prevail' (Isa. 54:17). But now I see there is more – the weapons forged against me can be used by me. Thank you my Father. Amen.

FOR FURTHER STUDY – Eph. 6:10–20; Heb. 4:12; Rev. 19:15
1. What is armour good for?
2. What is the only weapon listed and what does it enable us to do?

FOR READING AND MEDITATION – JOSHUA 14: 6–15

'… the Anakites were there … but, the Lord helping me, I will drive them out …'
(v. 12: NIV)

My final word to you is this: you are never too old to slay a giant. Some of you may be thinking, 'Well, I'm a bit set in my ways now that I've past 30 (or 40, or 50…) so I'll just have to stay the way I am.' Nonsense. Look at Caleb. He was 85 and eager to drive out the giants that were in the hill country of Hebron. (The Anakites, as we see from Deuteronomy 9:1–2, were a giantlike people.) At a time when it would have been easy for Caleb to have pulled out and settled back in his chair, he fearlessly set out to banish them finally from the Promised Land. While his peers were yawning, Caleb was yearning.

An American sociologist said recently that by their mid-thirties, most people have ceased to acquire new skills and attitudes. Stop and think, those of you who are over thirty. Are you in danger of settling down spiritually and mentally? Are you losing the zest for life naturally and spiritually? Don't settle for the status quo. If there are giants threatening you that need to be slain, go and get 'em. You now know how to do it.

By way of reminder, let me give you the principles once again. First, don't run. Stand your ground. The Lord of hosts is with you. Second, don't dress up in Saul's armour. Natural defences and resources are not much help in times of spiritual battle. Third, dip your hand in the cool, clear stream of God's Word and pick up one of the smooth stones of truth. Fourth, put it in your sling to signify your willingness to do battle. Then fifth, with a strong confidence in the Lord take aim. One to be ready. Two to be steady. Three to be off. Shoot!

Gracious and loving God, help me not to limit you by protesting, 'I'm too set in my ways to change now.' I commit myself afresh to being all you want me to be. I hear your call to battle. Here I am Lord. Send me. Amen.

FOR FURTHER STUDY – Psa. 20:1–9; Rom. 8:28–37; 1 John 5:4
1. What do some trust in? / 2. Where is our trust?

Don't lose your balance

FOR READING AND MEDITATION – PHILIPPIANS 1:1–18

'… that your love may abound more and more in knowledge and depth of insight,
so that you may be able to discern what is best …' (v. 9–10: NIV)

The theme was suggested to me when I came across this statement made by the great French Christian and philosopher, Blaise Pascal, 'No one is strong unless he or she bears within their character antitheses strongly marked.' In other words, in order to be a fully developed person one's virtues must be held in tension. For it is in that very tension – that strength is to be found.

Take, for example, the virtue of determination. In some people determination quickly becomes stubborness, and when it does then the virtue is dangerously close to becoming a vice. I use the word *vice* in the sense of something bad – a fault. Take again the virtue of enthusiasm. It is easy for enthusiasm to turn into fanaticism – a vice. One writer puts it like this, 'Zeal can often degenerate into hysteria, integrity become hard and unforgiving, and thrift pass over into stinginess. The art of living is to find the balance.'

Human nature being what it is, we seem to find it difficult to retain a balance. Most of us, if we are honest, would admit that although we are growing spiritually, our growth is lopsided. Our virtues are unbalanced. John Stott says, 'It seems there is no pastime the devil enjoys more than tipping Christians off balance.' Martin Luther put it even more graphically when he said, 'Some Christians are like a drunk man getting on a horse; he pulls himself up on one side and falls off the other.' What can we do about this imbalance in our virtues? We can bring the whole issue to God and with his help seek to correct it. God loves balance as much as the devil hates it.

*My Father and my God, give me the grace to face the fact that my virtues may be out of balance.
I don't want my growth as a Christian to be lopsided. Instead I want to be beautifully balanced. In
Jesus' name. Amen.*

FOR FURTHER STUDY – Luke 11:42; Eph. 4:13–15; 1 Pet. 2:2–3; 2 Pet. 3:17–18
1. How does Paul describe spiritual maturity? / 2. How does Peter say we can achieve it?

God's perfect Poem

FOR READING AND MEDITATION – EPHESIANS 2:1–10
'For we are God's workmanship, created in Christ Jesus to do good works …'
(v. 10: NIV)

The verse before us now could justifiably be translated, 'You are God's poem' (the Greek word translated 'workmanship' is *poiema*, from which we get our English word *poem*). I am a great lover of poetry as well as prose, and although I am not an expert in the structure of poetry, I know that traditional poetry must be rhythmical, each part balanced against the other. It is the same with life. A medical doctor says, 'There is a rhythm of the body. If this rhythm is disturbed there is a functional disturbance that leads to a structural disturbance.'

As there is a rhythm in our bodies, so there is a rhythm in our souls. If this rhythm is upset by some virtues being over-emphasised and others being under-emphasised, then our spiritual growth will be lopsided. It might sound irreverent to refer to Jesus as *God's Poem*, but that is what he was. In him all virtues were perfectly blended. If the statement I referred to yesterday is true – 'No one is strong unless he or she bears within their character antitheses strongly marked' – then no one was stronger in his personality than Jesus. One can see antitheses clearly marked in him. He was militant and passive, world-renouncing and world-embracing, tender and terrible, a man of prayer and a man of action, self-renouncing and self-asserting.

A missionary to India whom I heard speak said that many of the deities who are revered have qualities missing, so people invent other deities whose supposed qualities compensate for those which are lacking. We can be thankful that the Saviour we worship was the most balanced character ever seen on our planet. He was God's perfect *Poem*, with each one of his qualities perfectly balanced against the other.

O God, I must ask myself: is there anything poetic about my life? Are my virtues rhythmic and balanced? Do they express the beauty of the divine Poet? I want to become your perfect poem, dear Lord. In Jesus' name. Amen.

FOR FURTHER STUDY – Matt. 5:48, 9:1–8; Heb. 4:14–16, 5: 8–9
1. What advantages are there for us in the perfection of Jesus?
2. What is the consequence of the perfection of Jesus?

Show me your gods

FOR READING AND MEDITATION – HEBREWS 12:1–13

'Let us fix our eyes on Jesus, the author and perfecter of our faith …' (v. 2: NIV)

We continue with the thought that our Lord was the most balanced character this planet has ever seen. I once read that in China there is a leaning tower built by a ruler who saw in a dream the deity he worshipped as being lame. His deity was lopsided, so the tower he built to honour him was also lopsided. 'We always make our earth in the image of what we see in the sky,' stated one philosopher. And he went on to say 'Show me your gods and I will show you your men.' We tend to become like that we worship. If our god is unbalanced, we become unbalanced. How thankful we should be that the God we worship is not unbalanced.

Look with me in more detail at how Jesus' virtues were so perfectly balanced. Take, for example, a few of the qualities we mentioned yesterday. First, world-renouncing and world-embracing. He said on one occasion: 'I am not of the world' (John 17:16: KJV), yet he lived out his life in touch with humanity and died on a cross for the sins of the world. Then take again the qualities of assertiveness and meekness. He was filled with righteous anger at the money changers who were defiling his Father's house and drove them out. Yet he meekly allowed himself to be hammered to the cross. Then what about prayer and action? The two were perfectly blended in him. He spent whole nights in prayer, yet we are also told he went about doing good and healing all who were oppressed by the devil.

We can see the antitheses so strongly marked in Jesus. Each one of his virtues was balanced by its opposite. How wonderful it would be if the same balance could be found in us.

My Father and my God, can all my virtues be as balanced as they were in Jesus? Am I reaching for the impossible? I dare to believe. Show me the way. I will follow. In Jesus' name I ask it. Amen.

FOR FURTHER STUDY – Matt. 10:16; Mark 1:32–39; Luke 16:1–12; John 17:14–17
1. How did Jesus cope with the demands of crowds of people?
2. Balance the passage from Luke with the verses from John.

Growing, not groaning

FOR READING AND MEDITATION – 2 PETER 3:8–18

'But grow in the grace and knowledge of our Lord and Saviour Jesus Christ.' (v. 18: NIV)

Yesterday we ended by wondering whether the balance found in Jesus can be found in us. I believe it can. Maybe not as perfectly, but close. It depends on a number of things – our willingness to understand how sin has damaged our personalities, our readiness to admit to our spiritual lameness, and a firm resolve to surrender to Christ so that he might make us in his image. We also said yesterday that all of Christ's virtues were perfectly balanced and held in tension. And that tension makes a growing point. If we are honest, we would admit that for most of us the tension is a groaning point rather than a growing point. But it need not be so.

I keep on encouraging readers to grow spiritually and to identify those things that endanger that growth. Though I have never before dealt with the subject we are presently discussing, I certainly consider unbalanced virtues an impediment to spiritual growth. The other day I came across this by Dr E. Stanley Jones, 'When a man's right leg is too long – longer than the other – then he is lame. When one good quality is long in proportion to others then we are spiritually lame.'

Most would classify strong conviction as a virtue, but if we are not careful, strong conviction can make a man or woman blind to other people's points of view and prevent them from seeing any flaws in their own convictions. A Scottish theologian said, 'God grant that I may be always right, for I will never change.' One must admire a person who has strong convictions but we must be sure they are convictions and not just opinions. The person who thinks he is always right and will never change is always wrong.

O Father, take your chisel and make me into the image of Jesus. Help me understand that you can only do a perfect job as I remain steady and do not pull away. In Jesus' name I ask it. Amen.

FOR FURTHER STUDY – Rom. 8:22–27; 2 Cor. 6:3–10, 9:8; Heb. 5:11–6:3; James 1:2–8
1. How will the tension that makes us groan be resolved?
2. What does James say is the way to grow spiritually?

On being a whole person

FOR READING AND MEDITATION – COLOSSIANS 3:1–17

'And whatever you do … do it all in the name of the Lord Jesus …' (v. 17: NIV)

We shall consider a number of opposite virtues and qualities, but the first pair I want to draw your attention to is the mental and the emotional. Christian discipleship involves every part of our personalities. Our minds are to be renewed (Romans 12:2), our emotions purified (Ephesians 4:26), our conscience kept clear (Acts 24:16), and our wills surrendered to God's will. All we are as persons is to be committed to all we know of God. Yet of the various parts of the personality mentioned in Scripture, the mind and the emotions are by far the most often referred to. Some have trained the mind to the neglect of the emotions; this makes them intellectualists. And some indulge their emotions to the neglect of the mind; this makes them emotionalists.

Our reading talks about letting the Word of Christ dwell in us richly as we teach and admonish one another (v.16). Here is the awakening of the mind so that it is enriched with divine wisdom. Then the verse goes on to say: 'and as you sing psalms, hymns and spiritual songs with gratitude in your hearts to God.' Here is the awakening of the emotions, giving vent in joyful song. Both are necessary to our growth in Christ – the awakening and enriching of the mind, and the awakening and enjoyment of the emotions.

One man I know is a wonderful Bible teacher but is often referred to as 'a dry old stick'. When I asked him why he never seemed to appear passionate about what he taught he said, 'I have been like this all my life. I have never had much feeling.' He is wrong. He has a lot of feeling, but it is all repressed. Any imbalance in the personality is a cause for concern, but none more than the mental and the emotional.

O Father, stimulate my personality so that there is a more perfect balance between my mind and my emotions. I don't want one to take precedence over the other. Help me, my Father. Amen.

FOR FURTHER STUDY – Psa. 8:1–9; Rom. 12:2; Acts 24:16; Eph. 4:26
1. Savour slowly the heady mix of intellect and emotion in Psalm 8.
2. What is the result of renewing our minds?

I don't need my head

FOR READING AND MEDITATION – MARK 12:28–34

'Love the Lord your God with all your heart and with all your soul
and with all your mind ...' (v. 30: NIV)

Let's think now about those whose emotions are ahead of their thinking. Our age, I am afraid, judges truth by how one feels about it rather than the other way round. A university student I sat next to on a plane told me that something had to feel true before he believed it. This is a perilous position to adopt, but many do so. Over the years, I have had to deal with several young Christians who have come into the church with the attitude, 'But I can't believe something simply because it is written in the Bible. I can only believe it if it authenticates itself to me in my feelings.'

A danger in some charismatic churches (not all) is the emphasis on emotion and experience to the exclusion of the mind. One man commented, 'When I go to my church I might as well unscrew my head and put it under the seat, for you can be sure it won't be needed.' Now that is not just sad; it is tragic. It is assimilating the spirit of the age and that, says one writer, is nothing but worldliness. For worldliness is adopting uncritically the attitudes of the world.

In our reading today a teacher comes to Jesus and asks him which is the greatest commandment. Jesus quotes from Deuteronomy 6:4–5 but he adds something to that statement. He says: 'Love the Lord your God with ... all your mind.' The phrase 'with all your mind' was not in the original. I know it can be argued that the mind is part of the heart or soul, but to my way of thinking it is interesting, to say the least, that Jesus inserts the word *mind*. Jesus would encourage us to use our minds, to think. He would awaken us mentally as well as emotionally.

O God, forgive me if I have focused on the development of my emotions to the detriment of my mind. Help me stand against a world that would try to squeeze me into its own mould. In Christ's name. Amen.

FOR FURTHER STUDY – John 5:39–40; Acts 17:11; 1 Cor. 2:1–16; 14:10–15
1. What should be our aim in using our minds?
2. What is the key to spiritual discernment?

I don't have a good mind

FOR READING AND MEDITATION – 1 CORINTHIANS 14:1–25

'Brothers, stop thinking like children. In regard to evil be infants,
but in your thinking be adults.' (v. 20: NIV)

'To be perfectly frank, I'm getting exasperated with your infantile thinking. How long before you grow up and use your head – your adult head?' That's the way Eugene Peterson paraphrases our text for today in *The Message*. Jesus told us that we must be like children in many ways – our willingness to trust, for example. But in relation to the use of our minds, we are to be mature and adult.

A preacher tells a story about two women chatting in a supermarket check-out line. One remarked to the other, 'What's the matter with you? You look so worried.' 'I am,' responded her friend, 'I keep thinking about the world situation.' 'Well,' said the first lady, 'you want to take things more philosophically, and stop thinking.'

God thinks, and he has made us with the ability to think also. When we think, we glorify God. A scientist has been defined as 'someone who thinks God's thoughts after him'. Now I know some will say, 'But I don't have a very good mind. I didn't do well at school and thinking doesn't come easily to me.' I can sympathise, for I didn't do well at school either. But then I took Jesus into my life and he awakened my mind in a way that no earthly teacher could.

Ephesians 1:3 tells us that God has blessed us with every spiritual blessing in Christ. Every spiritual blessing. Does that mean he can bless us mentally? Well, he did that for me and I am sure he can do the same for you. Listen to this: '… by his power he may fulfil every good purpose of yours and every act prompted by your faith' (2 Thessalonians 1:11: NIV). Purpose to think better and more clearly and ask God to help you achieve this aim. He will.

My Father, I turn my mind over to you so that you can come in and think in me. I may not know a lot but I know this: my mind works better when you are in it. In Jesus' name I pray. Amen.

FOR FURTHER STUDY – Matt. 11:28–30; 1 Cor. 3:1–2; 2 Cor. 1:13; 2 Tim. 2:15
1. Draw encouragement from the first, second and third references.
2. What should we try our best to do?

The mind matters

FOR READING AND MEDITATION – PHILIPPIANS 4:1–9

'... brothers, whatever is true, whatever is noble ... think about such things.' (v. 8: NIV)

Think! That's Paul's admonition in our reading today. And that has been the admonition of all the great Christian leaders of the past.

The other day I was looking at what some of the notable Christians in history had to say about faith. In the course of my research, I decided to see how Dr Martyn Lloyd-Jones defined faith. This is what he said when commenting on the Sermon on the Mount, 'Faith ... is primarily thinking ... and the whole trouble with a man of little faith is that he does not think. He allows circumstances to bludgeon him. The way to avoid that, according to our Lord, is to think. Christian faith is essentially thinking. Look at the birds, says Jesus, think about them and draw your deductions. Look at the grass, look at the lilies of the field, consider them. The trouble with most people, however, is they will not think. Instead of doing this they sit down and ask, what is going to happen to me? What can I do? That is the absence of thought; it is surrender, it is defeat. We are entitled to define "little faith" as being a failure to think, of allowing life to master our thoughts instead of thinking clearly about it.' Powerful words.

Drawing on my counselling experience, I can tell you this: the people who go through the most stress are those whose thoughts are not under control. They don't think. Well, they do think, but not in the way the Bible instructs us to. They fail to think about what God says and think instead about what the devil is telling them. Their thinking is not according to Scripture – hence defeatist. There are many remedies on offer for worry, but really there is only one successful way.

It is to think – to think with God.

Father, I see that many of my problems arise because I don't think in the way I should think. Help me develop the mind you have given me so that my thinking is in line with your thinking. In Jesus' name. Amen.

FOR FURTHER STUDY – Rom. 12:3; Matt. 17:24–27, 18:12–14, 22:41–45, 26:63–66
1. What are we to think of ourselves? / 2. What are we to think of Christ?

Blunted sensibilities

FOR READING AND MEDITATION – MARK 14:32–42

'… he began to be deeply distressed and troubled.' (v. 33: NIV)

Now that we have seen the importance of the mental aspect of life, we move on to consider the importance of the opposite end of the spectrum – the emotional. Some, it has to be said, are all head and no heart. I have heard such people described as tadpoles – a tadpole is a creature with a huge head and not much else beside! The mind has to be developed but so do the emotions if we are to be thoroughly integrated people.

A psychologist claims that killers who murder for gain or gratification are almost always lacking in affect, that is, the capacity for entering into the feelings of others. Pamela Jonson, in her book entitled *On Iniquity*, says of our present generation, 'We are in danger of creating an affectless society in which nobody cares for anyone but himself or herself, or for anything except instant gratification. We demand sex without love, violence for "kicks" … we are encouraging the blunting of sensibility.'

People are emotionally flat for many reasons. Often the problem stems from the developmental years. Some were never encouraged to show emotion as children, or have been taught to suppress their emotions. Others have a fear of emotion. They are afraid to feel emotions that arise because they are not sure how to handle them. Do you know some theologians believe God is incapable of emotion? This doctrine is known as the impassability of God. This view is held despite the fact that we can be certain his Son was capable of emotions. A careful reading of the Gospels shows him touching the whole gamut of emotion from joy to sadness, from deep inner peace to the turmoil of soul which our text for today talks about. To be fully human and fully alive, one must feel.

Father, you have made me to be a feeling being. Yet some emotions scare me. Teach me how to feel without being frightened, how to experience my emotions without being intimidated by them. In Jesus' name I pray. Amen.

FOR FURTHER STUDY – Mark 3:1–6; Luke 19:41–44; John 11:35; Luke 10:17–21
1. Why was Jesus right to be angry? / 2. What filled Jesus with joy?

Four ways

FOR READING AND MEDITATION – EPHESIANS 4:17–32

'In your anger do not sin.' (v. 26: NIV)

We continue thinking about the emotions. There are four things we can do with our emotions. First, we can repress them – we can push them deep into the unconscious and forget all about them. Second, we can suppress them – we can push them into the subconscious, where they are not entirely forgotten, but temporarily submerged. Third, we can express them – we can laugh, cry, stamp our feet, get angry, shout, and so on. Fourth, we can confess them – admit to our feelings but control the expression of them so that it is in accord with Biblical principles.

It is always right to feel an emotion but it is not always right to express it. Take anger, for example. Some say that because the Bible teaches us not to be angry we should never feel anger, so whenever these people feel anger welling up within them, they pretend they are not feeling it. That is dishonest. Integrity requires that whatever is true must be recognised. We go wrong not when we feel anger but when we express it in a manner that is inconsistent with Biblical teaching.

'In your anger do not sin' tells us that we can admit to feeling angry, but by an act of self-control (a fruit of the Spirit) we must ensure that our anger is not dumped on to someone in a way that hurts them. But what if they have hurt us? ' "It is mine to avenge; I will repay," says the Lord' (Rom. 12:19). You ask, 'Lord, can I help you a little bit with the avenging?' He answers: 'No, that part is mine. I can do it better than you, and my method will be constructive, not destructive.' Always be willing to feel your emotions, but be careful about how you express them.

Father, you have me cornered. No argument I can present justifies the expression of my anger. Your Spirit gives me self-control. May I yield more to your Spirit than my own spirit. In Christ's name. Amen.

FOR FURTHER STUDY – Matt. 5:22; Mark 10:35–45; Luke 9:51–32; Col. 3:8
1. Note how Jesus defused the anger of his disciples?
2. How did the prodigal's father deal with his elder son's anger?

The soul's tambourine

FOR READING AND MEDITATION – LUKE 24:13–35

'Were not our hearts burning within us while he … opened the Scriptures to us?'
(v. 32: NIV)

We have been seeing that emotional awareness is a rich part of living. But isn't there some way to avoid feeling negative emotions and just feel the good ones? The short answer is 'No'. As C.S. Lewis pointed out, if we are not willing to feel negative emotions, then we will not experience the richness of our positive emotions. You can't have one without the other.

I can imagine someone saying, 'But what about me? My problem is that I feel dead on the inside.' If you have been hurt, then bring that hurt to God right now and ask him to heal you. But remember, there will be no healing until there is forgiveness on your part toward the one (or ones) who hurt you. You counter, 'But I can't forgive.' Change the word *can't* to *won't* and you are closer to the truth. You can forgive. Christ says so (see Luke 6:37). Better not to argue with him.

If your emotional constriction is due to years of mishandling, of never being taught how to express your emotions, then do this. Read through the Psalms – the book where almost every conceivable emotion is registered – and meditate on the passages where the psalmist expresses a particular emotion. Linger over those verses and ask God to help you feel what the psalmist felt. Many emotionally constricted people have practised this simple technique and discovered through it an expansion of their emotional spectrum. One woman summed up her experience like this, 'I learned to feel my way into the sadness of the psalmists and also into their joy. Unafraid to feel the dark side, I discovered I could feel more of the joy. I never felt joy before, not as deeply anyway. Nothing is more wonderful than when my soul takes its tambourine and dances with delight.'

O Father, give me a cool head and a warm heart. Help me experience my emotions without being emotional. Move me further along the road to being a well-balanced personality. In Christ's name I pray. Amen.

TAKE TIME TO REFLECT – What practical steps can you take to renew your mind?

Words and deeds

FOR READING AND MEDITATION – ACTS 7:17–36

'Moses … was powerful in speech and action.' (v. 22: NIV)

Now that we have seen the importance of being balanced mentally and emotionally, we move on to consider another pair of opposites: words and actions. Some are good at talking but don't do much good. They are long on words but short on actions.

It was said of Jesus that he was 'a prophet, powerful in word and deed before God' (Luke 24:19: NIV). Compare that with our text for today that tells us Moses 'was educated in all the wisdom of the Egyptians and was powerful in speech and action' (Acts 7:22: NIV). Both prophets were strong in two things – words and action. It's interesting to note that at the beginning of Moses' career, he was better at actions than words. When told by God at the burning bush that he was called to be Israel's deliverer he complained: 'I am slow of speech and tongue' (Exodus 4:10: NIV). Once he got started, however, he made a speech that covered most of the book of Deuteronomy. Not bad for someone who said he was not good at talking!

In some of us these two things – words and actions – have gotten out of balance. We talk more than we act, and very often the talking substitutes for the doing. We are building a crooked tower leaning wayward. Then, on the other hand, there are those who are strong on action but not on words. They cover up their unwillingness to talk about their faith by saying, 'It's my life that counts.' Of course our lives count, but we are called to represent Christ not only with our lives but also with our lips. Our fallen human nature seems to enjoy inhabiting one or other of the polar regions of truth. Our Lord straddled both poles simultaneously. So also must we.

Father, forgive us that in many ways we lack Biblical balance. So often we push people over to one pole of virtue while keeping the opposite pole as our preserve. Help us, dear Lord, for without you we are sunk. Amen.

FOR FURTHER STUDY – 1 Pet. 3:15–16; Mark 8:38; Rom. 10:8–10; James 1:22–27
1. What reasons could you give for the hope you have?
2. Ponder this: 'Preach the gospel always.' If necessary use words.

I can't hear what you say

FOR READING AND MEDITATION – TITUS 2:1–15

'… to show that they can be fully trusted, so that … they will make
the teaching about God our Saviour attractive.' (v. 10: NIV)

Deeds and words were the alternate beats of Jesus' heart, and they should be the alternate beats of our hearts too. With Jesus the content of his words went into his actions. This is how it must be with us also. We need to talk, and we need to act out our talking in good deeds. Some talk more than they act, and others act more than they talk. Our talking and our actions must go hand in hand.

Let's think of those who are good at talking about the gospel but whose lives do not match up with what they say. The story has often been told of the man who was constantly talking about his faith but whose life lacked holiness. Eventually someone said to him, 'I am sorry, but your life is speaking so loudly I can't hear what you say.'

In the village where I was brought up in South Wales, there lived a man who was always ready to speak at an open-air meeting. People would listen respectfully to those who witnessed to their faith, but when it was this man's turn, they would shake their heads and walk away. Why? Because they knew that his life did not match his words. He was as ready as they were to steal such things as electric wiring, nails and small tools from the local colliery. His words sounded hollow because they were not backed up by a righteous life. You don't have to tell a non-Christian that words and actions must go hand in hand. They know instinctively that a life which purports to be committed to God but is short on actions is shallow. Many have been deterred from responding to the gospel by those who say they are Christians but do not show the fruit of it in their lives.

Father, I must search my own heart today and ask myself, do my actions match my words? Am I as good at doing as I am at talking? Forgive me if I veer in one direction, and help me be a more balanced Christian. In Jesus' name. Amen.

FOR FURTHER STUDY – Matt. 23:2–3; Mark 12:38–40; James 2:12, 2:14–18
1. Is more stress laid on either saying or doing? / 2. But which comes first – doing or saying?

Word become flesh

FOR READING AND MEDITATION – ACTS 10:23–48

'They have received the Holy Spirit just as we have.' (v. 47: NIV)

'One of the tragedies of our time,' said a fine elderly Christian to me just a few hours before he died, 'is that the Word has not become flesh.' I pondered what he meant for a few days and struggled to understand what he had been getting at. Finally, during his committal service, the sense of what he had said dawned on me, and I referred to it in my funeral address. What he had in mind, I think, was this: if we do not back up our words by actions then the Word remains word. We begin with words and end with words. But when we put the word into action, then the Word becomes flesh.

The Word remains word, for example, when we talk about racial harmony and equality but do nothing practical to advance it. Today's passage shows how one of the deepest chasms that separates people – the chasm of racial prejudice – was bridged. The early Christians could have proclaimed the doctrine of all men and women being equal, but it would have had little effect on the prejudiced hearts of many of that day. Preaching against racism would have been Word remaining word. But an amazing thing happened: the Gentiles received the gift of the Holy Spirit on the same basis, exactly as the Jews. Peter used a word that became the funnel through which God could pour the Holy Spirit. He said: 'Everyone who believes in him receives forgiveness of sins' (v.43). *Everyone.*

As soon as Peter used that word *everyone,* the Holy Spirit fell on all who were in Cornelius' house. 'Everyone' was Peter's invitation. The Holy Spirit coming 'on all' was God's reply. That day the great gulf between racial groups was bridged – bridged not by a word, but by a Word become flesh.

O God, forgive us again that prejudices and circumstances press us to say 'some' when Jesus presses us to say 'everyone'. Grant that my faith shall not end in words, but in words become flesh. In Jesus' name. Amen.

FOR FURTHER STUDY – 1 Kings 18: 21–39; Matt. 7:16–27; Heb. 1:1–4
1. Why were Elijah's words answered with action?
2. What does the rock the wise man built his house on represent?

Walking your talking

FOR READING AND MEDITATION – ACTS 18:9–17
'But since it involves questions about words and names and
your own law – settle the matter yourselves.' (v. 15: NIV)

We saw yesterday how one of the greatest chasms between people – the chasm of racial prejudice – was bridged by a simple thing – the word of equality became flesh. Would that have happened if Peter had not responded to God's challenge and gone personally to the house of Cornelius? I doubt it. It was not the custom to sit down with Gentiles – but he did so anyway. And what followed was one of the most powerful and breathtaking events recorded in the Acts of the Apostles. Racial prejudice melted before this tender act of God's acceptance of the Gentiles.

When I was in South Africa, I heard about the captain of a British ship who, visiting Cape Town at the height of the colour-bar problem, picked up a black baby from its mother's arms and cradled it. Many of the white people who saw him were horrified and said, 'This isn't done in South Africa, you know.' That simple act divided the group – those with scowls on their faces belonged to the present and the past. The captain belonged to the future. In him the word of racial equality became flesh.

In our reading today, we see a proud Roman official fed up with the bandying of words and legal wrangles. With a wave of his hand he dismissed what he thought was another philosophy – another instance of the Word ending in word. But history has not been able to dismiss Christianity so glibly, because multitudes have proved beyond any shadow of doubt that their commitment to Christ meant more than just spouting words. They 'walked their talk' as one old preacher quaintly put it. 'Faith without works is dead,' said James (James 2:26: NIV). It is. When we back up our words by actions, then the gospel leads not to a comment, but conversion.

O God, forgive us if our words just end in words. Help us to 'walk our talk', for we may be the first and only Bible some people will ever read. May we be doers of the Word and not hearers only. In Christ's name. Amen.

FOR FURTHER STUDY – Eccl. 3:1–8; Acts 8:26–40; 16:25–34
1. What action of Philip's led to the Ethiopian's conversion?
2. How did Paul and Silas' behaviour affect the jailer?

The word of coffee ...

FOR READING AND MEDITATION – 1 TIMOTHY 4:1–16

'Watch your life and doctrine closely. Persevere in them …' (v. 16: NIV)

'The interest of men and women in the world,' said a famous missionary, 'is to see the Word become flesh.' He told of sitting with a group in a restaurant when a waitress came to the table empty-handed and asked, 'Anyone want more coffee?' 'No thank you,' they all replied. A few minutes later another waitress appeared with a steaming coffee pot in her hand and said, 'Anyone want more coffee?' 'Yes please,' they all responded. The difference? The first waitress presented the word of *coffee* remaining word; the second, the word of *coffee* become flesh. Sometimes we have to see reality before we seek it.

Paul stressed this when talking to the young Timothy. In our reading today he tells him: 'Watch your life and doctrine closely.' It's easy to become preoccupied with doctrine and forget the need to match it with action. While I was in Malaysia recently, a young minister told me this, 'I have spent three years in a theological college, but I have never done an act of love for someone in need in all that time. When you referred to the verse: "Do good unto all men, especially unto them who are of the household of faith" (Galatians 6:10: KJV), I was struck by the fact that I didn't know that verse. I went down by the river and saw a beautiful young family who were obviously very poor. I took all the money I had in my possession, put it into an envelope and handed it to them, then walked away.' The Word had become flesh.

If all we have to give to the world are words, then that is likely to make people feel inferior. But if we put actions to our words, then that gives added weight to what we say. Words and actions make for balanced Christian living.

Father, help me if I am building a crooked tower that leans wordward. From now on I want deed and word to be the alternate beats of my heart. In Jesus' name I pray. Amen.

FOR FURTHER STUDY – Isa. 29:13; Jer. 7:3–8; Amos 8:4–6; Mark 12:41–44; Gal. 6:9–10
1. How closely do the verses in Amos reflect modern life?
2. What was the motive for the poor widow's action?

Be prepared

FOR READING AND MEDITATION – 1 PETER 3:8–22

'Always be prepared to give an answer to everyone who asks you to give
the reason for the hope that you have.' (v. 15: NIV)

In some of us the two things we have been referring to have gotten out of balance.
We talk more than we act. And very often the talking substitutes for the doing. But
on the other hand, there are those who are strong on deeds and weak on words. They
cover up their unwillingness to share the Christian faith by substituting deeds.
Someone has defined piety as 'the art of right growing'. But if that growing is to be
'right', then it must be balanced.

Every Christian must not simply know the faith but share the faith. This does-
n't mean that we must all become preachers, but we must all be ready, as the apostle tells us: 'to give an answer to everyone who asks … for the hope that you have.'
What I don't want to do is to lay a guilt trip on those who find it difficult to share
their faith in Christ – and neither would the apostle Peter. Listen again to what he
says: 'Always be prepared to give an answer to everyone who asks you.' Note: everyone who asks. We are not expected to buttonhole people in the street and ask
them if they know Jesus Christ (though some are especially gifted to do this and to
do it in an inoffensive manner). However, all of us are expected to be able to give an
explanation, when asked, of what we believe.

If someone asked you today to explain why you are a Christian, do you know
what you would say? If you don't, then may I suggest that you take a blank sheet of
paper and write down at least three reasons why you are a Christian. Then memorise them. If you prepare yourself, God will lead someone to you. He will not send
fish toward unprepared nets.

*O Father, forgive me if I hide my reticence to share my faith by relying on good deeds. Help me
become a prepared witness – one who, without losing spontaneity, can give clear reasons for my
commitment to you. Amen.*

FOR FURTHER STUDY – Acts 4:18–20; John 15:16, 15:26–27
1. What was the attitude of Peter and John? / 2. Who will help us in our witness?

The fear of rejection

FOR READING AND MEDITATION – 1 JOHN 4:7–21

'But perfect love drives out fear ...' (v. 18: NIV)

We looked yesterday at the text: 'Always be prepared to give an answer to everyone who asks you... for the hope that you have.' A few weeks after my conversion I heard my pastor preach on that same text, and when he had finished I went up to him and said, 'Why is it that people don't often ask me if I am a Christian?' His reply was devastating, 'Perhaps they don't see much difference between the way you used to live and the way you live now.' I examined my life and found he was right. When I gave up the habits that were clearly non-Christian, people soon started saying, 'What's happened to you?' The quality of our lives should provoke people to ask us, 'What's different about you?' And when they do, we should be ready to tell them.

Does that mean we should wait for someone to question us about our faith before we share it? No. We should be ready at all times to put in a good word for Jesus Christ and to tell others about our faith in him. I have little time for the aggressive kind of personal evangelism that buttonholes strangers in the street and demands, 'Do you realise you are going to hell?', though I have known instances where people have been converted through such an approach. It ought, however, to be more the exception than the rule.

Behind a reluctance to share one's faith lie many reasons, but the biggest one I have found is the fear of rejection. Overcome that and sharing your faith becomes a lot easier. And how is the fear of rejection overcome? The answer is given by our text today: fear is expelled by the invasion of love. When love flows in, fear flows out. Love for God is the key.

Father, I have to ask myself, is my love for you stronger than my fear of being rejected? I open my heart to be invaded by your love today. Open your reservoirs and flood me out. In Jesus' name. Amen.

FOR FURTHER STUDY – Rom. 8:15; John 6:69, 9:24–38.
1. What was Peter's reason for not deserting Jesus?
2. What did the blind man gain from his rejection by the Jews?

Time for a check-up

FOR READING AND MEDITATION – LAMENTATIONS 3:25–42

'Let us examine our ways and test them, and let us return to the Lord.' (v. 40: NIV)

Having looked over the past week at words and actions and seen how easy it is to get them out of balance, we must now ask ourselves this question: How balanced is my life in relation to this matter? Do I use words as a substitute for doing? Or do I expect my deeds to speak for themselves and absolve me from any responsibility to share my faith verbally? Some of us may be living polarised lives. Like Abraham and Lot we separate one from another.

Why not take a few moments following today's reading and before going any further, stop and look at your life as a whole. Just what kind of life is emerging? Are you an unbalanced person? Have you grown lopsided? What impression do you make on people? When people think of you, what do they think of: balance or imbalance? After looking at your life overall, go over it minutely. Invite the Holy Spirit to join you. Ask him to help you be objective. Go over your qualities one by one and see if they are still virtues, or if they have become vices. Have you pushed them to an extreme? Has your strength become stubbornness, your meekness become weakness, your righteousness become rigid and rutted?

Let God render the verdict on each one. He can see things you cannot. You may come out of the assessment better than you expected. Don't be defensive. Surrender yourself afresh into his hands and look away from yourself to Jesus Christ. Don't end up trying to be balanced by using your own strength. Fix your eyes on Jesus. He has all the virtues perfectly blended in him. Become Christ-centred, not self-centred, even in the balancing of your virtues.

Lord Jesus, how I long to be like you – well-adjusted and perfectly balanced. But I can't become like you through self-effort. I give you my heart that you might work afresh in me. Amen.

TAKE TIME TO REFLECT – How balanced are you in Word or deed?
Where do you need to change?

Was Jesus assertive?

FOR READING AND MEDITATION – JOHN 7:14–24

'Stop judging by mere appearances, and make a right judgement.' (v. 24: NIV)

We move on now to consider another pair of opposites: assertiveness and yieldedness. I have often heard people say, 'My problem is to know when to be assertive and when to give in. Am I to be someone's doormat or am I to stand up for my rights? I can never be sure which position I am to take.' A translation of the text 'Let your moderation be known unto all' (Phil. 4:5: Amplified) suggested by the commentator Handley Moule reads: 'Let your yieldingness be known to all men.' But total yieldedness would make us everybody's doormat (not necessarily a good thing), and total assertiveness would make us everybody's thorn in the flesh. We must possess both qualities and straddle both poles.

My dictionary defines assertiveness as 'insistence on a right or opinion; declaring yourself, making a positive statement'. Keep in mind that assertiveness is not aggressiveness. Sometimes the two words are used interchangeably, but their sense is quite different. The word *aggressive* carries the meaning of being hostile, offensive, disposed to attack. Christians should not be aggressive, but they should be assertive. The challenge we face is to know when to be assertive and when to yield.

Was Jesus an assertive person? Of course he was. The passage before us today gives us just one glimpse of him in this role. He was strong without being overbearing and forthright without being obnoxious. But his assertiveness was balanced by a spirit of yieldedness. He was at one and the same time the most assertive and yielded person the planet has ever seen. As with all his other qualities he was perfectly balanced. Happy is the man or woman who knows when to be assertive and when to yield.

Blessed Lord Jesus, you who were so openly and positively assertive, help me to function in this way too. Teach me to be as balanced as you were. For your own dear name's sake. Amen.

FOR FURTHER STUDY – John 2:12–17, 8:51–58, 11:38–44, 18:37
1. How does Jesus justify his assertiveness?
2. What characteristic is common to all followers of Jesus?

Are you non-assertive?

FOR READING AND MEDITATION – 1 SAMUEL 15:10–26

'I was afraid of the people and so I gave in to them.' (v. 24: NIV)

We continue considering the virtues of assertiveness and yieldedness, but focus first on those who are non-assertive. Are you someone who says 'Yes' when you want to say 'No'? Do you eat a lukewarm bowl of soup rather than complain to the waiter? If you have to return something to a shop when there is good reason to do so, are you afflicted with an attack of nerves? Is it difficult for you to express your opinion to a group of friends and be direct in what you say? Then you are probably more yielding than assertive.

Many Christians I have met explain their non-assertive attitude as evidence of meekness and yieldedness. But more often than not, this is an excuse rather than an explanation. What underlies non-assertiveness? A common cause is a fear of displeasing others. You tell yourself that you must have the approval of others in order to function and therefore you can't stand their disapproval. That means you are dependent on others for the energy to drive your life rather than dependent on God. Whenever you elevate someone to the position where their interaction with you, or their approval of you, is necessary to you to function as an individual, then that person is your life. The Bible has a word for it – idolatry. It is putting another person in the place of God.

King Saul was a people-pleaser, as can be seen from the passage before us today, especially today's text. What a non-assertive individual really fears is that the other person will withdraw his affection, or end the relationship, or use his power to get back at them. How sad that so much of our lives is driven by fear when it ought to be under the control of our Saviour's love.

My Father and my God, forgive me that often I am more dependent on people than I am on you. If my sin is idolatry – putting people in your place – then I repent of it now. In Jesus' name. Amen.

FOR FURTHER STUDY – Matt. 27:15–26; Luke 19:20–26; Gal. 2:11–16; 2 Tim. 4:9–10
1. What resulted from Pilate's fear of displeasing others?
2. What truth did Paul draw out from Peter's non-assertiveness?

Let your 'Yes' be 'Yes'

FOR READING AND MEDITATION – MATTHEW 21:1–17
'It is written … "My house will be called a house of prayer,"
but you are making it a "den of robbers".' (v. 13: NIV)

Someone might be saying at this stage, 'But is assertiveness right for a Christian? Aren't we supposed to turn the other cheek and go the second mile?' There are times when it is appropriate to yield, but there are times also when it is right to stand up for an issue and not back down.

Another underlying cause of non-assertiveness is a mistaken sense of responsibility. We wrongly hold ourselves responsible for others' hurt feelings, even when what we have said is right and was put across in a gentle and gracious manner. In such a situation it is foolish to think that the fault is ours. Sometimes assertiveness does cause hurt to people, although no hurt is intended. The thing to ask yourself is this: did you hurt the other person or did that other person simply feel hurt? If you made a snide remark, ridiculed the other person, or knowingly violated their rights, then you have hurt that person, and you must hold yourself accountable. On the other hand, if you have simply refused to do something the other person wanted you to do for a valid reason, then your assertiveness was not in itself hurtful, even though the person may have felt hurt.

Non-assertive people often wait until their anger builds up before passing on their opinion about something, and then what they say comes across as hostile. One person admitted, 'When I say "Yes" to someone even though I really want to say "No" – but am afraid to – then after a while anger builds up inside me and my feelings of hostility explode like a volcano.' That type of situation can only be avoided when a person learns not to say 'Yes' when they mean 'No'.

Gracious and loving heavenly Father, help me to be a person whose 'Yes' means 'Yes' and whose 'No' means 'No'. Deliver me from a mistaken sense of responsibility. In Christ's name. Amen.

FOR FURTHER STUDY – Judg. 11:29–40; 1 Kings 18:7–8, 18:16–21, 22:1–28; Jer. 26:1–16
What is the possible cost of letting your 'Yes' be 'Yes'?

Take the first step

FOR READING AND MEDITATION – JAMES 4:1–17

'You do not have, because you do not ask God.' (v. 2: NIV)

There are some who think the role of a Christian is to be a doormat. Well let me tell you something: you are not meant to be a doormat; you are someone made in God's image, with rights and responsibilities. The *Reader's Digest* once published the story of a group of non-assertive people who started an organisation called the *Dependent Order Of Really Meek And Timid Souls*. Look at the first letter of every word and what does it spell? *DOORMATS*. Their motto was: The Meek Shall Inherit the Earth – if that's OK with everyone else.

How can those who are non-assertive start to act more appropriately? The first step is to talk to God about the issue. I am astonished at the number of Christians who, when they have told me they have problems and I have asked them if they have talked to God about them, have looked blank, shaken their heads and said 'No.' Why are we sometimes more ready to talk to a counsellor about our problems than to God?

The verse before us today tells us that a reason why we don't have is because we don't ask. So talk to God in prayer about the matter and ask him to help you and guide you toward being a more assertive person. If God is not in your life, and not the centre, then you can never be a truly secure person. If the centre is not secure, you are not secure. Make sure you are surrendered to him and that he has full control. Then contact your local Christian bookshop and get hold of some good material on the subject of assertiveness. Check that what you read is based on Christian teaching, for much of what the world teaches (not all) is designed to make you aggressive rather than assertive.

O Father, forgive me if I am more ready to talk to others about my problems than to you. Help me and guide me in this matter of being assertive, for I want to live life in a balanced way. In Jesus' name. Amen.

FOR FURTHER STUDY – Ex. 4:10–12; Jer. 1:4–9; Luke 11:1–13, 18:1–8
1. How did God respond to Moses' and Jeremiah's first steps?
2. What is the condition for assertiveness in prayer being answered?

Big – yet small

FOR READING AND MEDITATION – TITUS 3:1–11

'… be peaceable and considerate, and … show true humility towards all men.'
(v. 2: NIV)

Now that we have looked at assertiveness we will focus on its opposite – yieldedness. Many are assertive but their assertiveness is not balanced by yieldedness. They are polarised. Those who are assertive and whose assertiveness is not balanced by yieldedness ought to follow the suggestion given to me by my pastor when I was a young man, 'Be ready to give way in small things that do not involve principles.' He also said, 'The bigness of a person can be measured by the size of the things on which he or she takes a stand.'

As I was writing these notes, I read about a night watchman responsible for looking after the equipment belonging to a building contractor. Every night he would walk around the large yard where the tools were kept and in the morning faithfully give account for everything. He tended, however, to concentrate on guarding the smaller items, such as shovels, picks, pulleys, and so on. One morning his boss came in and found that although all the smaller items were accounted for, a fork-lift truck had gone – stolen! He gave his time to the little and missed the big. That story reminded me of another I have heard concerning an English cricket player who, running to catch a ball, lost his cap, turned back to grab it, and missed what appeared to be an easy catch. He made an issue of the little – the cap – and missed the big – the catch.

I know a man – an assertive individual – whose life is a failure on the whole because he doesn't know how to yield. He gets tangled up over little issues and misses the large ones. He makes molehills into mountains and mountains into molehills. He thinks he is big and influential but his acquaintances consider him to be petty.

O God, help me not to be big when it comes to small issues, nor small in connection with big issues. Teach me to maintain the right balance between all of life's issues, particularly the things I am considering now. Amen.

FOR FURTHER STUDY – Matt. 6:25–34, 23:16–24; Luke 6:41–42, 19:11–19
1. What is the likely consequence of obsession with small things?
2. What is the reward for keeping things in perspective?

Be sure of the big

FOR READING AND MEDITATION – MATTHEW 23:1–25
'You give a tenth of your spices … But you have neglected the more
important matters of the law …' (v. 23: NIV)

If there is one group of people who illustrate how easy it is to be one-sided in the
possession of virtues, it is the Pharisees. They gave a tenth of their income – a good
thing – but as Jesus pointed out, they neglected the more important matters – justice, mercy and faithfulness. They focused so much on small matters that they
missed the big ones.

John Wesley once took as his text Philippians 4:5: 'Let your moderation be
known unto all men' (KJV). He told those listening to him that this verse could also
be translated: 'Let your yieldedness be known to all.' He then went on to talk about
people whose lives get tangled up over all kinds of matters, such as personal prestige, small hurts and resentments, but who miss the significant issues of life.

Similarly, I have met people who become so caught up in skirmishes over this,
that, and the other – small things, petty things – that they lose the battles over major
matters. It all comes back to what we concluded a few days ago when discussing
assertiveness: we must be wholly surrendered and wholly yielded to God. When a
person is yielded to God, then that person doesn't mind yielding to others over small
matters – matters that are not matters of principle, of course. But when a person is
not yielded to God, not sure of the big, he or she makes an issue of every little thing.
Every one of us ought to ask ourselves right now: does a false sense of prestige keep
me from yielding in matters where I ought to yield? Am I a big person as regards
small matters, and a small person as regards big matters? Be sure of the big and the
small things will take care of themselves.

*Gracious and loving Heavenly Father, I need a change of perspective if I am to live the way you
want me to live. Correct my vision so that I can see the big things as big and the little things as little.
In Jesus' name. Amen.*

FOR FURTHER STUDY – 2 Kings 6:8–17; Amos 5:21–24; Rom. 8:18; 2 Cor. 4:16–18
1. How did Elisha help his servant to get a balanced view of things?
2. How do worship and social values relate according to Amos?

Full surrender

FOR READING AND MEDITATION – MATTHEW 4:18–22

'Come, follow me … and I will make you fishers of men.' (v. 19: NIV)

We must learn how to yield to God before we properly yield to others. Being yielded to God means that we are his and wholly his. Now be careful about this, because although at the moment you may think you are yielded, in a few days' time you may discover that you are not as yielded as you thought you were. A situation arises and you show by your reactions that you need greater yieldedness.

Sanctification is both instantaneous and progressive. By that I mean God brings about a change in you as you yield, but up ahead you discover that there is more to yield. Take, for example, the disciples in the passage before us. Peter and Andrew are seen casting their nets into the lake when Jesus calls them to be his disciples. Immediately they leave their nets and follow him. Does this mean they were fully yielded? No. Later, Peter went back to his fishing nets, even though he had been clearly called to leave them behind. He yielded, but not fully. Take also James and John. We read they were in the boat preparing their nets, and Jesus calls them; so they leave the boat 'and their father'. Note the words 'and their father'. Does this mean they were fully yielded? It might seem so, but we know from other parts of the Gospels that they still had some very unsanctified attitudes. On one occasion they wanted to call fire down from heaven on people who were not hospitable to Jesus (Luke 9:54).

It wasn't until Pentecost that the disciples appeared to offer their all, and when they did, God gave them his all – the Holy Spirit. I urge you, yield all to God today, and when you are fully yielded to him, then you will know how best to yield to others.

Father, I accept that before I can understand how to be yielded to others, I must be fully yielded to you. I yield my all to you now. Help me to experience balance in both assertiveness and yieldedness. In Jesus' name. Amen.

TAKE TIME TO REFLECT – Are you assertive or a people pleaser?
Do you know when to yield? Do you need to grow in these areas?

The Divine Optician

FOR READING AND MEDITATION – MATTHEW 19:16–30

'… love your neighbour as yourself.' (v. 19: NIV)

We come now to a pair of opposites which, if not balanced, can cause us a great deal of difficulty in life – self-concern and concern for others. Many are in trouble spiritually because they cannot combine the two. They either focus on the spiritual life of others and pay no attention to themselves, or they pay attention to themselves and have no concern for others. We are intended to have both an inward and an outward focus; to be personal and social.

There is a verse in the book of Revelation that reads like this: 'In the centre, around the throne, were four living creatures, and they were covered with eyes, in front and behind' (Revelation 4:6: NIV). Moffatt translates this text thus: 'And on each side of the throne … four living Creatures full of eyes inside and outside.' They had eyes on the inside to see themselves and eyes on the outside to see others. Both are necessary. If you turn your eyes always on yourself and continually focus on yourself to the exclusion of others, then you become morbidly introspective. And if you continue to do this and do it intensely, you become neurotic. On the other hand, if you look at others too much and never focus on what is going on in your own life, then you become critical and you will be known as a nit-picker. People will avoid you when they see you coming.

I read this in one of Dr. E. Stanley Jones' books – words that I think will strike a chord with all of us, 'Some Christians have cataracts on their "inside" eyes and powerful bifocals on their "outside" eyes. As we go periodically to have our spectacles adjusted, so we must go to the Divine Optician to have our inside and outside eyes corrected.'

O Father, deal with this tendency in me to look only in one direction. Help me to see through your eyes and then I will see myself and others in the way I ought to see them. In Christ's name. Amen.

FOR FURTHER STUDY – Matt. 20:1–16, 25:1–12; Luke 12:13–21; John 1:47–51
1. What unattractive characteristic emerged in the hired workers?
2. What resulted from the wise virgins' far-sightedness?

Take heed

FOR READING AND MEDITATION – HOSEA 7:1–10
'His hair is sprinkled with grey, but he does not notice.' (v. 9: NIV)

It is one thing to grow spiritually; it is another thing to grow up straight with no lop-sidedness. Some become so self-focused that they don't look out to others, and some become so other-focused that they miss what is going on in their own lives. When I was being brought up, I used to hear my father say over and over again, 'If some people were as good at telling themselves what is wrong with them as they are in telling others, they would be wonderful Christians. Now they are just wonderful Pharisees.' A self-focus is good – as long as it is in balance. Repeatedly in Scripture we are called to self-examination. Those who concern themselves with examining the lives of others and do not occasionally embark upon a few moments of self-examination will wake up one day to discover that their virtue has become a vice.

Several years ago I did a study on how many times the New Testament encourages us to 'take heed to ourselves' (KJV). Here are just a few: 'Take heed to yourself and to the doctrine' (1 Timothy 4:16: NKJ). 'Take heed to yourselves and to all the flock' (Acts 20:28: NKJ). 'Take heed to yourselves. If your brother sins against you, rebuke him; and if he repents, forgive him' (Luke 17:3: NKJ). 'Take heed to yourselves: for they shall deliver you up to councils …' (Mark 13:9: KJV). There are many more. What these texts encourage us to do is to look at ourselves – to take an inside look.

In the text before us today, Hosea scorns the people of his time for having heads sprinkled with grey hair and not knowing it. Normally we are the first to spot grey-ing hairs! But just as normally, we are the last to spot signs of spiritual deteriora-tion. That's Hosea's point. We think far too often that we are better than we are.

Father, I hear your voice telling me to 'take heed'. I need this challenge. Forgive me if I am more concerned about taking out the speck in someone else's eye than the beam which is in my own. In Jesus' name. Amen.

FOR FURTHER STUDY – Psa. 139:23–24, 119:59–60; Eph. 5:15–16; Heb. 12:2–13
1. What must our response be to our self-examination?
2. What standard should we assess ourselves by?

Denial – my trademark

FOR READING AND MEDITATION – LUKE 11:37–52

'... you Pharisees clean the outside of the cup and dish, but inside
you are full of greed and wickedness.' (v. 39: NIV)

We continue thinking about the imbalance that characterises us when we look at what is happening in the lives of others, but give no consideration to what may be happening in our own lives. The arguments that people use to avoid taking an inside look are many. One argument goes like this, 'I'm afraid to look at what may be going on inside me in case I become discouraged and overwhelmed.' But if problems are not faced, how can they be dealt with? The reason why God said to Eve in the Garden of Eden: 'What is this you have done?' (Genesis 3:13: NIV) was not in order to find out why Eve had given Adam the fruit to eat, but to give her an opportunity to identify what she had done. Only exposed problems can be dealt with.

The proper term for avoiding facing up to what is going on inside us is denial. I have talked a lot about this in recent years, and every time I do, people write to me and say, 'I didn't realise how deeply I was into denial until the Holy Spirit pointed it out to me through some words you had written.' One person even admitted this, 'Denial was my trademark.'

Our Lord, you remember, kept his harshest criticism for the Pharisees, who made denial a way of life. They specialised in telling others how to live and pointing out their defects whenever they failed to meet the standards of Moses' law. Jesus called them hypocrites because they never paused to search their own hearts. They washed the outside of the cup but the inside was filthy. Little wonder that Jesus was not welcome in their midst. The principle Jesus was enunciating is this: before you look at how others are developing, take a long look at yourself.

O Father, if I am in denial, then shake me out of it I pray, for I want no pretence in my life. Forgive me that so often I lament the faults in others when I am afraid to face my own faults. Amen.

FOR FURTHER STUDY – Gen. 4:6–12; 2 Sam.12:1–13; Matt. 26:69–75; John 21:15–17
1. What is the inevitable consequence of denial? / 2. What is the way out of denial?

What to look for

FOR READING AND MEDITATION – PSALM 139:17–24

'Search me, o God, and know my heart …' (v. 23: NIV)

From experience I know that whenever I introduce the subject of self-examination, the question that comes into people's minds is this, But what do I look for? Exploring the soul is a complex business. Our heart, says Scripture, is 'deceitful above all things' (Jeremiah 17:9: NIV).

I have come to believe that the key thing we should look for in our hearts is motives. The older I get, the more I realise how one can do things that appear to be spiritual when the real motive may be a covert bid for attention, the itch to prove oneself, or the desire for approval. When I think back to the early days of my ministry, with the advantage of hindsight (and some degree of maturity, I hope!) I can see that much of what I did was motivated by self-interest rather than the glory of God. I wanted to be seen, to make a name for myself, and my deceitful heart was adept at finding ways that made my self-centred efforts look spiritual.

A little while ago I talked with a young woman in Malaysia who told me that she wanted to invite an old boyfriend of hers to a meal in her home because, as she put it, 'I just want to show him that I bear no grudge.' I encouraged her to identify her real motive. She was open to the idea and after thinking it through she said, 'My underlying motive is not to show him I do not bear a grudge but to see if there may be a chance of us getting back together again.' One thing I have learned in life is this: the human heart in its fallen state is an amazing instrument for self-deception. We are masters of the art. That is why we need regularly to take an inside look.

Father, I am just not able to search my heart in the way that you can. Let your Holy Spirit shine into its inner recesses and bring to the light my true motives. In the name of Jesus Christ my Lord. Amen.

FOR FURTHER STUDY – Matt. 23:25–28; John 12:1–6; 1 Cor. 3:10–23; 1 John 1:5–10, 2:3–6
1. How can we overcome our tendency to deceive ourselves?
2. How will the value of what we do be revealed?

Vision and energy

FOR READING AND MEDITATION – COLOSSIANS 1:24–29

'To this end I labour, struggling with all his energy,
which so powerfully works in me.' (v. 29: NIV)

We began this section of our meditations, you will remember, with a reference to the four living creatures spoken of in Revelation who had 'eyes inside and outside'. They had eyes on the inside to see themselves, and eyes on the outside to see others. The eyes on the inside were the first to be mentioned but the eyes on the outside were equally important. To have one without the other is to be unbalanced. Therefore the issue we face now is concern for others.

How concerned are you about the spiritual growth of others? I am referring, of course, to those with whom you have a close relationship. You can have a general concern for the development of the whole Body of Christ, but what is that concern like when it comes down to the particular? 'The Christian demand,' says a theologian, 'is twofold: we are to be unbreakably given to Christ and unbreakably given to each other.' Paul knew the importance of that better than anyone. Listen to what he says in Galatians 4:19: 'My dear children, for whom I am again in the pains of childbirth until Christ is formed in you.' Put alongside that our text for today in which Paul talks about labouring so that the Colossians would become mature in Christ 'with all his energy, which so powerfully works in me'. Two things are evident here: Paul had a vision for people to become mature, and he experienced an energy that worked through him towards that end.

When did you last focus your prayers on a Christian friend and pray for him or her to become mature? And when did you last feel a spiritual energy going through you to this end? It is not enough to be concerned about ourselves; we must be equally concerned about others.

Father, I have seen the importance of being concerned about my own growth; now help me be equally concerned about the growth of those who are close to me in Christ. Give me your vision and your energy. Amen.

FOR FURTHER STUDY – Rom. 1:16, 10:1; Eph. 1:19–23, 3:14–19; Phil. 1:3–11
1. What vision did Paul have for the Christians in Philippi?
2. What energy did Paul say was available to the Ephesians?

Giving yourself to others

FOR READING AND MEDITATION – 2 TIMOTHY 1:1–12

'Recalling your tears, I long to see you, so that I may be filled with joy.' (v. 4: NIV)

Yesterday we said that the apostle Paul demonstrated two things in his relationship with people: he had a vision for others and experienced the energy of Christ flowing through him as he related to them. These two things sum up what other-centredness is all about – having a vision for others and allowing Christ's energy to flow through you to them.

What kind of vision did Paul have for the people to whom he related? It was a vision for them to become mature in Christ. Do you have a vision like that for the people to whom you relate? Are you clear in your mind as to what maturity involves? How do you think Paul would reply if you could sit down with him and ask him a question like this, 'Paul, what is in your mind as you pray for Timothy? How would you like to see him develop?' I think he would say something like this, 'Ah, Timothy … he's a little fearful and somewhat self-conscious, especially about his youth, but I see him growing into a strong confident leader in the Body of Christ.' That was his vision for him. But what about the energy? That came through him as he related to Timothy both in the letters he wrote and his personal contact with the young disciple.

Think now of your closest friend in Christ. It may be a husband, wife, son, daughter, neighbour, workmate. What comes into your mind whenever you pray for that person? In what ways do you feel he or she is in need of spiritual development? Do you focus on those matters in your prayer time and ask God to flow through you whenever you meet, so that his energy can come through you to them? That is what it means to give yourself to others.

Father, give me deep insight into the needs of those to whom I relate closely, so that I can see how to pray for them. And then flow through me with your divine energy as we share your love together. For Jesus' sake. Amen.

FOR FURTHER STUDY – Luke 22:31–32; Eph. 1:17–18; Philemon 4–6
1. What did Jesus pray for Peter? / 2. What did Paul pray for Philemon?

What is a Christian?

FOR READING AND MEDITATION – 1 CORINTHIANS 12:12–31

'… its parts should have equal concern for each other.' (v. 25: NIV)

We spend one last day emphasising the need to balance self-concern with concern for others. A woman sent me a letter some time ago after I had written about loving others as oneself, and took me to task for saying, 'We must take our eyes off people and put them on Christ. He alone is to occupy our attention.' In my reply, I quoted the incident in John's Gospel when Peter asked: 'Lord, what about him?' and Jesus answered: 'What is that to you? You must follow me' (John 21:22: NIV). I pointed out that to be concerned about others is not to take our eyes off Christ but to look at others through the eyes of Christ. Those who are preoccupied with their own spiritual health but have no regard for the health and needs of others grow lopsidedly.

When someone asked Baron Von Hügel, 'What is a Christian?' he replied, 'A Christian is someone who cares.' He went on to say that we can tell how far we are along the road toward maturity by how much we care for others.

A poet whose full name I cannot trace (though her Christian name was Mary) put some of the thoughts I am sharing now into this poem:

If you've never felt the sorrow of another person's grief,
if you've never felt an inner urge to want to bring relief
to someone who's in trouble, with a kindly word or smile,
if you've never loved your neighbour as yourself, with all your might,
if you've never shed a tear drop at a pure and holy sight,
if others have not been blessed by something you have said,
you need have no fear of dying, Brother, you're already dead.

Father, I simply must get these two issues in balance – concern for self and concern for others. Save me from erring in one direction and thus turning these virtues into vices. In Jesus' name. Amen.

TAKE TIME TO REFLECT – How concerned are you for others and for yourself?
Do you need to bring this area of your life into balance?

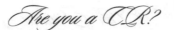

Are you a CR?

FOR READING AND MEDITATION – MARK 7:1–13
'You have let go of the commands of God and are holding on
to the traditions of men.' (v. 8: NIV)

The next pair of opposites we examine are these: being conservative and being radical. By *conservative* I mean having the tendency to conserve and maintain the status quo. By *radical* I mean the inclination to question things and agitate for change. Those who demonstrate only conservative values become reactionary and stuck in the mud. Those who manifest only radical tendencies become obnoxious rebels and revolutionaries.

Balanced Christians should seek to conserve all that is right and good, but they should look also to overturn those things that need changing.

Our Lord Jesus Christ was both conservative and radical. He was conservative, for example, in his attitude to the ancient Scriptures. 'I have not come to abolish [the Law or the Prophets],' he said, 'but to fulfil them' (Matthew 5:17: NIV). No one was more fierce in his denunciation of those who wanted to change the Scriptures than Jesus, insisting that the Scriptures cannot be modified. He did everything he could to conserve that which needed conserving. But he was radical too – as the passage before us today clearly shows. He supported his disciples when they were accused of eating food without having ceremonially washed their hands. He touched lepers on occasion, too (see Matthew 8:3: NIV), whereas the Pharisees made them keep their distance. He allowed a woman to pour expensive perfume on his head and reprimanded those disciples who said it was wasteful (see Matthew 26:6–13: NIV).

A disciple should not be above his teacher. If Jesus could combine radicalism with conservatism then so can we.

O Father, make me a balanced CR – a conservative radical. Sharpen my critical faculties so that I can see more clearly what needs to be conserved and what needs to be changed. In Jesus' name. Amen.

FOR FURTHER STUDY – Deut. 8:1–3; Jer. 6:16; Isa. 43:18–19; Matt. 13:51–52
1. What should be the result of remembering and conserving?
2. How can we be both conservative and radical?

Here I stand

FOR READING AND MEDITATION – 1 TIMOTHY 6:11–21
'Timothy, guard what has been entrusted to your care.' (v. 20: NIV)

Every Christian must be conservative. I am not talking now about political affiliation but about the need to conserve the good things that are ours from the past. In our text today, Paul tells Timothy to guard what had been entrusted to him. Later he urges him to 'guard the good deposit that was entrusted to you' (2 Timothy 1:14: NIV).

That advice is pertinent to our day, too. We live in an age when the Bible's reliability is being questioned, not only by those outside the church but by those inside it also. Often I meet young ministers who tell me they entered a theological college with great faith in God and in the Bible, only to come out of it with their faith in shreds. One young minister, knowing of my confidence in the Bible, said to me the other day, 'I don't need a face lift but I do need a faith lift. I would like to sit down with you for a whole year for that purpose.'

His comment reminded me of a sign I saw outside a plastic surgeon's office during a visit overseas: *Come in and have your face lifted*. Right next door to his office there was a church which had this on one of its posters: *Come in and have your faith lifted*. Not all churches could put such a notice outside, for some have a crisis of confidence concerning the Scriptures. The task of the Christian church is not to invent new gospels, new moralities, or new theologies, but to be a faithful guardian of the one and only gospel. There is need, I think, for another reformation, for all Christians to take their stand foursquare on the Word of God, as did Martin Luther, and say with him, 'Here I stand. I can do no other.'

Father, I see that our first task as Christians is to keep the good news of the gospel intact. Help me to form a strong conviction about this; not an opinion, but a conviction. In Jesus' name. Amen.

FOR FURTHER STUDY – Gal. 1:6–9; 2 Tim. 3:14–17; 2 Pet. 1:10–21; Rev. 22:18–19
1. Why was Timothy convinced of what he had learned? / 2. What is the origin of Scripture?

Christian conservationism

FOR READING AND MEDITATION – JUDE 1–16
'… I felt I had to write and urge you to contend for the faith that
was once [for all] entrusted to the saints.' (v. 3: NIV)

The faith for which we are to contend, we must notice, was once for all entrusted to the saints. I like the way Eugene Peterson paraphrases this verse in *The Message*, 'Dear friends, I've dropped everything to write you about this life of salvation that we have in common. I have to write insisting – begging! – that you fight with everything you have for this faith entrusted to us as a gift to guard and cherish.' On this basis I say again: every Christian is called to be conservative. Our task is to conserve the revelation given to us in the sacred Scriptures.

A book was published in Britain many years ago, written by four different authors, entitled *Growing into Union*. One of the authors expressed the point I am making with great force. He said, 'The church's first task is to keep the good news intact. It is better to speak of the habit of mind which this calling requires as "conservationist" rather than "conservative" for the latter word can easily suggest an anti-quarian addiction to what is old for its own sake, and for a blanket resistance to new thinking, and this is not what we are talking about at all. Antiquarianism and obscurantism are the vices of the Christian mind, but conservationism is among its virtues.'

I understand his desire to move away from the word *conservative* to *conservationism*, but whichever word we prefer to use (mine is *conservative*), it is clear that as Christians we are called to conserve, to guard, to protect the truth which has been handed down to us since the canon of Scripture was established. The Bible is changeless in its truth and authority. Changeless. It must not be altered in any way – either by addition or modification.

O Father, engrave this truth on the heart of your present-day church – the truth that we are to be guardians of your Word, not questioners of it. In Christ's name I pray. Amen.

FOR FURTHER STUDY – 2 Chron. 34:14–21; Neh. 8:1–12; Acts 2:42
1. What emotion did the reading of the law produce?
2. What happened when the people understood the Scriptures?

Repairing the Lord's Prayer

FOR READING AND MEDITATION – PSALM 119:1–16

'Blessed are they who keep his statutes and seek him with all their heart.' (v. 2: NIV)

If ever the church needed conservative-minded men and women it is now. The Scriptures are being tampered with to such a degree that all kinds of new theories and ideas are being mooted. We are being told, for example, that it is quite in order when praying to God to address him as *Mother* even though Jesus clearly said: 'When you pray, say: "Father"' (Luke 11:2: NIV).

I read about a church where the letters of the Lord's Prayer, which were inscribed in gold on one of its walls, were in need of regilding and repair. So also were the words of the Ten Commandments and the Apostles' Creed. The decorator hired to do the task submitted his invoice in this form:

> To repairing the Lord's Prayer: (so much)
> To three new commandments: (so much)
> To making a new creed: (so much).

A number of people in today's church like to set about 'repairing' some sections of the Word of God because they feel they are not in line with modern culture. But it is not that the Bible is out of step with culture; it is that culture is out of step with the Bible. Culture changes, Scripture never changes.

Advocates of homosexual relationships claim that they are natural on the basis that some have been made that way by God and they should accept their sexuality as being from him. They fail to see that homosexuality is not a sign of a created order but of a fallen disorder; something not to be celebrated but confronted.

Father, help me to be fixed on the things that are fixed and not to move from them, no matter how plausible the arguments that are presented to me. Establish me in your Word, for you are truth. In Jesus' name. Amen.

FOR FURTHER STUDY – 2 Tim. 2:8–14; 1 Tim. 1:15; Titus 3:3–8; Deut. 6:1–7, 11:18–21
1. What is to govern our way of life? / 2. What is the condition for enjoying long life?

As it was in the beginning...

FOR READING AND MEDITATION – ACTS 18:1–8

'From now on I will go to the Gentiles.' (v. 6: NIV)

Over the past few days we have been saying that every Christian must be conservative. But conservatism must be balanced by radicalism, otherwise, as we walk through the world we will veer in one direction. If our conservatism is not balanced by a Biblical radicalism, then it can degenerate into a vice. Some have pushed their conservative tendencies to such a degree that they are not just stuck in the mud; the mud has set like concrete.

Paul's conservatism was balanced by a Biblical radicalism, and when he realised that his ministry needed to change, he changed it. Others might have said, 'Stay exclusively with the Jews, that's what God wants', but Paul was radical enough to see that it was time for a change – an appropriate change.

An English duke is reported to have said, 'Any change at any time for any reason is to be deplored.' This is conservatism gone to extremes. Some ultra-conservatives have as their slogan, 'As it was in the beginning, is now, and ever shall be, world without end. Amen.' Conservatives hate change; radicals love it.

We must guard Scripture against the influences of our culture, but when culture is not anti-Christian, then we can consider change – if appropriate. A balanced Christian, however, will scrutinise everything before change is made, and test his conclusions against Scripture. We must not cling to the past simply because it is part of the past. We cling to what is good and we change what is not good. No tradition (if it is not Biblical) ought to be looked upon as sacrosanct and no institution as inviolable. We need to be conservative enough not to change for change's sake and radical enough to change when change is needed – sometimes even initiating it.

Father, do I need to be more radical? Has my conservatism got me stuck in the mud? If I am too conservative, then help me move toward Biblical radicalism. I don't want to be radical for its own sake but for your sake. Amen.

FOR FURTHER STUDY – Gen. 12:1–5; Isa. 1:10–14; Luke 1:51–53; Acts 16:6–10

1. What was promised to Abraham if he accepted radical change?
2. What was the result of Paul's acceptance of change?

No sacred cows

FOR READING AND MEDITATION – ROMANS 12:1–8

'Do not conform any longer to the pattern of this world, but be transformed
by the renewing of your mind.' (v. 2: NIV)

Today we ask ourselves: What really is biblical radicalism? It is the attitude of mind that questions things, reveres no sacred cows, and subjects traditions to careful scrutiny. In this sense Jesus was a radical, and so (as we saw yesterday) was the apostle Paul. I have just been reading the story of William Wilberforce, the man who did much to abolish slavery. His biographer said of him: 'There burned within him a passion to set men and women free from the evil chains of slavery. People called him a radical and a revolutionary. Thank God he was.' Thank God he was.

A radical, instead of lamenting change, will sometimes be in the forefront of it. Would to God there were more radical Christians when it comes to matters such as changing sections of the Acts governing abortion and homosexuality; our attitudes toward the poor both in our own country and overseas; fighting for the rights of dis-advantaged individuals, and so on. Without realising it, many of us have become captive to the lifestyle and value system of the world. We need to question ourselves and 'root out' (the true meaning of *radical*) those things from our lives that we have embraced uncritically.

All our denominations reflect past cultures. We talk about Anglicanism, Pres-byterianism, Methodism – all -isms. Each is an historic form of Christianity, but each has its own cultural baggage. All of this should be subjected to careful exami-nation, to see whether it is culture being defended or Scripture. Not all traditions need to be swept away, of course. Extreme radicalism – simply getting rid of things because they originated in the past and for no other reason – is as foolish as extreme conservatism.

Father, I realise that I must be ruled not by culture but by Christ. Help me to subject everything to careful examination to see what is influencing me – the things of time or the things of eternity. In Christ's name. Amen.

FOR FURTHER STUDY – Matt. 5:38–48; 1 Sam. 21:1–6; Mark 2:23–28; Luke 13:10–17

1. What reason does Jesus give for radical changes?
2. What does Luke reveal about Jesus' scale of values?

Time again for a check up

FOR READING AND MEDITATION – LUKE 5:33-39

'And no one after drinking old wine wants the new, for he says,
"The old is better."' (v. 39: NIV)

We come back to what we said at the beginning of this section concerning conservatism and radicalism, namely that all Christians should be *CRs* – conservative radicals. Some might think that these two qualities are in opposition to one another, but they are not. One has only to look to Jesus and to the apostle Paul to see that there is no need for polarisation on this issue. It may not be easy to balance conservatism and radicalism, but with God's help it is possible. We are to be conservative in the sense that we cherish what has been handed down from the past, but radical in the sense that we question whether what we cling to comes more from culture than Scripture.

But even when Scripture allows us freedom to change, we are not to be what someone has described as 'mindless iconoclasts' – changing for change's sake. Sometimes, as Jesus tells us in our text for today, 'the old is better'. Like old wine, what is established has stood the test of time. What we must pray for is discernment – discernment to know when to be conservative and when to be radical. It is no good saying, 'Well, I am conservative by nature and I leave it to others to be radical.' Biblical radicalism should be an integral part of everyone's development in Christ. If that balance is not there, then again I have to say – we will grow lopsidedly.

Take another look at your life today and ask yourself these pointed questions: am I off-balance in regard to conservatism and radicalism? Am I stuck in the mud when I ought to get up and go? Or do I approach things so radically that I fail to see the value of conserving that which ought to be conserved? It is time again for a check-up.

My Father and my God, I have come a long way with you over these past few weeks. Help me to look at myself in this area too. Where I have been unbalanced, please bring about the necessary correction. Amen.

TAKE TIME TO REFLECT – Does your daily life reflect the balance
between being conservative and being radical?

Two 'trying' sisters

FOR READING AND MEDITATION – 1 CORINTHIANS 15:1–11
'… I worked harder than all of them – yet not I, but the grace of
God that was with me.' (v. 10: NIV)

Another pair of opposites that deserve attention are these: trusting and trying. It is a virtue to trust and it is a virtue to try, but again, if one virtue is not balanced with the other and held in tension, then our growth will be one-sided. Some people's approach to the Christian life is all trust, and they do nothing to help themselves. Others are so taken up with *working their passage to heaven* that there is little room for trust. Perhaps the great preacher C.H. Spurgeon summarised the matter correctly when he said, 'We trust as if it all depended on God, and we work as if it all depended on us.'

I like what the apostle Paul says in the verse before us today, where he points out that when it came to work, he worked harder than anyone: '… yet not I, but the grace of God that was with me.' He tried harder than anyone, yet his trust was not in his own strength, but in the strength given him by God. That's the secret-working hard, but working in God's strength and not our own. Recently I met a man who asked me to pray with him because he was unemployed. I offered to do so gladly, but before praying I asked, 'What have you been doing about looking for a job?' 'Nothing,' he replied, 'I am trusting God to bring the right job to my attention.' In his case trust needed to be married to trying.

When I was young, I heard a preacher make a humorous comment on a verse in Romans 16 which reads thus: 'Greet Tryphena and Tryphosa, those women who work hard in the Lord' (Romans 16:12: NIV). He said he would like to rename these two 'Trying sisters – Try-phena and Trust-phosa'. There is a place for trying and there is a place for trusting. And knowing the difference is crucial.

O Father, when do I trust and when do I try? Draw me so close to you that any misunderstanding I have on this issue will be resolved. In Jesus' name. Amen.

FOR FURTHER STUDY – Neh. 4:14–18; Psa. 37:3–9, 46:1–11; Prov. 3:5–6; Phil. 2:12–13
1. How did Nehemia- combine trusting and trying?
2. What is the context in which we should work out our salvation?

Tired of trusting?

FOR READING AND MEDITATION – GENESIS 16:1–16

'… Sarai … took her Egyptian maidservant Hagar and
gave her to her husband …' (v. 3: NIV)

Let's reflect together first on the tendency found in many Christians to veer more toward striving than trusting. I am most certainly in this class. For me, it is extremely hard to sit back, do nothing, and let God bring about the solution to a situation in his own time and way. There are occasions in my life (and in yours too) when this is the position to adopt. But trusting is not easy. As I write about trusting and trying, I am aware that in this area, perhaps more than any other, I have grown lopsidedly. Some correction is needed, and with God's help I am dealing with it.

I have chosen our reading today because God has used it to pierce my soul recently, and I think he may well do that with some of you, too. Abram received from God a promise that through him and his wife Sarai would come a great nation. But Sarai fails to conceive and so she urges Abram to sleep with Hagar, her maid, and father a child by her. He responds to his wife's request, and sleeps with the maid, whereupon she conceives. How could Abram, the man whom God called his friend, act in this way? Why didn't he stand up to his wife and say, 'This is not the way to go; we must continue to trust God just as we have always trusted him'? Probably because he was tired of trusting.

Can a child of God be tired of trusting? I'm afraid so. When God says 'Wait' but the situation appears to be getting out of control, it is tempting to take matters into our own hands. But that way always spells doom. Perhaps you are in that position at this very moment. Stop striving and trust. He will bring his purposes to pass in his own time.

O Father, I recognise this tendency in me to act precipitately when I am in trouble. Show me when I should take action and when I should wait for you to work. Amen.

FOR FURTHER STUDY – Num. 20:1–13; John 13:15; Psa. 27:1–14; Luke 7:18–23
1. What resulted from Moses' and Aaron's lack of trust?
2. How did Jesus encourage John when he tired of trusting?

Trust, not negotiation

FOR READING AND MEDITATION – MATTHEW 18:15–35

'The servant's master took pity on him, cancelled the debt and let him go.' (v. 27: NIV)

Throughout time Christians have found it difficult to learn to trust. Dr Cynddylan Jones, a famous Welsh preacher, once said, 'The middle verse of the Bible is Psalm 118:9, "It is better to trust the Lord than to put confidence in princes." I look at it every day, but still the biggest challenge of my life is to trust.' There is something in us all that wants God to come through for us in such a way that we do not have to trust.

When Peter said to Jesus: 'We have left everything … What then will there be for us?' (Matthew 19:27: NIV), notice that our Lord replied by telling the story of the workers in the vineyard (Matthew 20:1–16: NIV). The vineyard owner hired men to work all day for the usual wage. Five times in all throughout the day he took on workers, but at the end of the day he paid them all exactly the same rate. Those who had laboured right through the day reacted strongly to the decision, but the owner said to them: 'Take your pay and go … Don't I have the right to do what I want with my own money?' (Matthew 20:14–15: NIV).

This story emphasises the need for servants to trust their master to do what is right. So often, like Peter, we talk *trust* but practise *negotiation*. We come to God believing that 'he rewards those who earnestly seek him' (Hebrews 11:6: NIV), but then we insist on being rewarded in the way we think we deserve. Where is trust in this? If trust means anything, it means coming to God and saying, 'Whatever you think is best is fine with me.' It doesn't mean that we have to stop asking for everything our hearts desire (as children do at Christmas), but it does mean being willing to remain content with whatever he chooses to do.

Father, help me understand that you always give the best to those who leave the choice to you. I want your best and to be the best. In Christ's name. Amen.

FOR FURTHER STUDY – Gen. 18:16–33; Luke 1:11–20; Phil. 4:11–13; 2 Tim. 1:12
1. Which ten words show Abraham's trust when negotiating with God?
2. What attitude will characterise us when we have learned to trust?

Careless in God's care

FOR READING AND MEDITATION – MATTHEW 6:25–34
'Look at the birds of the air; they do not sow or reap ... and yet
your heavenly Father feeds them.' (v. 26: NIV)

George MacDonald, the Scottish novelist, said, 'It is a greater compliment to be trusted than to be loved.' If that is so, then what sort of compliment are we paying God? We say we love him, but do we trust him? I have often thought how different life would be if God would say something like this in times of confusion: 'Look, this is what is happening. I am working on a person who can help you with your difficulty, but it will take two weeks before they are ready to move in the way I want them to move. However, at the end of two weeks they will move, and then your situation will be resolved.' But God doesn't show us what he is planning. He simply says: 'Trust.'

The verse before us today has been a great comfort to me when I have needed to trust. Eugene Peterson's *The Message* words it like this: 'Look at the birds, free and unfettered, not tied down to a job description, careless in the care of God. And you count more to him than birds.'

I am reminded of the true story of a contractor who was commissioned to remove several trees from a street that was to be widened. He and his workmen discovered a bird's nest in one of the trees, with a mother bird sitting on her eggs. They decided to leave the work until a week or two later. When they returned, they found the nest occupied by five wide-mouthed baby birds. So they waited a few more weeks until the birds had flown the nest. The whole enterprise was held up for several weeks and at some commercial cost. When a workman looked into the empty nest, something caught his eye: a soiled little white Sunday school card. On it were the words, 'We trust in the Lord our God.'

O Father, how often do your Word and my need fit together. My trouble is I want to trace you rather than trust You. Forgive me for this, and help me be a more trustful person. In Jesus' name. Amen.

FOR FURTHER STUDY – Gen. 6:9–22; Phil. 4:6–7, 4:19; 1 Pet. 5:7
1. Which eight words sum up the 'compliment' Noah paid to God?
2. What is the consequence of being 'careless in the care of God'?

Time to mop

FOR READING AND MEDITATION – ACTS 27:27–44

'… they dropped four anchors from the stern and prayed for daylight.' (v. 29: NIV)

We have been reflecting on the importance of trusting; now we turn our attention to the importance of trying. Trust has to be balanced by trying or working, otherwise there is an imbalance. Not long ago, I heard a story concerning an incident in the life of the eminent American philosopher, John Dewey. The great man was called by his ten-year-old son to the bathroom. The tap had got stuck and there was water all over the floor. The professor stood there for a few moments looking, thinking, attempting to take in the situation and come up with a way of dealing with it. His son looked at him in amazement and burst out, 'Father, this is not the time to philosophise, this is the time to mop.' There are times when trust has to give place to action.

In the passage before us today, we read of a wind of hurricane force which threatened the life of Paul and his companions. An angel had appeared to Paul (vv. 23–24) and told him not to fear, for no one would be lost in the storm. As the hurricane continued to blow and the ship was being driven toward the rocks, we read: '… they dropped four anchors from the stern and prayed for daylight' (v. 29). Why didn't Paul say to his shipmates, 'Look, God has told me no harm is going to come to any of us, so forget about trying to save yourselves and just trust God'? Because Paul knew that trust needed to be wedded to action, he gave them some practical advice on how to handle the situation (vv. 31–36).

St Bernard of Clairvaux, when preaching on this passage, ended his sermon with these words, 'He who labours as he trusts lifts his heart to God with his hands.' He does.

Father, how grateful I am that you have given me in your Word so many illustrations of your truth. They hedge me in and show me not just what to do but how to do it. Amen.

FOR FURTHER STUDY Neh. 4:6–9; Gen. 22:1–14; James 2:20–26; Mark 6:34–44
1. How did Nehemia- wed action to trust?
2. How did Jesus challenge his disciples to try?

God helps those ...

FOR READING AND MEDITATION – JOHN 9:1–12

'As long as it is day, we must do the work of him who sent me.' (v. 4: NIV)

J.G. Holland, a Christian preacher and writer, was close to the mark when he said this while talking about the need to balance trust and action, 'God gives every bird its food but he does not throw it into the nest.'

Earlier I mentioned that during my developmental years, I found study hard going. My parents, who were both devout Christians, prayed regularly for me, but their prayers didn't seem to accomplish very much. I remember saying to them one day, 'Why doesn't God give me the ability I need?' My mother replied, 'God helps those who help themselves.' No doubt you have heard that statement many times, but it was the first time I had come across it, and it acted, as the Americans say, 'like a burr in my saddle'. I realised that I was waiting for God to work a miracle while he was waiting for me to knuckle down to some serious study and apply my mind to what I should be doing, instead of using it to fantasise about this, that and the other.

A pastor was called to take over a church where the congregation had sunk into a low state spiritually. They believed that if they trusted God, people would come into the church without any effort on their part. The pastor thrilled the congregation with his first sermon, based on our text for today, 'As long as it is day, we must ... work.' The next Sunday he preached the same sermon. When, on the third Sunday, he preached the same ringing message and on the same text, one of the deacons felt something should be done. 'Pastor,' he said, 'don't you have more than one sermon?' 'Oh, yes,' he said quietly, 'I have quite a number. But you haven't done anything about the first one yet.'

Lord, I continue to be grateful that you insist on my being balanced. You demand nothing of me that I cannot attain – by your Spirit's help. Teach when to trust and when to try. For your own dear name's sake. Amen.

FOR FURTHER STUDY – 2 Kings 5:1–14; Matt. 7:21; 28:18–20
1. What did Naaman do to help himself? / 2. Who will enter the kingdom of heaven?

I did help you

FOR READING AND MEDITATION – JOB 13:1–12
'Would it turn out well if he examined you?' (v. 9: NIV)

Take a moment now to ask this question of yourself: how balanced am I in relation to trusting and trying? Do I find it difficult to trust, preferring to rush in and do something instead of waiting for God? Or am I the kind of person who tends to want to trust God to bring about the resolution of certain situations, when perhaps the appropriate thing to do is to exert some effort?

An apocryphal story goes like this. A small town was struck by a fierce storm and soon many of the streets and homes were flooded. In one man's home, the water rose so high that he had to climb on the roof for safety. A helicopter came along, dropped a rope, and a voice said, 'Grab the rope and we will haul you to safety.' 'No,' said the man, 'it's all right. I'm going to trust the Lord.' The helicopter moved away and later along came a speedboat. 'Jump into the water,' somebody shouted, 'we'll pick you up and take you to safety.' 'No,' said the man, 'I am going to trust the Lord.' The storm grew stronger and the man was swept away and drowned. When he arrived in heaven, he complained to the Lord, 'Why didn't you help me? My trust was in you.' 'I did help you,' said the Lord. 'I sent you a helicopter and a speedboat, but you refused to use them.'

The truly balanced Christian is trustful and active, not now and again trustful, and now and again active, but trustful and active at one and the same time. Jesus demonstrated the right balance of trust and effort. He said: 'The Son can do nothing by himself' (John 5:19: NIV) – trust. And again: 'My Father is always at his work ... and I, too, am working' (John 5:17: NIV) – effort. The two were beautifully balanced.

Father, I am on a quest for maturity, but now I want to make the quest specific: help me be balanced in this area of trust and effort. Save me from trying when I should be trusting, and trusting when I should be trying. Amen.

TAKE TIME TO REFLECT – Where do you need to trust God more?
Where do you need to step out and take action?

FOR READING AND MEDITATION – MATTHEW 10:1–16
'Freely you have received, freely give.' (v. 8: NIV)

Yet another sphere of life where we may discover an imbalance is that of experience and expression. Some concentrate on experiencing God but fail to express what they have experienced. Others concentrate on the expression of their spiritual life but do not have much experience of God, and thus have little to express. As I have been stressing, it is only when we straddle both poles that we exhibit a healthy Biblical balance. Unfortunately, as I have pointed out before, many of us push other people over to one pole while keeping the opposite pole for ourselves, foolishly believing that ours is the best.

No one ever warned me more clearly of this danger than John Wallace, the principal of the college I attended, when preparing for the ministry. He said, 'You will be tempted to take up extreme positions when you go out into the Christian ministry. You will say, "I believe in the sovereignty of God," and claim to be a Calvinist. Or you will say, "I believe in the freedom of the will," and claim to be an Arminian. But you will not be a balanced person unless you can harmonise the sovereignty of God and the freedom of the will. If you do not emphasise the freedom of the will you have nothing to save; if you do not emphasise the sovereignty of God you have nothing to save with.' Wise words.

On one occasion I met a man who told me that he was able to harmonise the Calvinist and Arminian views by being a Calvinist one day and an Arminian the next. He thought he was balanced; I thought he was barmy. We are not to be one thing one day and another thing the following day. We are to blend opposite virtues and make them one.

Father, I am so thankful for the experience I have of you. Help me to express what I have experienced so that it does not become stale and musty. This I ask in Jesus' name. Amen.

FOR FURTHER STUDY – Ex. 33:12–23; 1 Kings 19:9–16; Acts 2:22–36, 9:19–28
1. What did Moses learn from his experience of God?
2. How did Paul express his experience of God?

Synthesis

FOR READING AND MEDITATION – GALATIANS 5:16–26

'But the fruit of the Spirit is love, joy, peace, patience, kindness, goodness ...' (v. 22: NIV)

Yesterday we talked about the need for opposite virtues to be blended and brought together in a connected whole. Permit me to dwell on this point a little longer, before we look in more detail at experience and expression.

Two centuries ago, a German philosopher by the name of Hegel developed the theory of thesis and antithesis. First you lay down something, then you look at its opposite. This dialectic (form of argument) has been used by many teachers, including some in the Christian church. However, as Hegel said, the eventual resolution of the thesis and antithesis leads to a richer synthesis. There is a tendency among some Christians to think that when we exhibit one of an opposite pair of virtues, then we don't need to concern ourselves about the other. This is quite wrong.

A man once told me, 'My strength is confronting people with the reality of what they are doing or how they are living, and I do so without prevarication, letting the chips fly where they will.' He was good at exposing – he could cut right to the heart of issues – but was seriously lacking in love. His strength became a weakness because it was not balanced by the Christian grace of kindness. When I pointed this out to him, he said, 'But we are all gifted in different ways. What I lack in the gift of kindness can be made up by someone else. God will send another person to someone I confront and show them what it means to be kind.' I explained that virtues are quite different from gifts. Gifts are what we are given, virtues are an integral part of us. No one has all the gifts; they are distributed in different measure to God's people. But graces are different. All can be evident in us all.

Father, thank you for reminding me of the difference between gifts and graces. I may have some of the gifts but I can have all of the graces. Grant that it may be so. In Jesus' name. Amen.

FOR FURTHER STUDY – Luke 10:38–42; Eph. 4:8–13; 2 Pet. 1:5–8
1. Why did Jesus commend Mary? / 2. What is God's purpose in bestowing gifts?

What is 'life'?

FOR READING AND MEDITATION – JOHN 1:1–14

'Yet to all who received him, to those who believed in his name,
he gave the right to become children of God …' (v. 12: NIV)

After our slight diversion yesterday, we return now to the matter of experience and expression. Some, we said, concentrate on building up their experience of God but are not good at expressing it – giving out to others. Then others are good at giving out but not at taking in; they fail to deepen and develop their knowledge and experience of God. Whatever language we use – experience and expression, receptivity and response, taking in and giving out – it is clear that they are as integral to each other as an unborn baby is to its mother. Before we can give, we must receive.

John sums up this thought in the words of our text today: '…to all who received him… he gave the right to become…' How do we get the power to become? First by receptivity: '…to all who received him'. How does a plant get power to become? By surrendering, adjusting, receiving. Then and only then is it able to give. Suppose a plant tried to give out without receiving – if such a thing were possible. What would happen? It would shrivel up and die. No receptivity, no response. No assimilation, no expression.

A scientist has defined life as 'receiving from one's environment'. You and I live physically because we receive from our environment food, water, air, and so on. In the same way we live spiritually by taking in from our spiritual environment, the kingdom of God. What happens if we do not receive physically? We languish and die. What happens if we do not receive spiritually? Spiritual death creeps over us. No matter how naturally self-expressive and outgoing you are, you need to take in daily the resources of heaven if you are to remain a balanced Christian.

Father, you are leading me toward a more balanced life. For I cannot be mature without balance. Help me not to be like a dammed-up stream, with plenty flowing in but nothing flowing out. In Christ's name. Amen.

FOR FURTHER STUDY – Matt. 26:26–28; John 1:16–17, 15:1–8; 2 Cor. 8:5
1. How may we take in from our spiritual environment?
2. What is the twofold purpose of our bearing much fruit?

Time alone!

FOR READING AND MEDITATION – MATTHEW 6:1–14

'But when you pray, go into your room, close the door and pray to your Father …'
(v. 6: NIV)

We ended yesterday with the statement: No matter how naturally self-expressive and outgoing you are, you need to take in daily the resources of heaven if you are to remain a balanced Christian. This means that you must be willing to spend time alone with God.

Introverts reading this will say 'Amen'. Extroverts might say 'Ouch', for extroverts draw a lot of their energy from being with people, and don't much like being alone. I sympathise with your temperamental difficulty if you are extrovert, but if you are to express through your extrovert nature the power of God, then you need to draw from his resources, otherwise it is natural energy that is coming through – your energy and not the energy of Christ. Listen to these powerful words of James Russell Lowell:

If the chosen soul could never be alone
In deep mid-silence, open-doored to God,
No greatness ever had been dreamed or done,
The nurse of full-grown souls is solitude.

The cause of many of our problems, said Blaise Pascal, arises from the fact that we cannot sit still in a quiet room for an hour. But if we can, and if in that hour we make contact with God – what then? We will rise to go out into life with something to give other than our natural energy. We will go with God and we will give out God.

My Father and my God, you are offering to me breathtaking advice and breathtaking power. Help me humbly to take in and give out, to experience you and to express you. In Jesus' name. Amen.

FOR FURTHER STUDY – Ex. 3:1–6; 1 Kings 19:1–8; Mark 6:30–32; Gal. 1:11–17
1. What did Moses gain from his journey into the desert?
2. What resulted from Elijah's time alone with God?

Now let him out

FOR READING AND MEDITATION – HEBREWS 13:7–21

'And do not forget to do good and to share with others ...' (v. 16: NIV)

We have been emphasising the need to build up and develop our experience of God, for without experience we have little to express. But what about those on the other end of the scale who have a rich experience of God, but do not express it? That's what we must get to grips with now.

A poet whose name I have not been able to trace once wrote these words:

Every morning lean thine arm awhile
upon the window sill of heaven
and gaze upon thy God,
then with the vision in thy heart
turn strong to meet the day.

You can't turn 'strong to meet the day' unless you have the vision in your heart. And what is this 'vision'? It is the vision that comes from experiencing God.

Experience is wonderful, especially the experience of God, but the experience is not an end in itself; it must end in expression. It is one thing to have a beautiful experience of God, but it is another to share that experience with others. There must be inflow and outflow, otherwise the inflow will dry up. Billy Graham, when speaking about the Holy Spirit, said, 'The Holy Spirit is like electricity; he won't come in unless he can get out.' You have the Holy Spirit within you. That is your experience. Now let him out. That will be the expression.

Father, I am so thankful for the privilege of looking into your face each day, reading your Word, and reflecting on all you say to me. Help me to go with you into the day and give out for you. In Jesus' name. Amen.

FOR FURTHER STUDY – 2 Kings 7:3–9; Acts 2:4, 9:10–19; 3:1–10
1. What did the four lepers share with others?
2. What was the result of Peter giving what he had to the cripple?

An infallible spiritual law

FOR READING AND MEDITATION – NUMBERS 10:29–36

'If you come with us, we will share with you whatever good
things the Lord gives us.' (v. 32: NIV)

For one more day we discuss the need to express our experience of God. If we are to be balanced, then we must discipline ourselves to do this. There should be as much discipline in giving out as there is in taking in. Many Christians fail to share what they have received from God and thus what they have tends to go stale. We need to sit down with one another more frequently and say, 'What has the Lord been telling you recently? Tell me about what you are hearing from God in your reading of his Word or in your personal prayer times.' There is a verse in the Old Testament that goes like this: 'They that feared the Lord spake often one to another' (Malachi 3:16: KJV).

A man told me that while he was standing in the foyer of his church, he overheard two other men talking. One commented, 'I heard a wonderful sermon when I was on holiday.' The other said, 'I did too.' And that, apparently, was the end of the conversation. Some are earnest and regular in their quiet time and concentrate on building up their experience of God, but they are not as earnest or regular in their expression of it. They have never disciplined themselves to share. If someone engages them in conversation and jolts it out of them, then they share, but the sharing seems to depend on accident more than on choice – whim rather than will.

How are you doing in relation to this matter of experience and expression? Does your experience of God flow out in your expression of God? What God gives you is like bread. If it is not broken and shared, it grows mouldy and goes bad. The more you share, the more you will have to share. It is an infallible spiritual law.

O Father, help me not to become weary with the challenges. Show me clearly that not only do you lift the standards high but you supply the power by which I can reach up to them. Amen.

TAKE TIME TO REFLECT – Do you spend enough time alone with
God to receive from him? Are you sharing your experience with others?

I say this in love

FOR READING AND MEDITATION – EPHESIANS 4:1–16

'… speaking the truth in love, we will in all things grow up into him …' (v. 15: NIV)

We come now to the last pair of opposites – truth and love. Scripture holds these two in balance, and so must we. Some people are so intent on making love paramount in their lives that they overlook the importance of truth. Have you ever heard this argument, 'Let's forget our doctrinal differences in the interests of Christian love'? The idea sounds very plausible, doesn't it, but it is not biblical. Scripture commands us to love, but it also commands us to abide by the truth. Others adopt the attitude that truth is all-important and pursue it at the expense of love. So dogged is their zeal for truth that they become harsh, rude and sometimes downright obnoxious.

I have often heard one person say to another, 'Now I'm telling you this in love', and yet I could tell by their tone of voice and the angry look on their face that though there was evidence of truth, there was little evidence of love. Love that is not undergirded by truth can become sickly sentimentalism, and truth that is not shot through with love can become steel-like and hard. Let those who say it does not matter what you believe as long as you love, go back once more to their Bibles, for everywhere the Scripture binds truth and love together. They are like Siamese twins. And let those, also, who say the manner in which you raise a matter with another person is unimportant as long as you speak the truth, open up their New Testaments once again and read words such as those at the top of this page today: 'speaking the truth in love'.

It should not be difficult for Spirit-filled believers to maintain this biblical balance, for the Holy Spirit is himself, the Spirit of truth whose first fruit is love.

Dear Father, burn these words into my heart so that I shall be as truthful as I am loving, and as loving as I am truthful. Help me see that my way of life will not work unless it works your way – the way of truth and love. Amen.

FOR FURTHER STUDY – John 8:25–36, 16:12–15; Eph. 4:20–21
1. What must we do to know the truth?
2. How are we guided into all truth?

The highest emphasis

FOR READING AND MEDITATION – 2 CORINTHIANS 5:11–21

'For Christ's love compels us, because we are convinced that one died for all …'
(v. 14: NIV)

Very appropriately on this Christmas Day, our theme has brought us to the truth of Christ's love for us and the love that should not be lacking in our relationships. There are those in the Church who are determined to maintain the truths of God's Word, come what may. For that we must be thankful. But so often their pronouncements of truth are visibly lacking in love; thus the truth has little impact.

I would say to those whose truth-telling is not balanced by love that you are not following in the footsteps of the Master, nor indeed of one of his greatest servants, the apostle Paul. Jesus made love central in his life, and he insists that we do the same. Did Jesus pass on the torch of love to his disciples? He most certainly did. Peter talked about it as being supremely important. So did John. And so did Paul.

You will have gathered from the Acts of the Apostles, I am sure, that Paul was a fighter. He was ready to kill people to make them love God. Then came an amazing change. He was visited by the risen Christ on the road to Damascus and the germ of God's love got into his spiritual bloodstream, so much so that from that day to the day he died, he was like a man burning with a raging fever – the fever of God's love. When writing his first letter to the Corinthians, he made love his highest emphasis, as we see from 1 Corinthians 13. And when writing his second letter, he tells them that he was *compelled* by Christ's love (I wish the NIV translators had kept the much better word which the KJV uses: *constrained*).

Those who are prepared to do battle whenever they think the truth of God is being compromised need to remember that though it is right to stand up for the truth, it is wrong if it is not done in a spirit of love.

O Father, I am grateful for the words of your servant Paul, for he could not have uttered them unless your Spirit was speaking through it. As he held the torch of love aloft, so must I. Help me do just that, dear Father. Amen.

FOR FURTHER STUDY – Luke 6:35; John 13:1, 13:34–35; 1 John 4:7–5:4
1. Why ought we to love one another? / 2. What happens if we love each other?

A 'fallen' church

FOR READING AND MEDITATION – 1 TIMOTHY 1:1–11

' … stay there in Ephesus so that you may command certain men
not to teach false doctrines any longer …' (v. 3: NIV)

Paul asked Timothy to stay in Ephesus because the church there had got off the track. They had a marvellous beginning when the Holy Spirit came upon them (Acts 19:1–7), and such was the impact of the Spirit on the community that people who practised magic arts came and publicly burned books worth 50 000 pieces of silver. 'In this way the word of the Lord spread widely and grew in power' (Acts 19:20: NIV). It was a great beginning. So why did Paul have to urge Timothy to stay in Ephesus to try and set things straight? What had happened?

The story is related in Revelation 2:1–17. Here John transmits the message to the church at Ephesus: 'I know your deeds, your hard work and your perseverance … [but] you have forsaken your first love.' Then he continues: 'Remember the height from which you have fallen! Repent … If you do not repent, I will come to you and remove your lampstand from its place.' Later these words are added: 'You hate the practices of the Nicolaitans, which I also hate.' The problem with the Ephesian church was that they were better at hating than loving, a problem which some churches have today. I know communities of God's people who are good at hating evil but not good at loving. The Ephesian church was a top-notch church in the eyes of many – busy and industrious – but in the eyes of Christ they had 'fallen'.

By that standard I would say many modern churches have fallen – correct in doctrine, beautiful in ritual, eloquent in preaching, rich in culture, but lacking in love. Such churches should be careful, for if this lack of love is not repented of, Christ will come and remove his lampstand from their midst.

Lord Jesus Christ, your relentless but loving eyes see where we are ailing. Help us not to dodge the issue or make excuses. We repent, so give us another chance – another chance to love. For your own dear name's sake. Amen.

FOR FURTHER STUDY – 1 Cor. 3:1–9; Gal. 3:1–5; Heb. 10:19–25, 10:32–39; Jude 17–25
1. Why did Paul call the Corinthian church worldly?
2. Why was Paul so critical of the Galatians?

The power of love

FOR READING AND MEDITATION – 1 PETER 1:13–25

' … love one another deeply, from the heart.' (v. 22: NIV)

Today we ask: is the way of love a practicable way to live? If I were to select the most outstanding characters in the New Testament, I would choose the following: Jesus, Stephen, Paul and John. Why these four? Because they were all masters of the art of loving.

Jesus died with the word of love upon his lips: 'Father, forgive them, for they do not know what they are doing' (Luke 23:34: NIV). And Stephen did the same: 'Lord, do not hold this sin against them' (Acts 7:60: NIV). Paul said: 'Everyone deserted me. May it not be held against them' (2 Timothy 4:16: NIV). And some of the last words of the apostle John were these: 'We ought to lay down our lives for our brothers' (1 John 3:16: NIV).

A story I love to remind myself of whenever I think about the power of love was first told in a magazine called *Fellowship*. It concerns an American missionary to China who, during the difficult war years, refused to hand over the keys of an abandoned American university to the Japanese officer demanding them. The officer threatened the missionary with death by a firing squad if he did not do so. Still the missionary refused, and three soldiers were selected and lined up to shoot him. As they pointed their guns at him, the missionary smiled his broadest and most loving smile. They stood there sheepishly, lowered their guns and refused to shoot. An onlooker said the Japanese officer was so amazed that he did not discipline the soldiers. He also melted under the power of love.

Later, the missionary made tea for the officer and his soldiers before they went on their way. Love conquered. There is no greater power.

O God my Father, make me a more loving person, for this is the only way life will work. Teach me to reach out in love, and let it be my only attitude. In Jesus' name I pray. Amen.

For further study – John 15:9–15; Luke 10:25–37; 1 John 3:11–15; 1 Cor. 13:1–13
1. How do we remain in Jesus' love? / 2. What kind of love never fails?

Stand up and be counted

FOR READING AND MEDITATION – REVELATION 2:12–17
'To him who overcomes, I will give some of the hidden manna.' (v. 17: NIV)

We have seen that without love, truth becomes hard and steel-like. Christians whose noses begin to twitch whenever they sense truth is being compromised, and who are all set to fight but show no evidence of love, need to repent. Christ may come and remove his lampstand from their midst. But what if love is present but there is no passionate concern for truth? That also is a problem, and one we must examine now.

Those who are prepared to demonstrate brotherly love to all, but are not prepared to stand up for truth when it is being compromised, are also off-balance.

I began this section, you remember, by saying that our Lord Jesus Christ is deeply concerned for the preservation and propagation of the truth. Our reading today tells the story of the church at Pergamum – a church where truth was being compromised. They were not lacking in love but they were lacking in a willingness to deal with the error that was circulating among them. In the name of love, they were too tolerant of the false prophets who were part of their fellowship.

The privilege of guarding truth which has been vouchsafed to us through the Scriptures, should be of great concern to every Christian. It certainly is of great concern to our Lord, for here he rebukes the leaders of the church for not confronting those in error. He wants us to love him, but he also wants us to guard and preserve the truth he has given us. Those who think that it is possible to overlook error in the interests of love need to think again. In fact, they need to repent, because this too could bring our Lord into their midst, not to bless but to judge.

O God, forgive me if I have been too tolerant of error. I see that I am called as part of your church to guard and preserve true doctrine. Help me hold the truth in love, and love others in the truth. In Jesus' name. Amen.

FOR FURTHER STUDY – 1 Tim. 4:1–3; 2 Pet. 2:1–3; Heb. 13:9; 2 Tim. 4:3–4
1. What teachings characterise apostates?
2. Why will people not put up with sound doctrine?

The irreducible minimum

FOR READING AND MEDITATION – ROMANS 10:1–13

' … if you confess with your mouth, "Jesus is Lord," and believe in your heart
that God raised him from the dead …' (v. 9: NIV)

If we are to stand up for truth, then we must understand what truth really is. The question 'What is truth?', you remember, was one which Pilate asked Jesus (John 18:38: NIV). But in the famous words of Bacon: 'He did not stay for an answer.' There are many things about which Christians may disagree – as long as we disagree without being disagreeable. There are two things, however, about which there should be no disagreement, and anyone who does not subscribe to them ought to be deemed as being in error. This does not mean that such people should be treated as pariahs, but it ought to be made clear to them that close fellowship cannot be maintained when these matters are not accepted. The two issues I refer to are these: the authority of the Bible, and the Person of Christ. Speaking personally, these two issues have been the touchstone by which I have always agreed to have fellowship or not to have fellowship with others.

Take first the Person of Christ. One great preacher said, 'Christianity is Christ.' To be a Christian means accepting him as Saviour, as Lord, and as the second Person of the Trinity. Anyone who denies this truth cannot be a Christian and therefore cannot be accepted as being in fellowship in the Christian church.

The second belief to which every Christian should subscribe is the authority of the Bible. If we do not believe its truths, bring ourselves under its authority and obey its commands, we cannot call ourselves Christians. We may describe ourselves as moral, or respectable, but we cannot call ourselves Christian. True believers are Bible people who guard what has been entrusted to them – earnestly contending for the faith and holding the truth in love.

Father, I know I must be tolerant, understanding and respectful of other people's beliefs, but never let me become so tolerant that my convictions are compromised. In Christ's name I pray. Amen.

TAKE TIME TO REFLECT – Are there areas in your life where you are
compromising your convictions? What will you do about it?

Strong yet weak

FOR READING AND MEDITATION – JOHN 15:1–7
'You are already clean because of the word I have spoken to you.' (v. 3: NIV)

During these meditations on the theme of unbalanced virtues, it will have become clear to many that though they are strong in certain virtues, those virtues may, without them even realising it, easily become vices. I wonder, have some of you been talking to each other as you have followed me day by day in these meditations? I feel like saying to you as our Lord said when he joined the two disciples on the way to Emmaus, 'What have you been talking about?' (see Luke 24:17).

The Lord is asking you a similar question right now: what have your thoughts been as you have journeyed over these past weeks? Perhaps you have been thinking, 'I am strong in some virtues but weak in others.' These weaknesses must be brought to the Lord for his correction. Good. But keep in mind also that our strengths as well as our weaknesses need to be surrendered to him. We tend to think that it is only our weaknesses that get us into trouble, but often it is our strengths that do that. Peter's downfall resulted from his loyalty – which was his strength. He said to Jesus, 'I will never leave you', but he finished up denying his Lord and insisting that he had never known him (see Matthew 26). His loyalty was not counterbalanced by humility, so the driving force of loyalty pushed him toward spiritual pride, and his pride went before his fall – as it always does.

Surrender both your strengths and weaknesses into Christ's hands right now and trust him to work within you to bring about a better balance. He stands ready to prune your life, and all he needs is your consent and co-operation. You give him your willing heart and he will give you his wonderful power.

O God, set a watch not only at the place of my weakness, but also at the place of my strength. I dread to think that any light in me may become darkness. In Christ's name. Amen.

FOR FURTHER STUDY – Matt. 6:22–23; John 15:1–2; 2 Cor. 12:9–10
1. Why does God prune fruitful branches? / 2. Why did Paul boast about his weaknesses?

The last word

FOR READING AND MEDITATION – MATTHEW 1:18–25

'… you are to give him the name Jesus, because he will
save his people from their sins.' (v. 21: NIV)

As we end this series of meditations, we take a brief backward glance at the road we have travelled together. We began by making the point that virtues which are not balanced can easily become vices. In order to be a fully developed person, one's virtues must be held in tension by other virtues, for it is in that very tension that strength is to be found. There are many pairs of opposites we could have looked at, but space allowed us to consider just eight: the mental and emotional; speech and actions; assertiveness and yieldedness; self-concern and concern for others; being conservative and being radical; trusting and trying; experience and expression; and love and truth.

But what is to be my last word? It is based on our text for today: 'You are to give him the name Jesus, because he will save his people from their sins.' This was the text of the first sermon I ever preached. In these words lies our hope. During that first sermon I said, 'There are two things we need – light to help us understand the mystery of life, and power to give us mastery in life' (I have always loved alliteration!). In Jesus these two needs are met. He illuminates life by having come to this world and shown us how to live. But more, he gives power for the mastery of life. He saves us from our sins and from the things that have the potential for sin – such as unbalanced living.

Over these past weeks, he has thrown some light on the unbalance that may be present in our lives; now he wants to supply the power so that we can walk through life without a limp. We have found him as light, now let us go on to find him as power.

Lord Jesus Christ, I am thankful that you save me from all sin, and also from those things that can quickly become sin. You have given me light. Now give me power – power to become. For your own dear name's sake. Amen.

FOR FURTHER STUDY – Matt. 28:18; John 14:12, 20:22; Acts 1:8
1. Why can the believer do even greater things than Jesus did?
2. What is the condition for receiving power?